TREACHERY IN DALLAS

Also by Walt Brown

The People v. Lee Harvey Oswald
John Adams and the American Press
The JFK Assassination Quizbook
The Referenced Index Guide to the Warren Commission

TREACHERY IN DALLAS

Walt Brown

CARROLL & GRAF PUBLISHERS, INC.
New York

FIRST EDITION 1995.

CARROLL & GRAF PUBLISHERS, INC.
260 FIFTH AVENUE
NEW YORK, NY 10001

LIBRARY OF CONGRESS CATALOGING-IN-PUBLICATION DATA IS
AVAILABLE

ISBN: 0-7867-0238-9

MANUFACTURED IN THE UNITED STATES OF AMERICA

10 9 8 7 6 5 4 3 2 1

This work is dedicated to JILL BROWN,
my wife, my partner, my editor,
my best friend.

and to the countless individuals and family units
whose reputations have been tarnished or destroyed
by false accusations, political intimidation, and the
unseen fear that coincides when ''power'' loses
truth and justice from the vision of the just Maker.

As Aeschylus wrote many centuries ago, ''In our
sleep, pain which cannot forget falls drop by drop
upon the heart until, in our own despair, against our
will, comes wisdom through the awful grace of
God.''

Amen.

ACKNOWLEDGMENTS

The author would like to express his thanks to the countless librarians, archivists, bibliophiles, and correspondents who aided him in the task of bringing the concepts that follow to fruition.

Thanks are also owing to Marina Porter, Mary Ferrell, Gaeton Fonzi, Ed Hoffman, Jean Hill, Mike Robinson, Vince Palamara, Peter Dale Scott, Theresa Seay, Dick Russell, Harold Weisberg, Wallace Milam, Jim Marrs, Milicent Cranor, and Howard Donahue. In his or her own way, each individual cited has freely given time to contribute insights and materials.

On a more personal level, the ongoing work on this book has allowed to new "friends" to be thanked. The list of people to be thanked—and applauded—in this category would include Jan Stevens, who has helped immensely and made sacrifices to do so; Russ and Tiana McLean, who have kept the postal system afloat with their constant mailings of documents—a service they have unselfishly made available to any or all researchers; Dr. Gary Aguilar, John Judge, Jim DiEugenio, John Newman, and Cyril Wecht from "COPA"; in Texas, I am always indebted to Gary Shaw, Larry Ray Harris, Coke Buchanan, and Beverly Oliver M., and her husband Charles. Closer to home, weapons consultant Ron Chiste, Colonel, US Army, has provided invaluable help.

To Bill Greer and Roy Kellerman, who shared their perceptions of events within the limousine on November 22 before their subsequent passing, I deeply admire their candor. The late Harold Norman was also a decent and honest man who walked this earth for too short a time. No words can begin to address the loss, in 1994, of Larry Howard—not just to me, but to the ongoing search for the truth.

Local officers in Dallas are thanked for their willingness to listen to a thesis which they initially found both surprising and threatening, but eventually saw merit in. Among journalists, Jerry Rose of the *Fourth Decade*, Peter Kross of *Backchannels*, and Steve Gerlach, Paul

Jones, and Addie Tapper of *Probable Cause* in Australia have all been both supportive and willing to help in any way possible.

Since the "thanks you's" were published in *People v. Lee Harvey Oswald* in 1992, many of the family who were thanked therein have left us; their passing, like that of JFK's, are watershed events that determine the quality of life for those who survive. Their help while they were on this earth can never be understated nor fully acknowledged. It is a failure of words to suggest they are missed daily.

Jill Brown filled the voids and worked unceasingly for this publication and for the others that are currently nearing completion. Without her efforts, along with Gulliver's continued willingness to sleep in the general vicinity of the computer, this work would not be what it is. Between them, they kept an author going in a time of crisis that to him mirrored the fall of 1963.

God bless you all, especially you, Monkey and Bub.

Walt Brown
Summer, 1995

CONTENTS

BOOK TWO: RED PATSY

BOOK THREE: WHITE LIES

TREACHERY IN DALLAS

TREACHERY IN DALLAS

PROLOGUE:

November 22, 1963,
7:00 A.M.

Assassination is the extreme form of censorship.

—George Bernard Shaw

At 7:00 A.M. on the morning of Friday, November 22, 1963, two men awoke in Texas to begin a day that would forever redefine the American landscape and thrust America in new, often unpleasant directions.

Both men were busy doing what they expected to be doing shortly after 8:00 A.M. that morning. Both would be traumatized by the events that transpired at 12:30 P.M. that afternoon.

Neither man would return home alive.

And thanks to the Dallas Police Department, the Federal Bureau of Investigation, the U.S. Secret Service, and, last but certainly not least, the Warren Commission, *neither man* would receive justice.

The first individual, a societal misfit named Lee Oswald, awoke in Irving, Texas, at 2515 West Fifth Street, the home of Ruth Paine, ostensibly a pious Quaker, but also a woman with a curious political pedigree who was learning the Russian language firsthand from Oswald's wife, Marina. Consuming a cup of coffee for breakfast, Oswald left the Paine residence with a package he transported in the automobile of coworker Buell Wesley Frazier, from which it was delivered to the vicinity of the Texas School Book Depository, at the corner of Houston and Elm streets in downtown Dallas, Texas.

The exact contents of the "package" have never been truly determined, although it is highly suspected and has long been *assumed* that the brown wrapping paper contained a war-surplus rifle of extremely poor quality that made magical shots (one was a "magic bullet") and inflicted seven wounds in the limousine, killing the president and wounding the governor of Texas. Beyond that supposition, our history books are bereft of answers as to what was done with that rifle, or by Lee Oswald, as a majestic limousine carrying the second man, President John Fitzgerald Kennedy, passed Oswald's place of employment.

John Kennedy, a New Englander by birth and the ultimate spokesperson for the free world by election, awoke that morning in a hotel in Fort Worth, Texas, where borrowed art treasures had graced the suite where he spent the last night of his life. While Oswald was riding to work in a car that contained a package, the president was preparing to entertain a local crowd in front of the hotel with political small talk and wit. He then attended a breakfast at which he received a ten-gallon hat, which he refused to wear at the time, but promised to wear in the White House on the following Monday. (Instead, he would wear morticians' cosmetics and be buried; a Texan hat would nevertheless be in style in the White House on that Monday.)

Mrs. Kennedy, campaigning with the president for the first time since the hectic final days of the 1960 canvass, was dressed in a smart pink outfit with a complementary pillbox hat, an outfit she had not worn since a reception for an Algerian diplomat in 1962. She received a warmer reception than her husband, perhaps a portent of things to come.

At 12:30 P.M. CST, millions (if not billions) of lives were affected by the suggested confluence of the two men who awoke miles apart physically, personally, economically, and politically on a dreary Texas morning that had promised continued showers, a weather forecast that bears heavily on the subsequent events of the day. In a time span of six to eight seconds, the president was killed: dispatched with such speed and stealth that only one of his bodyguards had the time to react; dispatched amid an ambush that proved to be an acoustic nightmare, preventing his driver from hitting the gas pedal until after the president was for all intents dead; dispatched with such cleverness that no matter how many witnesses were interviewed, there was an equal number of conflicting reports. The witnesses, and there were many, could not agree on the number, origin, or timing of the shots, yet *nobody*, as of mid-1995, has ever come forward and indicated that they could provide positive identification of any individual with a weapon on the sixth floor of the Texas School Book Depository in Dealey Plaza that day.

While the president was being rushed to a nearby hospital where herculean yet futile efforts were made on his behalf, Lee Oswald was encountered by a police officer in the book depository, but was given a clean bill of health by the depository manager, Roy Truly. Oswald then left, went to his rooming house to secure a pistol, and had some form of encounter with at least two more groups of police officers. Arrested in a theater where he had been observed entering without a ticket, he was subsequently charged with the murder of a police officer, at 7:05 P.M., and, at 11:30 P.M., was charged with the murder of the president (an event he learned from a reporter, not anyone in the law enforcement business). The order of those respective charges and arraignments will have a tremendous bearing on the remainder of this narrative.

While Oswald was being charged in Texas, eleven hundred miles away, in a government hospital in Maryland, "pathologists" selected because of rank and proximity rather than expertise were completing their examinations of the deceased president, and morticians were about to begin their work upon him.

He would return to the White House, in an expensive coffin, at 4:21 P.M. on November 23, attended by his widow, still wearing the pink outfit that had been so lovely at breakfast an eternity earlier. It was not lovely anymore.

Oswald was quickly "convicted" by "lone-nut, communist" pronouncements from J. Edgar Hoover, and by similar and equally premature and prejudicial statements by the Dallas police, which the media pounced on.[1] As the hours passed, somehow Oswald became less of a communist and more of a lone nut.[2] Oswald would have his guilt restated in the official governmental inquiry headed by the chief justice of the United States, Earl Warren. That verdict, of course, would be rendered posthumously, as Oswald was killed in the presence of more than sixty[3] police officials a scant thirty-two hours after the late President Kennedy was returned to 1600 Pennsylvania Avenue.

To suggest that the events of November 22, 1963, are entirely encapsulated in the above narrative is naive in the extreme and has equal weight with theories that suggest that the universe is a massive timepiece that, once wound by an all-knowing timekeeper, will maintain its inertia forever. To suggest that the events happened because a lonely political malcontent sought fame, as suggested in the Warren Report, as well as in a recent work titled *Case Closed*, which also convicted Oswald, is to overlook the obvious. If Oswald had sought fame, he had but to claim it; yet the last forty-eight hours of his life were filled with denials of wrongdoing, pleas for an attorney, and requests to be allowed to shower, hardly the proud harangues of a crazed assassin seeking fame. It could also be argued that if Oswald had truly sought fame, he needed only to remain at the depository and (unarmed, of course) announce his guilt.

Far more sinister forces put John F. Kennedy in the coffin in which he would lie in state and subsequently be buried in a military cemetery. The same conspiratorial elements would guarantee that the "facts" developed to solve the assassination of the president would never be interfered with by a living defendant who could present the other side of the story in open court.

The assassination of John F. Kennedy was a meticulously crafted event with intertwined overtones that go far deeper than has ever been previously suggested. The killing of the president, as he began his reelection campaign in a crucial state that he had barely carried in 1960 and whose native son was in deep trouble politically, was no chance encounter of a Marxist with a cheap rifle crossing the path of a multimillionaire with the world at his feet. It was a coup d'état, with the president as the victim and the Marxist as the patsy.

More specifically, it was an act of political self-preservation initially undertaken by financial elite and the intelligence community of the United States, both of which had anticipated the election of Richard Nixon, but which were forced by events to make alternative contingency plans shortly after the 1960 election. The intelligence community had been partially remade by Kennedy following the abortive Bay of Pigs adventure, and had had its leadership changed by Kennedy because of its failures. The portent of future changes, such as an end to the Cold War, the Vietnam escalation, nuclear testing, and the missile race, plus the possibility that the president's brother would take over the U.S. intelligence community, posed a threat of such monumental consequences that the threat—and its author or authors[4]—had to be dealt with.

The intelligence community, serving as a broker for a covert operation, as had been their habit for decades, turned to organized crime, its recent partner of convenience in its attempts to kill Fidel Castro, and past partner in areas where underworld influence was far superior to intelligence "expertise" for assistance in this act of self-preservation. It was an equal act of self-preservation for the forces of organized crime. But not exclusively because the Kennedy brothers were prosecuting them; rather, organized crime was about to lose its base of wealth in the heroin triangle in Southeast Asia with Kennedy's abandonment of Vietnam, and, of equal importance, the mob wanted to stay within the orbit of the American government. The continuance of past successful operations with the intelligence community, be they a result of a "routine" intelligence black operation like the removal of Castro, or the ultimate act of national patricide in the removal of the president, would guarantee the mob a reasonable amount of immunity for the indefinite future. This immunity would depend, of course, on their continued silence, which was in their basic code of *omertà*, and which they would assist with *in keeping others quiet.*

Yet the killing of a president, be it the newly installed James Garfield in 1881 or the immensely popular and worldly John Kennedy in 1963, is a crime that transcends all others in scope and totality. Because of this, the financial elite-intelligence-mob planners, eventually joined and overtaken by Texas elements that included their political native son, needed a guarantee that would have seemed unthinkable in 1963: They had to neutralize the FBI, the one agency in America with the resources, talent, and dedication to duty that would have guaranteed that the president's killing would have been honestly solved in a relatively short period of time.

They accomplished this task with relative ease by using the secret, homosexual lifestyle of FBI director J. Edgar Hoover as blackmail, for if Hoover could be silenced, the FBI was silenced. Hoover would shed no tears over the prospect of John Kennedy's removal and replacement by Lyndon Johnson, Hoover's neighbor and good friend of two decades. Johnson, as well as the immensely wealthy yet politically threatened elements in Texas, would be equally receptive to a change in leadership in the White House. According to Madeleine Brown (LBJ's mistress of twenty-one years), he undoubtedly knew of the event *before* it happened, and had discussed the event with Hoover in advance, in effect giving Hoover deniability as he could always claim he passed the news to someone "within the White House," and it allowed Johnson to use discretionary power to stop the planned murder if he so chose.

Johnson chose to ignore Hoover's "warning," because LBJ's friends had brought him, by November 1963, to the brink of political disaster. So, as the sun glinted off the majestic fuselage of *Air Force One* at Love Field, Lyndon Johnson took the oath of office as America's thirty-sixth president. His predecessor's bullet-ridden body lay in an expensive bronze coffin in the rear of the same airplane.

The event had to coincide with the beginning of Kennedy's reelection campaign, before his popularity was so great, and his electoral momentum so strong, that no mere Warren Commission would be allowed to "solve" the case.

November 1963 was the perfect time.

The event had to be done in a place where the forces of law and order were of a strongly conservative bent and would not fray their nerves or lose sleep following leads in search of a solution for the case. This suggested the South in 1963, where the phrase "law and order" was more a cliché for racial separation, another lesson that could be taught on November 22. "Law and order" in the South of 1963 did not involve solutions to crimes of no damage to the South per se, particularly if the crime placed a Southerner in the White House, where decisions about military spending, mob prosecutions, civil rights, and oil taxes began—or ended.

Dallas, Texas, was the perfect place.

The event required two victims: one, obviously, the president, and the other, a scapegoat whom the public could quickly accept as the guilty party based on his résumé, not necessarily on the evidence in the case. It would also be helpful if all "fingers of guilt" associated with the scapegoat pointed directly at America's enemies of 1963, the Soviet Union and Cuba, which could further provide a "national security" umbrella for any facts that pointed in other directions, as well as to bring out the latent patriotism in those who would investigate, as well as in Americans who would be asked to believe the "facts" in the case.

Lee Harvey Oswald was the perfect patsy.

The event, already an almost perfect plausible deniability syndrome, also required something that most, if not all, researchers have overlooked: a deniability between the organizers and the shooters, and between the shooters and those who would ultimately bury the truth. According to this scenario, since it is obvious that elements in the U.S. government ultimately covered up the truth, as passed from Hoover to the Warren Commission, *they could not have been the killers*. Since it was also suggested that the U.S. military intelligence community, representing interests in black ops, a euphemism for covert intelligence operations, as well as hundreds of billions of dollars in defense spending which would be the trough for the financial elite, were the originators, but not the only group concerned with the self-preservation act of assassination, they, too, must be ruled out—as *assassins*. Too many— far too many—researchers have made valuable contributions to the literature by positing groups that had a reasonable motive for the assassination, as JFK's futuristic visions were not without a price tag, but those same researchers have always assumed, and usually reached a dead end thereafter, that the planners were the shooters: the CIA planned it, and some of them did it. But who? The mob planned it, and their killers did it. But who? Research has heretofore come up short at this point.

What was missed in these efforts was the vital element of plausible deniability, which has been the key to the conspiracy not coming unglued long ago. The planners were not the shooters. Assuming the killing had to be done for the reasons cited above, as well as for the self-preservation of Southerners threatened by Kennedy's oil-tax agenda and his willingness to place black people on an equal footing in a previously white-dominated society, the circle was almost complete.

It had to be done in the early stages of the campaign, and in the South; right-wing elements (eager to point the accusatory finger at the leftist patsy and all fellow travelers) would jump aboard the band-wagon, and massed southern wealth could easily outspend the Kennedy "fortune." Petrodollars, as well as right-wing pass-the-hat-at-the-meeting dollars, could aid and finance, if necessary, the event, which as Southerners they would have the chance to witness firsthand.

The question then becomes focused:

- Who was of a strong enough right-wing philosophy?
- Who had the necessary sniper/weapons skills?
- Who could blend into the scenery of Dallas, Texas, at high noon during a highly visible presidential motorcade and have no notice taken of them?
- Who was in a position where they could not, under any circumstances, be investigated in any serious way by the local police?
- Who could make all decisions as to whom was arrested?
- Who could see to it that the lone suspect, and hence the case,

would never make it to a courtroom where both sides of the issue could be presented?

There was and is only one answer: *the local police.*

After they had completed their brief but grisly chore, they blended perfectly into the scenery, went looking for the patsy previously *chosen and groomed* by the planners in the intelligence community and elsewhere, and arrested him at about the same time that insider J. Edgar Hoover was announcing Oswald's guilt, and domestic and foreign newspapers were printing information about the suspect's arrest for the *president's murder* that could only have been prepared *well in advance.*[5]

What remained was to silence the suspect, which was done on live television to the joy of millions of Americans and to the sorrow of those few who realized that the death of Lee Oswald meant the end of the search for truth. Beyond that, the closure of the dual killings merely required that the new chief executive of the United States prevent any serious investigations by appointing a presidential commission that worked under two fatal constraints. Primarily, it was the "Johnson Commission"; *he* made the appointments; *he* looked to the public for acceptance of the ultimate findings, which were to be given to *him.* The second constraint was the commission's limitation of being allowed to deal only with materials, testimony, and evidence previously approved by J. Edgar Hoover, and buried, where necessary, by commission member Allen Dulles, whose appointment to serve on that fact-finding board has got to be one of the all-time worst in American history. The other 98 percent of the files and facts not seen at the time by the Warren Commission have created a battleground for more than thirty years, an odd situation, to say the least, for a scenario in which one nut killed the president and was then silenced by yet another nut. Oswald and Ruby are both long dead; if they were, as we have been told, "lone nuts," *why are so many hundreds of thousands of documents being withheld?*

America and the world, in sorrow, would accept the commission's findings, which were then, and still are, championed in the media, but would somehow be troubled by the placement of the vast majority of evidence under seal until the year 2039. Much of it has been released since 1964, but much content has been curiously obliterated, and its veracity, years after the fact, can never be proved.

The man who awoke at the Paine residence in Irving, Texas, on

November 22 was found guilty by default, as he was the only suspect ever considered, and his murder, by a thug with credentials from two elements involved in the assassination—the local police and, to a lesser extent, the mob—closed the case far too prematurely. If I were to title a book *Case Closed*, truth would dictate that it could only concern itself with the one bullet fired by Jack Ruby on November 24. Oswald's participation in the assassination, viewed here as the manipulation of someone ultimately memorialized as a Red patsy, took far more craft than the firing of Ruby's single bullet.

As for the other man, who awoke in Fort Worth on November 22 to continue a political fence-mending trip through Texas, no words, no books, no solemn burial place in Arlington can ever begin to balance the loss suffered by America and the world in those few horrible seconds in Dealey Plaza.

But the truth can go a long way toward making that loss less painful.

The remainder of this work will be divided into five sections, each of which will be interrelated and integrated to each of the others.

The work will begin with "Theories." This section will present the major conspiracy theories as well as the lone-assassin theory. It will analyze the components of each theory, highlighting the basis in research for each, and explaining it in what is hoped to be enough depth so as to be understood by the casual student of the assassination without becoming tedious to the assassination buffs.

Each theory will be analyzed for its strengths and weaknesses, with an eye to maintaining that which is documentable and logical in each, while eliminating that which is untenable or undocumentable. In the process, some of the theories will be eliminated from consideration, although the reader is at all times encouraged to pursue a theory— even the lone-assassin fantasy—that is of interest to him or her. There is much truth to be found among the selections, and it is doubtful that there is an assassination genre book that will *not* increase our understanding of the event, although it is occasionally done by subtraction.

Each separate theory will conclude with a final analysis, and the section itself will end with an overall synthesis that will bring together several differing approaches to the event, as suggested earlier in this Prologue, but that have never been suggested in this manner before.

"Blue Death" will detail the myriad events that point the accusatory finger of guilt at a handful—but an important handful—of Dallas police officers or individuals who could count on the police for weapons, uniforms, and a means of guaranteed escape when their labors in Dealey Plaza were concluded. There are several key elements: the separation between the planners of the event (detailed in "Theories") and the perpetrators; the Dallas police's unbelievable ineptitude in planning a motorcade, "protecting" the president in that motorcade, and then conducting an investigation into his death that mocks the word "justice."

It should be noted here, for the reader's benefit, that prior to November 22, 1963, Dallas district attorney Henry Wade (later memorialized in *Roe v. Wade*) had prosecuted twenty-five homicide cases and had won convictions in twenty-four of them. This is highly suggestive that the Dallas police, *prior to* November 22, 1963, knew how to investigate homicides, understood the concepts of motive, means, and opportunity, and had some familiarity with legal technicalities such as chain of possession of evidence and locally performed autopsies. They also understood that they had to keep the various defendants alive for district attorney Wade to secure their convictions. Yet on November 22, 1963, they abandoned their previous, successful pattern of investigations and emerged as pathetic, bumbling buffoons unable even to keep the accused assassin alive in police headquarters. Part of this sudden failure may stem from the fact that the Dallas police were no longer just the investigators, but also the possible defendants, and it is certainly prudent to prepare a poor judicial case against yourself. Finally, it reminds the reader that it was precisely because of the same Dallas Police that so much truth in the event is lacking, because due to their willingness to televise Oswald's captivity, and insistence on televising—to the point of promoting—his transfer, he died violently in their custody. It should also be noted that the sheriff's department normally handles all such transfers, but did not, for some reason, want to get within a hundred miles of this case.

We must also allow for the possibility that J. D. Tippit was an equal sacrificial offering to the conspiracy, for not only did his killing suggest Oswald had a propensity for violence, it also gave Dallas authorities a neat and clever alternative had Oswald survived: put him on trial for the Tippit slaying, win an easy conviction in the standard "anarchist killed the policeman" scenario, and the world would still never learn the full truth of Dealey Plaza. Recall that

Oswald was booked and arraigned for the Tippit killing hours before charges were filed in the other murder Oswald was believed to have committed.

"Blue Death" was one slick operation.

It needed, however, a defendant. Imagine the state of the American psyche if, on Monday, November 25, 1963, as John Kennedy was being laid to rest in Arlington, the authorities in Texas had made no arrest or arrests with respect to the assassination. "Conspiracy" and "international terrorism" would have been on every American's lips, and the faith that has provided the ideological cement for the American way of life and for the American concept of government would have come totally unglued. It would have been the most hellish nightmare America had ever faced.

Enter Lee Oswald, with a checkered history: a résumé that included rifle skills, albeit mediocre; a Soviet defection, albeit staged; and a miserable life of desolation, desperation, and such violent acts as pouring a drink on a marine sergeant. Oswald's quick arrest and equally quick liquidation prior to Mr. Kennedy's funeral kept America focused on its grief, not on the long night of the American soul suggested above. There was suddenly no need to gather evidence, as Americans watched reruns of the execution of the Red patsy and sent telegrams of congratulations and/or money to Jack Ruby, the most highly visible assassin in American history. These factors are considered in the section "Red Patsy."

But Americans, in their collective subconscious struggle to live up to the standards and goals of the Founding Fathers and all the truly good things in our system of government, will eventually seek the truth. J. Edgar Hoover, for reasons he could not reveal, chose to extend octopuslike tentacles over every facet of an investigation of a murder that was the strict jurisdiction of the state of Texas—that is, until President Lyndon Johnson issued Executive Order 11130, establishing the President's Commission on the Assassination of President Kennedy. Seven prominent Americans supervised a team of unknown attorneys in their efforts to wade through the mass of rubbish furnished to them by the director of the FBI. Realizing that they were being just as victimized as the American people with respect to the truth, they did their patriotic duty and endorsed the findings of both the Dallas authorities and the director of the FBI. How this came to be will be considered in "White Lies." The compilation of them is still available in print in the Warren Report.

Lastly, the events of a few terrible seconds in Dallas will be viewed through a prism in "Hypothesis," based on the arguments presented in "Theories" as well as in "Blue Death," "Red Patsy," and "White Lies." It is the author's second biggest wish that this "Hypothesis" will make logical sense to the reader, and will point future researchers in the direction of the ultimate truth. No single book will solve this case, nor answer all the unsolved questions. That can and will only be done over time, and by taking "baby steps" to get there. Hopefully, a road map for many of those steps is contained herein.

The author's biggest wish, of course, was that Camelot had come to fruition, or, failing that, that the first investigation into the death of John F. Kennedy had been an honest one.

Theories

CHAPTER ONE

A PLETHORA OF THEORIES

—Chicago Mayor Anton Cermak, in the interval between his wounding and his death as a result of that wounding, made the supposition that the mob was behind the attempt on his life. (Cited in Scheim, Contract on America, p. 9.)

—If given the opportunity to make a similar supposition, what would John F. Kennedy have thought?

A PROMINENT WASHINGTON ATTORNEY who has studied the murder of John Kennedy for many years once chided the assassination research community by commenting, "We've now pretty well figured out who the dozen or more assassins were that fired the three or four shots at JFK." While this work will catalogue *twenty-eight* previously cited assassins (see Table I in the Appendices), it will also remind the reader that any such number—not to mention some of the suspects—is absurd.

Such a list of political, domestic, and international assassins has created both a cottage industry and a focal point for criticism of any research regarding the events of November 22, 1963, and that is regrettable. The equally serious frustration has been the absence of the entire corpus of source material that exist, but has not yet been made available, along with the source material that once existed but has been destroyed. Even the August 1993 document "releases" were for the most part straw men, timely released to coincide with a book pointing toward the familiar lone-assassin fantasy, and designed *as well as absurdly redacted* to blunt the impact of the thirtieth anniversary of the tragedy. There is much in there about Oswald's autopsy. So what? We know how Oswald died. What we need is the release of all materials on JFK's autopsy. We are still trying to determine how *he* died.

Hundreds of dedicated researchers and a reasonable percentage of the population of our nation are still very curious about what happened in Dealey Plaza. The research community has put forward a number of theories suggesting who or what group was behind the event, and the concerned population has read the published findings eagerly. On occasion, a theory has been presented and almost instantly rejected, but even then, there is usually something of value amid the debris. Lectures, college courses, and weekend symposia are now available for researchers and the curious to spend time together brainstorming and wading through the mass of existing material. Ultimately, however, the participants return home to their customary, nonconspiratorial pursuits with different visions of what led up to those terrible six seconds, what occurred during those six seconds, and what has been done since then to preclude a realistic understanding of of those few seconds.

For these reasons, this narrative will begin with a menu of the theories that have been developed over the years and the reasons for the genesis of the given theory. Each theory will be discussed with an eye toward saving what is valid and discarding what is not. Source materials will be documented, but will also be subjected to a collateral question, "What is logical?" Although only a hypothetical construct, logic is a powerful argument and cannot be ignored. Stripped of its philosophical garment, logic is common sense writ large. While the crime of murder, and in this case it was the murder—the assassination—of the leader of the free world in broad daylight, might not seem like a commonsense thing to do, think again. History has taught us only too well that individuals and groups will do what is in their best interest, be it stock manipulation, war (legalized murder), or genocide, if it makes sense to them. One person's grotesqueness is another's common sense.

An additional concern in the murder of President Kennedy is the apparent willingness of so many to subscribe without question to the *cui bono* ("who benefits") theory of history. Admittedly, the theory offers much validity, but it need not be the *only* building block of any study. To view the assassination strictly from a "who benefits" perspective is to allow ourselves to stumble upon a contradiction: Kennedy was so well respected by the general population that he was headed for a probable 1964 electoral landslide against his suggested Republican opponent, Arizona senator Barry Goldwater (a landslide subsequently given to Lyndon Johnson, partly out of respect for JFK). Yet conspiracy researchers have posited and documented the possibility that many special-interest groups took an intense dislike to the president's visionary policies, his popularity, and his likelihood for reelection. Each group is then seen as the one that would consider, carry out, and cover up the crime of political assassination. One of our concerns here is to consider, from the standpoint of evidence and logic, which of the cited groups could plan, which could carry out, and which could cover up the assassination, in a plausible deniability scenario as was suggested in the Prologue. It is unlikely that all such attributes could be laid at the doorstep of any single group, and hardly one individual, leaving us with the obvious conclusion that *the late* Lee Oswald could not have covered up his alleged crimes. It is also highly probable that the conspiracy succeeded because of a series of overlapping purposes that allowed—or guaranteed—the participation of several groups, leaving the curious researcher, much less the average American of 1963–64, in a wilderness of mirrors. (See Table 2.)

As you review and ponder the various theories, bear in mind three things. First, if the Warren Commission's verdict of the lone assassin is not accurate, then other individuals, not lone nuts, had to plan, execute, and hide the results of their deeds on November 22, 1963. Second, as we have seen, JFK was for the most part idolized by a good-sized majority of Americans, yet he was held in utter contempt by some of those who walked the corridors of power. This leads to a final question: Was the pathetic historical figure we know as Lee Oswald part of the majority of Americans sympathetic to John Kennedy, or was he part of the "contempt" cabal that stalked the corridors of power?

Also reflect for a moment on the operative word in all that is written herein, as well as in the millions of other words written about the events of November 22 in Dallas: assassination. For the throngs who visit Ford's Theater every year, as well as the crowds who have made Dealey Plaza a national historical landmark and a bigger tourist attraction in Texas than the Alamo, let us never assume that "assassination," defined elsewhere, is a phenomenon unique to America. In a survey I undertook recently, the ten greatest assassinations and/or attempts were seen to be those involving Caesar, Lincoln, Hitler, Gandhi (and family . . .), Charles DeGaulle, John Kennedy, Malcolm X, Martin Luther King, Anwar Sadat, and John Paul II.* Of these, eight were clearly the results of conspiracies, and the remaining two, John Kennedy and Dr. King, are still subject to such intense scrutiny that most Americans, when polled, believe them to be the results of conspiracies also, despite the contents of the official versions.

What has this survey taught us? One, that despite Allen Dulles's transparent attempts to convince his fellow members of the Warren Commission otherwise, leaders *are* killed by conspiracies—be they Bulgarian secret police, a truckful of Egyptian soldiers, or honorable Roman senators.

It also teaches us that lone-nut killings, like lone-nut Reichstag fires, have more often *needed* to be the official version, but have never truly merited much attention in any *honest* examination of the events.

---

*This excludes several Russian czars, most notably Paul I, whose own son was implicated, and Alexander II, the object of the wrath of Lenin's brother. It also excludes the misguided intrigues that befell the Julio-Claudian dynasty, as well as inept emperors after A.D. 180. In both exclusions, the local populace was toasting the ascension of the new ruler before the old one had been killed.

CHAPTER TWO

THE LONE ASSASSIN

In 1975, Warren Commission assistant counsel David W. Belin was trying to prove to CBS correspondent Daniel Schorr that there had been no conspiracy in the Kennedy assassination. "No one has come forward," he told Schorr, "and nothing has been proven. Therefore, there must be no conspiracy," Belin argued.

"Or there was a very good one," Schorr countered.

IF WE USE MR. BELIN'S LOGIC, since no one has claimed that he or she created the planet Pluto, and since no theory regarding the creation of the planet Pluto has been proven, we may therefore conclude that the creation of the ninth planet *was the work of a lone assassin.*

The lone-assassin theory originated on the afternoon of November 22, 1963, and was duly transmitted to the Warren Commission, which, in the absence of any independent investigatory powers, was at the mercy of FBI and other, lesser, governmental sources. In ten months of work, they "exhaustively" ratified the lone-assassin theory in time for its publication a scant six weeks before the presidential election of 1964.

Since that time, the Warren Commission's conclusions have found support in works by Jim Moore and Dr. John K. Lattimer.[1] In mid-1993, an additional, if specious, volume was added to those cited above.

The essentials of the lone-assassin scenario can be put on canvas with broad strokes: Oswald worked in the Texas School Book Depository and had occasion to fill orders from the sixth floor; he had, earlier in 1963, ordered a Mannlicher-Carcano rifle, virtually advertising his purchase of the weapon, similar in many characteristics to a weapon found on the sixth floor of the depository; a bullet, known to history as the "magic bullet," was found at Parkland Hospital, and that bullet linked the rifle to the assassination, although it could only suggestively link the rifle to *the crime*; it was alleged that the assassination was the result of an easy shot; a palmprint was found on the underside of the rifle, and it, along with some of the palmprints found on boxes at the scene, matched palmprints of one of the subjects taken into custody, Lee Oswald; one of the boxes had a crease in the center of it, as if it had been used to rest something on it.

This is the essence of the circumstantial case against Lee Oswald, and it is not the purpose here to go through a lengthy itemization of what is wrong with that case or why those pieces of evidence have less worth than originally thought. The evidentiary deficiencies of the case have been pointed out by a host of authors who published commentary on the Warren Report, or even on the official version before its government publication. I, too, have had a chance to challenge that evidence in *People v. Lee Harvey Oswald*.

In brief, the lone-assassin concept has been found wanting. What follows is a summary of the major points stated above, and commentary based on ideas and evidence that have *not* been common to published findings.

Problem number one, reduced to lowest terms, is that if Lee Harvey Oswald committed the murder of President Kennedy completely on his own, it is unlikely that the Dallas police would have arrested so many other people or listened to reports from witnesses who had such contradictory stories. On the contrary, if Oswald performed the killing alone, a committee of bakers, dentists, and door-to-door hearing aid salesmen could have looked at the evidence and rendered such a verdict, saving the taxpayers the cost of a blue-ribbon panel made up exclusively of individuals accustomed to being on the payroll of the federal government. Jim Garrison, noting the contradiction that a change of address card for Oswald's post office box in New Orleans was filled out two weeks after Oswald *departed* New Orleans, commented, "Who says that lone assassins have no friends?"[2] Such a question, while seemingly trivial, typifies the weaknesses and limitations of the official version.

Oswald worked in the Texas School Book Depository. Indeed he did, as did at least seventy-three others. But Oswald was hired there prior to the decision, much less the publication, of the president's itinerary in Dallas, making him nothing more than a clerk in a warehouse whose upper floors were 324 feet from Main Street in downtown Dallas, where a presidential motorcade, not yet announced but possibly within the ken of someone on the inside, would have appeared for only a few seconds. Oswald also had no way of knowing, at the time of his hiring, how long his *temporary* employment there would last, or whether he would be assigned to the *other* building, located several blocks north of Elm, and absolutely useless as a sniper post. Further, it is vital to recall that it was not Oswald who sought employment for himself at the TSBD; someone else found the employment and virtually delivered Oswald to it. Also, it should be noted, perhaps because Oswald knew of his temporary status or because of his inability to keep a job, that he confided to Marina that he found the work not to his liking and that he was looking for other work.[3] Lastly, despite his penchant for secretiveness and aliases, Oswald took the job at the depository under his own name, an exercise that hardly comports with the theory that he sought employment there to exercise his sniper skills. While it is true that Wesley Frazier knew Oswald's real name, Oswald's excuse that his real name and "defector" background cost him jobs might have been enough to hoodwink Frazier into letting him apply as "O. H. Lee" or "Alek Hidell." But he didn't.

As to the individual seen in the "sniper's nest" window, no one came forward to identify Oswald, and the only consensus was that Robert Edwards and Howard Brennan saw an individual in "light colored clothing"[4] and Ronald Fischer was convinced that the individual was "light headed,"[5] a reference to coloration, not mentality.

The lone-assassin concept is further weakened by the affidavits of both Carolyn Walther and Ruby Henderson (neither of whom was called to testify before the Warren Commission), which suggest that both witnesses saw two people in the so-called assassin window of the book depository. These statements are reinforced by both the Hughes and Bronson films, which show at least two figures moving around on the sixth floor of the depository within a very short time of the shooting,[6] and if we believe the Warren Commission, *neither* of those figures could have been Oswald, as he had to depart in great haste after the final shot he allegedly fired. In a further affidavit, Lillian Mooneyham, who witnessed the assassination from an excellent vantage point in the County Records Building, saw a male figure around the fabled boxes four to five minutes *after* the shooting.[7] Inasmuch as Oswald had left the building by that time and police did not reach the sniper's window for more than thirty minutes, the Warren Commission did not see any purpose in taking such testimony from Ms. Mooneyham. The 1978 House Select Committee on Assassinations, however, did conclude that the boxes on the sixth floor were rearranged after the shooting.[8]

Despite these hints that it was someone other than Oswald, it must also be asked what could be seen. From ground level, very little could be seen, and *nothing* would have been visible if lone-assassin Oswald had chosen to take the far easier shot or shots as the limousine traveled north on Houston Street, or negotiated the Houston–Elm turn, agonizingly slowly. If one studies Dillard exhibit C, a photo taken within seconds of the assassination that depicts two African-American males on the fifth floor, the problem of identification is clarified. As published, the man leaning out of the window is identifiable; the man inside the window is far less easily identifiable, and that window is open to a height of nine bricks, while the "sniper's window" is open to a height of only *six*.[9] It should be added that in the original Dillard photo, a clear print from the negative, both men are identifiable. It should also be noted, clear print or otherwise, that the windows on both floors are beyond filthy. Nobody could have identified anyone if they were behind that disgusting glass with the noontime sun hitting it.

The people with the best view, bar none, of the events of November 22, 1963, were the inmates on the upper floors of the jail on the southeastern corner of Elm and Houston. Search in vain for their names and testimony in the efforts of the Warren Commission, although we will hear of them again later.

Boxes were moved; the rifle, its exterior surface wiped clean of fingerprints, was hidden well enough to avoid police detection for almost an hour, only to be discovered at the virtual instant that Oswald should have been arrested by the *first* officers to reach him. The meticulous care given to the gun and its exterior surface by its presumed user, plus the time required to hide it from police view, suggest that an assassin would not have the opportunity to depart in haste; yet seconds after the shots ended, Oswald was confronted in the second-floor lunchroom by Officer Marrion L. Baker, who had his gun drawn. Oswald appeared calm, and the only controversy seemed to be whether Oswald was drinking a soda. Oswald mentioned the soda in an answer to FBI agent James Bookhout during questioning later that Friday; in Baker's report of the event, he wrote, "drinking a coke," but that was scratched out (it is still readable, however).[10] The reason for the concern over the soda is not that the police had to face the dilemma of whether to charge Oswald with possession of soda with intent to drink it, but rather that the soda destroyed the ever-so-delicate timing of the Baker-Oswald confrontation. When reconstructions were staged, Baker moved as if in a dream sequence, and "Oswald" hurtled at fast forward, yet the posthumous Oswald stand-in arrived at the lunchroom only four seconds ahead of the officer. But in the reconstruction, "Oswald" had not yet scrounged change, operated the soda machine, removed his purchase, taken the cap off it, nor begun to drink it.

In a chance encounter in Hollywood in 1992, I had the opportunity to meet Larry Pressman, a veteran character actor who played an investigator for the defense attorney portrayed by Lorne Greene in *The Trial of Lee Harvey Oswald*. Realizing we had much in common, Pressman told me that in his travels in Dallas, the fact that struck him more than any other was the configuration of the stairs in the depository. There was no way, he told me, that anybody could have fired and hid the rifle, and covered the distance across the sixth floor, encumbered as it was with both cartons and new, tenuous flooring, and then gone down the pathetically narrow book depository stairwell for four flights either in any haste or without drawing notice. "Check it out next time you're in Dallas," he said in closing. Little did he know that by then, only the sixth floor "Oswald only" exhibit of the depository was open to the public and security was tighter than in an airport fearful of terrorists.[11]

Other concerns still fail to provide any logical answers. No book depository employee turned assassin would choose the sixth floor, when, because of the construction of new flooring on November 22, it had the most employees assigned to it of any of the upper three floors. And if, as the evidence suggests, Oswald did not consume the famous chicken lunch found at the crime scene, what was he doing while it was being eaten? Sweating nervously in some hideaway hoping the chicken aficionado would vacate the "sniper's nest" in time for a rendezvous with destiny? Not likely.

Oswald was linked to the Mannlicher-Carcano rifle, no. C2766. He bought it, perhaps not in the manner a covert agent would, but certainly in a manner that would attract attention in the future. Using a coupon and a money order (arguably the only two such occasions he ever had for such routine documents), he had the rifle shipped to his post office box, where he retrieved it under the name of Hidell. He was then photographed with the weapon, another action *not* in keeping with the behavior of an assassin, and despite all the noise generated about the backyard photos being fakes (and there is much to question about them), his wife does admit taking at least two of the poses, and she even told this author that she has some recollection of the gun having a "gizmo" (telescopic sight).[12]

Yet problems, both evidentiary and logical, remain. The Mannlicher-Carcano rifle was an anachronism even by the time its weary Italian users were surrendering them en masse in the 1940s. The gun had begun its production run *in 1891* and can be seen today for what it was: a product of the mass warfare concepts of its time, in which huge armies charged each other, volleys were fired, and the bullets hit someone or something. It was not designed as a sniper's rifle, and a "gizmo," or telescopic sight, is about as appropriate on such a blunderbuss as caviar on war surplus crackers. And the weapon, as the FBI would *prove*, certainly lacked accuracy.

And what exactly did Oswald get when he purchased C2766? He got a $21 cannibalized piece of junk. Arms dealer William Sucher advised the Warren Commission on March 12, 1964, that "he has bought hundreds of thousands of rifles overseas as Italian Government surplus . . . many were collected from battlefields *and places of improper storage* [emphasis added] and they were in very poor condition. They were usually bought by the pound rather than units. Upon arrival in Canada, defective parts were removed and salable rifles were sometimes composed of parts of three or more weapons."[13] Small wonder that at the same time a blue-ribbon government panel was telling us of the high quality of this weapon, it was subject to litigation by Adams Consolidated Industries as "defective."[14]

Much has been made of Oswald's abilities or inabilities with a rifle, the most telling indictment coming from the late Leo Sauvage, an early critic of the official findings. In studying Oswald's 191/"marksman" score, Sauvage noted that the score of 190 was for all practical purposes a score of zero. "In other words, in May 1959, shortly before leaving the service, Oswald scored just one point more than the minimum required of each of the 175,571 officers and men then in the Marines."[15]

This should not be taken as a revelation. Much in Oswald's history suggests a lack of physical coordination: The mastoid operation he had as a child could impact on the body's balance; he was never successfully able to master something as simple as driving an automobile; he had been fired from Jaggers-Chiles-Stovall, a job that required manual dexterity; and Marine Corps records indicated he was not a great shot. Only the Warren Commission seemed to feel otherwise.

Oswald's lack of dexterity could easily have been seriously worsened by the fact that the gun presented to the FBI for inspection was found to have been sighted "as if for a left-handed man." The FBI failed to realize that because of the construction of the weapon, it could only be sighted that way, further proof it was never designed to hold a telescopic sight. Nevertheless, this situation obviously concerned a reporter on November 24, 1963, as Chief Jesse Curry, at one of his many briefings, was asked, "Is Oswald right-handed?"[16] This was no throwaway question asked to add trivial biographical data about Oswald, and the unknown reporter who asked this in CE 2147 obviously had a purpose—to wit, to match a left-handed person to the left-handed sighted weapon, or discover a "scoop" with the mismatch.

An equally valid question, open to several interpretations but nevertheless mandatory, is "Was the Mannlicher operable on November 22, 1963?" Mrs. Gertrude Hunter and Mrs. Edith Whitworth, who spent time together in a Dallas used furniture outlet that once sublet to a gunsmith, both testified to Warren Commission counsel that Oswald, with Marina, a young child, and a newborn infant, *drove* to the shop *in midweek* in November 1963 and that Oswald emerged from the car with a package in his hands and requested information as to where he could get a "plunger" (part of the firing mechanism) for the weapon. This testimony alone destroyed the lone-assassin theory, as it is highly likely that it was *not* Lee Oswald who drove up, since his time at the depository was all accounted for, and he neither drove nor owned a vehicle. But the Warren Commission never flat-out said it was not Oswald, so we are left with the possibility that as late as early November, the Mannlicher would not fire, and there has never been evidence produced (despite exhaustive attempts) that Oswald had its firing mechanism repaired anywhere else.[17]

While using the phrase "no evidence," there is one other major concern: There is no evidence that the "historical" Lee Oswald (as opposed to rifle-range impostors) ever fired a rifle with a telescopic sight.

The question of fingerprints, often a prime consideration in a crime such as murder, is also open to several interpretations. Dallas crime scene expert Carl Day told the Warren Commission that the one Oswald print found on the underside of the barrel when the weapon was disassembled was still on the gun when he sent it to the FBI.[18] Bureau fingerprint expert Sebastian F. Latona told the same investigating commission that he did not develop any prints on the rifle whatsoever.[19] The confusion could possibly have been clarified by FBI special agent Vince Drain, who transported the gun and all other evidence taken from Dallas to Washington at 3:00 A.M. on November 23, but he was not called by the commission. When his input was sought in the 1967 Garrison investigation, he expressed the doubt that there ever was a palmprint.[20] Of equal importance is the question as to why Oswald's fingerprints were not all over the weapon. In theory, he owned it and used it on November 22. Here again we see theory dictating facts: Oswald is culpable in the absence of prints, just as he was culpable for being absent, not present, at the depository an hour after the shooting.

Briefly putting aside the attempt on the life of Maj. Gen. Edwin Walker, U.S. Army (resigned), what is the pedigree of C2766 from the time of its ownership? In her earliest testimony before the commission, Marina Oswald indicated that she "knows for sure" that Oswald did not practice with the gun in New Orleans, where they resided from April to September 1963.[21] In subsequent hearings she would suggest that there was perhaps one evening *prior* to the move to New Orleans when Oswald may have taken the gun somewhere for practice and returned with it the same evening (so this is not Walker-related testimony, as Oswald was alleged to have buried the rifle after the Walker event). Mrs. Oswald also insisted that she had never seen any ammunition, which squares with the amount of ammunition or gun-related material traceable to the Oswald who was so obvious about the rifle purchase, or with the amount of bullets found at the Paine residence: none.[22]

The attempt on General Walker only bears on the narrative because if the story told by Mrs. Oswald of her husband admitting the shot, burying the rifle, and subsequently retrieving it is accurate, there should have been a host of questions and evidence regarding the condition of the wood and metal of that old gun after it was buried. What was buried were the questions, and with them, the truth.

Eric Rogers, the Oswalds' neighbor on Magazine Street in New Orleans, was unemployed and thus had the opportunity to notice

Oswald regularly on his side porch. Many were the times Oswald was seen reading; Rogers never observed him with a gun, although he was observing Oswald on the very porch that the Warren Commission would have us believe that Oswald sat and dry-fired, worked the bolt, and cleaned the weapon. Also, the cleaning equipment was never found, although a blanket was.

After New Orleans, the possibility that Oswald had access to the weapon for the purpose of practice becomes remote to the point of impossibility. The gun could only have gone, dismantled and within a blanket, from New Orleans to the Paine garage. It strains the imagination to conjure up Oswald getting access to that dismantled weapon in the clutter of that garage and sneaking off somewhere to practice with it while in the constant company of his wife and Mrs. Paine. We are thus left with the possibility that the accused lone assassin did not have one chance to fire the gun from early April until 12:29 or 12:30 P.M. on November 22, when his target cleared the foliage and became visible on Elm Street. Adrian Alba, whose garage was frequented by the gun-curious Oswald *after* he had purchased the Mannlicher, was quoted in a November 25, 1963, FBI report that is at right angles to everything that can be proven about Oswald's activities:

> Mr. ALBA expressed the opinion that OSWALD would necessarily have had a great deal of practice in firing a rifle with a scope sight to have been able to "get off as many shots" as he did . . . he knows that it takes a period of time for one to adjust his eyesight to the image at which he is firing after each shot. He added that this is not as easy as an open sight and that a bolt action rifle would add to the time necessarily consumed in firing such a rifle. He therefore believed that OSWALD had much practice in firing a gun of this type.[23]

As we have seen, there is no proof whatsoever that he did practice. There is also no proof that he ever bought a clip for the weapon, nor a single cartridge, despite an exhaustive FBI search for proof of such purchases. It was learned, however, that the U.S. Marine Corps bought four million such rounds in the 1950s, despite having no general issue weapons that could chamber such rounds. This suggests either a large purchase error, or covert use for such cartridges, assuming that somewhere there were weapons into which to put them. The FBI went so far as to sift through piles of hulls at every local rifle range in the Dallas area, desperately trying to find one cartridge that would prove Oswald had been practicing. Of hundreds of thousands seen, they submitted 1,336 such cartridges to their Washington lab; 80 proved to have originated from Mannlichers, but none matched C2766.[24]

Based on Constable Seymour Weitzman's "Affidavit in any fact," dated November 23, 1963, we learn that the gun he discovered in the book depository ". . . was a 7.65 Mauser bolt action equipped with a 4/18 scope. . . ." The arraignment papers for the murder of the president as well as the document charging attempted murder of the governor all cite a 6.25 Italian rifle.[25] C2766 was, of course, a 6.5 rifle, thus giving us more verifiable guns than usable cartridges, since of the three expended cartridges found in the depository, only two were able to hold and chamber a projectile.

If there is one certainty in the ongoing uncertainty about the Kennedy assassination, it is that the lone-assassin theory is further weakened by confusion regarding the bullet or bullets. The keystone in this evidentiary arch is, of course, CE 399, the "magic bullet." We know that the Dallas doctors removed far more metal from John Connally than is missing from the exhibit, and the doctors who performed the autopsy on the late president told the Warren Commission the same story—too much metal in Governor Connally. There was also the problem of identification of the magic bullet, for although it reached the FBI by passing through the hands of Darrell Tomlinson, O. P. Wright, Secret Service special agent Richard Johnsen, and James Rowley, head of the Secret Service, none of the four individuals could identify the pristine exhibit when the FBI came calling.[26] I would like to suggest to any reader of this narrative that if you had held a bullet in your hand in Parkland Hospital on November 22, in a location a few feet from where the president had just been pronounced dead, you would never in your lifetime be able to get the exact configuration of that bullet out of your mind. You would see it often in your nightmares.

Those concerns have been fully explored by competent researchers, as has the physics-defying path required of CE 399 to have done the damage attributed to it. Of equal curiosity is the question raised in the coauthored *High Treason*: CE 399, a jacketed military bullet, did massive damage to two individuals and emerged pristine, so reasoned the Warren Commission; yet a second bullet from the same gun came apart into dozens of dustlike fragments in the president's skull.[27] *How?*

There is also the potential problem of *far too many bullets*. The president was hit twice at the minimum and possibly four times; the governor was hit at least twice. Observers on the railroad overpass as well as at least one occupant of Chief Curry's car saw a bullet strike the road near the overpass, while one bullet was observed striking the pavement by the limousine near the book depository. It is also possible that a Secret Service agent in the vice-presidential follow-up vehicle saw a bullet strike behind the car he was in, according to an interview conducted by researcher Vince Palamara. Although the importance of that sighting is not noted by Palamara, this could have been the proposed frontal throat entry shot, having transited the president's neck. James Tague was wounded by a bullet that missed the presidential limousine by at least thirty-three feet, and Dallas officers Buddy Walthers and J. W. Foster were photographed next to an FBI agent who pocketed a cartridge that came to earth very close to the positions of Jean Hill and Mary Moorman.[28] James Altgens, who took one of the two most famous still photographs in Dealey Plaza (Mary Moorman took the other), is noted for providing the photo that suggests the presence of Billy Lovelady, who resembled Oswald, in the doorway of the depository during the shooting sequence. Altgens's *testimony* is more enlightening: He took the photo, which corresponds to Zapruder frame 255, at the instant "that he heard a burst of noise which he thought was firecrackers."[29] The Warren Commission never even considered the possibility of a shot being fired at, or near, Zapruder frame 255.

The last bit of unrehashed evidence that needs examination is the boxes, especially the one with the crease. The boxes admittedly had latent prints traceable to Oswald, but they also contained prints of several other as yet unidentified individuals, and every depository employee who handled boxes was fingerprinted. Prints do not last long on cardboard, so discard any theory that the company that shipped the boxes to the depository caused those prints. On the contrary, they were made in the depository, by an employee named Oswald and *others not employed in the TSBD.* Todd Wayne Vaughan, a subscriber to the lone-assassin theory who has had his expertise called upon by investigators, told this author (at the corner of Tenth and Patton, of all places) that the "unknown" prints of 1963 were later identified, and that they belonged to Dallas police officers. I believed him, of course; I just wished he could have told me which one of them had the rifle up there.

Of greater importance is the total absence of an Oswald fingerprint on anything permanent—the floor, the window glass, the sill, the bricks, the piping. His latent fingerprints seem only to appear on portable items—rifle, boxes, and bags.

The "crease" in one box troubles me, and would trouble the vast majority of marksmen, because no shooter worth his Marine Corps sharpshooter badge would use anything for a gun rest that was unstable enough to let itself crease. Why would anyone use a virtually collapsible carton when there exists a solid brick windowsill a mere thirteen inches above ground level? And to fire the weapon, work the bolt twice, and relocate on that crease would take considerably longer than the low-end time constraint of 2.3 seconds suggested by the official version. For a sniper armed with the Mannlicher, the process of setting up on the crease, firing, reloading, refinding the crease, reaiming—three times, yet—would have required the Zapruder film to be a full-length motion picture, not a matter of 5, 6, or 7 seconds.

Equally troubling in the timing department is the report of Dallas policeman E. D. Brewer, who radioed his dispatcher, "We have a man here who says he saw him *pull the weapon back through the window* of the southeast corner of that depository building."[30] Was the weapon also reloaded outside the window? It seems highly unlikely, but even if the bolt was worked inside the casement, it would still take time to get the rifle outside, and time was something that the Zapruder film proved a sixth-floor assassin, and the Warren Commission, did not have. Of course, we must account for the possibility that the gun was exterior to the window *so that it would be seen (but not necessarily heard).*

So much for the standard version, insofar as the Warren Commission's version could be subjected to a different line of condemnation than the reader is used to. But there are still problems with the "Lee Oswald–lone-assassin theory," and they begin with the Secret Service itself. Other researchers have documented the perceived threats to the president in Chicago and Miami in the month he died, which should suggest that the Secret Service was nonchalant at best and negligent at worst when they allowed the president into a city that had shown both Adlai Stevenson and Lyndon Johnson its unpleasant side. There has also been the suggestion, through the inscrutable Richard Case Nagell, that a separate attempt was planned in Miami for the winter of 1962–63, as well as a plot to kill the president during a Los Angeles preview of *PT-109* in June 1963.[31]

The point here is not to criticize or question Secret Service efficiency or lack of it (given that they kept one million filed concerns on well-worn index cards), but rather to ask the obvious: Is there one scrap of evidence that Lee Oswald was in Miami, Chicago, or L.A. at the times suggested? *Of course there isn't;* Oswald's mistake was being *in Dallas* when the conspiracy caught up to John Kennedy.

No recitation of reservations about the lone-assassin theory would be complete without reciting some of the doubts expressed by witnesses in Dealey Plaza. *Dallas Morning News* reporter Mary Woodward, standing adjacent to the first highway sign in the kill zone on Elm Street, told the FBI that she believed the shots came from above her "and from possibly behind her" in the direction of the overpass.[32] That testimony kept her from being called before the Warren Commission, and her absence was further guaranteed by her willingness to write a story for her paper telling what she heard, and having that story pulled after the official version began floating.

I had the distinct pleasure of having dinner with Mary Woodward (now married and living far from Texas), on November 22, 1992, along with assassination researchers George Michael Evica and Dick Russell. I asked Mary about the shots, based on what I knew from her deposition, and she seemed far more certain over dinner than her elliptically reported words in the FBI report indicated. The cadence she gave for the shot sequence put the last two almost simultaneous. I then asked her the obvious remaining (and admittedly leading) question: "The knoll?" She nodded in the affirmative, with a very persuasive intensity in her eyes.[33] Admittedly, sounds can play tricks on the human ear, but I was impressed by the perceptions of a journalist who was out in the open and not surrounded by the taller structures farther up near the corner of Elm and Houston.

Others have made the same claim, but it was surprising to read the reports of two Secret Service agents from the follow-up car, who also were *not called* before the Warren Commission. Paul Landis, riding outboard on the passenger side of the follow-up, indicated "my reaction at this time was that the [head] shot came from somewhere towards the front, right-hand side of the road."[34] George Hickey, of whom we will hear more later, was seated up on the left rear of the follow-up, and he can be seen turning in the Altgens photo, equivalent to Zapruder 255. Hickey deposed that he thought shot one was right rear (as he proved by looking that way for photographer Altgens), but shots two and three were at ground level.[35] Emmett Hudson, the Dealey Plaza groundskeeper, who should know the prevailing acoustics as well as anyone, was deposed in CE 2003: "The shots that I heard definitely came from behind and above me." *He was standing on the stairs that lead up to the picket fence.* In his subsequent testimony, he rephrased the "above and kind of behind" testimony, but Warren Commission counsel Wesley Liebeler had the last words when he added, ". . . the motorcade?"[36]

The circularity of the Warren Commission's premise and conclusion is now more evident: Since all they were given by the FBI and, to a lesser extent, local officials was evidence accumulated in the book depository, they could only conclude that the event occurred there. Anyone who suggested otherwise became not an eyewitness but an "earwitness" and therefore, because of acoustical confusions, far less credible. But Jean Hill was an eyewitness, claiming to have seen a muzzle flash, smoke, and the shadowy figure of a man with a rifle barely visible on the knoll, an area she unknowingly named.[37] We will have further references to Ms. Hill's testimony later, as it was ultimately to be turned into one of the the Warren Commmission's whitest of "white lies."

At least one other witness, lost to history through accident or intent, gave evidence to corroborate Ms. Hill's statement. In Decker 5323, Dallas sheriff's officer Jack W. Faulkner told of running toward the knoll, where he thought the sounds came from, only to encounter a woman [unknown] who told him that Kennedy was dead—shot through the head. Faulkner said: "I asked her where the shorts [sic] came from, and she pointed toward the concrete arcade on the east side of Elm Street."[38]

So despite the Warren Commission's willingness to turn observers into "earwitnesses," there were eyewitnesses, as well as, to coin a phrase, "nosewitnesses." And their olfactory perceptions are vital: They include Mrs. Earle Cabell, Senator Ralph W. Yarborough, and others who smelled gunpowder either well down Elm Street or in the area behind the picket fence. This nasal evidence comports with the testimony of Jean Hill and Deputy Sheriff Faulkner's "unidentified" witness, as well as the better-known testimony of S. M. Holland and most of the railroad workers who were standing on the triple underpass that a shot or shots came from the grassy knoll.[39]

Other telling contemporary observations were recorded for posterity when they were logged in on the police radio channels. Police Chief Curry, keenly sensing that something had gone wrong in the motorcade, quickly told his dispatcher, "Get a man on that triple underpass and see what happened up there." Sheriff Decker, more astute in terms of the event and the use of manpower, quickly radioed, "Have my office move all available men out of my office into the railroad yard. . . ." Of course, Decker had the luxury of ordering more men, since he had told his officers *not* to provide any motorcade security.[40]

Other reports spoke of a light green two-tone car carrying an occupant with a rifle (reported at 2:19 P.M., after Oswald was in custody); a suspect carrying a rifle on the railroad tracks near Cobb Stadium; a pickup order for the occupants of a 1957 Chevy sedan, license NA 4445, suspected of carrying a concealed weapon; an additional call for a "wrecker" needed on the parking lot west of Cobb Stadium for the "suspect's car."[41] While the shots were still echoing, the police radio carried a transmission for a suspect with a 30-30 rifle, a very precise description, yet one that is at odds with the poor-quality Mannlicher, and the same suspect was referenced by 12:48 P.M.: "He is thought to be in this Texas School Book Depository here on the northwest corner Elm and Houston."[42] Why a suspected presidential assassin would be thought to be still lurking at the site of the crime as late as 12:48 P.M. is an investigative concern worthy of critical inspection. If there was still an assassin in the TSBD at 12:48 P.M., we know it was not Oswald.

This suggests that the individual mentioned was disguised to fit the event. The wearing of a Dallas police uniform would have been an excellent, and successful, disguise.

Other eyewitness observations at variance with the official version include the oft-repeated identification, by Roger Craig, a highly lauded sheriff's officer, of Oswald. Yet the "Oswald" he saw was an individual running from the depository well after Oswald's documented 12:33 P.M. departure and entering a Rambler station wagon driven by a dark-complected individual. Craig subsequently viewed Oswald in the Homicide Bureau and positively identified him as the man who got in the Rambler, just as cabbie William Whaley and bus driver Cecil McWatters identified Oswald as being in their respective vehicles at the same time.[43]

One mute exhibit of earwitness testimony would eventually rewrite history, at least temporarily. For reasons not fully explained, a Dallas motorcycle officer, H. B. McLain, riding well behind the limousine, had the transmit key on his radio "open" during the tragic shooting sequence (Officer McLain today strongly denies both that it was his motorcycle and that his radio was kept on). Acoustics experts called by the House Select Committee on Assassinations first washed the fifteen-year-old tape of extraneous noise, then determined that there was a high probability of more than three shots. Tests were then done, with a greater scientific precision than what had gone before, and it was determined that of the six to nine sound impulses, perhaps shots, on the tape, four had been fired from either the book depository or the knoll, with shot number three coming from the knoll, *and missing.* There is still some minor agreement there with the official version, until one analyzes the time factor of the shots. Counting the first shot as "0," the second shot, from the same location, was fired 1.66 seconds later, far too fast to have been fired from Oswald's Mannlicher. The third and fourth shots were fired 7.49 and 8.31 seconds, respectively, after "0," close enough (.82 second apart) to create the "double bang" sound effect spoken of by many witnesses. The House committee, using the last depository shot as the fatal shot (and still relying on potentially fraudulent autopsy evidence, not acoustics, to place the source of the shot), concluded that the shots corresponded to the following Zapruder frames: "0"=Z157–161 (a time when JFK's car was hidden from the sixth floor of the depository by dense foliage); 1.66=Z187–190; 7.49=Z295–6; and 8.31=Z 312–3. This suggests one of two equally disconcerting possibilities: Either both Kennedy and Connally were wounded in the Z187–190 range, well before they show any reaction whatsoever, *and* they were shot by a lousy marksman *through the foliage,* or the two depository shots both missed and Kennedy and Connally were hit from behind by an assassin not in the depository. However, if one adds one second (and eighteen frames) to the timing, one arrives at the following sequence: "0"=175–179; 1.66=205–208; 7.49=313–316; 8.31=330–333. This sequence would allow for Kennedy's back wound, without foliage, as shown in the Zapruder film at Z205–208, and would place the head shot's origin on the knoll (7.49); the final depository shot, 8.31, would be a few inches farther down Elm Street, and can be seen in the Zapruder film to rip into Connally, causing his wrist and thigh wounds.[4] On your next occasion of viewing the Zapruder film, concentrate on Connally; he shows serious movement very shortly after Z313—movement too fast, and possibly too animated for someone going into shock, to be a reaction to Kennedy's wounds. It is highly possible that he was being wounded, as close study of earlier

Zapruder frames clearly shows blood on his suit coat and shirt front, but none on his right cuff.

Before continuing with House select committee findings, it should be noted that the acoustical reconstruction that was believed in 1978 has since been seriously challenged. Of greater import, and not open to challenge, is the fact that police microphones somewhere were kept open within time proximity to the assassination; perhaps a communications snafu was one of the more simplistic contributions the police made that day.

The House committee also revised earlier dogma about the wound that apparently was inflicted on the president from behind, stating its findings indicated there was a slight *upward* trajectory to the "*back* wound."[45] This simple finding was as much of a milestone as the committee's willingness to accept the acoustic evidence of the shots. First, it posited the wound for what it was: a back wound, not the nonsensical "neck wound" that was a forced prerequisite for the Warren Commission. Second, it reflected the reality of the wound. I have seen and heard much controversy about the president's back wound, as speakers point to the holes in the president's garments, then cite Secret Service agent Clint Hill's testimony about "a wound six inches down from the neckline" (an accurate description), and conclude with the autopsy deduction that the bullet went in at an angle of forty-five degrees. If you look at the garments and ask where a bullet would go that entered those holes on a six-foot individual of average build and then went down and to the left at forty-five degrees, you are forced to conclude that the president died from that shot, as it would have pierced his heart. It did not, as we know. It entered where shown on the garments, which were not seriously bunched, but rather fit comfortably on a man with a raised shoulder configuration—almost hunched, as suggested in the photograph where President Kennedy was mobbed as he emerged from a swim. It then traversed slightly upward, knicking the spinal column, and possibly emerging from his throat. It then either hit the windshield, the chrome, or flew out over the chrome and could have been the bullet that Sheriff Decker saw hit the pavement behind Curry's cruiser. The bullet did not, as the Warren Commission wants us to believe, enter just below the hairline, go *down* at an angle of eleven degrees, and then make several roller-coaster turns to and through the governor.[46]

With respect to angles, we have been scammed. For all the precision of measurements taken during the Secret Service "reenactment" of the assassination, our attention was diverted and our suspicions aroused by the use of a 1956 Cadillac instead of the presidential limousine. What was lost in this shuffle was the angles: The commission gave us the angles to Elm Street, located in the horizontal plane; angles relative to the president, who was in the vertical plane, are quite different and can tell us much about the events of that day.

Although not emanating from eye-, ear-, or nosewitnesses, we cannot move on to our next suspect before we take a detour through what will be called "official doubts." Henry Wade, the man who, after Oswald's death (and pressure from D.C. to close the case), would hang it all on the deceased suspect, initially told reporters, ". . . preliminary reports [i.e. pre-Hoover] indicate that more than one person was involved in the shooting."[47] There were other concerns of a similar nature while Oswald was alive. Jesse Curry was asked, "Is there absolutely no doubt now that nobody else is involved as an accomplice?" Curry replied, "I would not make that statement."[48] When pressed on that comment, he would not elaborate, and the Warren Commission obviously did not want him to either, as they did not ask him about it. When Henry Wade testified before the commission, he maintained his earlier position: "From what I picked up, it appeared to me there was no question that he [Oswald] received his inspiration on this and maybe other help from somewhere."[49] "Other help" could imply financial backing or additional shooters; either way, "other help" is synonymous with "conspiracy."

The Warren Commission also heard from George DeMohrenschildt regarding Oswald: "Now, we heard, also, that he was getting some regular checks from somewhere."[50]

Perhaps the most surprising witness to appear before the Warren Commission and provide unsolicited information was General Walker, whose testimony is really quite engaging and worth reading for the sheer exuberance that Walker brought to his own investigation. When pressed for a suggestion that the Commie Oswald was equally guilty of the "assassination" attempt on Walker, the resigned general answered, "And I am not very prone to say in fact he did. . . . In fact, I have always claimed he did not. . . ."[51]

Reasonable doubt? Certainly. Howard Brennan, hardly a witness either the Warren Commission or this author would want to stake an entire case on, told the commission that his observations did not include seeing the rifle fired, "but you heard the last shot?" "Yes, sir." This strongly suggests that the last shot was *not fired* from the weapon in the sixth-floor window that Brennan was observing.[52]

Assassination researcher Dick Russell, who spent seventeen years studying the strange doings of Richard Case Nagell, wrote: "The USSR ordered Nagell to eliminate Lee Harvey Oswald because they thought it might be an extreme embarrassment to them if he was caught, not because he was one of them, but because of his history."[53] This one sentence, in the midst of a lengthy, scholarly look at the Kennedy assassination, epitomizes much of the frustration of the research community, as it suggests that the Soviets knew more about the event than our own government has been willing to tell us for thirty years. It also guarantees that the Soviets, perhaps better than Americans, understood the concepts of "patsy" and "conspiracy."

Just as the then-Soviets were an unlikely source on the "patsy" theory, we have an equally unlikely source on the cover-up concept, and it is General Walker again, speaking of the kind of cover-up that has prevented us from hearing from many witnesses who might have had much to tell: "I think there is a definite—I don't know if you would call it evidence—but you can anticipate that people would like to shut up anybody that knows anything about this case. People right here in Dallas."[54] Could General Walker have been speaking about right-wing local officers, of whom an ample supply existed back in 1963, who could intimidate, or eliminate, witnesses as needed? The allegations regarding the participation of Roscoe "Rock" White in the assassination and, after the fact, as the point man in the drive to tidy up loose-mouthed witnesses may provide an interesting answer to that question.

I could overlook much of what has been written above if I could be presented with Oswald's motive. Alas, that, too, is lacking. One suggestion that I find absurd was put forward by Renatus Hartogs, who treated the thirteen-year-old truant Oswald. Along with coauthor Lucy Freeman, the pair suggested that Oswald's poor spelling was his motivation to hate, and he took it out on Kennedy.[55] An equally curious theory, often put forward, was that Oswald committed the assassination as a way to gain a permanent niche in history. Yet when history stared Lee Oswald straight in the eye—in the halls of the Dallas Police Department several times, and in the basement press conference, did Oswald seek to trumpet his achievement to the world and gain the fame he was supposedly seeking? No. He denied participation in any capital crimes committed on November 22, requested that an attorney come forward, and asked that he be allowed to shower.

The niche he gained was in Rose Hill Cemetery in Fort Worth.

Equal-time department: Any analysis of the lone-assassin concept would prove inadequate without consideration given to the "detailed research" done by Gerald Posner that led to his book *Case Closed*.

We are asked to believe that Mr. Posner conducted countless interviews, in many cases reinterviewing dozens of the people involved, leading to a cogent reappraisal of the assassination that suggests that the work done previously by "critics" was based on erroneous information. Mr. Posner's interpretation of the witnesses' testimony suggests that they were all wrong in earlier testimony, even the entire group of Dallas doctors who never actually saw JFK's head wound, according to Posner. Other witnesses whose stories are examined are shown to be wrong, and the remainder, such as Sylvia Odio or Delphine Roberts, Guy Banister's secretary, to name just a couple, are just plain crazy. Miss Odio's testimony, believed in 1978 by the House select committee, is seen as a result of her being driven to a psychiatrist because of her "fractious marriage"[56] and therefore useless in getting at any truth.

As one wades through the first 223 pages (47.2 percent of the text) of Mr. Posner's work, one is treated to a compendium of reports that portray Lee Oswald as an individual far more demented than any previous human on this planet. Perhaps Mr. Posner forgot that he also authored a biography of Dr. Mengele. While I would not want Lee Oswald as the local recreation director or coach, I would suggest that most of us run across far worse psychopaths in our daily pursuits, some of whom make Oswald seem tame.

Beyond that, the reader gets the suspicion that the methods, sources, and errors in *Case Closed* are similar in many ways to the works of previous writers that Mr. Posner criticizes. The "critics," he claims, are out for a fast buck and will part with a few bucks for cheap, sensational claims that have no support. In this regard, the pot is calling the kettle black, as it has been clearly shown that Mr. Posner did not, in fact, even speak to some of the witnesses he claims to have interviewed and even *quoted* to prove a point. Several major witnesses in *Case Closed* have already gone on the record to state unequivocally that they never spoke to Mr. Posner, although he quotes them, and even embellishes with details about the interview or interviews that never happened. Still other witnesses have said that they did speak with Posner but that their words or thoughts were sadly misrepresented.

Beyond that, *Case Closed* is a weak attempt at objectivity inasmuch as it reveals its clear bias in the fifth line of the first page of text: "Dozens of witnesses sent the police scurrying in different directions in futile search of an assassin."[57] Analyze that statement closely: "Dozens [plural] of witnesses [plural] sent the police [plural] scurrying in different directions [plural] in futile search of an assassin [singular]."[58] So dozens of people sent a cadre of officers in many different directions, all to look for a psychopath named Oswald. It would make more sense to be candid at least with respect to the perception: Witnesses, right or wrong, believed that there were shooters in several places. Also bear in mind: if *one* of those witnesses [plural] is correct, put the Warren Report and *Case Closed* in the fireplace.

What Mr. Posner conveniently neglects is that there was virtually no reaction by police to witnesses who reported seeing a rifle in the sixth-floor window of the depository, where I have no doubt there was a rifle. *Why did it take the police so long to "scurry" after the most obvious assassin?*

The biggest concern with this latest Warren Commission rehash, besides its claim to being something it is not, is a new variation on the "What's wrong with the Warren Commission?" theme. *You can't have it both ways.*

Oswald is credited, on December 20, *1956,* as qualifying as a sharpshooter, which is noted as the second highest qualification in the marines. Mr. Posner does not tell his readers, however, that sharpshooter is also the second lowest, as it is the middle of three categories. Either way, the point is moot. To make the shots made almost seven years after this 1956 Oswald effort would require a master expert marksman, literally the best of the best. Oswald, however, was barely able to qualify before being discharged from the marines, but Posner fails to note that Oswald's score was a pathetic 191, a score frequently awarded to someone unable to hit a bull in the butt with a baseball bat so that some weary range officer does not waste valuable time with a noncombat "grunt" about to be phased out of the marines.

Having learned from Mr. Posner of Oswald's rifle acumen in the marines, although it was neither with a cheap Italian rifle nor an equally cheap Japanese scope, we discover that KGB files indicated that Oswald was a lousy shot—so poor, in fact, that he could not hit a rabbit *with a shotgun*. This datum, which would tend to mitigate his earlier stated marksmanship prowess, is buried in a Posner *footnote*.[59]

It is the same story with the Dallas doctors. They were wrong in statements about the president's wounds, according to Posner, because they did not possess the requisite pathology skills. And Humes et al. did? So it can be argued that "The mistakes in judgment from Parkland are exactly why we have autopsies."[60] Agreed; but the law was rather clear on the fact that the autopsy should have been *at Parkland,* not at a government institution. And, of course, at Parkland, it would have been done by Dallas doctors, whereas at Bethesda it was done by professors on the payroll of, and in the career service of, the U.S. government.

Not that the government would ever interfere, although, well, call it a curiosity, but there is the matter of KGB defector Yuri Nosenko. After our government nearly drove him insane and beat his teeth out of him, they kissed, made up, and relocated Nosenko so carefully that when a researcher found out *the state* Nosenko was living in, the government relocated him again, undoubtedly for his safety, as a curious JFK researcher obviously posed a deep threat to a man already desensitized to pain by CIA tortures.[61] Yet Gerald Posner was granted a direct interview with the traitorous Nosenko, and was allowed to ask 130 questions that the CIA did not get around to asking in the several years they were treating Nosenko to the best mind-altering games American technology could invent. Nosenko's revelations to Posner suggest that American mind-altering technology had worked, for the former KGB stooge told that at the height of the Cold War, the KGB perceived Oswald to be mentally unfit, so they allowed him to stay in the USSR. If we were to use logic like that in our dealings, when the Watergate goings-on came unraveled in 1974, Nixon would have been made president for life.

We are also told, "Firearms experts testified after the assassination that a marksman such as Oswald [did any of them have personal knowledge of Oswald's "abilities"?] would need to fire only ten rounds to adjust the scope and become familiar with the peculiarities of that rifle."[62] As a master-expert shot, I find no argument there, except to note that the ten shots would have to have been fired after the Mannlicher was allegedly reassembled in the depository. Does that mean there were thirteen shots?

It is also emphasized that months before the assassination, Oswald spent a great deal of time playing with the bolt on the rifle and cleaning the gun. We are to infer from that datum that the shots in Dealey Plaza were therefore easy. Somehow, however, I doubt that if I oil my baseball glove regularly and practice holding the seam of a baseball, I will become Nolan Ryan. Equally illogical, if I hire a domestic to clean my house regularly (as Oswald allegedly did with his rifle), does that guarantee that such an employee could build the same house?

In what is an interesting narrative, and one told as if derived from revelation, there are some absolute impossibilities and some truly bogus data. We are told, "His dark blue one [jacket] was found at the School Book Depository and she [Marina] identified the jacket found in the gas station as *the other one* [emphasis added]. He had even worn it to the Paine's [sic] house the night before the assassination."[63] Oswald could not have worn the gas station jacket to the Paines', as the blue one was worn on Friday to the TSBD, where it was subsequently found, and Oswald only donned the "other one" at the boardinghouse on North Beckley at 1:00 P.M. Posner's profered jacket scenario is nonsensical. Perhaps Mr. Posner's research also proved that Oswald took the pistol to the depository, then went home after the shooting to get the rifle, which he used to shoot a theater before being arrested inside a police car. *Hey, you never know. . . .*

Equally erroneous is the testimony of Dr. Bill Midgett, the first doctor to reach the stricken limousine when it arrived at Parkland. He told (if, in fact, he was interviewed, as claimed) the author of *Case Closed* of his observations with respect to the president's wounds while Mr. Kennedy was being wheeled into the emergency room. Dr. Midgett must have been a giant of medicine, as the president's head and upper extremities were covered by Clint Hill's suit coat to prevent the curious from seeing the wounds.[64]

In the media's impetuous "rush to judgment" of Mr. Posner's book, it was noted that although he reached the same conclusions as the Warren Commission, he was highly critical of them. Yet he still used the testimony of star witness Howard Brennan, perhaps the least honest of any witness in the case. In his posthumously (for good reason) published work, Brennan told that after his March 1964 appearance before the commission, his good friend Earl Warren asked him if he would like to be introduced to Jackie Kennedy. There is a term for stories like that, and you wouldn't want to step in it barefoot.

For an author "critical" of the commission, at times Mr. Posner sounds like an apologist: "Since all the Commissioners had full time careers [one wonders what Allen Dulles's was: ex-spook?] they could only spend part of their time at the hearings. Senator Russell had the poorest attendance, hearing only six percent [sic] of the testimony. Only three of the seven commissioners heard more than half the testimony."[65] Therein, Mr. Posner reveals a glaring inadequacy with respect to an understanding of how the commission worked, and demonstrates the complete shallowness of his own research in the process. With respect to Senator Russell, he attended the hearings of only 6 of the 488 witnesses, making him present for 1.2 percent (not Posner's 6 percent) of the testimony. Further, Russell asked only 249 questions, or 0.2 percent of the commission's total. Russell would have had to have asked 6,596 questions to have attained 6 percent participation, so Mr. Posner's assertion is, well, let's be kind and call it inaccurate. Either way, you still would not want to step in it.

The other members, in varying numbers, attended parts of the testimony of 93 of the 488 witnesses, so no commissioner could claim to have been present for more than 19.05 percent of the testimony, even if they had heard every question posed to every witness deposed by commissioners, which they most assuredly did not. As a group, the seven presidential dwarfs asked only 6.3 percent of the total questions.[66]

Among witnesses, Officer H. B. McLain, believed to have been the motorcycle officer with the "open" microphone on his cycle, told author Posner that such a theory was nonsense because of the massive crowd noise in Dealey Plaza, which did not appear on the tape in question. Agreed again; but in a subsequent revelation, we are asked to believe that depository employee Harold Norman (who was under the "sniper's nest" window), despite the massive crowd noise and eighteen motorcycles, was able to hear, according to Posner, "Boom, click-click, boom, click-click, boom."[67] What obviates the validity of that testimony is that there had to have been another click-click, as three hulls were found on the floor, and the rifle, when discovered, had a bullet, not a hull, in the chamber. Mr. Norman is also the cited authority on the architecture of the depository. He was able to hear the booms and the click-clicks because the flooring was being redone and only thin plywood was holding everything together. Yet whoever was on the sixth floor in the "sniper's nest" was surrounded by boxes containing thousands of pounds of books. How can a floor so thin that it allows sounds to be clearly heard support such weight plus an assassin? *Or assassins?*

I did learn from *Case Closed* that Oswald had a tendency to smirk quite a bit. Perhaps smirking should be added to the Secret Service manual as a protective concern.

Analysis: The lone-assassin theory has, virtually since its inception, been penetrated at will by at least a thousand points of light. Numerous researchers have ably targeted obvious specific weaknesses in the theory, or the entire corpus of the theory. While room must be made for differing observations due to a host of variables, there are no such variables that could explain that which was seen, heard, and smelled in the vicinity of the grassy knoll, nor are there any acceptable explanations that would allow for Lee Oswald, in a poor vantage point and in possession of the cheapest weapon on the advertisement page from which he purchased it, suddenly to become a world-class marksman. Given what we know about the suspect and the gun, we would have to credit *gravity* as the reason the bullets went down.

The public has recognized the weaknesses in the official version, and there are many who now suspect that Oswald fired no shots in Dealey Plaza on November 22, 1963. This is not to suggest, however, that he was not the patsy he claimed to be, and as the patsy he may very well be culpable as an accessory, although to a crime whose full nature he did not understand until it occurred. Either way, the only credence still placed in the Lee Oswald–lone-assassin theory is held by a handful of staunch Warren Commission defenders, and their reasoning is sadly as circuitous as the path required for CE 399 to have inflicted wounds on both Kennedy and Connally.

Lee Oswald knew, better than anyone, whether there was a lone assassin, but he was killed before he was able to tell us, a curious thought in itself. Perhaps wherever Oswald is now, he's reading all the words written about him *and smirking*.

CHAPTER THREE

THE SECRET SERVICE: THEORIES OLD AND NEW

". . . they even have to die in secret."

—Seth Kantor, reporting on a rumor on November 22
that a Secret Service agent had been killed and his
death hushed up because he may have been involved in
the plot.   (Kantor, ex. 4, 20H 410

ANY CONSIDERATION OF THE SECRET SERVICE as a participant in the
tragedy of November 22, 1963, must begin with the reminder that
the men (in 1963), like the men and women now, are dedicated
individuals willing to put their lives on the line to save those of our
elected officials, most specifically the president. Given that postulate,
we must consider the acts of the Secret Service during the Texas
trip, consider theories that include the service, and remind ourselves
that only special agent Clint Hill, of ten agents in the immediate
vicinity of President Kennedy, took action. For reasons never fully
explained, the others remained inert.

John Kennedy was not an easy individual to protect. Despite World
War II injuries that very nearly halved his life, and at least one disease
that was life-threatening, he was an activist president. He sought
crowds; he understood that politics required reaching the people; and
he knew that occasionally it took courage to succeed at it. For a
president who authored *Profiles in Courage,* the last profile this author

has of John Kennedy in life is Zapruder frame 312, and it is more likely Kennedy's courage than Secret Service intrigue that allowed one or more gunmen to see that profile in their sights.

Robert Blakey has noted, "As his family and close associates were aware, John F. Kennedy had a preoccupation with death."[1] He had faced it in the South Pacific, in Boston operating theaters, and in public appearances in places where a liberal New Englander who had "betrayed" the movement to free Cuba would not be welcome. As we are coming to learn, his policies of moving America in a different direction were creating powerful enemies, some of whom had "friends in high places," which gave license and leverage to some of those enemies.

We also know that the president traveled several dozen times in 1963[2] and that on the night before his death, he prophesied how easy it would be for someone with a rifle to kill him. Overlooking the oft-told story that the Texas trip convinced JFK to indicate privately that LBJ would not be the '64 vice-presidential nominee, this premonition may have been President Kennedy's last correct prediction.

The Secret Service has always been suspect primarily because they failed to protect the president, and secondarily because of nagging little questions that don't make logical sense: Why did only Clint Hill, a last-minute addition to the trip, go to the rescue? Why did the car slow down or stop? Who had the fake Secret Service credentials in Dealey Plaza, and how were they obtained? Why was the protection so thin, with motorcycles kept at a distance, agents kept off the car, and military backup totally absent? Why was nothing done about the agents' after-hours escapades in Fort Worth on November 21? What was the basis of Seth Kantor's rumor that an agent involved in a plot had been killed? Why had the president been allowed to charge so boldly through Dallas, a town that in 1963 was a seething cauldron just waiting for a victim to scald? Why was a fifty-four-year-old Secret Service agent the driver of the car? Why, since it was Dallas, did the head of the White House detail stay in Washington instead of making the trip? Why did the Secret Service remove evidence in haste from Dallas, not allowing either the local coroner or the local police the opportunity to deal with the evidence? Why had the recent concerns for Kennedy's safety in Chicago and Miami not guaranteed maximum security in Texas? Was there anything unusual about the motorcade route?

These are serious questions, but there are reasonable, logical answers for most of them. First of all, despite the concerns in Chicago
and Miami,[3] Secret Service procedure was such that it localized its
concerns to maximize its efforts. So when John Kennedy decided on
a trip to Texas, the Secret Service did its normal investigation into
possible problems *in Texas*. While 20-20 hindsight allows us to see
the folly of that policy, that nevertheless was standard contemporary
policy, regardless of who the president was.

Over the years I have had the opportunity to speak with a few
Secret Service agents, and while they are quick to admit that the
Protective Research Section of the service has been vastly modernized
"since Dallas," the procedure has remained very similar. I asked one
agent why there was no concern in Texas for Thomas Vallee, who
had been arrested in Chicago in November 1963, clearly with intent
to kill President Kennedy. "Our focus," he told me, "would be in
Texas." Virtually all the agents I have spoken to say almost the same
thing, and it does not sound rehearsed. Most are quick to add in
defense of the Secret Service, "You have to remember, it happened
in about six seconds." When I initially heard that disclaimer, it was
not all that long after I had taken my driver education course, which
taught me that in an automotive crisis, I could hit the brakes in about
a second. Was there something manifestly different about the *gas pedal*
on such an expensive car?

The most fundamental answer to the question as to why the Secret
Service failed to protect the president is perhaps the most difficult.
First of all, there was tremendous concern for the president's safety
in Dallas. I was told this by both of the Secret Service agents in the
front seat of the president's car during the shooting. When Roy
Kellerman said it, the statement was made with such conviction and
intensity that no listener would doubt it. The driver, William Greer,
said just about the same thing, but without the intensity, as he almost
seemed detached from the event—he was the driver, as he had driven
Truman and Eisenhower before and would drive Johnson to church
on November 24, and "protection" was for the others, he seemed
to say.[4] Agent Kellerman also told me of very serious concern by
both Ken O'Donnell and John Connally as to the removal of the
bubble top on the limousine.

The Secret Service failed to keep John Kennedy alive for three
primary reasons. First, there was no documented attempt on the life
of an American president since 1950, when President Truman was
the focus of an attempt at Blair House, the temporary presidential

residence while the White House underwent restoration. Secret Service agent Floyd Boring was the hero of that piece, and it is an irony that Boring was one of three individuals who could have been sitting in the passenger seat of the limousine on November 22, 1963. It just happened that it was Roy Kellerman's turn. What this proves is that the agents protecting the president that day, despite rigorous training, had no real experience in crisis management. None had ever fired a gun in the defense of a president. And although they were a worried group all the way through downtown Dallas, with possibly as many as twenty thousand open windows, there is a strong hint—not an admission—that when they turned onto Houston Street and the crowd was suddenly only "one deep" on the sidewalk and thinning in the open plaza ahead, they breathed a sigh of relief. After the huge turn onto Elm, there were only scattered spectators, and Winston Lawson, riding shotgun in Curry's lead car, was already looking past the motorcade when he wrote: "12:35 Arrived Trade Mart." In those few seconds of letdown, perhaps understandable after the huge crowds showing warm affection, the Secret Service lost their protectee.

Second, in defense of the Secret Service, the president did not make their jobs easy. Kennedy knew, as he approached the 1964 election, that Texas was crucial, and within that state, Dallas was *the challenge*. To tour such a tough town with the Secret Service draped all over the presidential limousine, with motorcycles surrounding the car, and with the usual military presence very obvious, was just not Kennedy's style. He didn't want to read the news the next day at LBJ's ranch that the president, shielded by a massive cordon of bodyguards, had timidly sped through "the big D." He wanted to let them know he wasn't afraid of them.

As we now know, *he should have been.*

The third primary reason that John Kennedy never delivered a midday speech at the Trade Mart involves a judgment call that in turn calls into question the entire issue of conspiracy and whodunit. The question is simple: "Why, in the face of danger, did the car slow down?" Average motorcade speed in the suburban portion had approached 20 to 25 miles per hour; in the city, the average was about 15; the Zapruder film yields an *average* of 11.2 miles per hour during the time of the shooting. But the film taken by Orville Nix, according to Richard Trask, who self-published *Pictures of the Pain,* shows that during the immediate time frame of the final bullet, the car was traveling at only 8.7 miles per hour. Why?

In the late 1960s, the question of John Kennedy's death turned from an intense curiosity into a personal obsession for this author. I wanted nothing more than the whole truth, and figured if I talked to as many people as possible who were involved in one way or the other, the truth would hit me as an apple had once changed Isaac Newton's universe. The first people I wanted to speak to were those who, to my thinking, held the ultimate key to solving the riddle: the three autopsy doctors. But they were not talking, period (and as of this writing, they still aren't). They were tough to find and impossible to get to the phone. National security, you know. My next choice was Clint Hill, but he had done his job that day, so my focus turned elsewhere. Years later I saw an interview with Mr. Hill on *Sixty Minutes,* and he spoke of serious deterioration of his health because he arrived at the limousine a couple of seconds late. I was no longer of a mind to probe his psyche, though at the time of this writing, he is the one man I would still like to speak with, if for no other reason than to acknowledge his courage. But in the 1960s, I started small, dragging out the Greater Washington phone book and finding a listing for William Greer. What he told me in a couple of conversations has forever changed my perspective on the event.

William Greer was not an educated man, having only two years of high school in Ireland in the 1920s. As a result, he did not come across with either intensity or articulation in our conversations, but he did speak, if hesitatingly, with conviction. He had relived the event in his mind a thousand times and had come to grips with what had happened.

My first question, after formalities and asking if he'd mind talking a little (and he sounded like the answer was going to be "no"), was about the huge turn at Elm and Houston. Greer was quick to point out that he had never driven the route, and the turn surprised him. But then he got to the point with candor. He had to slow down in the turn, *and after it,* to maintain the "integrity of the parade." With the crowd gone, he could have made the turn and stepped on the gas, bringing the speed up to a safer 25 to 30 miles per hour, but he didn't, in order to allow the following cars, and the much larger press buses, to negotiate the crazy turn and stay close to the president's car. Then, as he straightened out and looked ahead, he encountered another problem: The triple underpass, which should have been devoid of civilians, was, on the contrary, overpopulated. This greatly concerned Greer, as there was always the fear that even friendly civilians could cause problems for the limousine as it passed beneath them. (I wanted to ask Greer if he'd seen *Ben Hur*, where a similar, preautomotive incident provided the set piece for the movie, but not if it meant interrupting his train of thought.) So, at that moment, he had three concerns: one, the letdown as the parade came to an end; two, allowing following vehicles to catch up; and three, looking for a way to avoid going under the populated overpass at that spot. He told me he saw no escape to the right, where the knoll gradually rose, and prospects were not much better on the left, where a few stragglers such as Jean Hill and Mary Moorman (whose identities were unknown to Greer) were located. Greer did not say it in so many words, but he intimated that he would have felt a little silly taking a wild detour through the crowd to avoid the group on the overpass, but he also knew that he had to make a judgment, and that the civilians who should never have been there in the first place had forced him to make that judgment.

With all this going through his mind, he heard "a backfire," which he did not immediately recognize as a shot, and then he looked back in time to see Connally begin to react to a wound. He never saw the president, he told me. He added that it was at that time that he hit the gas. I told him that it was several seconds later that the car finally accelerated, and I almost expected to hear a click from his end, but instead I heard a deep sigh followed by his answer. The car was in low gear for parades, he told me, and it had to be shifted and then there would be a pause regardless, because of the weight of the heavily armored vehicle, such heavy armor plating being virtually meaningless since the vehicle was a convertible with the top off. I then groped politely for the bottom line, asking if he could have slowed the vehicle either in the act of looking back or because *his perception of the threat was from the front.* He told me that he had asked himself that same question many times, and had no answer for me.[5] He did not deny the possibility. All I was able to learn in subsequent conversations was that there had never been any worries that his age (fifty-four in 1963) would be a problem, and he added that the president showed appreciation for him as his driver.

Why was Clint Hill the only one to react? Again, the Altgens photo provides an answer. While the rest of the agents are looking in various directions, Hill is looking forward, and he was undoubtedly the first to recognize the president's distress and be in a position to react. He did so with great courage, possibly saving Mrs. Kennedy from serious injury or worse, and he then hung onto the back of the limousine for a ghoulish, high-speed ride to Parkland Hospital, where he removed his suit coat and covered the president's upper extremities. This leads us to two thoughts: First, since the Secret Service agents were looking in different directions at the time of the shots, it strongly suggests that their trained perceptions allowed for the possibility that shots were coming from different directions. Secondly, the willingness of Clint Hill to cover the president gives us an indication of events to come: The Secret Service did not begin a cover-up by removing the president's body prior to a Texas autopsy, nor were their actions in removing the two limousines in haste irregular. Both actions—the removal of the president and the limos—are indications that the Secret Service is inculcated to protect the president, and in this case, John F. Kennedy's detail, which became a lame duck group midway on Elm Street, were protecting their man—from a Dallas scalpel at a time when the president's widow was in shock, and they were protecting his memory in not allowing the morbidly curious to view either the president or the bespattered limousine. It clearly presents conspiratorial overtones, but just as Mrs. Kennedy insisted on not letting go of her husband as the car reached Parkland, so, too, were his bodyguards unwilling to release him.

One unanswered question is why Roy Kellerman did not go to the president's aid, for he admitted that nothing—neither the upper frame of the automobile nor the Connally family—could have prevented him from getting to the president, yet he never got there. As the 1963 Secret Service manual indicated, "The first duty of the agents in the motorcade is to attempt to cover the president as closely as possible and practicable to shield him by attempting to place themselves between the president and any source of danger."[6] Kellerman did not tell me, or to my knowledge anyone else, but perhaps he stayed in the front because he considered the front "the source of danger."

I may not agree with these decisions, but I can understand how they could be made: loyalty. What is difficult to understand is how the Dallas authorities let them exert this loyalty. Or perhaps the Dallas authorities wanted it done that way for their own sinister purposes, and gave the Secret Service carte blanche to abuse procedure. Dr. Earl Rose, in that scenario, was the only fly in the ointment, as it was his job to perform a local autopsy on JFK.

The other questions can be quickly reviewed, at least where answers are possible. There are many contradictory theories about who made the decision regarding the motorcade route. Current research tends to suggest Jack Puterbaugh, a political (not security) advance man for the trip from Love Field to the Trade Mart. A curious sidebar arises here; one possibility considered was to continue down Main Street well past the triple underpass, and then loop back to the Trade Mart. The problem with that plan was that it would have taken the motorcade with all its dignitaries through the low-rent, red-light district of Dallas. Instead, the cars went through a very tranquil and lush green area that became a kill zone.

The one thing we know for sure about the route is that it was carelessly planned, and that is not in keeping with the style of the Secret Service I had occasion to deal with in my brief stint at the Justice Department. Bear in mind that prior to Dealey Plaza, they had not lost a president, and despite an increase of the lunatic fringe since 1963, they haven't lost one since. Ultimately, the Warren Commission would cooperate with both the Secret Service and the local authorities in altering the truth. The conventional story is that the limousine was forced to access Houston and Elm streets because that was the only way to reach Stemmons Freeway. The Warren Commission went out of its way to be sympathetic to this decision, always stressing in its questions that had the car continued down Main Street and not entered "deadly plaza," access to Stemmons Freeway would have been impossible, because of "a barricade." This is blatantly *not* true. Beyond the triple overpass, the "barricade" suggested by the Warren Commission is a three-inch curb, which could have been easily navigated by every vehicle in the motorcade, with discomfort to none. From there, it was only a matter of sealing off Elm Street traffic, and the motorcade could have cut across the deserted Elm Street and entered the ramp to Stemmons Freeway as planned. (Note to reader: On your next trip to Dallas, check out the curbing past the triple underpass—you could negotiate that bump easily with a bicycle, much less a limo; and while I would *never* suggest violation of local traffic regulations, it is possible to replicate the suggested motorcade route yourself—just observe Elm Street to your right, jump the curb, and hit Stemmons Freeway.)

As far as the fake Secret Service credentials appearing shortly before and after the shooting sequence, I am convinced they are extremely important pieces of evidence that guarantee conspiracy. Members of the intelligence community wanted a group of individuals in place in Dealey Plaza to safeguard the escape of the shooters and with the authority to manage a damage assessment situation—chase away anyone going near the knoll before the parade, such as Gordon Arnold or the railroad workers who were kept on the triple underpass, or chase away anyone who got too close immediately after the parade, and otherwise just be there to collect any stray film that may have been exposed. The point is, however, if the Secret Service were part of the conspiracy to kill the president, they certainly would not pass out their own credentials to members of the plot. We would have heard of FBI credentials, or some variation, to throw us off their trail. As for the origin of the specious credentials, we must ask ourselves where the starting place would be in a search for a source of extremely believable forged government credentials. Such a question would quickly point in the direction of Langley, Virginia.

Could the Secret Service's performance have been impeded by alcohol imbibed the night before? That would require medical testimony, and it would no doubt say both yes and no. The one thing that is clear is that the hours kept by the Secret Service on the night of November 21–22 certainly did not improve their performance in Dealey Plaza. Secret Service regulations clearly state that such behavior *will be* (not "may be") *cause for removal from the service*, yet no punishments were meted out because to have done so would have stigmatized the agents involved in what was perceived as a six-second acoustic nightmare in which they were basically helpless regardless of their readiness. The drinking, however, suggests a key overlooked question: Would the Secret Service have behaved in such a way if there had been a perceived threat?[7] The absence of Secret Service concern suggests a further failure by *local,* not national, authorities, as well as a weakness in the general tenor of the Protective Research Section of the Secret Service.

Lastly, we have the Seth Kantor rumor, of the dead Secret Service agent who had been part of a plot. It may be possible that one or more witnesses, seeing the actions of Clint Hill in charging the limousine and then hanging on in an odd position, came to believe that Agent Hill, too, had been caught in the crossfire.

There is more serious verification from another source, however. Mark Crouch, who has provided yeoman service to researchers by providing copies of autopsy prints from the James K. Fox negatives, and has maintained the "chain of possession" of those negatives (the veracity of which will be discussed elsewhere), heard an intriguing tale from Fox. As they became acquainted in the early 1980s, retired

Secret Service agent Fox indicated to Crouch that he had been in the White House on November 22, 1963, and would later add that "We lost a man that day." Crouch naturally assumed that the reference was to JFK; Fox indicated otherwise, adding that he had been ordered to put together a group of senior agents to meet a plane that day to receive the body of the dead agent. It is my suspicion that the story has not received a wider circulation, as it would fit quite well into "body alteration" theories, as perhaps it was not an agent on the other plane. The Crouch story is well told in *Dateline Dallas,* April 1994, and was "verified" by early news reports on November 22 that spoke of a Secret Service agent being killed (along with the president and a policeman, so this is not misunderstood Tippit data).

There also have been persistent rumors of a "burn party" held by the Secret Service on December 7, 1963, at which many of the autopsy materials were consigned to the flames.[8] This theory is given some credence by an estimate of autopsy materials running to 257 in number, and in thirty years, we have seen a handful. Where are the rest, or what happened to the ashes? And while we are asking tough questions, why did the Secret Service round up several windshields for the automobile after its usefulness was at an end, and why did both Greer and Kellerman testify before the Warren Commission that the windshield they were shown was not equal to their recollection of the windshield when they saw it in the White House garage on November 23?

In the category of "new Secret Service theories" we have the argument that the president's bodyguards could be proven to be guilty of criminal negligence, a.k.a. willful misconduct, according to researcher Vincent Palamara. Agreed; but criminal negligence is not the same, nor should it be seen that way, as premeditated murder or accessory to murder, and if Mr. Palamara, a youthful researcher who has indefatigably followed all Secret Service trails, and better than anyone else, is suggesting that the president was killed because he was inadequately protected, he may have put the cart before the horse.

Earlier, it was noted that JFK was difficult to protect. It's almost inconceivable, given Kennedy's preoccupation with his own mortality, his November 21 prophesy to an aide, and the political climate of Dallas, that John Kennedy would have allowed his car to leave Love Field if he did not feel secure and in charge of the situation. It's equally inconceivable to imagine him thinking, "My bodyguards are acting very strangely today; did Caesar ever feel this way . . . ?"

Mr. Palamara's arguments for negligence are well taken. We know that the Secret Service should not have been out drinking on the last night of John Kennedy's life; we know, too, that absent Clint Hill's bravery, the service had little to be proud of on November 22; it is also no secret that the Secret Service were rather hasty in the removal of the president's body and automobile—a valuable crime scene—from Parkland Hospital.

But many of those concerns have been explained, and other arguments put forth in this new theory overstate the case. Author Palamara suggests, "The Secret Service altered the Dallas Police Department's plan to have a squad car in close proximity to the JFK limousine."[9] The facts in the case are that Chief Will Fritz wanted a closed sedan, full of Dallas officers, immediately behind the president's car. The Secret Service vetoed this idea because their own follow-up vehicle was *always* the car immediately behind the president's. And given the Dallas police performance that weekend, added to the central thesis of this book, keeping the police *away* from the limousine was an act of inspired wisdom. Further on, it is argued that "The Secret Service was responsible for LBJ taking over Air Force One [sic] after the murder of JFK." Anyone familiar with the differences between *Air Force One* and *Air Force Two,* the vice president's plane, will understand why the decision was made, as well as the soundness of it. From both security and communications standpoints, the president's plane was vastly superior, and this was a time of national crisis of not-yet-resolved international proportions. Add to that the fact that LBJ was president legally from the pronouncement of the death of his predecessor, it was his plane. We may bemoan the absence of sympathy shown to the president's family and his longtime political aides, who have been pictured, not always accurately, as incensed by the usurpation of the plane, but like it or not, LBJ belonged where he was. It is inconceivable that John Kennedy's body would be on the most high-tech political airplane on the planet, while the new president was flying, perhaps in crisis, in a far less secure aircraft.

Vincent Palamara makes his negligence case, to no one's surprise, and has some interesting revelations along the way. But that is not to say that the Secret Service killed their protectee. For one thing, what would have been their motive? As members of the White House detail, they put in long and difficult hours, but it was the best duty available. If they lost the man they were sworn to protect, their future postings would be of no consequence on the national scene, and their careers would never advance. In addition, any theory that suggests the service was an accessory to the event overlooks the obvious: Two agents were in the car, and two of the four men in the car received serious wounds, while fragments narrowly missed the agents and shattered protective glass in the windshield.

Yet another recent publication indicts the Secret Service and names "name." In a chapter titled "The Plot," in *Killing the Truth,* veteran Kennedy researcher Harrison E. Livingstone posits the theory that much of the resentment against Kennedy came about because of his successes with women. "Secret Service agents close to the president who knew of some of his feminine liaisons resented it, sat in judgment of him, and cooperated with the plotters to kill him."[10] This suggestion would have us believe that the president's own Secret Service detail would throw their own careers to the winds because of JFK's womanizing, and would do so with the realization that JFK would be followed by LBJ, who brought presidential "liaisons" to a higher level of art form.

Mr. Livingstone insists that an unnamed source told him that the Secret Service had to be in on the plan, and the finger of accusation is then pointed at driver William Greer. One of the reasons cited is that "Greer laughed as he came down the steps of the Supreme Court of the United States after his interview with the Warren Commission."[11] In point of fact, special agent Greer was photographed with agents Hill and Kellerman as they walked on the pavement in front of the Veterans' Building, at 200 Maryland Avenue, N.E., in Washington. The testimony was given on March 9, 1964, a sunny day with a temperature in the low sixties. Mr. Greer, possessed of a wry face to begin with, may simply have been reacting to the sun in his face.[12] And it seems odd that he would laugh on the steps of the Supreme Court, since no testimony was ever taken there.

Analysis: The Secret Service was stuck between a rock (a boss who thrived on public exposure) and a hard place (Dallas, Texas). They reacted slowly, perhaps from lack of experience, or more importantly from a lack of understanding of what was happening in those few terrible seconds. Had someone charged down the knoll with a rifle, I have no doubt JFK would have survived, as his bodyguards would have functioned as trained. (They were alert and on the job in the two instances when the motorcade stopped at JFK's request, and the car would have been mobbed but for their quick action.) But in an unfathomable six-second *crossfire,* human limitations cost the life of a president.

They maintained their loyalty to their fallen boss, removing his body and automobile from the scene of the crime before they became morbid evidence, perhaps denying us an honest autopsy and a local search of the automobiles in the process. In this sense, the Secret Service was more protective of John Kennedy in death than they were able to be in life.

It is ironic, in retrospect, to think that the president drove through a seething city in an unprotected convertible while J. Edgar Hoover, an employee of the president's brother, had four armored vehicles at his disposal.[13] Hoover died of natural causes at age seventy-seven, nine years after the death of John Kennedy and four years after the death of his former boss, Robert Kennedy.

SECRET SERVICE II: S/A HICKEY AND THE AR-15

The second theory that suggests Secret Service involvement in the president's death was contained in a work titled *Mortal Error,* which details the ballistics theories of Howard Donohue as told by Bonar Menninger.

Mr. Donohue is extremely well read in the field of ballistics, and is also a crack shot, as he was the first individual (although he did so only years later for a 1967 CBS documentary) to match Oswald's alleged performance in the allotted time. (Donohue is a world-class marksman. Was Oswald?) His study of the ballistics angles of the shooting has convinced him that the shot that impacted on the rear of the president's head came not from the depository but rather from the Secret Service follow-up car, and specifically from an AR-15 rifle carried in that vehicle if the need for firepower arose. In Mr. Menninger's book, the trigger on the AR-15 was activated by Secret Service agent George Hickey.

I appreciate Mr. Donohue's dilemma. He believes, as other researchers do, that the one or two shots that hit the president from behind were medium-angle-trajectory shots originating from a point other than the sixth floor of the depository. Low-floor Dal-Tex Building shots are easy to suspect but difficult, if not impossible, to make, because of the downward slope of Elm Street and the presence of the Secret Service car so closely behind the president's car. But the suggestion that George Hickey fired the shot *as the cars lurched* is untenable. For one thing, the president had been struck in the head, flung backward, and Mrs. Kennedy had time to climb onto the trunk before the cars sped up, so the implication is that the fatal shot was fired about four seconds after the fatal shot, something of an impossibility, even in Dealey Plaza, where anything seems possible.

Beyond that, there are no witnesses to such a shot, and while most eyes were riveted on the president, certainly a few had to be looking elsewhere, and if the event had happened as described, someone would have seen it, and it also would have been heard for what it was and not confused with a shot from either the knoll or somewhere well behind the limousine. There is also photographic evidence that strongly tends to exonerate Agent Hickey. The Altgens photo, taken at Z255, shows Agent Hickey, seated on the top of the rear seat in the follow-up car, looking directly behind him and not reaching for the AR-15. At 58 Zapruder film frames, or 3.169 seconds later, the fatal bullet struck the president. We are thus asked to believe that in 3.169 seconds, Hickey ceased his visual search of the area behind the car, faced forward, got down from his elevated perch, retrieved the secured AR-15, stood, and had the gun discharge. Such a scenario makes Oswald's timing problems look easy.

The theory is further weakened by statements made by Secret Service agent Glenn Bennett, riding alongside Hickey. In his original notes on the assassination, Bennett noted, "I [after the shots] immediately hollered to Special Agent Hickey, seated in the same seat, to get the AR-15. . . ."[14] In a subsequent deposition, Bennett noted that he saw a shot hit the president in the head and then he reached for the AR-15.[15] Hickey, it should be noted, drove Kennedy's car from Parkland to Love Field, where it was put aboard a military transport. It was also Hickey who drove the "stand-in" Cadillac in the Dallas reenactment of the crime. It stands to reason that if Clint Hill suffered ill health after Dallas, George Hickey would have been a basket case if he had fired the mortal shot.

Critics have been quick to trash the entire corpus of *Mortal Error* because its central thesis is ballistically reasonable but otherwise unsupported. I spoke with Mr. Donohue on December 8, 1993, and he readily admits that while he works worldwide as a ballistics consultant, that is the extent of his expertise on the case. He still insists that Oswald fired from the depository, but that Kennedy's death was a tragic accident caused by agent Hickey. I admire Mr. Donohue's willingness to believe in his work, and for his equal willingness to give his time, effort, and travel expenses to aid other researchers.

Analysis: Mr. Donohue's ballistics arguments are well taken and deserve a look, but his conclusion is far easier to doubt than to prove.

Special agent Hickey is unavailable for comment, having suffered a massive cerebral hemorrhage in 1993.

SECRET SERVICE III: WILLIAM GREER

The final theory involving the Secret Service comes to us courtesy of a lecture tour by Milton William Cooper. In his JFK/UFO presentation, Mr. Cooper shows the Zapruder film and sees Kennedy's driver, William Greer, turning around, with a gun in his left hand, and firing a bullet into the president's head. The audience then also gets a UFO story for the price of admission. That's only fair—there should be something in there approaching the truth.

Analysis: Having studied the same Zapruder film as Mr. Cooper, I have come to the conclusion that what Mr. Cooper sees as a gun flash is the result of a bullet doing damage to the limousine windshield, with shards of glass resulting. Beyond that, William Greer was *not* Annie Oakley (1860–1926).

CHAPTER FOUR

THE CIA

Colonel Flagg: "The CIA can supersede anybody's orders."
Frank Byrnes: "Not the president!"
Colonel Flagg: "We're working on it."

—a pithy but pertinent exchange from *M*A*S*H*

ITS VERY TITLE IS A MISNOMER, although it was unintentional. At its inception in 1947, the Central Intelligence Agency—the CIA—was to be the centrally located intelligence-gathering agency for the U.S. government (although its charter limited its purview to external intelligence), which in that and subsequent years placed a premium on its intelligence operatives as the front-line troops in the Cold War.

By 1963, the agency was hardly "central"; it could only be seen as "central" in that it was the generic intelligence organization behind whose facade all kinds of cloaks and daggers existed. Beyond that, it was isolated geographically (as opposed to most U.S. government agencies, located in the busy federal hub of Washington), its budget was carte blanche and unpublished, and it was compartmentalized to such a degree that not only did the left hand not know what the right hand was doing, but also the left hand was frequently unaware of the existence of the right hand. Part of this is inherent in the nature of intelligence-gathering. The CIA is made up of management/career officials, plus scholars who study various arcane concerns, support staffs and clerical help, and the often faceless and multiple-identity covert agents. The concept of "central" could no longer be appropriate in 1963 given the agency's responsibilities by that time.

"Intelligence" is also in a sense misleading. A great deal of what the CIA does is trivial nonsense that generates virtually no useful intelligence. For years they opened countless pieces of mail originating from or addressed to places behind the Iron Curtain, going to or from American citizens. Most of what they learned was little more than that Uncle Nikolai lost a tooth or became a grandfather. Occasionally a gem of data would fall out of an envelope, such as an indication that Uncle Nikolai slept poorly because loud jet fighters were flying very low over the village on a regular basis. This kind of intelligence does not change history, but you have to mow the whole wheatfield, chaff included, to harvest the crop.

Further, the quality of some decisions made by—or for—the CIA also calls into question the very concept of intelligence, as the United States sponsored revolts, unrest, political sabotage, coups d'état, and even assassinations in the names of intelligence or national security, or worse, *democracy*.

As Col. L. Fletcher Prouty has astutely pointed out, however, the CIA *is an agency*.[1] In theory it receives directives from the powers for whom it acts *as agent,* then translates those directives into actions performed either by staff employees or, on occasion, by subcontractors.

Researchers strongly suspect that elements of the CIA, aided by just such power brokers above and subcontractors below, were a major factor in the assassination of President Kennedy. It would also be fair to suggest, as did author James Hepburn (a pseudonym for a French attorney who liked Audrey Hepburn, hence *J'am Hepburn*), ". . . the upper spheres of the CIA were certainly not informed of the preparation for the assassination."[2] "Hepburn's" thesis has gained acceptance within much of the research community, as it has compelling logic on its side. The CIA's surviving top echelon, following the post-Bay of Pigs removals of Allen Dulles, Richard Bissell, and Charles Cabell, were *not* for the most part professional spies (which is not to suggest that Dulles, Bissell, and Cabell were). With few exceptions, they were political appointments, often career bureaucrats, who earned far less in government service than they would have in the private sector—whence many came and to which some might return, but with a much-enhanced résumé.

No, there wasn't a top-level conference at CIA headquarters in Langley at which it was decided that John F. Kennedy had become a threat to the CIA's perceived interests.

The covert operatives, however, were another story. It was their goal to succeed so magnificently as covert operatives that they would one day occupy the thrones at Langley, which open wide the temples of power and wealth within government, as well as at some future time in the private sector. To those operatives on the way up, it is an article of faith among the research community that John F. Kennedy was a very real threat. That realization was not a long time in coming, either, as the CIA prepared a dossier analysis of what to expect from John Kennedy very shortly after he earned the title "president-elect"[3] (an event that apparently caught the agency by surprise, as they were expecting a continuance of the Eisenhower/Nixon laissez-faire acceptance of agency chicanery).

As actor Donald Sutherland told us in Oliver Stone's *JFK,* up to the time of John Kennedy's election, the "secret team" had much to congratulate themselves about, if you consider rearranging governments on several continents a good day's work.

But one problem loomed on the horizon: Cuba.[4] In 1960, then vice president Richard Nixon became the White House prime mover in an attempt to restructure the government of Cuba, with no real thought given to Fidel Castro having any role in that new order. Nixon worked closely with Dulles, Bissell, and General Cabell at the CIA, and everything seemed to be going smoothly until some irregularities in the voting tally in Cook County, Illinois, excluded Nixon from continuing his plans. But the invasion of Cuba stayed on the drawing board.

John F. Kennedy inherited the plan, which was seen as having a chance of success if all the prerequisites had been met. Unfortunately, one of them involved eliminating the entirety of Castro's small air force, and the other involved an agency-promised popular uprising of Cubans to coincide with the invasion of the CIA-sponsored Cuban exiles. Neither of those promises was kept. Either the president, or McGeorge Bundy in his stead, called off the second series of air strikes, and worse, there was no uprising. The Bay of Pigs had been aptly named.

Kennedy was given the blame for the failure and he accepted it, although an accurate assessment of the failure could hardly point the finger of blame at Kennedy because it was certainly not his fault that no Cubans in Cuba revolted. Inwardly, however, the president was seething. Unaccustomed to failure, he saw the CIA as having made promises that were ill-conceived, and in retrospect the president realized the invasion was preordained to failure. In the days to come, Cabell, Bissell, and Dulles would be replaced by Kennedy appointees.

CIA director Dulles had been on vacation during the Bay of Pigs, which raised questions about the quality of his leadership. This needs to be viewed in another perspective. If the CIA director is away, other intelligence heads, knowing this, will not suspect an impending threat; hence, Dulles's vacation. When the impending threat failed to justify the ruse, Kennedy made the vacation permanent.[5]

The dismissals took the CIA by surprise, but their larger and more immediate concern was that it was being suggested through the Washington sieve that more replacements were coming. The first concern was that a newly created agency might steal some, much, or all of the CIA's thunder; this concern had been enunciated in National Security Agency memorandums (NSAMs) 55, 56, and 57, which took power from the CIA and gave it to the Pentagon, but the Pentagon was uncomfortable with the change, as they still had to work closely—sometimes very closely—with the CIA. The second was that a reelected Kennedy might install as CIA director the right man for the job but the wrong man for the CIA: Robert Kennedy. The third concern, which arose later, was the fear that John Kennedy, having brought the nation to the brink of nuclear war in October 1962, had seen in that potential holocaust enough to consider new alternatives for bringing an end to the Cold War, as well as to the potentially splendid conflict gradually developing in Vietnam, which would ultimately, after the passing of JFK, pour hundreds of billions of dollars into the coffers of the very "military-industrial complex" that Kennedy's predecessor had warned about in his farewell, as well as to banking interests who would become immensely wealthy feeding at the trough of what has become known as "the deficit." John Kennedy's vision of a world without such wars would obviously mean less need for cold warriors and badly overpriced weapons systems. The death of John Kennedy was a stay of execution for the CIA; the subsequent death of Robert Kennedy was a *pardon*.

There have been serious questions asked about the CIA's possible relationship with Lee Oswald. Orest Peña, cited as an FBI informant by Mark Lane, told Lane that Oswald was also an FBI informant, and that the CIA knew about and used this knowledge. This suggests the CIA was free to use Oswald in any capacity it saw fit, with no fear of a close investigation by the FBI.[6] It is interesting to note here that both the FBI and the CIA denied that Oswald had any working relationship with either agency. Is that common practice? Did either or both agencies issue blanket denials that David Berkowitz, John W. Hinckley, Mark David Chapman, and Geoffrey Dahmer were on their payrolls? Of course not. What is that old saying about protesting too much?

There are other suggested links between Oswald and *some* agency (recall the CIA's function as a generic "intelligence front") related to American intelligence. Gary Powers believed that Oswald had knowledge of U-2 routes, but Oswald would not, or should not, have known anything about Powers' doomed flight from Peshawar, Pakistan. It is also known that Oswald had a voluminous CIA 201 file, and virtually everyone knowledgeable in CIA methodology agrees that such a file is highly suggestive of a close *working* relationship with the agency, its sponsors, or its subcontractors. It is further strongly suggested that the letters that traveled to and from Oswald in the USSR and the Oswald family in America were opened as a result of the CIA mail intercept program, adding a few pages to Oswald's file, and it is believed that Oswald's domestic mail was opened after his return to the United States.[7] This is significant because much of Oswald's correspondence can be viewed as having been written *for public consumption,* and it takes on additional significance because *it suggests that the intelligence community was aware of Oswald's weapons collection.* If Oswald was suspected as an enemy, this data would assume great significance and should have been acted upon well before November 1963; it would only have remained secret if Oswald was *not* perceived as an enemy.

In a sworn affidavit of May 18, 1964, CIA director John McCone, Dulles's successor, indicated to the Warren Commission that the CIA never heard of Lee Harvey Oswald.[8] Given what we have learned subsequent to the execution of both Oswald and Director McCone's affidavit, it is clear that the CIA should have been highly knowledgeable with respect to Lee Oswald, especially since they were photographing and taping him in Mexico in October 1963. The documents declassified in an eight-hundred-thousand-page governmental regurgitation in August 1993 prove that the CIA knew a great deal more than they told the Warren Commission about Lee Harvey Oswald, making CIA director McCone's denials the work of a stooge at best and a perjurer at worst. It is possible that McCone in fact did not know; *but he damn sure should have been told.*

To accept the CIA's May 1964 denials at face value, we must overlook the fact that the CIA of the early 1960s was routinely debriefing thousands of *tourists* returning from anywhere behind the Iron Curtain. It seems odd that they would consciously avoid someone who had been a tourist in Russia for two and a half years and had told consular officers at the U.S. embassy in Moscow, at least one of whom had a CIA background, that he planned to give U.S. military secrets to the Soviets. To believe the denials of a CIA-Oswald link, we must also overlook the names of Spas T. Raikin, George DeMohrenschildt, David Ferrie, Guy Banister, and Clay Shaw, CIA operatives whose paths often bisected Oswald's. (Of note, only one of them testified before the Warren Commission, the group created to find the full truth; researchers, on limited budgets, discovered the remainder of the list.)

When Oswald returned to the United States, there were neither law enforcement officers nor full-time intelligence operatives awaiting him and his family. His welcoming committee was comprised of Spas T. Raikin, one of the leaders of a CIA-sponsored organization that welcomed home people from overseas. If Raikin and Oswald did anything more than exchange perfunctory hellos, the record does not so indicate.

Within six days of his arrival in Fort Worth, Oswald took a manuscript he had prepared and "smuggled" out of Russia, detailing his Soviet stay, to typist Pauline Bates to have it visually improved. Ms. Bates told the Warren Commission that "an engineer" encouraged Oswald to have the material published.[9]

The "engineer" reference would seem to point directly to George DeMohrenschildt (if not several candidates among the Russian émigré community who had unusual connections, to say the least), and it is hard to imagine two more unlike personalities than Lee Oswald and George DeMohrenschildt. Yet there is the strong suggestion in Pauline Bates's testimony that CIA contract agent DeMohrenschildt had befriended Oswald immediately upon his return *or knew him before his defection.* A well-to-do world traveler with a handful of graduate degrees and a host of friends in high places is not the sort of person one would expect to take an immediate liking to Lee Oswald. It is also part of DeMohrenschildt's pedigree that the Communist Revolution of 1917 had ruined, at least for a time, the bright future he had envisioned for himself. Why then befriend the Marxist Oswald, who had defected to the very government that denied DeMohrenschildt his heritage?

George DeMohrenschildt will be a major character in this narrative in the section entitled "Red Patsy." For now, questions remain: Why did he, and by extension, the Russian émigré community, befriend

Oswald? To what extent was he one of two Oswald Dallas baby-sitters for the intelligence community? Why did DeMohrenschildt suddenly cast off Oswald in the spring of 1963, as Oswald was leaving for New Orleans and DeMohrenschildt was departing for Haiti? The last question suggests two answers: Oswald had been handed off to Clay Shaw, a personality and political type similar in many ways to DeMohrenschildt, and also a CIA contract agent; secondly, the possibility is raised that DeMohrenschildt was the mystery man in Haiti contacted in May 1963 by "Saul," the elusive centerpiece of several conspiracy theories, including the original "Ricky Don White scenario," which also implicated his father, Dallas cop Roscoe White.[10]

Two names remain from the menu cited a few paragraphs above: David Ferrie and Guy Banister. Ferrie was a pilot of remarkable skills and a man of considerable intellect, though to describe him any further would stain his piloting skills and his intellect. A CIA contract agent like DeMohrenschildt and Shaw, Ferrie also had connections to organized crime in New Orleans through his contacts with Carlos Marcello. Authors Harold Weisberg; Anthony Summers; Henry Hurt; John Davis; David Scheim; James DiEugenio; Jim Marrs; and, more recently, Robert Morrow, who told of his own experiences with the serendipitous Ferrie, have given us a good picture of the man and his associations.[11]

Yet the portrait is not complete. Jack Martin, pistol-whipped on November 22 by FBI, ONI, and CIA operative Guy Banister, spoke guardedly of both Ferrie and Oswald being part of Banister's operation. This has been corroborated by Banister's secretary, Delphine Roberts, and her daughter, yet it creates a situation that begs for an explanation. Was Oswald a genuine supporter of Fidel Castro, willing to sacrifice income needed for his family to pursue his Fair Play for Cuba leaflet campaign, the totality of which added up to *minutes*? Or was he an anti-Castro activist of the Ferrie-Banister stripe who printed leaflets in Banister's office with the goal of sabotaging the pro-Castro movement? Consider the facts: The Fair Play for Cuba Committee in New Orleans was an Oswald-led paper chase with Oswald as the only member, and Oswald had been warned by FPCC president V. T. Lee that New Orleans was not the climate in which to do such work. Weigh that against Guy Banister's operation, the epicenter of the anti-Castro movement in New Orleans, and surrounded by the bastions of the U.S. intelligence community. Banister had money, power, operatives, weapons, a mean temper, and a hatred of all things even remotely red or pink, and was not afraid to use any or all of them. V. T. Lee had an office in New York and pamphlets.

Was Oswald slick enough to fool Banister and Ferrie and infiltrate their group while he was really a leftist, or was his design to cast guilt on Castro and similar fellow travelers down the road?

Either way, these ominous concerns have "intelligence community" written all over them, and the trail does not end there. Oswald was positively identified in Clinton, Louisiana, at a black voter registration drive in the late summer of 1963, in the company of David Ferrie and a larger, ruddy-complected individual. The House Select Committee chose to believe the witnesses who placed Oswald with Ferrie (not a tough I.D., as Ferrie was just slightly less physically obvious than Joseph Merrick, a.k.a. "the elephant man") and either Banister or Shaw. Jim Garrison was, of course, convinced it was Shaw.[12]

Ferrie next attained prominence as a paid observer in the courtroom where Carlos Marcello's deportation hearings were decided on November 22, 1963, conveniently providing Ferrie with an alibi for the time the shots were fired in Dealey Plaza. He then set off on an exotic 364-mile drive across Louisiana, winding up in Galveston, Texas, at an ice-skating rink. It has often been suggested that Ferrie's mission was twofold: one, to pilot the getaway plane for one or more conspirators; two, to serve as liaison if any remaining conspirators in Dallas needed advice. What is often overlooked is that Ferrie began his trip *after* it was known that Oswald had been caught, so if his intent was to aid escaping assassins, Oswald could not have been one of them. Logically, it is also difficult to posit a scenario in which one or more assassins, fleeing the massed phalanxes of American law enforcement, would want to stand still in any one place until David Ferrie drove 364 miles through a torrential downpour to aid their escape[13] (unless these assassins were either native to Dallas or had the luxury to "flee" at their leisure while a patsy took the blame).

Ferrie never did ice-skate. He did, however, "skate" through judicial proceedings in the following days as he was sought, as early as November 24, as an accessory in the president's assassination. Upon his return to New Orleans, he turned himself in, and was interviewed by federal officials who quickly issued a finding of no complicity. His biggest concern thereafter was his library card, believed to have been discovered in the billfold of Oswald shortly after his arrest in Dallas. Ferrie told the Secret Service he never loaned his card to

Oswald. Oddly, he had not been asked. Official records do not help clear up this concern, except by inference, for although the Warren Commission published photos of every garment or shoe of Oswald's that was seized by Dallas authorities, there are no published photos of either the billfold or its collective contents.

The New Orleans events conclude along similar lines: In 1964, before he had a chance to talk to the Warren Commission, Banister died, and federal authorities seized his files before Banister's own staff members could get to his office. Elsewhere in New Orleans, Eva Springer was contacted by her employer, attorney Dean Andrews, with the news that he had been hired to defend Oswald on November 23 by someone named "Bertrand." Andrews would later change his story to suit the time, although he did tell the Warren Commission that he intended to find both Bertrand *and* the real assassin. Given this, is it likely that his secretary would invent both a "Bertrand" and Andrews' call to her?[14]

Neither Shaw, Bertrand, Banister, Ferrie, nor Ms. Springer was called before the commission. In the CIA's fraudulent blanket denial of knowledge regarding Oswald, they made no mention of any of the above-named individuals who might have known him.

The strongest case for CIA involvement, besides personal memoirs such as Morrow's *Firsthand Knowledge,* comes from Mark Lane's *Plausible Denial.* This work, the outgrowth of a trial in which E. Howard Hunt brought litigation to clear himself of any involvement in the events of November 22, 1963, *and lost,* revolved around the testimony of Marita Lorenz, who allegedly accompanied a CIA caravan of weapons and agents to Dallas a day or so before the assassination. A CIA "romantic plant" for Fidel Castro, Miss Lorenz gave testimony to the House select committee that her CIA superiors ordered her not to appear before the Warren Commission, and that when she did tell everything she knew to the FBI, they did nothing. She also included Gary Hemming among the caravan, but points heavier blame at E. Howard Hunt, and also Frank Sturgis, who reportedly told her, "We killed the president that day."[15]

Sturgis certainly had a checkered career. In a 1968 deposition cited by Lane, Sturgis admitted that he had worked for the CIA against Castro and "was approached by an agent of the Central Intelligence Agency to do a domestic assassination."[16] His name would become more famous in 1972, in another operation involving both Cubans and power brokers in Washington.

E. Howard Hunt was a career full-time CIA employee, as opposed to being a per-job contract agent. Anthony Summers, in *Conspiracy,* and Tad Szulc, in his biography of Hunt, insist that Hunt was heavily into the anti-Castro efforts of the CIA and that he was also temporary station chief in Mexico during the fall of 1963, which coincided with Oswald's visit there. With respect to that visit, either the CIA was monumentally inefficient, or duplicitous. Their claim that Oswald's visit was not noted because their cameras and listening devices were all inoperative suggests both inefficiency and lack of truth. The photo they submitted of "Oswald" shows an individual who could fit Oswald in his pocket. It is CE 237, and according to Hugh McDonald, is the assassin "Saul." In their report on CE 237, the CIA indicated that the photo showed an American, approximately thirty-five, who "may be identical to Lee Harvey Oswald, born 18 October 1939." Thus the CIA *did know Oswald,* despite their denials, and they also tried to tell us that they photographed a thirty-five-year-old who may also have been a twenty-three-year-old. The August 1993 release of material confirms this.

With respect to Marita Lorenz, I do not find her story credible. She may well have been Castro's lady, and she may equally well have tried to kill him with a pill that subsequently dissolved in cold cream, but the caravan story presents difficulties. It asks us to believe that although she had operative status, she was taken along for the ride as part of a two-car caravan whose passengers included Hunt, Sturgis, and Hemmings, as well as a serious stockpile of weapons, for the purpose of killing the president in Dallas. This is hard to believe. When she wanted no further part of the event, so the narrative continues, she asked to return to the Miami area, and the president's killers simply let her walk away as they were planning the ambush.

That part does not wash, period. What is interesting is the list of players she brings to the event, and the most curious is Gary Patrick Hemming, about whom precious little is known, as compared to the more visible and subsequently more notorious Hunt and Sturgis combo.

What has intrigued researchers about Hunt, and to a lesser degree, Sturgis, is their subsequent involvement in presidential dirty tricks, and the handling of those matters.

It is understood in intelligence circles that if an agent is lost, there will be reasonable compensation to the family. Yet Hunt's demands for $2 million to the Nixon White House, as discussed on a presidential recording of March 1973, amounts to either fifty years' salary as reasonable compensation, or it was blackmail. By the time payment was considered, investigative journalists had pretty much uncovered anything Hunt knew about the Watergate break-in. So *what did he know* that could have been worth $2 million to President Nixon or the U.S. government?

The intelligence community left many other fingerprints on the Kennedy assassination. Richard Case Nagell is a case in point, as is Garrett Trapnell, who was involved in an incident similar to Nagell's in 1963 and is also mentioned in Dick Russell's work on Nagell. Trapnell also claimed knowledge of the events of November 22, and was hospitalized (as Nagell was jailed) on that date. Trapnell was told by the FBI to be quiet and was paid off when released from the hospital.[17]

George DeMohrenschildt and Clay Shaw have already been cited as Oswald baby-sitters in Dallas and New Orleans, respectively. But who was there when Oswald freelanced, as on his trip to Mexico? Oddly enough, CIA agent William Gaudet received the tourist card issued immediately ahead of Oswald, and gave every indication that he knew of Oswald from his awareness of the Banister-Ferrie satrapy. While aboard the bus to Mexico, Oswald was engaged in conversation with John Howard Bowen, a.k.a. the Rev. Albert Osborne, who had been deported from Mexico in 1958. Given the highly religious content of Mexican culture, it is hard to imagine someone being deported for being a "Rev.," so there may also be something sinister in Bowen/Osborne's presence.[18] In the documents released in August 1993, hundreds of pages indicate Oswald did not have contact with Bowen. These are weasel words: he could have easily had the suggested contact with "Osborne."

Despite hundreds of documents on bus routes and time schedules, passenger lists, and interviews with bus officials and tourists to learn about Oswald's Mexican trip, the commission ignored Nagell, Trapnell, Gaudet, and Bowen/Osborne. They did take lengthy testimony from George DeMohrenschildt, who entertained them with his life history, his travels, and his theory that the FBI killed Kennedy. At the time he was discovered years later by House select committee investigators, DeMohrenschildt killed himself with a shotgun.

Other data round out the narrative. Madeline Brown, longtime mistress to LBJ, suggested that Kennedy's successor told her of the CIA's involvement in JFK's death. Former CIA agent Victor

Marchetti also went on the record often regarding the CIA, saying at one point that they even considered admitting what they knew about Dealey Plaza and the possible involvement of some of their people.[19]

But that is moot. The better question would revolve around what the CIA had been willing to divulge in 1963 and 1964, and the answer, beyond vague denials, is *nothing*. They had the good fortune to have Soviet defector Yuri Nosenko fall into their laps, but they kept him from the Warren Commission with a stall involving Nosenko's bona fides, which would ultimately last for years. And we must not lose sight of the fact that there was an easy way to verify Nosenko's legitimacy, even if the vaunted CIA was ignorant or it or simply wanted to keep Nosenko on ice. Nosenko had left his family behind when he defected; U.S. intelligence needed only to learn their fate and they would unlock the Nosenko enigma. If the family members were suffering in some Soviet dungeon, Nosenko was real. If their lives were not affected, he was bogus. (This theory, in the original manuscript of this book, was confirmed by a KGB source in March 1995.) But it was either not checked out, or the results were such that we will never be made privy to them. Nosenko was, however, the ultimate "man for all seasons," as he seemed often able to manufacture answers on both sides of the Oswald spectrum, depending, of course, on which way the prevailing CIA gusts were blowing.

The CIA thumbed its nose at the official investigation in every way possible. Volume XXVI, the final volume of the Warren Commission Exhibits, contains what little CIA material was provided, and the dates are instructive. Answers to simple questions posed by the commission months earlier were provided on September 14 and 18, the two most common dates on CIA material in the published evidence. It should be recalled that the Warren Report galley proofs began circulating on September 4.

All told, the CIA has amassed something on the order of three hundred thousand pages of material on Oswald, and we saw precious little of it prior to the August 1993 release, and that "material" was not always complete nor intelligible. We will know all of what it contains if it survives and if they show it to us. An agent who requested anonymity told this writer through an intermediary that the CIA has been working since 1988 to declassify its material on Oswald, and they hoped to conclude their labors in

1994. Compare that statement with the House Select Committee's comment that their representative visited the CIA and read Oswald's file *in an hour.*

Analysis: The U.S. intelligence community, with the CIA in the vanguard, immediately perceived President Kennedy as a threat. Unlike Eisenhower, he would not rubber-stamp their harebrained schemes and he began replacing some overzealous cloak-and-dagger types with professional administrators. His policies would further limit the CIA's heretofore sacrosanct set of rules, and a reelected JFK would end American involvement in Vietnam, which would have involved many billions of dollars and untold intelligence games. Robert Kennedy, with Hoover in retirement, would no longer be needed at the Justice Department and would move to Langley and preside over the ultimate bureaucratic housecleaning.

At the same time, in its well-documented willingness to accept the challenge to kill Fidel Castro, an assassination more challenging than previous assignments, the CIA looked to outsiders, using fancy code names such as AM/LASH and ZR/RIFLE. Their inabilities to reach Castro led the CIA into an alliance of convenience with organized crime figures who theoretically had much to gain if they could retrieve their casino empire in Cuba *but who in reality had far more to gain from the subsequent ability to hide behind and take protection from the CIA.*

The CIA clearly had additional motives for perceiving that a change of administration would be to their advantage, as Kennedy was seen as seeking accommodation with Cuba and a limit to the testing of nuclear weapons.

But the CIA, for all its cloaks and daggers, does not have a special group of work-space cubicles for paid assassins. They wanted the president removed, but within the agency, they apparently did not have the personnel to do so, as their Castro failures and their subsequent willingness to look outside the agency prove. They did, however, have access to groups that would also support the assassination and that would provide sponsorship for the ultimate killers. Thereafter, the CIA's role was to stonewall the official investigation, hardly a challenge. Powerful private interests not always in the public spotlight also had access to the CIA *as an agency,* and they, too, had desires that Kennedy be removed. On that two-way street was decided the fate of Camelot.

There is no reason to scrub the CIA as an early prime mover in the planning of events, in which they acted in the capacity of an agency. Their early willingness to see the removal of John Kennedy gave strength and hope to private interests far more powerful than the CIA, and those groups, with help from local talent, accomplished their purpose in Dallas, Texas.

CHAPTER FIVE

THE FBI

*Our worst enemies here are not the ignorant and the simple,
however cruel; our worst enemies are the intelligent and
corrupt.*

—GRAHAM GREENE, *The Human Factor*

THE FEDERAL BUREAU OF INVESTIGATION did *not* do three things
with respect to the assassination of President Kennedy.

First, the FBI did not assassinate Kennedy; second, the FBI did not
adequately alert the Secret Service to threats against President Kennedy that were in their possession; and third, the FBI did *not* assist
in a meaningful, positive way in the investigation into the killing of
President Kennedy. On the contrary, they sidetracked the Warren
Commission into accepting the FBI director's stated theory as to the
early afternoon of November 22, 1963.

Recent revisionist biographies have not been kind to J. Edgar Hoover, and rightly so, for it was his willingness to operate and thrive
above the law, while pretending to enforce it, that badly tarnished
the image of a highly professional and otherwise honest agency. No
understanding of any major criminal investigation headed up by J.
Edgar Hoover is possible if one does not recognize at the outset that
Hoover's ideas, motivations, and policies were, *without question,* the
FBI's ideas, motivations, and policies.

In a pair of ironies, it is interesting to note that in 1908, the Office
of Chief Examiner (it became the Bureau of Investigation in 1909)
was founded by Charles J. Buonaparte, grandson of a dictatorial fanatic whose megalomania nearly destroyed France. Buonaparte could

not have known that the bureau he organized would someday be dominated for forty-eight years (longer than the lifespan of either murdered Kennedy) by someone with a Napoleonic complex.

Nor could Hoover have known, early in World War II, that the FBI bug that picked up pillow talk between John Kennedy and suspected Nazi sympathizer Inga Arvad would get Kennedy transferred to a desolate *PT-109* command and subsequent heroism that would start him on the road to the White House . . . and Dallas.[1]

Hoover's "dirt," exemplified by what he had unleashed against Kennedy in the 1940s, was the essence of his power. Hoover's personal files, containing a lifetime accumulation of wiretap data, investigative reports, and just plain gossip, guaranteed that no legislator, committee, or president would arise to challenge an FBI budget or the performance or tenure of the director. It has been suggested that one reason Kennedy appointed his brother Robert as attorney general (nominally Hoover's boss) was his concern over Hoover's files. And for good reason: The same source indicated the FBI discovered thirty-two women in JFK's presidency.[2] On a given day, if "Senator John Doe" was deciding which way to vote on a piece of legislation and found himself subject to presidential arm-twisting on one side and Hoover's blackmail on the other, it is arguable that "Doe" would follow Hoover, demonstrating de facto what individual had more power in the United States. Hoover went after his enemies and protected his friends.[3]

Hoover's most serious enemy in 1963 was John Kennedy, with Robert Kennedy second and "Father Time" a close third. Hoover had been born on January 1, 1895, and by federal statute would have been mandatorily retired from the FBI on his seventieth birthday, January 1, 1965, just over eight weeks after JFK's projected reelection. Since Hoover had received no believable signal that Kennedy wanted the FBI director to stay on beyond the statutory age, he could only have concluded that the inactivity of the Kennedys was the handwriting on the wall. While he no doubt considered using his files against JFK, to use them against Kennedy before election day would have been an act of political suicide, and Hoover knew it. His files, then, constituted the "bark," which *was* worse than the bite; after November 3, 1964, they would have been academic: Kennedy would have been elected to his second and final constitutionally permitted term; Hoover would have been pensioned off; and RFK, no longer as vital at the Justice Department, would have been moved into leadership at Langley. Unable to use his files, Hoover dealt with his threatened retirement in a more direct way.

Prior to the day that direct action occurred, however, Hoover chose to deal with this concern through inaction. An FBI teletype dated November 17, 1963, directed all field offices to contact CIs (confidential informants) to determine whether a militant revolutionary group was a potential threat to the president during his Dallas trip of November 22–23. Interestingly, the teletype "officially" received no response and curiously disappeared from most FBI files after November 22. Equally interesting are the eight misspellings in the teletype, almost as if a dysgraphic Lee Oswald had written it (and recall that Oswald had delivered a note to the FBI previously, the contents of which have been much discussed, but can only remain conjecture, since they wound up in a federal commode after the assassination).[4] As it happened, this event, like so much else of what we know of November 22, is a through-the-looking-glass transaction; a "militant" revolutionary group *was indeed planning to kill Kennedy in Texas,* but Hoover *was part of the group.*

And they succeeded, and got away with it.

Richard Case Nagell had dispatched a letter to Hoover in mid-September, suggesting an attempt would be made on JFK between September 26 and 29, presumably in Washington. But Nagell signed the letter "Joseph Kramer," and his prediction did not come to pass. Patsy Oswald was in Mexico during the proposed Nagell/Kramer scenario.[5]

A November 15, 1963, memo received by the Protective Research Section of the Secret Service was published by the Warren Commission. It tells of "information received telephonically from FBI headquarters, Washington, D.C.," that indicated a "militant *group* of the National States Rights Party plans to assassinate the president and other high-level officials."[6] The subject who provided the material, a Klan member, was not named, and because he was in jail for car theft on November 22, no further action was taken. Was he the one-man "militant group"?

Thus there are strong indications that the FBI knew *something* was going on, and given Hoover's unquenchable thirst for intelligence, combined with the ongoing widespread ELSUR and COINTELPRO wiretap campaigns, it is possible that these reported "militant hate group" memos may have been smoke screens for more serious information possessed by the director of the FBI. Yet we have no record of any FBI preventive measures, save one phone call.

Hoover has also been viewed as an accessory to the assassination *before* the fact by his surreptitious and unexplained presence at a party hosted by the oil-rich Murchisons (long-standing friends, financial supporters, and investment counselors to Hoover and LBJ) of Dallas on the evening of November 21, 1963.[7] Although the complete guest list is unavailable, Hoover's presence has been confirmed by his African-American driver, who had been promoted to FBI special agent to allow Hoover to say he was not hiring whites only; in addition, the gathering was attended by Madeline Brown, who had not expected LBJ to attend. She insists that not only was Hoover present, but also prior to the arrival of Johnson (from nearby Fort Worth, after the presidential party had settled there for the evening), the gathering had the aura of a tribute *to Hoover*. Others suggested to have been in attendance include future president Richard Nixon; future Warren Commission member John J. McCloy (frequently a financial emissary of the F-8 group, as the ultrarich, ultraconservative Texans who frequently gathered and gambled—both with money and power—on the eighth floor of the Lamar Hotel in Houston were known); Herman Brown, of Brown and Root, who would receive a $1 *billion* Vietnam contract; and two Houston residents, George Bush and his father. A private meeting of the more powerful elements was held after the late arrival of LBJ, and the exact details of what was said behind those closed doors are known best to the surviving participants. It was after that meeting and before the next day's motorcade, however, that Madeline Brown learned from her paramour that John Kennedy would not be president by the end of the weekend. We can also conclude, however, that Lee Oswald was *not* there, as his whereabouts on the evening of November 21 is one of the Kennedy assassination's greatest certainties.

It is known for certain that John Kennedy visited Dallas the following day, and there was someone—or some group—present in the vicinity of the motorcade who did not support Kennedy's continuance in office. As the sound of the shots, as well as their target, died in Dealey Plaza, Hoover, back from Dallas and aware of events that would unfold, sprang into action. Apparently possessing a phone that did not go dead when many other D.C. phone lines went down, he contacted the attorney general at his home to tell him bluntly that the president had been shot. Soon after, in a second call to RFK, Hoover told him that the president's condition was very serious, whereupon RFK informed Hoover of the president's death, and, without saying so, the end of his own power at the Justice Department. In between those calls, NBC News, which had interrupted regularly scheduled midday drivel, was announcing that J. Edgar Hoover was unleashing all the resources of the FBI to assist with the investigation of the events in Dallas (despite the fact that they had no jurisdiction whatsoever). Of note, they would be given jurisdiction before nightfall by LBJ, and there is no record of the call from Hoover to the Dallas field office.

Before *Air Force One* landed in Washington, Hoover made it known that Lee Harvey Oswald, someone he described in his Warren Commission testimony as a "dedicated Communist,"[8] was the lone assassin and there was no conspiracy.

That pronouncement is the key to our inability to get at the full truth today. Once Hoover made that statement, it meant that every FBI agent who cared about his livelihood or the location of his duty station would strictly follow the party line as established by Hoover; follow any lead, regardless of time, cost, or investigative value, if it pointed in the direction of Oswald as the lone assassin; studiously avoid any information, even if it meant misstating data, if it pointed to anything but the lone assassin.[9] The first two rules of the FBI were tacitly invoked: Cover the bureau, and cover your ass. The cover-up had begun, a week before the Warren Commission was born. The import of this cannot be ignored; while countless scholars have blamed the Warren Commission for the cover-up, it predated the commission's existence, and the commissioners were presented with a Hobson's choice: Destroy previous government pronouncements made at the highest levels, or don't make waves.

Before the tragic weekend was over, Hoover and Nicholas Katzenbach, standing in at Justice for the grief-stricken RFK, firmed up the lone-assassin line. They both accepted the need "to convince the public that Oswald is the real assassin" but warned, "Speculation about Oswald's motive ought to be cut off."[10] Considering that the continuance in office of J. Edgar Hoover and the promotion of his friend Lyndon Johnson were two of the motives, that was prescient reasoning.

They rushed *to*, but not *with*, judgment.

After the Warren Commission's inception, Hoover took three significant actions. First, he tried to convince the commission to relax, because the FBI had the case well in hand, since they had been involved, albeit without jurisdiction, from the beginning. With respect to jurisdiction, Hoover would later tell the Warren Commission that the FBI had been immediately called in by the new president, "because, as you are aware, there is no federal jurisdiction for such an investigation."[11] If true, this further implicates LBJ in the assassination; if false, it demonstrates Hoover's ability to invent presidential policy *and get away with it.*

Second, when the Warren Commission refused to rubber-stamp Hoover's conclusions without at least the formality of an investigation, Hoover released the five-volume FBI Report on the assassination in December, two full months before the Warren Commission called its first witness.

Third, Hoover gave marching orders to selected, trusted agents to locate damaging information regarding the members of the Warren Commission.

Beyond this, Hoover was as uncooperative with the Warren Commission as he could be, but this was not a problem, since he had solid information about the growing scandal engulfing President Johnson's close associate Billy Sol Estes, as well as about a February 17, 1961, Texas plane crash that would guarantee that Hoover had a friend for life in the new occupant of 1600 Pennsylvania Avenue.[12] Hoover's agents took useless data from Jack Ruby's friends from the 1920s and Lee Oswald's schoolmates from the 1940s and 1950s, and when the Warren Commission requested a document, Hoover sent them five thousand. Working under limited time constraints and in the face of Hoover's paper chase, the Warren Commission was effectively sidetracked.

It was no accident of timing that J. Edgar Hoover appeared before the Warren Commission on May 14, 1964, and answered a mere one hundred questions, committing at least three acts of perjury. He had been appointed as FBI director for life by Lyndon Johnson on May 8, six days before his scheduled Warren Commission appearance.

In September 1964 the Warren Commission issued a report reflecting the conclusion J. Edgar Hoover announced on the afternoon of November 22, 1963.

Analysis: The FBI, through its omnipotent director, had prior knowledge of the assassination and did nothing with it, as Hoover stood to gain by Kennedy's removal. Field agents had no choice but to follow the path set by Hoover; senior FBI officials had no difficulty with the knowledge they possessed.

Hoover was also subject to both CIA and underworld blackmail for some events that occurred out of the public eye. Hoover's word being law, the former close friend of Joseph McCarthy convicted Lee Oswald of the crime of killing JFK before Dallas authorities had even booked Oswald for the murder of Officer Tippit. Hoover subsequently made sure that the Warren Commission, lacking independent investigators, only received information that ratified the guilt of Oswald, and did not embarrass the bureau for its lack of preassassination caution. The Warren Commission, hardly eager for full disclosure based on Johnson's concern that a nuclear holocaust would follow, acquiesced in and enlarged on the FBI cover-up. This will be expanded upon in the chapter "Hoover to Warren to Chance" in "White Lies."

In the time interval of the FBI's most intense scrutiny of the case, it has been documented that seventeen agents were disciplined and transferred to other bureau posts. What has never been revealed was the reason for those transfers; incompetence is the usual conclusion, but is erroneous. Incompetence would have led to dismissal; the agents in question were transferred to ensure that they could no longer get together to discuss what they—and not the public—knew. Dismissal would have led to at least one coming forward. Hoover even covered up within his own bureau.

Given the FBI's talent and track record, an unimpeded FBI investigation would have solved the Kennedy assassination *sine die*. Instead, the investigation was handled by the Dallas police and J. Edgar Hoover.

The suspects handled the investigation.

CHAPTER SIX

THE RIGHT AND OTHER WINGS

A conservative government is an organized hypocrisy.

—BENJAMIN DISRAELI, 1845

MANY STUDENTS OF THE KENNEDY ASSASSINATION, despite the emergence of the CIA and organized crime as the two leading "suspects," refuse to give up their beliefs that a coalition of elements of the right, or big oil, or white supremacist groups, could have been involved, possibly along with the CIA or military intelligence. There is good reason to agree with them.

We have already seen that there was concern—from Kennedy's White House staff, to the governor of Texas, to the Secret Service—that the Texas trip was going to include a stop and a motorcade in Dallas. It should be noted that Dallas in 1963 was not considered either a CIA or an organized crime stronghold, so the concern must have had a different origin.

Winston Lawson, Secret Service advance agent for the Dallas trip, singled out the right wing as his primary concern when he testified before the Warren Commission regarding his premotorcade jitters.[1] Roy Kellerman, in earlier testimony, had been surprised as special agent in charge of the Texas trip that no protective research concerns had been transmitted to him.[2] Oddly, following the poor receptions given to LBJ in 1960 and Adlai Stevenson in October 1963, and the tremendous concern that the "right" would be very visible on November 22, there was nothing evident in the motorcade, and only a demonstration planned for the Trade Mart, which was bypassed by the motorcade on its unscheduled high-speed trip to Parkland Hospital. Does this overt display of "good behavior" prior to Elm Street mask some very serious "bad behavior" in Dealey Plaza?

The concerns were real to others as well. The *Dallas Morning News* of October 6 (pre-Stevenson) told that "Democratic leaders are worried over the possibility of 'incidents' " during President Kennedy's Texas visit. "They fear segregationists or ultraconservatives may picket the President or even try to harm him physically."[3] Dallas police chief Jesse Curry took to the airwaves shortly before the president's visit to remind Dallas citizens to be on their good behavior. He had reason to be concerned: As Larry Schmidt, leader of Conservative USA, had written to Bernard Weissman on October 29, 1963, "Never before have Dallas conservatives from the GOP to the John Birch Society ever been so strongly united."[4]

The recipient of the letter was the same Bernard Weissman who was cited as a close acquaintance of Warren Carroll, a writer for H. L. Hunt's *Lifeline,* and was also the Bernard Weissman who told the Warren Commission that H. L. Hunt was the financier for the right wing. Weissman also testified that the money for the "Welcome, Mr. Kennedy" ad came from Texas oil and that the concept for the ad originated with the John Birch Society.[5]

The ad was, in fact, paid for by Edgar Crissey, Nelson Baker Hunt (son of H. L. Hunt), and H. R. Bright, onetime owner of the Cowboys ("America's Team"). Weissman, with a Semitic last name, could only have been a stooge for the right and a name to appear on the ad and sow confusion in the process. In the Warren Commission testimony of General Walker and Professor Revilo Oliver, two men clearly cut from conservative cloth, there is no talk of "Jack Ruby" but rather of "Rubenstein," giving Ruby's Semitic birth name an evil connotation.[6]

It should not seem odd that oil money would finance conservative publications in Texas, as oil was Texas. Consider Texas's political clout prior to 1901, when the first oil wells were begun, to where it is today, and consider the proportion of Texas's contribution to the U.S. oil industry, and how it could have felt threatened by both the "Kennedy Act" of 1962 and subsequent legislation that filled a few minor oil loopholes, and one can understand how oilmen attached ever greater significance to their previous conservative posture.[7] Should it seem odd, then, that when Ilya Mamantov was contacted to translate Marina Oswald's answers for the Dallas police, the contact was made by Jack Crichton, an independent petroleum operator and reservist in army intelligence?[8] Or that LBJ's confession to mistress Madeline Brown regarding the Kennedy assassination was that "It was the oil people and the CIA"?[9] Certainly Mr. Johnson had a clearly established "pipeline" to both groups. And make no mistake about it: Madeline Brown is very clear that not only did Johnson make that statement years after the assassination, but also that he was well aware of it, and indeed part of it, before the assassination.

The other element mentioned earlier is the John Birch Society, referenced briefly in the rambling, often incoherent Warren Commission testimony of Jack Ruby: ". . . there is a John Birch Society right now in activity, and Edwin Walker is one of the top men of this organization."[10] This was brave testimony to give in a Dallas jail, because Dallas, with Walker, Mayor Cabell, *and* H. L. Hunt, has been aptly described as "a mecca of the radical right." It is also of paramount importance to understand that membership in either the KKK, or later, the John Birch Society, was a prerequisite for a Dallas police recruit in the early 1960s.[11] Also recall that it was the same Ruby who gave testimony that he drove Connie Trammel, a relative stranger, to keep an appointment with Lamar Hunt on the afternoon of November 21.[12]

Gen. Edwin Walker, U.S.A. *resigned* (as he insisted), was also no worshiper at the Kennedy shrine. After Walker got some inexpensive publicity by his anti-integration antics, he was briefly institutionalized on orders from the attorney general, making Walker about as appreciative of the Camelot mystique as was Carlos Marcello, who had been unceremoniously dumped in the jungles of Central America on orders from RFK. Ultimately, of course, Walker would be used as a front man, a martyr whose free speech to the troops had got him run out of the army and around whom an inchoate conservative movement ("distraction" might be a better word) could gather. Given the overall conservative bent of the respective institutions, it is odd that neither the Dallas police nor the FBI could get any handle on the April 10, 1963, attempt on Walker's life, at least not until after November 22, 1963, when the steel-jacketed 30.06 fired at Walker, almost like a magic bullet, became a suspected Mannlicher-Carcano round.[13]

All of these facts suggest that a moderate New Englander was simply not overly welcome in Texas, a state Kennedy had carried by only 46,000 votes in 1960 despite having a prominent Texan on the ticket. More noteworthy is the fact that Kennedy failed to carry Dallas, and the overall ethnic vote totals, showing Kennedy with a huge percentage of the black vote in a nationwide election won by a whisker, is conclusive proof that he was *not* the electoral choice of white America in 1960. And Dallas, powerwise, was the ultimate personification of white America in 1963.

Need further proof? Look again through *all* your Kennedy assassination materials and take careful note of how many black Dallas police officers, Secret Service agents, or FBI agents you see in those photos. (If you find *one,* please forward a copy to the author.)

The conservative mind yearned for the wholesome past, not the "New Frontier." The right, fearful of outside threats and insistent on "Fortress America," would fight the closing of military bases, and they would line up alongside the steel titans in their fight against the president. They would oppose many of the 1,054 bills JFK would send to Congress in his 1,037 days. When "U.S. Notes" appeared in 1962, they cost big business, as well as banking interests, a great deal of money because the government, not the banks, had become the brokering agent. Those "U.S. Notes" disappeared, after November 22, as suddenly as they had appeared.[14]

Kennedy allowed the White House to be used for on-location shots for *Seven Days in May,* a fictional account of a coup led by right-wing generals. In the all-too-real Dallas motorcade, the pilot car contained two Dallas officers, a Secret Service agent, and a Major Weiddemeyer of the U.S. Army.[15] What was he doing there? Do army majors routinely ride in presidential parades? And what of James Powell, army intelligence, taking films of the assassination, and then gaining access to the TSBD during the search? What of Alcohol, Tobacco, and Firearms special agent Frank Ellsworth and postal inspector (and FBI informant) Harry Holmes being part of the Dallas questioning of officers? Was November 22 a convention of federal people who had no business in a Texas homicide?

Since no innocent explanation has been offered for these presences, one can only place a sinister interpretation on them.

Other factors also point the finger of suspicion at the groups cited above. Jean Hill's motorcycle officer-boyfriend "J. B." told her, regarding Dallas Police Department scuttlebutt, "Somebody high up in the government wanted Kennedy out of the way and Johnson in the White House. Maybe not Johnson himself, but somebody powerful enough to pull it off."[16] The right wing, the Klan, the Birchers, Walker, and the Hunts were clearly "powerful enough," but they weren't "high up in government," leading to a nasty query: Who was? *We know for sure who was* after *November 22.*

Loran Hall, an interesting stage extra in the events of Dallas, reportedly turned down a $50,000 offer from right-wingers to kill Kennedy. Having spoken at length with Dick Russell, whose *The Man Who Knew Too Much* carried the allegation, I have no reason to doubt the veracity of the claim. But with oil money, the right wing had carte blanche to offer a contract far higher than a paltry $50,000; it would have amounted to a blank check.

Other well-connected right-wingers also deserve a brief look. David Ferrie, discussed earlier for his CIA and organized crime connections, was virulently and openly anti-Kennedy, and according to "participant" Robert Morrow, Ferrie was the brains behind the assassination.[17] William Reily, who briefly employed Lee Oswald as a coffee-machine greaser and then allowed him leisure time to visit Adrian Alba and God knows who else in the heart of the New Orleans intelligence neighborhood, was well known as a financial supporter of right-wing, anti-Castro organizations. This hardly makes him a candidate to hire Oswald, the one-man New Orleans "chapter" of the FPCC. Reily's reward was that several of his employees, shortly after Oswald's employment was terminated, went on to lucrative government contracts at NASA—an agency that obviously placed high value on coffee expertise on a résumé. Jim Garrison correctly alleged that the Reily Coffee Company was being "sanitized."[18]

Joseph Milteer, who lent his voice to recordings suggesting that Kennedy would be killed in the fall of 1963 and authorities would arrest someone to divert suspicion from the real plotters, was a member in good standing of various and sundry groups *not* enamored of Kennedy policies. William Duff, believed by General Walker to have been his assailant,[19] was reportedly seen in the company of Lee Oswald in April–May 1963 (April, possible; May, Oswald was in New Orleans). George DeMohrenschildt is alleged to have discovered John Birch "infiltration" into the Kennedy plot,[20] but "infiltration" suggests there was already something afoot that could be infiltrated.

Georgia senator Richard Russell, who in his first 281 days of service on the Warren Commission asked four questions, spoke out sharply against JFK's June 11, 1963, civil rights remarks, delivered the day after his American University speech, a set of equally troubling pronouncements to the right wing. In suggesting continuance of southern tradition, Russell preached an advocacy that customers had rights to buy products, but merchants had equal rights to choose customers.[21]

Dallas seethed; Stevenson suffered; JFK was warned, but took the political gamble—and lost. Although Jack Ruby's Carousel Club was closed on Saturday, November 23, perhaps to give its owner the chance to do some freelancing, the rest of the strip joints were open, and Dallas was alive and partying while much of the nation and the world mourned.

Analysis: Groups and individuals cited in the foregoing narrative certainly had no affection for John Kennedy or his policies, and occasional violence had been known to be a method employed by such groups. It is possible that in their loathing of Kennedy, added to the potential willingness to embrace a Texan president, some elements cited above may have been the final catalyst—not just infiltrators in the Kennedy assassination. It should also be noted that such groups are based on the "good old boy" network, which guarantees a code of silence among all even if there are transgressors in their midst. Several good old boys made plans in Texas, and one good old boy became president. Other good old boys "investigated" the event.

And it must also be noted that the Dallas law enforcement community was an additional dependable group of good old boys.

One of the unspoken keystones in all of this is the Walker shooting, seen by many as a red herring. If Oswald shot at Walker, how could any subsequent alliance include both Walker and Oswald? Since everybody knew Oswald was involved, Walker could not have been, so the thinking goes. (Continue to bear in mind the premise of that logic.) Although Walker testified that he did not believe it was Oswald who shot at him, it is equally easy to imagine a shot fired into an *empty room* in the Walker residence to divert suspicion from a group that would be active later in the year.

John Kennedy had planted the seeds of a new America—one that would tax the mighty oil barons, one that would close superfluous military bases, and one that looked to liberty and justice for all—not just for all whites.

The conservatives would see to it that the fall harvest of 1963 was not based on the seeds planted.

"Guns don't kill people, people kill people" is the basis of one somewhat pretentious philosophy. Its corollary might be, "Guns don't kill people, money kills people."

CHAPTER SEVEN

ORGANIZED CRIME

Three Can Keep A Secret If Two Are Dead . . .

—Philosophical construct attributed
to Carlos Marcello★[1]

AMERICA HAS FOR MANY YEARS maintained a curious love-hate relationship with the tightly knit fraternity that has come to be known as "organized crime." We demand of our legislators and law enforcement agencies tough statutes and rigorous enforcement in the "anti-rackets war," while at the same time we sanctify the mob with our fascination with *The Untouchables* and silver screen genre such as the *Godfather* saga.

Although the FBI, through propaganda minister Hoover, had insisted for years that there was no such thing as organized crime, a postulate agreed to by U. E. Baughman, head of the Secret Service when JFK took office, America knew better. Some felt the direct pressure as vending and service industries were infiltrated and eventually bought out with mob money. Others recognized that certain illicit trades were carefully controlled. Anyone who could read a newspaper knew that Albert Anastasia was not gunned down by an irate paperboy, and that the Appalachian meeting of November 1957 was not a high school reunion.

The suspicion that organized crime was the moving force behind the Kennedy assassination has been well chronicled by authors G.

---

*If one assumes that the "Marcello safety factor" is a constant—that is, that 300 can keep a secret if 299 are dead—the safety factor can then be expressed algebraically as $S=T-(T-1)$, although confirmation would be impossible.

Robert Blakey and Richard Billings (based on House select committee findings) as well as by David Scheim and John Davis. The Kennedy brothers, having been put into office with the understanding that Joe Kennedy would temper their anticrime concerns, did not live up to billing, and although the campaign coffers had contained some syndicate money (as had Nixon's), the Kennedys prosecuted their campaign donors with a vengeance. They also failed to make any changes in the geopolitical structure of Cuba, which had been a lucrative mob stronghold prior to the arrival of Castro. Organized crime leaders also recognized that John Kennedy was sharing a mistress, Judith Campbell, with a "reputed" mob boss. These are strong motives, and the mob knew how to take human life and cover their trail.

We know that Carlos Marcello, reputed head of the Louisiana crime syndicate who had been unceremoniously deported on Bobby Kennedy's orders, had uttered the famous oath "Take the stone out of my shoe!" We also know that Marcello contributed heavily to Cuban exile groups (a constant ingredient in the assassination stew) as well as to LBJ, to block anticrime legislation in the Senate.[2] We know that Jimmy Hoffa, whose vast union pension fund occasionally provided Mafia capital, was not on any Kennedy Christmas card list, but rather was a prime target for prosecution and as such had sworn vengeance against his tormentors.[3] (It will be recalled that it was Hoffa who insisted that all U.S. flags at Teamster buildings that had been lowered to half staff because of the assassination be raised.) It is also known that a frustrated Central Intelligence Agency, unable to get to Fidel Castro, turned to organized crime for muscular assistance. We are aware that Jack Ruby, with well-documented syndicate connections and equally well-documented police connections, made an increasing number of long-distance phone calls as the presidential trip to Texas approached. Yet it should be noted that Ruby had served as an FBI informer in 1959, raising questions about either his loyalty to the mob, or FBI foolishness in being infiltrated.

Do these factors add up to an assassination? Not for certain. There is a strong suggestion of motive, but there is just not enough smoke to suggest that there was any fire. Taken logically, many factors suggest that organized crime may well have gone along for the ride on November 22, having everything to gain and nothing to lose, but to posit the assassination as purely a "mob hit" may be to take the easy way out.

It is true that the Kennedys were making inroads against organized crime, but the leaders of the major families stood *to gain* in certain respects when RFK's task forces beat up initially on the small fry. For all the noise about the Mafia having motive to remove the president, they could have done it "cleanly"—either by going public with what they knew about JFK's private life, or by fighting power and money with their own power and money and literally buying the next election. Had Kennedy's sexual peccadilloes been revealed in November 1963, a year before the election, the then prevailing atmosphere in puritanical America, combined with a short list of legislative successes and a growing list of enemies, could have made JFK vulnerable. Organized crime could have installed the Republican of their choice and sent a political sympathy card to Joe Kennedy, Sr.

Organized crime successes in this venue must also be considered. It is easy to announce, "the mob got JFK." But a quick check of the mob's prior score sheet with respect to *political* murders is a short list indeed. There are literally no national politicians whose deaths the mob can be blamed for prior to 1963. They may have bumped off some local mayor who got a sudden attack of morality after accepting bribes, but one searches in vain for organized crime involvement in the deaths of any large city mayors, or any congressmen or senators, much less any presidents. It is also overly simplistic to insist that JFK was a target because he and RFK were going after the mob. Anyone familiar with reruns of *The Untouchables* knows that past presidents have wreaked greater havoc, and on bigger fish, than what the Kennedys succeeded at. What they ultimately may have done is an open question.

The Cuban-mob motive may also be overstated. Organized crime is a vast, carefully managed corporate empire, and it keeps itself in better financial shape than many of America's corporations, and certainly in far better fiscal health than the U.S. government, even in the 1960s. Castro closed the casinos and expelled the prostitutes. If the mob had an ongoing concern in Cuba, it was first and foremost hubris. They wanted their Cuban connections back because they were rightfully theirs, but not because they needed the money. In the 1960's there were many avenues of opportunity available to enterprising business people with investment capital, and a location called Vietnam would soon be a rich entrepôt into the illicit drug marketplace, unless, of course, a visionary president terminated the American commitment there. Carlos Marcello and others would back Cuban exiles financially because it was very much in their interest to maintain the tenuous CIA-mob anti-Castro connection.

It cannot be emphasized enough how vital this was to them. This CIA connection made organized crime *legitimate*. It put them inside the circle, where they had been off and on since World War II, when gangsters of Italian descent were sent home to provide intelligence for the coming U.S. invasion. The mob also had access to other data that American intelligence could not get, and those data had long been the basis of a quid pro quo. Events of 1961–63 only served to continue this preexisting "odd couple" relationship. No matter what they did in contravention of the law, the government would somehow have to sweep it under the rug rather than have the public learn that its government was subcontracting through gangsters for intelligence or to kill foreign leaders. Imagine a typical televised Senate "rackets" hearing in 1963. Instead of an accused mobster appearing "with his mouthpiece" and "taking the Fifth" ninety-odd times, he admitted that organized crime was laundering money *and working with the CIA to kill Fidel Castro.* It would have been nothing less than the biggest news story of the decade, dwarfing Sputnik, the Bay of Pigs, the Missile Crisis, or the shooting down of the U-2.

John Kennedy *was* having an affair with Judith Campbell, a young woman reportedly sharing sexual favors with an underworld leader. (Ms. Campbell was by no means alone, and JFK's paramours may provide the best definition of "mob.") Although the organized crime code of conduct might call for a murder to dissuade future such liaisons, traditional rules are altered when it is the president, not a rival in the underworld, who is involved; or the rules might have created the liaison *with* the president. Either way, the easiest approach would have been to the woman in question, perhaps making *her* an offer she could not refuse. The second easiest approach did, in fact, occur. J. Edgar Hoover had a sit-down lunch with JFK, alerted the president to what he knew, and the relationship cooled thereafter.

Jack Ruby's suddenly enhanced phone bill may indeed provide circumstantial evidence of mob involvement in the events of Dallas. But his itemized phone bill, in and of itself, is a weak evidence dossier with which to convict organized crime of the assassination.

Certainly the mob did some talking that was overheard by electronic surveillance prior to November 22. But because they were overheard saying "JFK will be hit," that is probative of the event, not its perpetrators, and by 1963, underworld figures knew that eavesdropping was occurring, and they spoke in generalities. Thus we have no recording that announced "Frankie and Lenny from St. Loo are gonna whack the president in Dallas in a crossfire"; on the contrary, what was heard might have been hearsay from the mob's new political partner, the CIA, or wishful thinking. Similarly, when Carlos Marcello, in the presence of FBI informant Edward Becker, demanded, "Take the stone out of my shoe!" was he saying, "Have it done," or "Wouldn't it be nice if it happened"? There are far more than mere semantics in those choices. Our understanding of events is also hindered by the fact that such data are contained on FBI wiretaps, and if there is one certainty in the JFK murder, it is that Hoover told very little of what he knew before, during, and after.

Rose Cheramie, a key witness not called by the Warren Commission, told that "word in the underworld" was speaking of an attempt on JFK.[4] A different kind of warning came from SV-T1, a Savannah FBI informant, who reportedly saw Lee Oswald receive a sizeable amount of money under the table at a Marcello-owned restaurant.[5] Karen Bennett Carlin was fearful of speaking with Secret Service agent Roger Warner about a possible connection between Ruby and Oswald, and apparently she had good reason to feel that way, as it was long believed that she met a violent death within a year.[6] In fact, she is still alive and insists that the Ruby/Western Union "telegram to Karen Carlin" scenario was a ruse to make Ruby's crime not appear premeditated. The data of Miss Carlin (a.k.a. Little Lynn) thus guarantee that Ruby had one or more confederates within Dallas police headquarters, and the choices are narrow: the boys in blue or Lee Oswald. Oswald seems unlikely.

Authors Davis and Scheim are at odds regarding Oswald's employment in the summer of 1963. John Davis sees Oswald as "a runner and collector" for a bookmaking operation run by Oswald's uncle, Dutz Murret, but David Scheim sees the Oswald-Murret connection as overstated.[7] A contact of Murret's, Emile Bruneau, posted Oswald's bail after the New Orleans fracas of August 1963, but that may have been as much to keep Murret out of the limelight as to bring Oswald into it.

Robert Blakey has written that the House Select Committee on Assassinations believed that Jack Ruby was stalking Oswald, had organized crime connections before and after the weekend of the Dallas killings, and that underworld figures attended Ruby's trial.[8] That statement requires some analysis. The stalking component is true in that Ruby did spend a few hours at Dallas police headquarters after

Kennedy was shot, and all of his life in police custody after Oswald was shot. Yet Pete Fisher, a photographer for UPI, saw Ruby standing in the doorway of the police "show-up" room as Oswald was brought in for the midnight press conference. "OSWALD passed not more than three feet from Ruby as he was led up on the stage."[9] Ruby would have had to know he would get another chance, or that testimony weakens the "stalking" theory. And only select individuals in one clearly identifiable group could have guaranteed that Ruby would get another chance.

There are many indications of Ruby's involvement with the underworld, but they, too, are circumstantial and contradictory. Lewis McWillie, cited in a Warren Commission document as a "gambler and murderer," was mentioned in the arrest of another suspect whose phone numbers included that of Jack Ruby. Other documents show that Ruby, who admittedly spent a week vacationing in Cuba in 1959, actually flew in on September 12, 1959, and left the following day.[10] There are also the suggestions that police knew Ruby had underworld connections, and that Ruby acted in typical mob fashion in his treatment of the Dallas cops, without whose assistance Ruby's Carousel operation would have been more difficult.[11] While there are many FBI reports of interviews that paint Ruby as little more than an average citizen, the depositions of Irving Alkana, Paul R. Jones, and Jack Hardee indicate Ruby at least had connections to organized crime. Lenny Patrick dissented, telling the FBI, "No matter how much you investigate, you'll never learn nothing, as he [Ruby] never had nothing to do with nothing."[12] If the picture is not clouded enough, CE 1536 showed mob connections to Ruby, but as published by the Warren Commission, it was sanitized to remove those references.[13]

The key to a better understanding of Jack Ruby is a quick study of his finances. Despite compromises worked out with the IRS in March 1962, at the time of the assassination, Ruby owed the Internal Revenue Service a documented $44,413.86 and possibly as much as $20,000 more. In addition to monies owed to family members, including $16,000 to his brother Earl, Ruby also had debts to other financial backers. When arrested, Ruby had on his person or in his car $3,169.11, which IRS revenue officer Harris Jackson seized: "I will retain this money in the Intelligence Division office for the purpose of examining serial numbers."[14] One can only wonder what that critical scrutiny revealed.

Organized crime figures are usually very successful, not in serious financial straits, as was Jack Ruby. A quick scan of Ruby's assets could suggest that he had between sixty and a hundred thousand reasons to do what he did on November 24. Of equal value in our assessment of Ruby is the reminder that organized crime members occasionally work "off the books," and Ruby's Social Security account showed no earnings *from the second quarter of 1940 through 1955,* nor any in 1961 or the first three quarters of 1962. Lastly, many of Ruby's phone calls were to officials of AGVA, a "mob-dominated" union whose members undressed in the Carousel Club.[15]

Further consideration will be given to the question "Who was Jack Ruby?" later in this narrative. Given his poor finances and bleak prospects beyond 1963, it is difficult to see him as anything beyond a syndicate errand boy, if that. We must, however, weigh that assessment along with the testimony of Regis Kennedy, FBI agent in charge of the Marcello case, who told the House select committee that Carlos Marcello was a tomato salesman with no involvement in organized crime.[16]

Analysis: Given the mob's anti-Castro alliance (of convenience) with the CIA, its desire to have its Cuban assets liberated, and its well-earned distrust of the Kennedy brothers, it is easy to see organized crime as a suspect in the assassination. They also may have wanted to remove the president and replace him with Lyndon Johnson, already seriously compromised by an FBI director who was professing total ignorance of the existence of organized crime.

However, it is almost impossible to see organized crime as the senior partner or the prime mover in the assassination if we analyze the event in light of syndicate methodology.

First and foremost, it is hard to imagine any "family"—the Marcello family, the Gambino family, or the Trafficante family—taking on the president of the United States without the full agreement and understanding of all the major families. Even when there was agreement between or among families, it was usually to ratify an intramural conflict; the mob, prior to 1963, had no history of taking on mayors, governors, or senators, much less a president whose brother headed the Justice Department. And while we have many hints and suggestions that the mob was involved in the event, there is not a shred of evidence that any such meeting of the families was convoked with the item of presidential assassination on the agenda.

Second, the ambush scenario—much less that of the lone assassin—

crosses the line into fantasy with respect to past practices of organized crime. It is inconceivable that anyone would have said, "Yes, unfortunately, the president must be taken care of. Give the contract to Dutz's nephew—what's his name?—Oswald—yeah, the kid that was a marksman in the marines years ago who just bought a cheap surplus rifle." Organized crime would have had to have a *guarantee* that John Kennedy would not be alive on November 23, that those who needed to know would know it was the mob's work, and that they could not be tied to the crime. In that sense, Oswald *was* useful to them. It thus becomes very difficult to believe a conclusion that specifically suggests that organized crime killed the president, with Oswald as a major player in the event. Also, the Mafia maintains its power by letting the world know they committed a crime and got away with it. Would anyone have accepted Lee Oswald as a "mob torpedo"?

Two alternate scenarios, far more in keeping with syndicate methods, immediately come to mind, if, in fact, the removal of JFK had been on their agenda. Scenario one: Reactivate Judith Campbell. Reestablish the liaisons between her and Kennedy, and on one White House visit, have her kill JFK in the presidential boudoir with a silenced weapon. The body might not be discovered until an hour or more after her departure, and the day's television programs would have been interrupted with the news that President Kennedy had been found dead, presumably of natural causes. We certainly would *not* have been told that the president had been killed "gangland style" by a mob consort he was shacked up with in the White House.

Scenario two: Assuming the motorcade route was known forty-eight hours in advance, a phony highway repair crew is dispatched to the triple underpass late Thursday night, where the crew proceeds to pack the Elm Street underpass with high explosives. Two innocuous railroad cars, containing highly flammable materials, are parked above the underpass. As the slowly meandering limousine reaches the target zone, an unknown spectator at Houston and Main streets activates a remote control switch in his pocket, and the explosion, concussion, and fire kill and incinerate everyone in the limousine, touching off the railroad cars, which are ultimately blamed for the tragedy. As a backup, a pro-Castro group telephones authorities and the media and claims responsibility. While the world mourns the loss of all six occupants of the car, the Dallas cops and railroad workers on the underpass, and at least a couple dozen spectators killed nearby, the focus would be far greater on the totality of the tragedy than on JFK. Tomato salesman Marcello would receive the transmitter as a souvenir.

These scenarios make a lot more sense than the mob putting Oswald in the window and hoping he hits his target as it leaves his field of fire, for if the mob had made the attempt *and failed*, we would have seen a real "war on crime."

And the players knew that.

CHAPTER EIGHT

POLITICAL FOES: JOHNSON AND NIXON

The proper memory for a politician is one that knows what to remember and what to forget.

—VISCOUNT MORLEY, 1917

IT IS AXIOMATIC THAT AMERICANS past puberty in 1963 recall where they were and what they were doing when they learned of the assassination of President Kennedy. How many, however, can recall their immediate reactions? I shall never forget how an otherwise overcast New Jersey afternoon suddenly turned cold, although the temperature stayed relatively constant, and my thoughts were on the loss suffered, not on the perpetrators of the event. My father, however, had a different take: "He was killed in Texas; look where the new president lived." The loss of John Kennedy was hard enough for me to believe, and I was totally unprepared to deal with my father's theorizing.

Times *have* changed.

John Kennedy's visit to Texas in late November 1963 amounted to the kickoff of his bid for reelection in 1964, an issue that seemed at the time a reasonable certainty. Reelection would have kept John Kennedy in power until January 20, 1969, and a successful second term might well have laid the groundwork for a political dynasty of Kennedys.

In retrospect, although we view JFK larger in death than in life, the biggest threat to his reelection was a host of LBJ-related scandals that were rapidly emerging from the horizon into the foreground.

Those same events became cloudy, meaningless concerns after LBJ became president, as Mr. Johnson used the power of *that* office to bury *all* his concerns.

Kennedy's reelection prospects were clearly unacceptable to many political leaders of both parties, but not nearly as unacceptable to two men who thirsted for the presidency before time ran out: Lyndon Johnson and Richard Nixon, *both of whom* became president because of JFK's death.

Both had lost to John Kennedy in 1960, and both felt they deserved to be president. Nixon was subsequently humiliated by his 1962 defeat in the California governor's race, a battle he entered to create his political rebirth, not his epitaph. Johnson was humiliated in 1960 by the subpar Democratic showing in Texas, and subsequently by the cold shoulders transmitted from the elite Kennedy corps of intellectuals to "Colonel Cornpone" from Texas.

Nixon hoped to campaign for Republican candidates in 1964 and have his résumé thereby validated; Johnson was hoping his name would still appear on the 1964 Democratic ticket. As fate would dictate, it did: *at the top.*

Focusing first on Lyndon Johnson, it has been widely suggested that his time was running out. He was nine years older than JFK, and he had suffered a massive heart attack in 1955. As noted, his name was beginning to be seriously clouded by the Billy Sol Estes scandal, in which Henry Marshall, the Agriculture Department agent investigating Estes' improprieties, was killed on June 3, 1961. (Although he was shot five times by a rifle, Marshall's death was ruled a suicide; *those* are magic bullets.) By 1963, the name Bobby Baker was being added to LBJ's woes, as Johnson's former protégé and influence peddler was reporting a net worth of well over $1 million (a much bigger pile of change then than now), on a yearly salary of $19,263.[1] J. Edgar Hoover had gotten LBJ out of yet another scrape, in which the crew of Johnson's private plane had been killed when ordered to the ranch in bad weather. According to author Craig Zirbel, LBJ not only got away with murder, but also he pocketed $700,000 from insurance claims.[2]

Given John Kennedy's increased popularity in states that had been close races in 1960 (aided by targeting those areas with lucrative government contracts), coupled with Johnson's weak showing in Texas in 1960 and the growing Texas scandals that threatened to reach Kennedy, there was talk—but never confirmation—that JFK would have a different running mate in 1964. Given differing sources, JFK's departure from Fort Worth can be viewed through two vastly different prisms. One story has JFK being introduced to LBJ's sister, and JFK guaranteeing her that the Democratic ticket would carry Massachusetts and Texas, suggestive of Johnson's incumbency on the ticket. Another version, following the spat between Texas politicians over who would ride in which car, has JFK telling his secretary, Evelyn Lincoln, in his last memo to her, that Johnson would not be on the 1964 ticket.[3] One can also view the November visit to Texas in two ways: One, why bother, if the native son is terminal? or two, get the momentum going early, before the political tumor is removed.

This is how John Kennedy may have viewed the issue. Lyndon Johnson saw it differently, according to Madeline Brown. Ms. Brown told this author that the vice president told her, before the guns fired in Dealey Plaza, that John Kennedy would not be a roadblock to the Johnson political aspirations anymore, and Ms. Brown was gracious enough to offer, but never *supply*, documentation to me that proved the veracity of her assertions. (The most significant document promised was a 1958 communiqué from Clint Murchison to LBJ virtually outlining how the native Texan would arrive at 1600 Pennsylvania Avenue; JFK's election was but a temporary roadblock to the Murchison plan. It came to fruition the day after the gathering he hosted.)

So began LBJ's final day as vice president.

Lyndon Johnson, two cars back in the motorcade (and in the only VIP car that did not have a Secret Service driver), witnessed the assassination. His car also sped to Parkland Hospital, where he was segregated from the ensuing tumult. To return to Love Field, he had Mrs. Johnson put in another car, either to protect her from assassins who might still be lurking, or as a decoy to draw them out. He rode aboard *Air Force One*, a wise security precaution more than a usurpation, but he insisted on having the blood-spattered widow Kennedy at his side during the swearing-in, almost to legitimize the passage—or seizure—of power. When the Kennedy entourage headed for Bethesda Hospital, Johnson raced to 1600 Pennsylvania Avenue and power, and within a few hours would fire Evelyn Lincoln and request that the grieving widow get out of the White House in haste. It has also been documented that calls from the *Johnson* White House attempted to limit the scope of the Texas investigation, and following the shooting of Oswald, that White House calls were made to the police to close the case and to attending physicians to get a deathbed confession from Oswald.[4]

On November 29, 1963, Johnson created the Warren Commission, effectively blocking House, Senate, and Texas inquiries into the assassination. Ten months later, the president received the Warren Report, detailing the same conclusion that had been made public by his neighbor, J. Edgar Hoover, on November 22, 1963.

To suggest that Richard Nixon had any direct involvement in the assassination is at best a circumstantial chimera and at worst a poor attempt at cheap sensationalism. Nixon did stand to gain from the events of November 22, and is arguably the person who profited the most from the *two* Kennedy killings. But to benefit *from* is not necessarily to be involved *in*.

Nixon was in Dallas from Wednesday to Friday of the assassination week, but he had a valid reason to be there, and left, according to most accounts, well before JFK arrived.[5] The point of interest of Nixon's presence in Dallas, aside from his presence at the Murchisons' (confirmed by two sources, including a local Texan named Peter O'Donnell, who drove him there), had to do with the site of the Bottlers' Convention Nixon was attending. With that building unavailable for JFK's midday Dallas speech, the choice of sites was narrowed to the Trade Mart or a far less suitable meeting hall. The latter was rejected for lack of presidential dignity, leaving only the Trade Mart, which dictated violating Secret Service procedures by going through Dealey Plaza, and draining precious protective manpower, as the Trade Mart had sixty entrances and a network of catwalks and balconies.

It had been a hectic sixteen years for the poor Californian who entered Congress with JFK, rose swiftly, and seemed on the verge of the presidency until his makeup betrayed him in the "first debate," a contest he did not even need to enter, and as history tells us, he should have avoided. As the point man for a Cuban invasion that would have been the first major success of a Nixon presidency, he was naturally disappointed in the outcome, both at certain doctored ballot boxes in November 1960 and at the Bay of Pigs in 1961. It is a very honest emotion to suffer if you feel something has been stolen from you. It's an equally honest emotion to suffer when a person of humble origins loses the ultimate prize to a playboy millionaire.

The last suggestion of Nixon's involvements in events of 1963 stems from the reappearance of some of Marita Lorenz's crew, the suspected cast of characters in the 1972 political felony that came to be known as "Watergate." The infamous "Nixon tapes" contain a number of veiled references—clearly concerns of Nixon—to past Cuban events. Which ones? Nixon did not get elected, so all he did regarding the Bay of Pigs was get the ball rolling and then pass it along to the choice of the electorate. Why the secrecy? What did E. Howard Hunt know that was worth $2 million in blackmail money to Nixon? Did Nixon resign for reasons other than "a third-rate burglary"?

Could the Murchison-LBJ communiqué have been a hint of things to come, and could Nixon's presence at the Murchisons' have been a convenient way to guarantee the silence of the man who would emerge as the leader of the Republican party after the Goldwater debacle?

Analysis: We do not have all the answers to all the questions, but perhaps by asking them, our energies can be focused. Richard Nixon hardly seems culpable in the events of Dealey Plaza, and is at worst the victim of his own image. Yet the more we learn of Nixon, the more his ominous tentacles point in directions that seem suspicious. Perhaps future biographers, not preachers of current events, will provide the answers.

Lyndon Johnson does not seem as blameless. "Knowing" him from his papers, diaries, and from friendly as well as hostile biographies, and from interviews with those who knew the real LBJ—not the on-camera character actor—it is clear that his sins before the White House and in the White House outweigh by good measure those of his predecessor and his successor, neither of whom finished his elected term.

While I was unconvinced that Johnson could have been a "plotter" in the assassination when it was but a theory of my father's and not yet the satirical "MacBird," it is now very easy to suspect that a mutuality of purpose between LBJ and powerful forces in Texas, as well as a similar mutuality of purpose between Johnson and Hoover, had much to do with the behind-the-scenes doings that led to the gunfire in Dealey Plaza.

Hoover and Johnson well knew that their political lives depended on John Kennedy's political death. For LBJ, it was never a lone-assassin theory: He was facing a triangulation of fire from Bobby Baker, Billy Sol Estes,[6] and "TFX," a defense industry scam gone awry. The triangulation of threats never caught up to LBJ, because the triangulation of people whom he and his powerful Texas friends could control caught up with Kennedy.

My father partially solved the case on November 22, 1963, but never lived to publish or see his son recognize the obvious.

CHAPTER NINE

IDEOLOGICAL FOES: CUBA AND THE USSR

Communism is the corruption of a dream of justice.

—ADLAI STEVENSON, 1951

JUST AS JOHN KENNEDY had political enemies in 1963, so the United States had ideological enemies. Though few in number, they provided a nuclear threat to American security that was enough to push the American defense budget from the category of tens of billions to *hundreds* of billons. War was good business, but so was keeping the peace.

As 1963 began, people the world over were very pleased that a peaceful solution had been found to end the stalemate that had been referred to as the Cuban Missile Crisis. That October event had taught the world—especially Americans and Russians—of the importance of American nuclear superiority. But the crisis had also taught the world how close it had come to the unthinkable Armageddon, where destruction would be measured in megatons and survivors would be counted in handfuls.

Perhaps Castro, now feeling militarily naked without his Soviet toys, was eager for revenge. And perhaps Khrushchev was equally eager for some form of payback, having been outwitted by the younger American and embarrassed in front of his own Soviet power structure, as the "Missiles of October" have been seen as a private gamble by Khrushchev. But such a scenario assumes that the Soviets, and to a lesser degree the Cubans, lost the missile crisis.

Did they?

Only in the American media, where "the other guy blinked," and where we were treated to aerial views of crates, allegedly containing missiles, aboard Soviet ships bound homeward. The reality of the event was far more balanced. The missiles had gone to Cuba for two purposes: to safeguard the island, and to offset American nuclear superiority.

Both Soviet purposes *were* achieved. We eventually learned that Kennedy pledged not to invade Cuba again (a promise he seemed intent on keeping, breaking up staging areas and training bases for Cuban exiles), and the threat of war convinced both sides of "mutually assured destruction," which made the nuclear numbers game essentially irrelevant except to U.S. defense contractors. In addition, we also learned afterward that U.S. missiles, similar in nature to the Cuban missiles in question, were withdrawn from American bases on the Soviet perimeter in Turkey, and slightly farther away in Italy. They were sitting ducks anyway, but it was a face-saving gesture that Khrushchev could take to the Politburo and claim the whole crisis was a trade-off. The U.S.A. won, the USSR won, but Castro felt left out. If he had the idea to seek revenge against JFK, would he have picked Lee Oswald, whose track record and Fair Play for Cuba Committee publicity stunts were so obvious?

Kennedy seemed thereafter to recognize the Cuban concern with attempts at reconciliation, both for the realpolitik gains that could be made and to soften the Cuban-Soviet axis that was proving economically burdensome to the Kremlin. Castro tentatively went along with the initiatives, which were still in progress when Cuba received news of the tragedy in Dallas. There it ended, as we are still, in the mid-1990s, at odds with Castro, although we recently offered many dollars to the remnants of the Soviet empire.

The only real indication of Cuban hostility came in a statement made by Castro in September 1963. Aware that he was an American target but unsure of the ultimate title behind the operation, he warned that attempts against Cuban leaders could have harmful effects on American leaders. What was he really saying? You come after us, we'll get you? Or, If you succeed, it will only hurt you in the long run? Or, worse still, *The fanatics you have rounded up for this operation are unilaterally dangerous?*

The third statement seems more realistic than the first two. Also bear in mind the consequences that would have followed the assassination of an American president if the event was proven to have been the work of Castro's guns. All the king's horses and all the king's men . . . Even Castro recognized this. Years later, when interviewed in Havana by members of the HSCA, he put the issue squarely on the line: Imagine, gentlemen, the state of the world in late 1963 if Oswald *had been granted a visa* by the Cuban consulate in Mexico and *had made* a trip to Cuba. No answer was necessary for Castro's statement of the obvious.

A chilling hypothesis is nevertheless possible from the distance of three decades: *Castro's rash September statement unknowingly signed John Kennedy's—and Oswald's and Ruby's—death warrants.* Once Castro made his hasty promulgation, it gave a license to those elements in America who were already stalking the president. Given Castro's rhetoric, the president could now be killed, removing him as a threat to the intelligence community, mob prosecutions, Texas oil power, and the future occupations of Lyndon Johnson and J. Edgar Hoover, and neutralizing the threat of RFK to both intelligence and underworld, and Castro would be blamed. The intelligence services would reap a rich harvest of caseloads to work on, and with no Kennedy looking over their shoulders. The threat of nuclear war would prevent punishment of Castro, as we are reminded that it was just such a threat that convinced Earl Warren, in the face of grave constitutional concerns, to accept the chairmanship of the president's commission.

As for the Soviets, the missile crisis taught them everything they would ever need to know about brinksmanship, and the demands placed on the Soviet economy by the military were already beyond all reason. Khrushchev was now ready to agree to begin disarmament, to allow a thaw in the Cold War, and to (albeit grudgingly) establish some trust—and a hot line—with the United States. "Détente" was stillborn in the streets of Dallas, and a massive escalation in Vietnam in 1964 would see an end to the concept of trust as well as to the reign of the "trusting" Khrushchev.

Analysis: Both Cuba and the USSR, with whom Oswald had made lengthy and obvious contact, had far more to *lose* by Kennedy's removal than they stood to gain. When Dean Rusk testified before the Warren Commission (be it to tell the truth or to avoid nuclear war), he gave a flat denial of any Soviet involvement in the assassination. "There were tears in the streets of Moscow," he concluded.[1] This was in stark contrast to the reaction in Dallas, where even today, old-timers scoff at Soviet or Cuban connections, asserting, "Well, hell, why would one communist kill another?"

Because the Soviets could not match the United States ruble for dollar in the ever-escalating arms race, Khrushchev needed breathing space in 1963 for his economy—just the kind of breathing space that Gorbachev was denied, leading to the collapse of the "evil empire." On the American front, the once-feted Castro had had his missiles removed by people who did not even speak Spanish, and he had every reason to feel abandoned. Both Khrushchev and Castro understood the fundamentals of the American Constitution, especially the part about presidential succession. And both knew where Lyndon Johnson was coming from. Both needed American goodwill, but they could not be sure they would receive it from a president born in Texas and elevated to power by unseen forces of evil. Castro's rhetoric about threats coming back to haunt *came back to haunt him for three decades.*

Oddly, it must be added that Castro, in his discussions with American envoys from the House Select Committee on Assassinations, and the KGB since the collapse of communism, both gave the impression of being forthcoming with whatever knowledge, ideas, or data they had regarding Kennedy's assassination.

It is only in America that documents, or perhaps truth, is a secret of the highest national security priority, despite the continued reiteration that the crime whose documents have been hidden, destroyed, or sanitized was the motiveless crime of a lone nut.

CHAPTER TEN

CUBAN EXILES

I know how men in exile feed on dreams of hope.

—AESCHYLUS, *Agamemnon*

IT WAS NOT WITHOUT REASON THAT consideration of the Cuban exile community within and without the United States would be the final topic of discussion under the heading of possible suspects. While individuals such as Castro, Khrushchev, Johnson, Nixon, and the two Secret Service men are obvious and easily identified, "Cuban exiles" or "anti-Castro Cubans" are far more difficult. Even the CIA and the FBI are better known, inasmuch as the members, such as we are able to learn their memberships, take oaths to preserve and protect, and their names are supposed to exist somewhere. "Organized crime" and "Cuban exiles," on the other hand, are amorphous labels that cover broad, often ill-defined spectra of the population and are therefore convenient when seeking to assess blame.

There can be no doubt that Cuban exiles (or at least a militant percentage of them) were active prior to November 22, 1963. Having been displaced from their homeland and from the lives they had always known, they sought refuge with American help and hoped their adopted country would want Cuba freed as badly as they did. They were no doubt crushed—some physically, many others emotionally—by the failure of the invasion forces at the Bay of Pigs, by a lack of any further invasions, and by the unrealized potential of the Cuban Missile Crisis.

They possessed motive, means, and machismo, yet somehow the combination of ingredients reads more like a recipe than a result. If they had been so easily swept *from* Cuba by an upstart outside the continuum of power, how were they really expecting to rid the island of that upstart, now entrenched in power and heavily supported by the second strongest military power on the planet? If the CIA's promised "popular anti-Castro uprising" at the time of the Bay of Pigs proved to be a fantasy, what should that have told the exiles about popular satisfaction, at least in the early 1960's, with respect to the Castro government? If their most brave and militant efforts only floundered on the beach at the Bay of Pigs and were totally undone because Castro still had *a mere three jet trainers*, were the exiles really big enough to believe they could retake the island if they could assassinate an American president? Lastly, if they were splintered into many subgroups, was there enough unity among those groups to carry out the events of November 22?

Despite Kennedy's promises that there would be no further invasions of Cuba, the exiles, with support from the American intelligence community, continued to train for some future adventure, while at the same time carrying out sabotage missions against the island of Cuba. Although there had been a time when the Kennedy brothers seemed active supporters of such activities, 1963 would mark a turning point.

Flyers were circulated throughout the Cuban exile community in Miami (the largest such exile population) in April 1963 that pulled no punches in their political orientation: "Only through one development will you Cuban patriots ever live again in your homeland as free men ... if an inspired Act of God should place in the White House within weeks a Texan known to be a friend of all Latin Americans."[1] While the message's content is crystal clear, its origin raises questions. Was it a purely in-house memo, Cuban to Cuban, and if so, how did its writer or writers know with such clarity about events that were being planned in Washington and Texas? Or was the message an intelligence vehicle to stir up a hornet's nest and provide a distraction when and if an "inspired Act of God" came to pass? Finally, can anyone conceive that Lee Oswald authored and, in lone-nut style, distributed these Miami missives?

Dallas sheriff's deputy Buddy Walthers gave indications that members of the Freedom for Cuba Party had been mysteriously holed up in Dallas until November 15, 1963, and he added that his unnamed informant indicated that Oswald had paid them a visit.[2] This leaves unanswered questions about where these folks went *after* November

15, and again places Oswald on both sides of the Cuban fence. The subsequent suspect is also placed on both sides of the fence in his encounters with Carlos Bringuier when he offered his expertise to anti-Castro Cubans, with the as yet unresolved "Odio incident" of late September 1963 when an "Oswald" again threw in his lot with the anti-Castro Cubans, as well as his dealings with Ferrie, Banister, and Shaw in New Orleans, clearly of an anti-Castro stripe. On the other hand, we are asked to believe that Oswald was Castro's most ebullient protégé on the continent, based on brief possession of *five hundred* leaflets.

In those contradictions are the seeds of confusion that can make or break any theory that Cuban exiles were responsible for the assassination of John Kennedy.

Authors Robert Groden and Harrison E. Livingstone have asserted that the gunmen in the assassination were Cubans and Cuban Mafia, and six gunmen, including "professionals," were involved.[3] Their research is perhaps the clearest suggestion of strong Cuban involvement, prior to the publication of *ZR Rifle: The Plot to Kill Kennedy and Castro*. This author's research also points to the presence of a Cuban hit squad in Dallas, but they were not the critical one in Dealey Plaza.

Subsequent to the assassination, a confidential FBI source indicated "that the assassination of KENNEDY was the result of a plot prepared and executed jointly by Chinese Communists and FIDEL CASTRO." An additional source subsequently enhanced the story, suggesting that the financing came from Wall Street. An equally unnamed source "in another government agency which conducts security investigations" told that "about a dozen persons who were privy to the plot have been provisionally jailed in Cuba to prevent any indiscretions. . . ."[4] Somehow, given the state of world politics in 1963, an alliance of Castro and Chinese Communists strains the imagination, and financing for *their* activities from Wall Street boggles the mind. Wall Street had much to gain from the removal of JFK, but such a financial center is of a conservative bent that would suggest an unwillingness to form an alliance with the inchoate Cuban movement and the massive ideological leper colony that was mainland China in the early 1960s.

It should also be noted that Miami, already suggested as the site of two possible attempts on Kennedy, as well as New Orleans, in addition to its Marcello-Ferrie-Banister coalition, both possessed sizable Cuban populations. What about Dallas? While there was a

Cuban presence there, it was considerably less than in either Miami or New Orleans, and it was a captive of the right-wing elements that were so pervasive in Dallas. The right wing wanted communism out of Cuba, but for political, not sociological, reasons. They could care less about the local Spanish-speaking population, and merely used them as pawns in their game. So, too, did the CIA.

Analysis: While it is clear that the motive, means, and machismo existed, the machismo aspect would suggest that at some point in the past thirty years, the responsible Cuban exiles would have exercised their bragging rights. Their silence suggests they're not entitled. It must also be recognized that whatever role they played at the time would clearly have been staged to place the blame on Castro, and the tenuous Oswald-FPCC connection failed to accomplish that goal fully. That logic argues against their involvement. And if they had even been able to get close to JFK, logic would suggest that Fidel Castro could have been killed by the same group. The other anti-Kennedy suspects might have trouble inside Cuba, but exiles had the best crack at Castro; if they could not succeed there, how could they succeed in Dallas?

Beyond those caveats, there is almost a Cartesian consensus among students of the assassination that Cubans had to be involved somehow, in the sense that "they seethe, therefore they kill." It cannot be denied that they seethed; proof is lacking that they killed.

This is not to say that we should get a crayon and eradicate the Cuban exiles from the list of suspects. There are strong suggestions that they served in various roles as CIA assets, and the CIA remains a prime suspect. The exiles, like the arrested assassin, would provide valuable distractions if anyone decided to investigate thoroughly.

CHAPTER ELEVEN

PRELIMINARY CONCLUSIONS

A MULTILAYERED, INTERWOVEN CONSPIRACY whose initial guiding purpose was self-preservation came to a meeting of the minds and set in motion the events that took the life of President John F. Kennedy. They subsequently subcontracted the shooting, as explained in "Blue Death," and arranged for enough hit teams to be present to bring all suspect groups within the federal conspiracy statutes, thereby guaranteeing a measure of silence from all concerned parties.

Of the suspects listed, some can be eliminated. The Secret Service, while arguably negligent, did not kill the man they took an oath to protect. The Secret Service is a dedicated fraternity, and they know their job. In 1963 they were a vastly underpaid group of individuals who did the job they were assigned as well as it could be done within the resources they were given as well as within the limitations imposed on them by a president who often used them as intermediaries for his sexual matters. After 1963, protective resources were increased, but too late for JFK as well as for his Secret Service detail, who were phased out and replaced by a group led by Rufus Youngblood, the agent who protected vice president Johnson, arguably the safest person in the motorcade.

Kennedy's death was a tragic loss for the Secret Service, and it is hard to conceive why they would have a reason to support his murder. With respect to the allegations made against agents Greer and Hickey, they are nonsense.

Richard Nixon can also be crossed off the list. Although subsequent events would demonstrate a ruthless side to Mr. Nixon, the cast of characters around Nixon included names such as Donald Segretti and groups such as CREEP, rather than names like James Bond and groups like SMERSH.

It should also be noted that while Nixon stood to gain from the events of Dealey Plaza, he also stood to lose. On November 22, John Kennedy presented a five-year roadblock in Nixon's quest for the White House. On November 23, Lyndon Johnson could have lengthened Nixon's wait to a nine-year stretch, as LBJ had the opportunity to serve out Kennedy's unserved fourteen months and still be elected to two full terms. Nixon would still have been young enough in 1972, but his chore would have been much harder, as he would have been an anachronism, twenty years down the road from his 1952 "Checkers" speech and twelve years distant from his 1960 loss to JFK. A new political generation would have emerged in the meantime, and Nixon would have been further hampered by his similarities to Johnson. While JFK and Nixon had been perceived as a clear choice in 1960, there were far more similarities between Nixon and LBJ, and when Americans change leaders, they frequently change ideologies. Nixon would win in 1968 by demonstrating how he was *different* from the faltering LBJ, and the Democrats made his job easy by nominating LBJ's vice president, Hubert Humphrey (after the "lone nut" murder of Robert Kennedy), whose difficulty in 1968 was that he had to spend more time convincing voters that he was not Lyndon Johnson than he spent to convince them of who and what he really was.

Lastly, and I know this will trouble some conspiracy theorists, I would also eliminate Castro, *his Cubans,* as well as Khrushchev and the Soviets as suspects. It is difficult to conceive all of Oswald's FPCC posturing, plus the well-documented Oswald impostors, all of which pointed the accusatory finger directly at the Soviet-Cuban axis, and then suggest that Castro or Khrushchev would have ordered Oswald to perform those pro-Cuban, pro-Soviet posturings while he was, or others were, ordered to kill the president. It is also highly unlikely that Castro or Khrushchev, with ample firepower at their respective disposals, would rely on the likes of a Lee Oswald. If the Soviet-Cuban axis were involved, the name Lee Oswald would be unknown to history, unless, of course, agencies within the American government learned of the threat and manipulated Oswald for months if not years to stage the fakery. That, too, is hard to imagine.

Ultimately, the Soviet-Cuban theory was LBJ's bogeyman to get Earl Warren to head a presidential commission; it was the reason that "national security" could be invoked to hide mountains of documents that otherwise should have been available, since the alleged assassin was dead (the weight of JFK's lungs at autopsy had to be concealed for reasons of national security?); and finally, it helped maintain the tension—and profit—of the Cold War.

Neither the Soviets nor the Cubans needed Oswald. The Soviets had the KGB, which was far more ruthless and deadly than portrayed in spy movies and TV thrillers, and they would not have been caught. In its day, the KGB was the most efficient killing machine on the planet; agents followed orders and left no trace.

Castro had reasons to mistrust Kennedy, but they were diminishing in 1963, and Castro had no reason to expect improvement from LBJ, as other groups might. Events have also demonstrated that Castro is a survivor, now in his fourth *decade* as ruler of Cuba. He has survived American insouciance as well as sabotage, frequent changings of the guard in the Kremlin, the "end" of communism, continued poverty, numerous poor harvests, and rival claimants to the mantle of power. If he could survive all those things, he could certainly have weathered the Kennedy presidency without the need to terminate it.

We are left with six general possibilities: the CIA; Hoover/FBI; right-wing/oil/hate groups; LBJ; organized crime; and Cuban exiles. If this were a multiple-choice question, the choices would be designated "a" through "f," with "g" being "none of the above" and "h" being "all of the above."

The correct answer to the question "Who was behind the killing of John F. Kennedy?" is "h": *All of the above.*

This hypothesis will be developed through the remainder of this book, and reinforced in the concluding "Hypothesis," but for now the general outline and the two key riddles in the puzzle can be suggested.

John Kennedy's "New Frontier" was an intelligence concern at the beginning. Even before the beginning of JFK's term, the invasion of Cuba loomed brightly on the horizon. The taking back of Cuba in 1961 would have been the gleaming jewel in the crown of the CIA et al., but it did not come to pass. The target then became simply Castro, on the continued CIA misunderstanding that the people of Cuba were ripe for revolution. This challenge to kill Castro was brokered through the CIA by the power groups for whom they act as agent, but the job proved too difficult, so the agency subcontracted with organized crime and Cuban exile groups, both eager to help, but for widely divergent reasons. Leading right-wing groups would support them, as one possible result would be an American-dominated Cuba instead of an island so close to our shores governed by foreigners who were also cursed Reds. LBJ and Hoover's FBI were still out in the cold at this point.

Gradually, as time passed with no success, and without even the hint of a prospect of success in the often mindless attempts on Castro, the challenge remained the same but the motives and method changed. Kennedy had allowed missiles, albeit only briefly, in Cuba; he had argued for treaties and discourse with the Soviets that would bring a generation of peace, but at the price of forfeiting billions of defense dollars in Vietnam and at superfluous bases around the world. Kennedy had also enforced the admission of black students in some southern schools, and had invited black leaders to share their agenda with the president in the White House. He had begun the restructuring of the CIA itself. And he would end the careers of J. Edgar Hoover and Lyndon Baines Johnson.

Or they would end his.

Clearly, Kennedy was the most serious threat yet to the power elite.

If, however, *Kennedy* could be killed in such a way that the finger of guilt pointed at Castro (if, e.g., someone with Marxist leanings who was a leader in the Fair Play for Cuba Committee did it), then all the above groups would be supported with all the might of the U.S. government and the American public in the effort to rid Cuba of Castro and communism. This would entail having such a suspect—a "patsy," if you will—framed for the crime almost immediately, and it would have to be a patsy with an excellent pedigree. Lee Oswald fit this profile perfectly. Unfortunately, this short-sighted intelligence scenario did not account for the Soviets, who were not going to sit back and watch Havana be bombed back into the Stone Age, so while the patsy took the heat, he would take it alone, as Americans were too shocked by the horror of the Dallas tragedy to call for Castro's head.

J. Edgar Hoover would publicly announce Oswald's guilt almost immediately, and it would be just as quickly accepted by the new president of the United States, who would appoint a blue-ribbon panel to rubber-stamp the director's conclusion and guarantee that the sole investigating body did not look too closely at either the head of the Executive Branch, the director of the FBI, or any real evidence. In this sense, the president's commission, using programmed FBI bloodhounds, had the liberty not to investigate two prime suspects. The president would also make telephone calls to investigating authorities in Texas and insist that the investigation and the indictment stop at Oswald, and he would also call Oswald's attending physician and demand a deathbed confession. Failing to get that, he would accept the Warren Report as holy writ.

The two riddles that provide the ideological glue for this theory have never been previously explored to my knowledge, and although no one will answer them today, we must nevertheless activate them as possibilities.

The first problem is the attempt on the life of Gen. Edwin Walker. The "whodunit" is not vital (Marina Oswald's testimony notwithstanding), because I do not believe the general was sitting at his desk when the bullet was fired. I suspect that the right wing, and the petrodollars behind it, had something—quite likely a presidential assassination—on its future agenda, and they needed publicity that would point subsequent fingers of guilt away from them. A bullet fired in anger by a leftist nut can create the kind of scenario that would overlook the right as elements of the assassination.

What is unbelievable about the Walker shooting of April 10, 1963, is that as of seven months later, or roughly November 22, 1963, it was still *unsolved*. General Walker was the hero, the freedom-fighting anti-Communist incarnate, and his true believers included the vast majority of those who were employed in law-enforcement capacities in and around Dallas, Texas. It strains belief that they could not solve the crime. *Or would not.*

The attempt on his life, real or otherwise, *remained unsolved because it was staged to create a diversion for some future event.* As it happened, that future event occurred on November 22, and thereafter the Walker case suddenly "made sense." We are asked to believe that the same lone nut who would shoot at a fire-breathing John Birch Society right-wing general leading the fight *against* desegregation was obviously the same person who would shoot the eastern moderate who occupied the White House and was trying to *accomplish desegregation* and retain possession of that dwelling.

Equally curious was the unwillingness of the Warren Commission to take testimony from Walter Kirk Coleman, the key eyewitness to the Walker event.

The events of April 10, 1963, were portents of things to come.

The second riddle is cut from entirely different cloth. More puzzling, but equally understandable, are the actions—or inactions—of the FBI. As noted, Hoover's word was FBI law, so some understanding must be arrived at to answer the fundamental question of why the FBI did not investigate the Kennedy assassination. While it is true that they took thousands of interviews and rounded up a National Archives full of "evidence," from the reverberations of the shots in Dealey Plaza, the focus of the FBI was exclusively on Lee Oswald. Why?

J. Edgar Hoover had become famous, feared, and omnipotent in two ways: one, by solving any or all crimes that would grab headlines and hype the FBI in the media and in the public imagination. Hoover's second method was to have incriminating material on anyone who stood in his way.

So the question must again be asked, "Why didn't the FBI go all out to solve the Kennedy assassination?" If one had studied the FBI prior to 1963, it would have been logical to conclude on November 22 that the vaunted FBI would spring into action and solve the crime of the century. The media would then be filled with pictures of handcuffed defendants, statements (accompanied by obligatory photos) from J. Edgar Hoover, and before long, Hoover's law enforcement satrap would supersede the Secret Service as the agency of presidential protection. Having so much to gain, what insurmountable barrier stood in the way of a full FBI investigation?

Four possibilities come to mind. The first is that the FBI had prior knowledge of the event, and Director Hoover, caring more about the continuance of his leadership in the bureau than Kennedy's in America, ignored the warnings and let the assassination happen. He then pinned the blame on Oswald, who could hardly have been seen as a threat (or an FBI concern) prior to going home on November 21 and possibly bringing a rifle to work the following day.

Possibility number two is a more specific offshoot of number one. Through the bureau's many wiretaps on organized crime, conversations were overheard in which organized crime figures, part of the CIA-exile-right-mob cabal, were overheard discussing in general terms the impending accession of LBJ. The knowledge in and of itself compromised the bureau, since Hoover chose to ignore it, and it further compromised the bureau since Hoover had been denying the existence of, and avoiding where possible prosecutions of, organized crime, inasmuch as they were much tougher than the "Pretty Boy Floyd" types that the FBI thrived on, and also because the CIA and the mob had compromising material on Hoover's very private "other life" that could rob him of what was most dear: his dictatorship over American law enforcement.

The third possibility is that Oswald was, in his murky netherworld, somehow traceable to the FBI. As noted elsewhere, FBI agents, in common with agents in most other American and foreign law enforcement bodies, rely on informants for street information or for infiltration. It is impossible to conceive of an FBI agent, attired in standard white shirt, tie, cuff links, and polished shoes, attending a Cuban revolutionary meeting. It is equally inconceivable that street agents would identify all their sources and that the FBI director would have at his fingertips the names of all the confidential informants employed by the eighty-four hundred FBI agents. It is very possible that Lee Oswald, connected to every side of the political spectrum at the time, would have been a prime candidate for an FBI agent on the make for a new and knowledgeable snitch—particularly one who seemed to be so easily manipulated.

In this scenario, Hoover pronounced Oswald's guilt so quickly that there was no time to find out who he was, yet there was time enough for FBI agents to sit in on all interrogations, take custody of all significant evidence, exert federal control, threaten Oswald's widow with deportation, and sanitize all files in the meantime.

The last scenario seems the most likely, albeit the most bizarre. The year 1963 was but one of many years of internecine warfare between the FBI and the CIA in their respective struggles over power and territoriality. CIA leaders knew how Hoover did business, *and they, quite possibly with mob help, "Hoovered" Hoover.* Carefully biding their time, they got incriminating evidence—probably tape recordings as well as photographs—of the private side of the FBI director, and they used that material to make sure he would not take any kind of close look at the Kennedy assassination. On the contrary, Hoover would protect his privacy by joining the early planners, and in so doing he would bring aboard his powerful Texan friends, LBJ included, who would then bring the lamb to the slaughter and manage the event, carried out by locals in their own backyard. Hoover would then point the finger at Oswald, the unaided communist, suggesting that more federal funding be devoted to those who deal with the communist menace—the FBI and the CIA—all the while continuing to deny the existence of, or suggest prosecutions of, organized crime.

It has been said that politics makes strange bedfellows. It may also be true that strange bedfellows made politics.

Analysis: Billions of dollars were at stake in the changing vision of John F. Kennedy, and people in power, and people with power, were keenly aware of the price tag of the "New Frontier," and passed their concerns along to those in the corridors of power who might share their agenda. Intelligence operatives responsible for providing covert activities and intelligence gathering that translated into American policies that could create civil and military contracts totaling billions of dollars annually, had, by late 1962, also become disillusioned with the Kennedy-led prospect of a generation of peace. Most troubling their political horizon was the realization, following the "American victory" in the Cuban Missile Crisis, that Castro would remain in power without whatever was in the boxes that the Soviets sent home aboard their ships. Also troubling was the realization that without the intercession of assassins' bullets, JFK, and possibly his brothers, would stake a long-term claim to occupancy of 1600 Pennsylvania Avenue. This element cannot be overlooked: Until the accession of FDR, it was axiomatic that presidents came and went without "power" being disturbed. FDR broke that tradition, but a constitutional amendment prevented any such future incursions by temporary presidents into the real corridors of power. JFK had to operate under the limitations of that amendment, but his family did not, and those who had the most to lose suddenly had a great deal to fear.

Using Cuba as their focus, the intelligence elements already linked to organized crime restructured their objective to rid the world of Castro by using Kennedy's death as a pretext. This was a method not unacceptable to organized crime elements, who felt betrayed and threatened by the Kennedy brothers and who would willingly return to their former assets in Cuba. Those elements of organized crime aided a "plausible denial" syndrome, as it would not be good for any investigative agency to discover an alliance between the intelligence community and the mob.

Texas wealth and right-wing elements disenchanted with JFK's moves toward racial accommodation and toward a policy that would later, under a different president, become known as détente, jumped aboard the bandwagon to rid America of an eastern "liberal" (as they saw him) who would allow racial harmony; call out federal troops to protect American citizens; and threaten, through the closing of tax loopholes, the vast profits of the domestic petroleum industry. The CIA/mob alliance thought up the concept. Texans, assured of Hoover's compliance, brought the idea to fruition using local talent that they could easily purchase and control.

It is arguable that such elements controlled the local talent long before November 22; that date may just have been a matter of calling in long-standing IOUs.

To add seasoning to the stew and to provide further deniability, Cuban exiles, willing and eager to revenge their April 1961 humiliation, were added to the picture. As unstable as they were amorphous, they would create a focus of unrest in America while at the same time fronting for faceless intelligence operatives who could not go public with their plans. The Cuban exiles were also the best able to point the finger of blame for the event at Castro, the ultimate (or penultimate, depending on one's perspective) target of the exercise.

Since Hoover's private life was known within the intelligence community and in the organized crime circles *that Hoover frequented* (as well as to FBI people, tacitly), the planners had the tapes and photos that would guarantee that the vaunted FBI would not get in the way of an assassination scenario that included a preplanned patsy. Having no choice but to accept the *fait accompli*, which suited Hoover fine on a career level, he joined the Lyndon Johnson-oil axis. Johnson, a junior partner in the "Texas connection," might have had consultative power to suggest such "executive action," but his agenda would have been obvious. Johnson would subsequently contain the investigation by appointing a presidential commission that would prevent any other investigations, while relying on the already compromised FBI for their source material.

Realizing that something was very wrong with the nonsensical evidence they were being handed by the FBI, the president's commission had no choice but to follow, with all due intensity, the absurd trail Hoover provided, and lend all their magisterial dignity to a report that is one of the ultimate American lies. But that would come later.

Thus an interwoven, interlocking conspiracy was created. All that was required was for the president to sniff the cheese and step into the trap. The cheese, of course, was reelection, and the trap was sprung in Dallas. Given the nature of the conspiring elements, it is likely that there were at least three other possible "kill zones" created, although never intended for use. Whether populated by exiles, mob torpedoes, or intelligence assets, they were there to guarantee the silence of those groups by making them culpable. They were never given the "go" on November 22, and when the president's car passed their vantage point—or failed to reach it if they were on the route of the return motorcade—they were able to conclude that their compatriots had been successful in Dealey Plaza and that they were just as guilty of conspiracy, in the legal sense, as had been the triggermen themselves. That would guarantee their silence, and they have lived up to the guarantee.

Such was the planning.

Who pulled the triggers, and who let it happen?

Book One

Blue Death

CHAPTER ONE

OF MECHANICS AND INVESTIGATIONS

Politics are almost as exciting as war, and quite as dangerous. In war you can only be killed once, but in politics many times.

—WINSTON CHURCHILL, 1920

HAVING POSITED THAT AN INTERWOVEN, multifaceted conspiracy with overlapping goals of self-preservation had come to the conclusion that President Kennedy's term should be shortened, it is now our challenge to consider the "mechanics" (a polite euphemism for "assassins") chosen for the operation and the methods necessary to contain the investigation within the first few hours until the dust settled and the world could be convinced of Oswald's—and nobody else's—guilt.

The word "assassin" is derived from the Arabic word *"hashshashin,"* literally "eaters of hashish," and specifically an order of Middle Eastern Muslim fanatics active from 1090 to 1272 whose goal was to kill Crusaders. (Believers in "Camelot," take note.) Since those times, "assassin" has come to mean a paid killer willing to murder someone of political importance.

There had been numerous assassinations in the twentieth century prior to 1963: McKinley, Trotsky, and Gandhi were among the bigger successes, and both Roosevelts, Harry Truman, and Charles DeGaulle had been targets.

Yet in the history of modern assassinations, there had been few targets as large as John F. Kennedy, and the players knew this only too well. Their job, then, was to arrange for "mechanics" who would maintain the plausible deniability already created by the interlocking directorate behind the event. The planners had money at their disposal, to be sure, but "outsiders" can be conspicuous, expensive, and often more secretive and devious than their employers. Given the nature of this assignment, there was no guarantee that in a week, a month, or a year there would not be blackmail demands of astronomical proportions, or worse, public confessions by foreign mechanics who suddenly came face to face with American policies they disliked.

No, the forces behind the assassination were going to have to originate within America's borders—hardly the haven for terrorists that other nations provided or encouraged, but there was a talent pool. What was needed was a group that already had a strong dislike for Kennedy, so there would be no change of heart, loss of will, or pangs of conscience. Also needed were people talented with weapons. In addition, it would be very helpful if the mechanics chosen were able to blend in with the scenery of a major American city such as Dallas at high noon on a sunny Friday, and it would be an absolute blessing if those mechanics were in such a position that local authorities could not possibly investigate them.

One group and only one group fits this profile perfectly: a rogue handful of Dallas police officers, with one or two key people near, at, or above the chain of command.

As suggested in "Theories," the plausible denial syndrome was probably greatly aided by the presence somewhere in Dallas of a well-armed CIA/Cuban assault team composed either of genuine exile fanatics, or the Hunt-Sturgis-Hemming-Lorenz decoy caravan, as well as mob torpedoes, and even a right-wing/white supremacist team, but they were never considered active. Dealey Plaza was the kill zone all along, and elements of the Dallas police, hardly friendly to Kennedy, had the weapons, skills, and ability to blend into the scenery and come and go casually; and the rest of the department, loyal Americans and honest cops in varying degrees, could hardly begin an investigation of themselves. They had Oswald in their subversive file and they were not surprised when he became the suspect as soon as the shots were fired.

This section of the book will show how the Dallas police controlled the motorcade route, the manpower allotments, the crime scenes, the "evidence," the media, the interrogation of the one serious suspect, the release of all other suspects, the custody and safety of the prisoner, the prisoner's immediate family, and all phases of the preliminary investigation.

When elements of the Dallas police were chosen, it was a selection whose wisdom time has sanctified; for while the world watched in horror at the repeated flaming ineptitude of the Dallas cops during that tragic weekend, little did anyone know that they had *succeeded* in every responsibility they had been given. And their success has survived until now.

With respect to the "investigation," it is an article of faith among law enforcement officers, be they local, state, federal, or Interpol, that there is really only one way to run an investigation, and that is with thoroughness. Take every scrap of evidence, add to each of those scraps by dauntless investigation until the saturation point is reached, then begin to see where all the evidence points, and only then narrow the focus.

The Dallas police certainly did not do that. No crime scene involved in the assassination was ever truly sealed. They rushed to the grassy knoll, yet stayed only long enough to take a cursory look and sniff gunpowder, to which they attached no significance, or which they had no choice but to ignore. They had several witnesses who pointed to the exact window in the TSBD where a rifle had been seen, yet it took them forty-two minutes to climb six flights of stairs and become curious about that window—almost as if it were not yet time for the curtain to rise and have the stage props revealed. There is a pervasive pattern of *not* taking names and addresses of witnesses, as if they did not want to know. Certain witnesses were totally ignored. No impediments were placed in the way of potential fleeing assassins, and although they knew Oswald was missing from the TSBD, no all-points bulletin was ever broadcast, *even for him.* None was needed; they knew roughly where he was at all times, and they found him quickly enough, though it took two tries and one officer's life to put him permanently within their clutches. The search for any additional evidence, or assassins, was totally halted once it was "officially recognized" that Oswald was a suspect in the Tippit murder and was missing from the TSBD. Police who used the telephone at the Texas Theater, as well as the police who escorted Oswald or witnessed his arrival at police headquarters, were convinced of Oswald's guilt in both murders from the outset.

The press was allowed to overrun police headquarters, partly to generate reams of stories convicting Oswald, who was often taken through their midst, which also provided cover in case a grieving citizen sought revenge for the loss of the president. Evidence was faked, altered, or suppressed. Ridiculous lineups were held at which witnesses, after seeing Oswald's picture all over the newspapers, were asked to identify him amid teenagers and an overweight Mexican. Photographic evidence was seized and has never been seen since. The large police presence at Parkland, ostensibly still under the command of Chief Curry, who was also present, refused to enforce Dallas law and insist that Dr. Earl Rose perform the necessary autopsy on JFK. Despite telephone threats against Oswald, the press was given all rights, and the prisoner was executed in front of sixty million Americans.

The evidence was almost immediately given away to the FBI (who had no jurisdiction, but were brought in quickly by two "accessories before and after the fact," Hoover and Johnson), and with the evidence went the legal case, but it didn't matter, since Oswald was not to live. With Oswald's death, the case was effectively closed.

And Jack Ruby was not totally a creature of the mob when he executed Oswald. *He was part of the Dallas police/mob scenario all along.*

The remainder of this section will flesh out the allegations suggested above and demonstrate overwhelmingly that the assassination of President Kennedy could not have been accomplished with such amazing simplicity, nor buried with such nonchalance, if there had not been a serious conspiratorial presence on the ground in Dallas who did not have to concern themselves with either escape or investigation. It very nearly was the perfect crime.

CHAPTER TWO

EARLY SUSPICIONS

Stuff the head
With all such reading as was never read:
For thee explain a thing till all men doubt it,
And write about it, Goddess, and about it.

—ALEXANDER POPE, *The Dunciad*

IT DID NOT TAKE LONG before people began to suspect the Dallas police of involvement in the assassination, but though many authors have suggested or hinted that there was such involvement, most have portrayed them as somehow tangential to the event. Part of this no doubt stemmed from the merciless beating the Dallas cops took for losing both the president and his *alleged* assassin within forty-eight hours.

Thomas Buchanan, in one of the first two books critical of the emerging "official version," noted that it was a tradition in Europe to suspect the police of complicity in an event like the JFK assassination, but he outran available 1964 sources in suggesting, "The chief of police, encouraged by the most respected citizens and with the aid of petty criminals recruited from the local bars, set out to kill the president of the United States."[1] Given chief of police Curry's blatant perjury before the Warren Commission, when he testified that Ruby was known to only a handful of his officers when many others testified that Ruby knew *hundreds* of Dallas officers, there is at least some credence to Buchanan's suspicions. Buchanan's theories were already in print when J. Edgar Hoover testified before the Warren Commission on May 14, 1964, and blandly asserted that such "journalistic garbage" could be expected from a member of the Communist Party.[2] Buchanan's book further forfeited credibility in postulating that Ruby was the second gunman (Oswald being the first), and when Ruby completed firing from the triple underpass, he dropped the rifle and sprinted back to the *Dallas Morning News* office, where he was seen at 12:40 P.M. Such theorizing did not strengthen Buchanan's other conclusions.

There were other early indications of Dallas police involvement. Ilya Mamantov, translator of Marina's Russian for the Dallas cops on November 22, indicated he was contacted to serve as translator by Jack Crichton of army intelligence and was then called a second time in quick order by the police, and subsequently picked up and driven to police headquarters in a Dallas police squad car, strongly suggestive of a police-intelligence linkup.[3] In a memo already cited, deputy attorney general Katzenbach wrote to Bill Moyers, "The matter has been handled thus far with neither dignity nor conviction; facts are mixed with rumor and speculation. We can scarcely let the world see us totally in the image of the Dallas police when our president is murdered."

Gen. Edwin Walker, a man with many friends on the force, put his concerns bluntly: "The city police has misused the [Warren] Commission and the FBI." He also told the commission, "You can anticipate that people would like to shut up anybody that knows anything about this case. People right here in Dallas."[4] Taking Walker's second statement piecemeal, it must be asked, Who could shut people up? and second, Who would know what individuals had information that needed to be kept under wraps? The Dallas police would have to be at the top of that short list.

From Jean Hill's police boyfriend "J. B." we learned of the general state of mind of Dallas police officers following the shooting of Oswald in police headquarters: "It sure makes the Dallas police look like a bunch of damned morons."[5] *And very unlikely suspects.*

It must also be recalled that membership in right-wing organizations such as the John Birch Society or the Klan was a prerequisite for acceptance on the Dallas police force, and that must be tied to a snippet of Jack Ruby's often elliptical testimony: ". . . there is a John Birch Society right now in activity, and Edwin Walker is one of the top men of this organization."[6] It should also be remembered that Ruby promised a great deal of interesting testimony if the Warren Commission would take him *out of Dallas police headquarters.* Not to

D.C. or even to Spokane, for that matter, just out of Dallas, and *Dallas police headquarters.*

Warren Commission counsel Albert Jenner showed at least a hint of curiosity when he asked Linnie Mae Randle, sister of Wesley Frazier and neighbor Ruth Paine, if there "had been any conversation in the neighborhood prior to the assassination of any FBI *or police officers* [emphasis added] having visited the neighborhood."[7] An FBI presence would be unnoticed, as they appear as well-dressed citizens and drive standard vehicles. A police presence would be far more obvious—and for what purpose? Would the local police be charged with the responsibility of maintaining surveillance on someone suspected of being a national security risk? Not likely. If the police were spending time in Oswald's neighborhood, it was for sinister purposes heretofore not considered.

Suspicion was further cast in an FBI interview with police lieutenant George Butler, who did not know who was responsible for the transfer of Oswald in the midst of a media mob. Butler believed that both Chief Curry and City Manager Crull would have had more sense than to take the risk of exposing such a prisoner, suggestive of a decision made at a higher level—and what level was higher in Dallas?[8]

A statement from "J. B." to Jean Hill epitomizes federal suspicions about the police and the case, but we must recall that the FBI already had its marching orders, and they were stamped "Oswald only." Nevertheless, the feds poked around, causing J. B. to write:

> From everything that's been going on in the department, I get the distinct feeling the feds think somebody in the Dallas police had something to do with the hit on Kennedy. . . . I can't see any other reason why they'd be spending so much time grilling so many of our people . . . the parade route, the way the cars were arranged, the way our escort formation was set up, the fact that so many Dallas cops knew Jack Ruby, the fact that somebody let Jack Ruby into the basement right before he shot Oswald, the fact that some of the cops were heard cussing Kennedy for being a flaky liberal.[9]

J. B., in one concise paragraph, told the essence of the "blue death" scenario, as well as federal curiosity about it. Of course, a "Red patsy" and some "white lies" prevented it from becoming a public concern for a lengthy time.

In later years, Jim Garrison would join the parade of individuals who were suspicious of police elements, cautiously at first, suggesting that plotters and assassins are often outsiders, but "Otherwise the men working to set up the operation are residents of the city where the action is scheduled to occur, resulting in a miminum influx of strangers."[10] Garrison would later warm to his task and become more direct: "Most observers are in general agreement that the weekend of November 22, 1963, was not one of the better weekends for the Dallas police force. However, in fairness to that organization, it must be said that most of its members did not know that the assassination was going to occur."[11]

Subsequent researchers, including Robert Groden, Harrison Edward Livingstone, "James Hepburn," Penn Jones, John Davis, and G. Robert Blakey, would all focus on tangential points at which the Dallas police could fall under suspicion, and correctly so. Eventually, a deputy sheriff named Hiram Ingram, a friend of Roger Craig's, stated that he had knowledge of a police conspiracy. Ingram fell, breaking his hip, on April 1, 1968, and died of cancer three days later on April 4, 1968, while national attention was focused on the King assassination in Tennessee.[12]

Authors Davis, Blakey, and Richard N. Billings focused on the activities of Sgt. Patrick Dean, a supposed mob-connected Dallas police officer and witness that the HSCA had high hopes for.[13] Little did they know of the value of the catch they could have netted; but like the official investigating body in 1964, the right questions were never asked of Dean.

By then it was 1978, fifteen years after the fact.

CHAPTER THREE

THE MOTORCADE

What kind of god art thou, that suffer'st more
Of mortal grief than do thy worshippers?"

—SHAKESPEARE, *Henry V*

THE WARREN COMMISSION, in both its hearings and documents and its subsequent Report, failed to clarify the simple issues of who planned the motorcade and how much attention was given to *the route ultimately taken*. In commission exhibit 1365, the front page of the *Dallas Morning News* for November 22, 1963, is cropped to exclude the original motorcade route down Main Street to the triple underpass, with no dogleg through Dealey Plaza.[1]

In his testimony, Roy Kellerman, Secret Service special agent in charge for the Dallas trip, indicated the motorcade route was in the hands of Winston Lawson, Secret Service advance agent for the Dallas trip, and the Dallas police.[2] The question then becomes, "Who knew Dallas better?" and the answer is obvious. Dallas agent Forrest Sorrels told the commission that *police officials* agreed that the route taken was the best,[3] and given the thesis being argued here, indeed it was. There are also strong hints that Chief Curry drove Lawson and Sorrels through the motorcade route to the point where Main Street crosses Houston, and then indicated "there's the highway over there." Also, as indicated earlier, there was no reason why the motorcade could not continue down Main Street, and, with Elm Street closed off, jump the small curb to reach Stemmons Freeway. It is neither a dignified nor a presidential approach, but if the cops on the overpass had done their job and kept civilians *off*, it would have been the safest way to proceed.

There is not one hint of evidence, on the other hand, that the Secret Service mapped out the eventual route or traveled all of it to see if it posed any dangers, such as expansive turns expressly forbidden in the Secret Service manual. Political advance men, may have created the odd route in the final week, because the Trade Mart was the last-gasp choice for the luncheon site. Dallas police officers and higher-ups, however, had to know of the security risks in the Dealey Plaza turn, as well as its potential as an ambush site, but one that offered the ultimate bonus: A suitable patsy (already in their "subversive file") worked on the very corner where John Kennedy would last recall being in a slowly turning automobile.

The Dallas police helped put the president in the kill zone.

Beyond the suggestion of Jack Puterbaugh insisting on a route to the Trade Mart, we are somewhat in the dark as to the exact identity of the local official or officer responsible for the precise motorcade route. We must concede, however, that there was a route, and that it would go downtown and eventually find its way to Stemmons Freeway. Of equal certainty is that during the week leading up to November 22, police officers were looking for duty rosters and postings that would indicate their assignments with respect to the known motorcade. All of this has a bearing on an incident that occurred on November 20 when two Dallas officers saw "mock target practice" going on at the picket fence atop the knoll. They arrived in time to see the participants depart in haste, and only wrote a report of the incident subsequent to November 22. The report was buried by the FBI and only came to light as a result of Freedom of Information Act (FOIA) litigation.[4] The event can either be seen as two cops doing their duty and thinking nothing of it, or as a fatal lapse of judgment by officers who should have immediately taken steps to make sure that all concerned parties were aware of this sighting so close to the impending motorcade route. Clearly, that was not the case. The motorcade route was thus known to those taking the target practice on November 20, and those who were "practicing" could only have known from police sources. Information regarding this security breach never reached the Secret Service.

Equally lax (intentionally or accidentally) were the officers on the triple underpass well before the motorcade arrived. In the deposition in which Julia Mercer claimed she saw a gun case being unloaded from a pickup truck at the base of the knoll, she also added, "There were three policemen standing talking near a motorcycle on the bridge just west of me."[5]

What else did the phrase "presidential protection" mean in terms of motorcade security? In essence, very little. An early transmission from the airport, prior to the arrival of *Air Force One,* indicated, "The crowds are getting large and we have very few officers. The only ones we have are assigned on the corners. There should be *reserves* [emphasis added] along the route."[6] The value of the reserves was best epitomized by the captain of the Dallas reserves, Charles Arnett, who told the Warren Commission that reserves were ordered to take no action if spectators booed the president, but if there was a threat of bodily harm, they were to report their concerns to the nearest "regular officer."[7] So if a reserve officer saw someone in the crowd draw a pistol and aim at JFK, that officer was under orders to run a couple of blocks and return with a regular officer. The president would have been safer in Washington under the watchful eye of the White House pastry chef.

A total of 178 officers, including reserves, were assigned to the parade route. Part of the justification for that low number was the equally large force needed to provide protection at the Trade Mart, with its many entrances and catwalks. But that begs the question: More police should have been made available. Given the estimated crowd of 250,000 people, 178 officers amounts to one officer for every 1,404 possible assassins. Further, there is no hint in the testimony of any officers that they were given instructions at any time to be concerned about the estimated 20,000 open windows along the parade route.[8] Of equal interest is the number of officers who kept their regular Friday off on the day of a motorcade, which had prompted enough concern in Dallas that the chief of police took to the airwaves to warn the population to be on their good behavior.* Some of the police who testified before the Warren Commission were on duty, and told what they did with respect to immediate events. Others, however, numerous in quantity, were off-duty at the

*An interesting point of cross-reference is the security for the 1993 visit of Pope John Paul II to Denver. Security measures there included the forbidding of costume shops to sell or rent religious garb, so no strangers could pose as clerics. In addition, the pope's car was armored and bulletproof. All police vacations were canceled, and every officer of the 1,347-person force worked daily twelve-hour shifts. Manholes were welded shut, and rooftops were swept regularly or guarded by sharpshooters. "It is the same thing we do for the president," said David Metzler. *The Record,* August 13, 1993.

critical moment. A review of the duty status of 25 officers of the Homicide and Robbery Bureau shows that at the time of the motorcade, 10 (40 percent) were on duty; 6 (24 percent) were off duty; 2 (8 percent) were on vacation; and 7 (28 percent) had the day off. *sixty percent were not available in the city that had just roughed up Adlai Stevenson.*[9] As a point of reference, the next time you have the opportunity to view news tapes of the weekend of November 22–25, 1963, watch for the security reports; they speak of maximum protection and the like, and, as such, are rubbish. Of equal interest, anyone present for the dedication of Dealey Plaza on November 22, 1993, can guarantee that there were far more than 178 officers present there . . . 30 years too late.

There were additional logistical concerns with respect to the makeup of the motorcade. Marrion Baker, the only officer to suspect the TSBD as the source of the shots virtually immediately, testified that he had been assigned to ride alongside the president's car, but had been told by his sergeant five or ten minutes before leaving Love Field that no officers would be riding alongside the presidential limousine.[10] The order may have come from the president; we must also consider the possibility that it came from the noted sergeant's superiors. The Dallas police were directing the protection in the motorcade whose route they had determined, and by limiting the motorcycles to the rear of the limousine, they guaranteed that the president was left exposed to shooters *in front of him.*

Other problems of an equally suspicious nature raise questions: Why was a major from army intelligence riding in the pilot car, and why did that car do nothing about the civilians on the triple underpass? Why was the next car, the "lead car," a closed vehicle, with the Secret Service man in the *front* assigned to look out the *back* window to monitor the limousine and the Secret Service man in the *back* assigned to look through the windshield for potential problems in *front*? The Dallas police had even suppressed protection in the lead car, where it was vitally needed.

Why were press cars moved several places behind the presidential car, when usually they were allowed better access? Of all presidential motorcades, this particular one presents us with a virtual dearth of press photos, removing one concern of the plotters; amateur photographs, as we know, were dealt with on an ad hoc basis, sometimes by the fake Secret Service in place. Why was the presidential car, originally scheduled to be seventh in line, moved up to third, behind

Curry's car, which had the potential to box it in if it tried to escape a fusillade?[11] (While researchers are concerned that the presidential limousine slowed down during the shooting, Curry's car had to have stopped, as shown in the second Altgens photo taken during the shooting. Testimony from the occupants of the lead car indicates that the car was virtually to the triple underpass at the time of the first shot, yet the photo, taken as Clint Hill was reaching Mrs. Kennedy, shows Curry's car a reasonable distance *short* of the underpass.) And why did Will Fritz insist on having a closed car filled with Dallas officers carrying machine guns, right behind the presidential limousine, when that spot was always taken by the Secret Service follow-up? Fritz would later contend that if his suggestion had been taken, his officers, even in a closed car, would have gotten off return shots before the shooting sequence ended.[12] *That could only have happened if they had known where the shots were going to originate from.* And even then, the suggestion was ludicrous, as the Secret Service is charged with protection in all such situations. The local police have the responsibility for dealing with suspects, and, for those watching television on November 24, 1963, it is clear that they dealt with the suspect.

As the motorcade entered the kill zone, there were other concerns: As noted, the driver of the presidential vehicle, William Greer, had a concern regarding the civilians on the triple underpass. There were two Dallas officers up there as well, but they had clearly disregarded instructions in allowing *anyone* to be there during the motorcade. Their superiors would later claim that they were supposed to keep out "unauthorized" people, but they were then unable to define "unauthorized." They had chased away AP photographer Altgens. Why leave others there? One answer to this question is that if those allowed to stay on the overpass had been ordered off, where would they have gone to get a good view? The nearest good viewing position is *behind the picket fence*. The presence of civilians where they should not have been also broke Greer's concentration during key seconds of the motorcade.

Winston Lawson, riding in the lead car, tried to wave the onlookers off of the triple underpass, but it was a futile gesture. As he was doing so, he heard the first shot.[13] At the same moment, Sheriff Bill Decker got on the radio and called for men to get into the railroad yards.[14] Decker's action, coming from someone seen by the House select committee as having underworld connections which went back as far as 1946, suggests that he either thought that was the source of the shots, or his call was a diversion. Either way, it was his only concern of the day, as he had ordered the sheriff's department not to participate in the protection of the motorcade, and subsequently the Warren Commission would not be curious about this or Decker's uncharacteristic unwillingness to transfer Oswald.[15] Sheriff Decker would also have virtually nothing to say to the Warren Commission, and they did not even attempt to break through his at times hostile veil of silence.

Dallas Secret Service agent Forrest Sorrels, sitting behind Decker during the motorcade, had some interesting observations about events in Curry's car. He noted that he could never recall a time when he had seen "the chief [Curry] so nervous and talkative," and he added, "I looked toward the top of the terrace to my right as the sound of the shots seemed to come from that direction . . . and Chief Curry immediately broadcast to surround the building."[16] The Dallas radio logs duly record a call by Decker, perhaps too precisely, at 12:30:40 P.M., indicating officers ordered into "the railroad track area, just north of Elm."[17]

The shattered motorcade, carrying two shattered men and the shattered dreams of a nation, left the scene of the crime forever. Left behind were shooters, weapons, witnesses, films, and many, many unanswered questions that the Dallas police, like J. Edgar Hoover, answered too quickly.

CHAPTER FOUR

DEALEY PLAZA

Alas, I am struck a deep mortal blow.

—AESCHYLUS, *Agamemnon*

DEALEY PLAZA, named for George Bannerman Dealey, was a 3.07-acre haven of lawn and monuments at the rump and rust end of 1963 Dallas. Although there are glass skyscrapers nearby today, thirty-two years ago it was an oasis amid an eyesore.

It was also a crime scene, and it was never sealed. While motorcycle officers, street patrolmen, and the otherwise unoccupied men of the sheriff's department sprinted *to the grassy knoll* upon hearing the shots, no officers had the presence of mind to seal the area, maintaining spectators for witnesses, searching for that one elusive clue, and somehow getting a better handle on events than they did.

It has already been noted that there was "mock target practice" in Dealey Plaza on November 20, and Julia Mercer, a witness with no ax to grind against anyone, reported seeing a gun case unloaded there on the morning of November 22. Both reports immediately tend to take at least some of the sting out of the lone-assassin theory, for it is unlikely *Oswald* was on the knoll practicing, and he hardly needed a second gun, as it would have taken a miracle to operate the one he purchased in the time frame allotted.

At 12:19 P.M., a call went out over the police radio network, "code 3" (haste), for an ambulance for Dealey Plaza. The ambulance arrived and picked up a suspected epileptic, departing at 12:25 P.M. At that time, the driver of the ambulance, a Mr. Pollard, using call number 111, radioed, "We are going to have to take this *prisoner* to

Parkland. Is Harwood blocked all the way?"[1] Upon arrival at Parkland Hospital, the "epileptic" departed without waiting for treatment. This raises several questions. First, the timing is too pat. In criminal terms it is called a diversion. An event is staged, the crowd focuses on that event, and something previously planned to coincide with the diversion occurs without public notice—such as snipers taking up positions, for instance. Secondly, since when are suspected epileptics, or most any other ambulance passengers, considered "prisoners"? Finally, why was the passenger in the ambulance, Jerry Belknap (who paid his ambulance bill on December 2) not called before the Warren Commission and asked to explain his odd behavior as well as his medical history?

Fewer than five minutes after the ambulance departed, sirens could be heard announcing the arrival of the motorcade. Ninety seconds later, hybrid events seemingly involving a firecracker, a motorcycle backfiring, and rifle shots, led to the wailing of additional sirens, which, among other things, announced a change of presidential administrations. Something very illogical, however, followed the volleys of shots. Although witnesses would later be divided as to the source and timing of the shots, the surge of humanity (with the lone exception being Marrion L. Baker) was toward the grassy knoll.

One of the most striking pieces of contemporary Dealey Plaza footage is a black-and-white film clip (the Weigman film) taken from a car well back in the motorcade. The film depicts the car in front, a dark 1959 Chevy, turning the corner from Houston onto Elm. In front of the car is a sizable group of eyewitnesses to the assassination, looking down the street at the carnage. Of note, there is not one individual in that clip, out of dozens of spectators standing in front of the depository, who is looking up at the building, fleeing from it, or in any way giving any indication that shots had just come from there. It may be the most valuable brief clip whose absence of data tells us a great deal.

Photographer James Altgens' reaction, as reported by the FBI, was typical: ". . . as the president's car disappeared he observed some Secret Service agents and police officers with drawn guns on the north side of Elm Street running in the direction of the triple overpass. He said he thought they were chasing someone who had fled from somewhere behind the president."[2] Altgens could provide no more information, as the "suspicious" police were in the process of returning by the time he caught up to them.

Victoria Adams, who had viewed the motorcade from the fourth floor of the TSBD, heard shots, ran down the stairs (the narrow TSBD stairs, and she encountered no one, particularly no one in flight), and headed for the railroad yard. "We had not gone far when a Police officer stopped us and instructed us to return to the building, which we did."[3] This action suggests that the officer considered the railroad yards a crime scene that should not be invaded, and it is a powerful indication that he did not believe the sniper was lurking inside the TSBD, as it is hard to imagine someone giving an order, "Okay, lady, get back inside that building with the gunman. . . ."

Luke Mooney, one of the second wave of officers to reach the fence area (the motorcycle officers who broke off from the motorcade were first), testified, "We were trying to clear the area out and get all the civilians out that wasn't officers."[4] Taken literally, this means that the police may have been ordering curious civilians to leave the scene, so that only investigative officers would remain—was this to minimize the possible testimony of civilian eyewitnesses to an ominous police presence behind the fence, because standard police procedures would have meant *keeping* all civilians there—unless someone knew that no civilian could have been involved. Mooney also indicated that he had not been in the railroad yards long when he was ordered to the TSBD. When asked how he received the order, he told, "It came by word, by another officer."[5] This clearly raises the possibility that officers who suspected a shot or shots from the knoll were casually ordered out of a crime scene, perhaps by the perpetrators of the crime.

In another odd event involving the police and the knoll, Officer J. C. White, stationed on the west side of the triple underpass, testified that he did not hear any shots because a train was going north on the underpass.[6] This is odd because the second Altgens photo, showing Clint Hill and Mrs. Kennedy from the back of the limousine, is framed in the background by the underpass. There were spectators present, in violation of Secret Service orders—but no train. Fortunately for Officer White, his observations were contained in a report. Giving false information on paper is less serious than if under oath.

Hugh W. Betzner, Jr., a bystander who took photos in Dealey Plaza, noticed the rush to the picket fence and theorized that it was the area where the shots came from. He then realized he had taken a photo of that area during the shooting sequence, and contacted sheriff's deputy Eugene Boone. Boone removed the film from the camera, and Betzner was left to believe that he would never see the prints. (Neither did the Warren Commission, nor was Boone asked about this, although he mentioned taking film from a "Betzer.") Betzner also observed police and men in plain clothes "digging around in the dirt as if they were looking for a bullet."[7] One wonders how the police could have suspected that a bullet impacted at a certain location unless a witness supplied them with that information, and we have no record of such a witness or such a statement. Or, for obvious reasons, such a bullet.

So far we have police apathy, false statements, strange handling of vital evidence, and failure to maintain custody of key witnesses. We plummet to incompetence, or worse, however, when we realize that within minutes of the shooting, Houston and Elm were reopened to traffic, and countless hundreds of drivers and passengers were allowed to motor casually over pieces of the president's shattered skull. Anything else they may have driven over must be left to conjecture.

The final law enforcement effort in the railroad yard was the removal of three "tramps" from a train that had been stopped by signalman Lee Bowers. The tramps were then marched through Dealey Plaza, where photos were taken of them. Many theories abound about the "tramps," but two things are certain: The photos do not suggest anything remotely approaching normal police procedure, especially the kind of vigilance that might be appropriate following a presidential assassination, as the police escort of two officers is nonchalantly leading the "tramps" to police headquarters and the revolving door that led to oblivion for many years. Secondly, the officer in front has a standard security-related earpiece, hardly normal procedure, and the officer bringing up the rear is wearing trousers far too short, and it is unlikely that he experienced a recent growth spurt. Author Fletcher Prouty insists that those officers are fakes.[8] He may be right, but they were certainly not the only fake cops (or Secret Service men) in "Deadley Plaza" that day.

Within hours, the Stemmons Freeway sign was moved. Why and by whom? It was part of a crime scene, making it evidence.

Lastly, the reader is by now familiar with Lee Bowers' testimony about the three strange vehicles that entered the TSBD parking area within thirty minutes before the shots were fired. That area was also to have been sealed by police. Dealey Plaza was not sealed, or contained, and the railroad yards were not sealed before or after the shooting.

There can be no doubt where the blame for these lapses lies.

If the focus at the time of the shooting was the knoll, and that was treated with lackadaisical ennui, what of the TSBD? That must have gotten the full treatment, as the police had to concentrate somewhere, and they did have witnesses who pointed out the exact window where a rifle had been seen. Although the police did not take all witnesses' names, it can be inferred that they were Brennan, Euins, Fischer, Edwards, and Carolyn Walther.

Witnesses and a window they had. Something was lacking.

Arnold Rowland's testimony of seeing a man with a gun on the opposite end of the TSBD is well known. Lesser known is a snippet from his testimony that he recalled seeing a Dallas police officer on the sidewalk in front of the door of the TSBD.[9] Doing what? No one is going to fire a gun out of the doorway of a *high building*, and there certainly was no traffic there to stop. Beyond that, there were several officers assigned to traffic duty at the corner of Elm and Houston, and then no police presence until the underpass. Again: Why in front of the TSBD? The only logical answers are all sinister. He was on his way in, for evil purpose, or to deal with a preselected patsy; or he was there to help someone else, perhaps in uniform, escape.

Tests showed that it took Oswald just over a minute to get to the location where Officer Baker encountered him, so the low-end estimate of his departure time from the TSBD would be approximately three minutes after the shooting. Three minutes might have been a long time for a patsy whose scenario had suddenly soured, but it would have been an *eternity* for a genuine assassin bent on escape. But there again, logic forces reconsideration. Clearly, a *sixth-floor* sniper drew attention to himself. A rifle was seen, shots were heard, and the target was the president of the United States. Is there any reasonable or logical way to allow for the theory that a sixth-floor sniper, having fired at the president, had any real chance to leave the depository? Certainly not. Under normal conditions a suspect building would have been surrounded and sealed within seconds and nobody would have been allowed to exit. But these were not normal conditions, and normal, basic procedures were ignored by the police. Either the building had no reason to be suspected, or the authorities intentionally avoided doing their duty.

James Jarman, on the floor below the sniper's window, told of going to the opposite end of the floor and observing the commotion in the railroad yards, and then casually leaving the building with no questions asked. Chief Justice Warren asked, ". . . did anyone stop you as you went out the building?" Jarman answered, "No, sir." Warren persisted: "You could have gone right away if you wanted, could you?" Jarman answered, "Yes, sir."[10]

Bonnie Ray Williams, watching the parade with Jarman, told how the police had gotten to the fifth floor while he, Jarman, and Harold Norman were still there: "While we were standing at the west end of the building on the fifth floor, a police officer came up on the elevator and looked all around the fifth floor and then left the floor. I did not see anyone come down from the sixth floor via the stairs."[11] This statement is fraught with ominous overtones. First, it suggests that either the police knew exactly who they were looking for, an unlikely possibility that fast, or that African-Americans were not considered either assassins or witnesses, as they were thereafter ignored. What boggles the mind is that there is no hint whatsoever that the officer asked any questions: Did you see anyone? Did you hear anything? Has anyone come down the stairs? Did you see any strangers? *Nothing*. In a June 15, 1994, interview, Harold Norman told me that he found it quite perpelexing that the police passed up him and his friends without even a hint that they were a concern. Perhaps Jarman, Norman, and Williams didn't have that "returned Soviet defector" look.

The officer could *not* have been Marrion Baker, who, along with Roy Truly, left Oswald on the second floor, then *climbed* to five, and took the elevator to seven to reach the roof, where Baker thought the gunfire had come from. They stopped briefly on six on the way down, then made their way back to the first floor.[12] What is significant about that itinerary is that their travel and roof search consumed at least fifteen minutes, and at the end of that time, there still were no police concerns for the sixth floor, despite at least five witnesses— nine, if you count Jarman, Williams, Norman, and James Worrell— who had expressed concerns about the sixth floor. Were the police *avoiding* the sixth floor? Police travels and statements of witnesses such as Norman, Jarman, and Williams also have to take depository architecture into account. In 1963, the stairs emptied out at each level. Thus an assassin coming down from six would find himself in the open on five until he traveled a few feet and reentered the staircase, which would dump him on four. It's an overlooked but significant concern.

In answer to an earlier question, the police did not seal the TSBD building as one might expect in accordance with normal procedure. After being in the railroad yards, Luke Mooney entered the TSBD through "gaping back doors" where he posted *a civilian*, telling, "so he stood guard, I assume, until a uniformed officer took over."[13] Between 12:55 P.M. and 1:00 P.M., Forrest Sorrels returned from Parkland and entered the same back door, guarded at that time by a "colored civilian." No identification was required, and Sorrels added that he did not know at the time that the TSBD was suspect; he was there looking *for witnesses*.[14]

In this regard, Dallas police radio logs are instructive. At 12:48 P.M., a transmission was made to indicate that the suspect was still believed to be in the TSBD and armed.[15] (If the "Blue Death" thesis is correct, so was that transmission.) This could only be based on the theory that since no one was seen leaving the building armed with a rifle, an assassin must have still been lurking with one, a truly clever deduction. A later transmission, which does not clarify the matter, indicated it was unclear if the suspect was still in the TSBD "or not known if he was there in the first place."[16] All of this raises questions, as Sergeant Harkness had a witness who had pinpointed *the* window by 12:37 P.M., and Howard Brennan told of diving for cover and then immediately informing police. Subsequent transmissions from Inspector Sawyer (listed as "9" in the logs) suggest the weapon was a .30-.30 or "some type of Winchester." He also provided a description, giving 5'10" and 165 pounds, and the dispatcher, for reasons known perhaps only to himself, then added the words "white male" to Sawyer's data.[17] At 12:49 P.M., Captain Talbert was still giving orders to seal the depository: "Have that cut off on the back side, will you? Make sure nobody leaves there." When Talbert got a response, he alertly replied, "More than that building. Extend out from that building so it can be searched."[18] But this was twenty minutes after the shots.

In further confusion, Inspector Sawyer broadcast, "On the *third floor* [emphasis added] of this book company down here, we found empty rifle hulls and it looked like the man had been here for some time."[19] Sawyer's transmission was a result of Luke Mooney finding the hulls on the *sixth* floor at 1:12 P.M.. It is hard to imagine someone standing in that sniper's window and seeing cartridges and thinking they were only on the third floor. Finally, at 1:35 P.M., the TSBD is mentioned on police channel 2: "It's being secured now."[20] This was an hour and five minutes after the shots, twenty-one minutes after the death of Officer Tippit, sixteen minutes before the arrest of Oswald, and long after the departure of any or all who had anything to do with the shots fired from the TSBD—including Lee Oswald.

Officer Marrion Baker reads and sounds like an honest man who did his job as he saw it on November 22. It is unlikely that he was in any way involved, or else he would have avoided the TSBD, as all other officers did in the crucial time frame. It is possible to posit that he was to have caught or shot Oswald and that Roy Truly prevented that, but that is unlikely. If that had been Baker's function, he would have done it regardless. His search of the building and the roof was good police work, but the absence of any officers on the sixth floor suggests that good police work was limited to Officer Baker.

How successful was Captain Talbert in his suggestion that the search be extended to other buildings? Apparently, not very successful. We know that at least two people were taken into custody in the Dal-Tex Building, but this was due more to the awareness of building personnel of strangers in their midst, whom they pointed out or delivered to the authorities, than to efficient police work. "Jim Braden" was taken into custody there and was subsequently allowed to admit that he knew nothing, sign his assumed name, and depart. A fingerprint check might have revealed his lengthy arrest record under the name Eugene Hale Brading, and might have mattered in subsequent hours when David Ferrie, with whom Braden was an office neighbor in New Orleans, was taken into custody . . . and released.

Detective James Leavelle provided the documentation regarding the other man taken into custody at the same location: "The uniformed officers came up with a white man named William Sharp of 3439 Detonta, who the officers said had been up in the building across the street from the book depository [the Dal-Tex Building] without a good excuse. I took charge of the man and escorted him to the sheriff's office, where I placed him with other *witnesses*"[21] (emphasis added).

Witnesses? Was Oswald treated as a witness?

Given their less-than-optimum performance in the first minutes after the assassination, is it possible that uniformed Dallas police officers were active during the assassination? There is persuasive evidence that the answer to that question is yes.

First, we must go back to our examination of the TSBD and reask the question as to whether a sixth-floor sniper, seen by multiple witnesses, really could have believed he had a chance to escape. The reality is that under normal circumstances, the building's sources of egress would have been immediately covered. As we have seen, they were not, but how would a sniper know that unless he either had knowledge of what the police were going to do or not do, or unless he had a foolproof way out of the TSBD at his leisure? A blue Dallas police uniform is just such a guarantee. Police officers eventually swarmed into the TSBD, and many came and went. One of them may have taken off his uniform shirt and been in the sniper's window, in a white T-shirt, the outfit common to witnesses' descriptions.

There is also a very strong suspicion that a deputy sheriff named Harry Weatherford was on the roof of the County Records Building, due east of the limousine, at the time of the shooting.[22] Weatherford gave a deposition that he was in front of the sheriff's office during the shooting, but Roger Craig, who was there, insisted Weatherford was atop the building, which is odd inasmuch as the sheriff's officers were not used in any *preventive* details in the motorcade, and the view from ground level, without crowds at that point, was undoubtedly better than the view from several stories up . . . unless, of course, you were watching the motorcade through a telescopic sight.[23] Weatherford will be heard of again in this narrative, in equally sinister activity.

What is of equal significance is the fact that *John Connally could not have been shot from the "sniper's nest" in the book depository.* The source for this conclusion is the acoustic findings of the HSCA, both for what they contain and for what is not mentioned. The tests were carefully circumscribed to include only the possibility of shots from the "sniper's nest" in the TSBD and the knoll. So although the experts found four shots from those locations, the tape contained the suggestion of additional shots, the source or sources of which could not be determined because the acoustics experts were focusing on only two sites. The shots were determined to have times of "0," 1.66 seconds, 7.56 seconds, and 8.31 seconds. Since it is clear that either 7.56 seconds or 8.31 seconds was the time of cranial impact so vividly depicted in the Zapruder film, we can time events from those two perspectives. If 8.31 was Z313, then "0" came at Z161, 1.66 came at Z191–2, and 7.56 came at Z299. Given those figures, it is clear that Connally was wounded well after Z192 but well before

Z299. If we posit 7.56 as Z313, then "0" becomes Z175, 1.66 becomes Z205–6, and 8.31 becomes Z327, possibly Connally's wrist and thigh wound but certainly not the more serious thoracic damage.[24]

Connally was not wounded through the chest from the "sniper's nest" of the Texas School Book Depository. Warren Commission exhibit 689 strongly reinforces this. As shown, for a bullet to have passed through Kennedy and hit Connally, JFK would have had to have been *standing* on the rear of the limousine, as the bullet path, noted by attending physicians, was from such an elevation that it would have cleared JFK's head by several feet.[25] The angle of the wound as shown, and as it existed in reality, is so steep that it would have had to have been fired from a closer location than the sniper's nest—high up and closer, and there's only one such spot in the universe: the west end of the depository, where Arnold Rowland saw a man with a gun at 12:15 P.M.

The mathematics are also *all wrong.* The Mannlicher-Carcano, which is in fact a *medium*-power rifle, had a muzzle velocity of 2,160 feet per second. Again using the Zapruder film as the clock for the event, at that rate a bullet would travel 2,160/18.3, or 118.03 feet *per frame.* Since the men were sitting at most 4 feet apart, the bullet would have traversed that distance in .00185 second (185 one hundred thousandths of a second). Also, using the 118.03-feet-per-frame reference, this means that a bullet could have entered and traversed JFK and gone on to hit Connally *twenty-nine times* in one frame. Bear that in mind the next time you view the Zapruder film: If you don't see both men react simultaneously, the "magic" of the magic bullet, like all magic, is revealed as illusion. And since the Warren Commission's credibility depended on the "magic" bullet, what does that imply about an alleged sixth-floor sniper? Quite clearly, it implies that he had to be a magician. Nobody believes in "magic" anymore, as even people who used to advertise themselves as magicians now prefer "illusionists."

What about the knoll, the remaining area under suspicion? Could someone in blue have been there as well? There is certainly ample evidence to support the possibility.

Officer Jack Faulkner, heading for what he thought to be the source of the shots, came upon a woman who told him JFK had been shot dead: ". . . and she pointed toward the concrete arcade on the east side of Elm Street."[26] Emmett Hudson, who was standing directly in front of the picket fence at the time of the shots, testified that he did not see any guns except in the possession of the police.[27] Mrs. Donald Baker ran quickly to the knoll and saw only policemen and those working around the tracks.[28] S. M. Holland, who hurried to the spot behind the fence where he thought one shot had been fired, found a number of Dallas police officers already there, in the area behind the picket fence reserved for parking for the sheriff's department and others who work at the courthouse.[29]

Lastly, Jean Hill, amid an interview conducted before it was known that JFK had expired, insisted that the shots came from "the hill" and told of seeing a policeman with a rifle. When she shared this information with "J. B.," he cautioned silence.[30] For good reason: In the 1963, pre-SWAT era, police rarely carried rifles. The first (and theoretically only) cops ahead of Jean Hill would have been motorcycle officers, and they certainly would not have had rifles. Officers arriving subsequently in squad cars might have had shotguns, but not rifles.

Another eyewitness, whose story will be detailed farther along, insists that on climbing the knoll, she encountered Roscoe White and Patrick Dean, but she did not make the ominous or obvious connection at the time.

Flash of light. Smoke. Head snap. Gunpowder smell. Crowd surge. *Police with rifles.*

Which brings us to Roscoe "Rock" White, who had joined the Dallas police force in the early fall of 1963, and Harry Weatherford. It was the contention of Roscoe's widow, Geneva (now deceased) and son, Ricky Don, that Roscoe White was on the grassy knoll, where he fired two shots at the president with a 7.65 Mauser. It is also their contention that White met and discussed the event well ahead of time with Ruby, and that White killed Officer Tippit.

Further elements of the story include the fact, although not elaborated on, that White sailed with Oswald to Atsugi, and that White remained in intelligence circles, performing the assassination with authorization addressed to him in the code name Mandarin.

Documentation exists. The question is, "Is it believable?" Quite possibly. First, researchers always have had a fascination with a photographic image they call the "badgeman," suggesting that someone wearing a blue uniform and a badge was firing from alongside the motorcade. The part about two shots clearly does not square with the acoustic evidence presented to the HSCA, and the identification of a 7.65 Mauser seems at first glance too easy and too pat. Yet Ricky Don White has the weapon in question, and it is a quality weapon suitable for sniper use. Like the Mannlicher, it, too, may be a stage prop, but it cannot be ruled out, since whatever did hit the president was never adequately identified and we are still chasing vague suspicions.

The sources seem reasonable, as White's widow, after Roscoe's death in 1971 in an accidental fire, as well as his son, who was ten at the time of his father's death, seem to have no ax to grind, with the possible exception of a pecuniary one, and even that suggestion is somewhat Faustian. The contention that White killed Tippit does not square well with witnesses' perceptions, but the Kennedy case is a classic of misperceptions. It does square, however, with Oswald's landlady's report that a police cruiser, carrying two officers, pulled up outside the rooming house shortly before 1:00 P.M. When Tippit's cruiser was found, a police shirt was found in the rear seat, and it did not belong to Tippit. Recall also that Oswald spoke to the occupant or occupants of the car from the *passenger* side, which allows for the possibility that Tippit and White (or a second officer, regardless) were in the car, giving Oswald someone to talk to on the passenger side, and giving Tippit the backup he otherwise would have called for, and when he went to confront Oswald, White shot him by leaning toward the steering wheel. Witnesses would probably not see that coming from the darkened interior of a vehicle, and their subsequent gestalt of the event would be an identification of Oswald. The unanswered question, of course, is how White got from the knoll to the front of Oswald's rooming house in fewer than thirty minutes, but if Oswald was able to accomplish the feat using public transportation, White certainly could have in a police cruiser at a time when most such cars were traveling at very high speed with nobody taking particular notice, given the circumstances.

The last bit of corroboration for this scenario came with the discovery in 1975 of yet another "backyard" photo of Oswald and the rifle, in the possession of the Whites. How would Roscoe White have obtained a photo never before seen? Quite likely, he obtained it early on from patsy Oswald (for reasons that will be cited later) and would have seen to it that it filtered into the investigation when needed. As it turned out, police insider Jack Ruby guaranteed that it wasn't needed. Search the official records of the investigation and you will not find the name Roscoe White, yet he somehow owned one of the biggest pieces of evidence, a photo similar to that which graced the February 21, 1964, cover of *Life*.[31]

Sheriff's Officer Harry Weatherford has also been given prominent mention, although not by his family. Roger Craig contended that Weatherford was on the roof of the county jail, which had a commanding view—far better than the depository—of Dealey Plaza. When confronted with such allegations, Weatherford exercised some ill-conceived bragging rights, allowing researchers to draw the conclusion that he was *not* atop the jail just for a better view of the parade.

Weatherford, like White, is also tied to the "backyard photos," which more than anything else seemed to convince the public of Oswald's guilt. When Dallas police officers went to search the Paine residence on November 22, they were met by sheriff's officers (including Weatherford) who had the jurisdiction but chose to leave the search to the locals. At quitting time, not much beyond a blanket had been found officially. Yet the next day, after Sheriff's Officer Weatherford had visited the Paine home, the backyard photos were found, just as one oddly turned up in the possession of Roscoe White.

A few other thoughts need attention before we leave Dealey Plaza. First, it seems odd that Oswald was calm in the presence of Officer Baker, yet allegedly behaved with hostility forty minutes later, in the presence of Tippit, and another forty minutes later, when arrested. One other interesting morsel in the food-for-thought category was the statement of James L. Simmons, a spectator on the triple underpass, who told that the presidential limousine slowed down, and only accelerated when the motorcycle escort, circling about, got out of the way.[32]

Not only were the crime scenes—Dealey Plaza, the railroad yards, the TSBD, other nearby buildings, and the grassy knoll—never sealed off, but neither were the Dallas airports, train and bus stations, nor major highway arteries leading out of the city. *There was no need for that: The police knew in advance whom to arrest.*

CHAPTER FIVE

APATHY

The death of democracy is not likely to be an assassination from ambush. It will be a slow extinction from apathy, indifference, and undernourishment.

—ROBERT MAYNARD HUTCHINS, 1954

AFTER THE INITIAL SURGE to the grassy knoll, captured in so many contemporary photographs, the efforts of the Dallas police can be quickly summarized: They caught and kept Lee Oswald. To characterize anything else they did that weekend as "investigating" is to fail to recognize lack of concern, absence of precision, misguided focus, and certainly lack of thoroughness. It can be truly said, "They left many stones unturned."

It also started at the top. Chief Curry, as noted, used his police radio, but did not lead the presidential limousine to the nearest hospital, as Jack Daniel's film, taken from the west side of the triple underpass, shows the president's car passing Curry's cruiser. Curry did *follow* the limousine to the hospital, where the chief remained.[1]

Who was in charge of the "investigation" at this point is unclear, for although there was an immediate "Signal 19" involving President Kennedy broadcast, Homicide Chief Will Fritz called in to the dispatcher from his post at the Trade Mart at 12:51 P.M. to ask if JFK would still be going to that site. He was told, "It's very doubtful."[2] The question remains: Who was in charge in the first key minutes? An absence of leadership suggests a preplanned desire to have investigative actions proceed in a vacuum, with chaos preferable to control. (No *Get Smart* pun intended.)

Curry remained at Parkland until Lyndon Johnson decided to leave, then *drove* the new president to *Air Force One,* in violation of all Secret Service regulations. At 2:38 P.M. he appeared in the photos of the swearing in of LBJ, arguably the first time a law enforcement director was given such a photo opportunity after losing the national leader he was supposed to protect. Curry then deplaned, but remained at the airport to speak with Mayor Cabell, finally arriving back at police headquarters at 4:00 P.M. By then, Oswald was the prime—and apparently the only—suspect in both homicides, and television bulletins and late editions of newspapers were announcing that conclusion to the world. In the course of the "interrogation" of Oswald, Curry *never* asked Oswald one question. Over the next forty-odd hours, Curry would warn subordinates not to publicize evidence, but would then do it himself, and would take his receiver off the hook on the evening of the 23rd so that a squad car had to be sent to his house to alert him to telephonic threats against Oswald received by his department and the FBI. In spite of those threats, he continued to accommodate the media circus in existence, guaranteeing the press—and Jack Ruby—maximum opportunity to witness Oswald's transfer. Curry would be in his office, on the telephone to Mayor Earl Cabell, when Oswald was shot, and learn of the event from a newsman. Meanwhile, Oswald's wife and mother were detoured on their way to see Oswald, and taken, of all places, to Curry's house. No cause was given for the change of plans, nor were they told immediately of the shooting.

With a police chief like Jesse Curry, with such an obvious fire in his gut to get to the truth of the matter, what could be expected of his department? Did they behave in a manner suggesting they were investigating the killing of the president, the wounding of the governor of Texas, and, of equal importance, the killing of a fellow officer?

Sadly, they did not even come close. They treated the events of the weekend, even the killing of a fellow officer, like an unsolved jaywalking.

Except for nabbing Oswald and rounding up enough circumstantial evidence in the TSBD to have the outline of a case against the designated suspect, the police did very little. At the time Captain Fritz was asking about the Trade Mart, an "unknown" came on the police radio and suggested that the epileptic seizure just prior to the motorcade be looked into.[3] This was never done. At virtually the same time, 1:00 P.M., however, officers were searching the bus that

Oswald had boarded and recently left. This again suggests Oswald as a premature suspect, since a city bus clogged in postmotorcade traffic has to be the *worst* possible choice for a presidential assassin bent on escape. And given the American fascination with driving the open road, the bus search suggests that someone besides Marina or Ruth Paine knew that Oswald could not operate an automobile and traveled by bus.

Outside the TSBD, officers were encountering people with information to give, but the officers generally radioed in to ask what to do, and then for the most part took names and addresses, or did nothing and released the individual. Later, some witnesses were taken to the sheriff's department to have statements taken, but that was also an irregular process. Officer 142 called in with a witness at 12:35 P.M. and was told to get the name and address. At the same time, Clyde Haygood also had a witness and was told to get the data, and the name and address. Patrolman C. M. Barnhart had an inebriated suspect who fit the first broadcast description, but little more is heard of him.[4] Jack Faulkner, L. C. Smith, J. L. Oxford, and Alan Sweatt all had witnesses but did not take any information.[5] Jean Hill, taken to the sheriff's office, either by people eager to get her off the knoll (Miss Hill's version), or by a reporter (official version), was given a blank piece of paper and told to sign it, which, if accurate, casts serious doubts on the veracity of the corpus of the sheriff's department reports.[6] Equally curious is something *not* discovered at the Texas School Book Depository: No individual employed there came forward to police to indicate they were afraid to reenter the building. That tells us that either all seventy-three known employees were convinced that shots had come from elsewhere, or that they knew, or suspected, the depository as a location for shots, but once Kennedy's car had passed, there was no further threat to human life. Ponder those choices the next time someone insists to you that all shots were fired from the depository; you immediately have seventy-three employees whose behavior strongly indicates otherwise.

Subsequently, officers who were ordered to take names both at the Texas Theater and in the police basement failed to do so.[7] The police would also place little credence in the Oswald-as-FBI-informant data provided to them by journalist Alonzo Hudkins, and they would virtually ignore Louisiana officer Francis Fruge's information regarding Rose Cheramie and her pre-assassination information.[8]

When Dallas assistant district attorney William Alexander heard on the police radio that an officer had been killed, "We all knew the same man who killed the president had killed Tippit. . . . We had made up our minds by the time we got there." Alexander, in fact, indicated he "would file" for both crimes while on the way to the Tippit scene; he was subsequently on hand, and armed, at the Texas Theater.[9] Such hunch-playing would have been reasonable if the assault on the officer had occurred within a block or two of the TSBD, or within minutes of the motorcade. But forty-five minutes later and miles away are no guarantees of the same individual, and the police would have looked foolish if they had put all their eggs into the Tippit basket and come up without the president's killer. Luckily, they had Oswald. *For both.*

Captain Fritz, having returned to the TSBD from the Trade Mart, must have had a similar intuition. At approximately 1:25 P.M. he had been given Oswald's name, address, and description by Roy Truly, who had inventoried his workforce and noticed Oswald's absence (among other absences). Fritz then went to the sheriff's department for a private meeting with Bill Decker, an odd transaction since Fritz possessed the name of a suspect in a presidential assassination but stopped to schmooze off the record, then returned to police headquarters without ever issuing an all-points bulletin for Oswald. When he arrived at headquarters, Oswald was there, apparently bearing out Fritz's intuition and lack of urgency.[10]

This also raises serious doubts. Why was no APB issued? Was Tippit, or a surrogate, supposed to kill Oswald at, or shortly after, 1:00 P.M.? If so, no APB would be necessary. Also, if Truly furnished the data, he would have given the Paine address, raising the question of how the police came up with the 1026 North Beckley address, as well as the 605 (602 was correct) Elsbeth address—a location where the Oswalds had lived prior to moving to New Orleans in the spring. Neither the North Beckley nor the Elsbeth Street address was available to Roy Truly, unless he were truly psychic.

These questions remain unanswered. It was not a problem, however, as the first sentence uttered to reporters by Captain Fritz indicated that Oswald was guilty, and he also indicated that *Tippit* had been arraigned at 7:10 P.M.[11] Clearly, this news satisfied City Manager Elgin Crull (the de facto executive of Dallas, not the mayor, a figurehead), who went away for the weekend.[12]

At this point it must be asked, "Who was J. D. Tippit?" If Richard Nagell is "the man who knew too much," then J. D. Tippit would seem to be "the man who never was," as he entered and left the pages of history in a few minutes. At 12:45–46 P.M., the Dallas radio logs show that Tippit was moved "into Central Oak Cliff area,"[13] a seemingly mundane and highly irregular transmission in the helter-skelter only fifteen minutes after the shooting of the president. Tippit was later radioed to "be at large for any emergency that comes in."[14] Such a transmission mentioned nothing about a "suspect" and is either a cover for Tippit's real purpose or just a prod to look for some idiot who would use the commotion of the shooting of the president as a perfect time to unload a bank. In no case does it suggest Tippit's future behavior. Sylvia Meagher saw the transmission as a total fabrication, added to the records afterward.[15]

Tippit was in car number 10. Mrs. Earline Roberts, in CE 2781, indicated that she believed car number 207 pulled up in front of the rooming house at 1:00 P.M., but since 207 was accounted for at that time, the Warren Commission concluded that she was mistaken about the police car being there and honking its horn.[16] (That means if you forget a phone number, the telephone was never invented.)

Shortly after 1:10 P.M., at a time Oswald could not possibly have been there,[17] Tippit pulled up behind someone, miles from the scene of the assassination, and although researchers are quick to argue that Tippit pulled over based on only the blandest of descriptions, this misses the point. Essentially he was working from no description, since he pulled up *behind* the suspect. A conversation occurred, Tippit exited his vehicle without calling for backup, and was killed as he unholstered his service revolver. If we cannot answer the question "What made Tippit so curious as to stop this pedestrian?" we must place a sinister interpretation on it, as if Tippit knew whom to look for but obviously not what to expect. In that sense, Tippit, too, may have been a patsy, sent by prearranged order to pick up a stranger, or located in a neighborhood where his presence was common,* but when he realized who the stranger might be, his sense of duty over-came him and he paid for it.[18] There is also no documentation what-soever to suggest that Tippit stopped anyone else in the twenty-five minutes between the transmissions to him and his fatal encounter.

*Tippit was literally part of the landscape where he was killed. Cabbie William Scoggings testified to seeing Tippit, but took no notice because Tippit was always there [3H 324–25]. Resident Charlie Virginia Davis told the Warren Commission that she thought Tippit lived there, highly suggestive that he spent a lot of time there, and someone looking for him would know where to find him [6H 458].

Tippit's patsy status is further enhanced by the grossly negligent investigation into his death. Although he was supposedly killed instantly, there were no photos taken of the spot where he fell, clouding the issue, as in the Kennedy case, of where the shots came from. In the published photos, there do not even appear chalk marks around where his body had fallen, a further indication that investigating officers did not want the location of his body known. There is nothing in the published record regarding any specifics of his autopsy, or regarding mundane things that should have been checked, such as his finances. Lastly, we must also allow for the very grisly possibility that Tippit was killed not by Oswald, but rather by the officer whose shirt was in Tippit's car (the "second" officer seen by Oswald's landlady). Yet Oswald took the heat there also, guaranteeing that the public acceptance of Oswald's "propensity for violence" would be far more demonstrable, and of even greater import, with the shoddy case made against Oswald for the murder of the president, particularly the absence of a local autopsy. It is possible that Tippit was killed so that Oswald could be tried and executed (recall he was charged with "murder with malice aforethought" in what seems a chance encounter) for killing *Tippit,* and the public would still be in the dark about what really happened to Kennedy.

Also unanswered is the question of where Oswald was going at the time of the Tippit encounter. Was he going *to* the Tippit encounter? This is suggested by the charge filed against him, "murder with malice aforethought," otherwise an inappropriate filing for an *accidental* event, unless the police knew that Oswald would react violently to the officers who pulled up in front of the boardinghouse after Oswald learned of his patsy status, and that he might get violent, creating a more obvious event for which he could become the subject of a Dallas-wide dragnet.

With the shooting of a police officer, much of the focus of events shifted from Dealey Plaza to the Tippit crime scene. Some officers remained in the TSBD, but there was far more Tippit traffic on the police radio than JFK traffic. It could be argued that this is natural when a fellow officer is killed, but why then did the cops put together such an empty case and perform such casual searches if they believed Oswald had killed an officer? There is also no radio transmission suggesting "knock on all the doors in the neighborhood and see if anybody saw anything," and many residents nearby were never contacted by any investigators. This, too, was highly irregular, but no more irregular than the avoidance of a real search extending out several blocks from Dealey Plaza and involving every trash can, trash dumper, sewer grate, postal box, nook, and cranny. In both sites, it just wasn't done. *It didn't have to be.*

The radio logs noted that the descriptions in both cases were similar, and at 1:30 P.M. police channel 2 knew JFK was dead on arrival at Parkland. By 2:01 P.M. there's no mention of anything even remotely involving JFK, as the concern was whether Mrs. Tippit had been notified.[19]

Beyond those bare facts, we have silence. Only two photos of Tippit were published, and very little was said of him, except by Calvin Owens, who made Tippit too good to be true—or believed.[20] Again, there are no crime scene photos or autopsy photos of Tippit, and the evidence in his case was handled worse than the evidence in the JFK case.

It would be unwise to forget the allegations about that "other" police shirt in Tippit's car, given the other suspicions already developed about a handful of individuals in blue.

At 1:22 P.M. a rifle was found in the TSBD and it was given a few minutes' study. At 1:51 P.M., twenty-nine minutes later, Oswald was arrested in the Texas Theater. These two closely related events effectively put an end to the investigation into the murder of the president and a Dallas police officer.

Oswald was relieved of his billfold on the way to headquarters, and it was discovered to contain identifications for both Lee Harvey Oswald and Alek J. Hidell, although the Hidell Selective Service card, containing a photo of Oswald, was as patently fake as anyone could imagine, since Selective Service cards at that time did not contain photographs. Either Oswald desperately wanted to prove to someone that he was Hidell, or *someone else* wanted to prove *Oswald* was Hidell, the man who had purchased the Mannlicher. Subsequently, CE 1148 would depict Oswald's property at the time of his arrest: money ($13.87—hardly a sum for someone planning an escape), a bus transfer, a belt, a ring, a post office box key, and an ID bracelet—but no billfold.[21] In the days following, a frantic David Ferrie would deny that his library card was found in Oswald's wallet, but he also visited Oswald's New Orleans address, looking to get the card back.[22] Ferrie's distress is understandable: His library card was among the nonpublished billfold contents.

Oswald was questioned for two hours and then taken to a lineup, where a search of his person revealed five live pistol cartridges, further testimony to a lack of thoroughness by the arresting officers. The cartridges were found by Elmer L. Boyd, who marked them and put them in a drawer and then forgot where he put them.[23] It would be another five hours before Oswald was photographed and fingerprinted.

The remainder of the afternoon of November 22 more closely resembled a production orchestrated by Barnum & Bailey than one that involved the police force of a major city, the FBI, and the Secret Service. As Chief Curry was leading LBJ's caravan to the airport, the dispatcher radioed Curry and asked if he was on his way to Love Field. Curry answered, "Yes, but don't put it on the air." At the same time, reflecting a total lack of awareness of events, Fritz got on the radio to announce, "Mrs. Connally is being flown in here from Austin."[24] Wounded bystander James Tague was mentioned on the radio, but does not appear in CE 2003, the accompanying summary.

At the depository, photographs showed that Oswald's clipboard was in plain sight, yet it was not "discovered" until December 12 (and in a different place), suggesting a very limited search of a major crime scene.[25] Much would be made of the chicken bones found near the sniper's window, but it should be asked, "Who can rapidly bolt and fire an old weapon with greasy fingers?"[26] Several photos taken by crime lab novice Robert Studebaker show the boxes near the sniper's window arranged in a variety of configurations, hardly a possibility for a sniper who had to work a bolt action rifle three times in fewer than six seconds.[27] No sniper arranged all those configurations, raising the possibility that they were only police hypotheses, because the real configurations did not exist or had had their original locations violated by incautious officers.

Between 4:09 P.M. and 5:12 P.M. there were two radio transmissions regarding the presidential cars at Parkland as officer 508 was on the way to fingerprint them. In fact, they had been taken away hours before and were on the ground at Andrews Air Force base by 5:12 P.M. Dallas time.[28] One's curiosity here is drawn to the idea that the police wanted to print the cars, not search them for ballistics evidence. Fingerprinting them suggests that evidence had been planted by someone not careful, or that one of the occupants of the car was a suspect. Interestingly, a photo was printed in a November 1983 *Life* magazine showing Dallas police present while the presidential limousine was being scrubbed prior to its hasty departure from Parkland.

While it has always been conjectured that Jack Ruby planted the "magic bullet" at Parkland, what would have prevented those officers from retrieving ballistics evidence in the car and replacing it with mangled Mannlicher fragments, or placing the magic bullet on a stretcher in Parkland? There were many police at Parkland and only one Ruby, if there was that many.

Parkland Hospital also allows for sinister overtones in the case of further police malfeasance. There is no evidence that even in the time the police had Oswald in custody they did *anything whatsoever* with respect to gathering evidence at the location where many medical people were treating the fatally wounded president, and where the "key" piece of evidence, the magic bullet, was found. In fact, the magic bullet was never even seen by Dallas authorities, as it went right to D.C. in an agent's pocket. (The agent would later deny it was the magic bullet, and, as of this writing, does not recall taking any bullet to Washington.) The Dallas blues also allowed federal officers to confiscate and subsequently obfuscate all video material emanating from Parkland Hospital. Did anyone on the force in Dallas have any idea it was their job to collect evidence? A thirty-second snippet of one video has become available, and it single-handedly destroys the official version. A doctor, in scrub suit fresh from Connally's operating theater, went before the cameras in late afternoon to tell reporters that the governor's chest wounds had been repaired and that subsequent surgery would be done immediately on the wrist and the leg, but there should not be any undue concern *about the bullet still in the governor's leg.* Indeed, the reporters should not have been concerned, since the bullet in the governor's leg at Parkland was also in a Secret Service agent's pocket, and he was almost back to the capital. Now, that is a "magic bullet."

The searches conducted by police were far from thorough, and both at the Paine residence and at North Beckley, they were suspended and would be resumed on Saturday, unheard-of procedure in any case, much less a dual homicide. Even then, however, they were less than thorough, as Ruth Paine testified that Robert Oswald, plus Marina's bodyguards Thorne and Martin, came by and collected some of Oswald's things—including the camera with which the backyard photos were taken. The camera was turned over to authorities in February.[29] Had Robert Oswald not turned in that camera, the Warren Commission would have had to discount the validity of the "backyard" photos.

The ultimate charade in police procedure involved the match between the rifle (given away to the FBI) and the magic bullet, never seen by the Dallas authorities. Chief Curry was asked, "What about the ballistics test, Chief?" He answered, "The ballistics test—we haven't had a final report, but it is—I understand will be favorable."[30] Having such prescience regarding vital evidence tests was almost as valuable as knowing in advance whom to arrest.

Prisoner Oswald was questioned on and off for twelve hours. Although he was informed that he had rights to counsel and that his statements could be used against him, this is an inaccurate representation of events. The police should have insisted that he be kept incommunicado until he had counsel. Second, anything he said *could not,* under Texas law, be used against him. No less an authority than Assistant D.A. Bill Alexander informed Warren Commission counsel Arlen Specter of that Lone Star legal peculiarity when Specter was going out of his way to keep Ruby silent during his polygraph exam—on the pretext that what he said could be used against him.

No records were kept of the interrogation, and a host of foolish reasons—lack of space for a steno among them—have been put forward to explain the absence of records. A better explanation would be that his statements could not be used against him, or that *there was a concern that he would make a statement that nobody would want preserved.* The latter seems the more likely choice. Either way, the absence of interrogation notes was a moot point: Oswald was never going to get near a courtroom, and that, too, was thanks to the local police.

From what can be pieced together, it is possible to conclude that a good number of questions were asked about Oswald's travels to the Soviet Union as well as his membership in the Fair Play for Cuba Committee. Some time also was devoted to breaking through the Oswald/Hidell shroud. Oswald told Secret Service inspector Thomas Kelly that he was not a Communist: "No, I am a Marxist, but I am not a Marxist-Leninist."[31] The distinction was probably lost on his audience, but when Oswald indicated that he had shown a Secret Service man where the phone was as he was exiting the TSBD, the implications of that statement were not lost on his listeners, as they could well have known by then that no Secret Service members remained in Dealey Plaza.

Oswald was frequently questioned about the shooting of JFK and Tippit, but there is no indication he was questioned with respect to

Governor Connally, and such questions could have been very revealing. If Oswald knew, without being told, that Connally had been shot, that would have suggested that he *saw* the assassination. If he did not know, it would have suggested innocence. The record indicates that he was never arraigned for the shooting of Connally, and that as late as November 23 he was not aware the governor had been shot. FBI agent Bookhout noted, regarding Oswald's interrogation, that he denied shooting the president, and indicated that Oswald "did not know that Governor Connally had been shot."[32]

Roger Craig told that the "station wagon" was mentioned to Oswald, and he replied that it belonged to Mrs. Paine and that she "had nothing to do with this." This statement is of paramount significance, but it was not pursued. It suggests that Oswald did at least know who *was* involved although if he was a patsy he would have had limited knowledge. Why would the police not be curious as to who was involved if Oswald could boldly tell them who was not? There are no records at all to suggest that Oswald was ever asked who was involved *with him*, and when he made his "patsy" confession, there were no questions like "Patsy for whom?"

There is also no hint of questioning as to why he went home on Thursday, a key event, although there was much questioning about his use of post office boxes. Here again, the questioning was not efficient, as Ruth Paine indicated that Russian magazines were delivered for Oswald at her home. If this is true, what was he receiving at his post office box, and why would a frugal loner need a post office box in the first place?

Apathy was also demonstrated in the clear absence of any of the usual "police games" during Oswald's interrogation. There is no record of any time when Oswald was confronted with the Mannlicher, and that is the ultimate confrontation. "Here is the gun we found, son. There are prints on it. Within hours we'll know where you got this and we'll have a ballistics match." Instead, the cops showed Oswald a photo of himself and the gun. Were they expecting him to confess to having fired at a photo of the president? There were other pieces of evidence he could have been confronted with as well, but all he was shown was a photo, and he denied the veracity of it—perhaps for good reason. Duplication of the photo with the shadows as shown is *impossible*. There is also no hint of anyone playing the traditional "good-guy/bad guy" cop routine with Oswald, nor is there any suggestion of scenarios where he was told he had been identified by enough witnesses to fry him till he sizzled—and "sizzled" defines onomatopoeia.

There was also an attitude bordering on benign neglect with respect to the individuals other than Oswald who were taken into custody. Larry Florer and "Jim Braden" denied any knowledge of events, as did Oswald, but only the first two were allowed to leave. Jack Lawrence, who worked with car salesman Albert Guy Bogard and who behaved extremely suspiciously on November 21–22, and William Sharp, earlier noted as having been taken into custody by Jim Leavelle, were given equally short shrift.[33] The three "tramps" breezed through headquarters and were given as much attention as "tramps" usually get. Wesley Frazier was wrongly taken into custody, had property seized, and was required to take a polygraph test.[34]

Michael Paine told of hearing of Oswald's arrest, for the Tippit slaying, and of his returning to see Ruth: "Well, of course, the police were reporting they had suspects here and suspects there, were chasing suspects over here. . . ."[35] Who were these "suspects"?

Secret Service agent Roger Warner, guarding *Air Force One,* left his post to go to Fort Worth to question Donald Wayne House of 404 Lula, Ranger, Texas.[36] House then disappears from the official record as if he had never existed.

Other police transmissions indicate there was concern with a white Pontiac station wagon, and officers were warned to "proceed with caution and advise." Three other suspicious vehicles (including a 1957 Chevy—of Walker photo fame?), containing weapons as well as occupants, are mentioned, and a wrecker was needed for the "suspect's car" just west of Cobb Stadium.[37] The same radio logs indicate, "They got a suspect hiding in the balcony at the Texas Theater," and later there were reports of "several persons armed" at the Braniff Building at Love Field.[38]

Some of these "others" gave statements to the sheriff's department. Others were not heard of again. Oswald, who was never in the balcony of the Texas Theater, remained in custody until his execution.

Further contributing to the circus atmosphere of the weekend was the unrestricted media access to police headquarters. The corridors outside the Homicide and Robbery Bureau were almost always jammed, and occasionally the prisoner was jeopardized by being taken through the crowd. Contemporary photos show multiple thick feeder cables being snaked in through windows to connect television cameras to remote trucks. Most significantly, anyone was allowed in. Ronald Jenkins testified that no identifications were checked for the midnight press conference, and that press cards were lying on the table for anyone's access. Jenkins indicated that he reported this ease of availability to the police.[39] Of course, it could be argued that the police wanted anyone and everyone to have access.

Thayer Waldo, the first journalist to arrive at headquarters, agreed with Jenkins' assessment that anyone could have wandered into the press conference, which Seth Kantor described as "something akin, I guess, to something you might conjure up for the Middle Ages."[40]

Lack of security notwithstanding, the late evening press conference raises many questions. Oswald had been charged with the president's murder at 11:26 P.M., then taken to the conference, where he denied being charged, only to be told by a reporter—not the cops—that he *had* been charged. The subsequent arraignment took place at 1:35 A.M. Also, the midnight press conference amounted to Oswald being brought out and whisked away—he was there just long enough to give off the "suspect" look and be photographed for subsequent media manipulation, but as soon as he protested his innocence, he was out of there. Lastly, since when do assassination suspects get press conferences?

There is much further testimony regarding ease of access. Some journalists suggested they were never asked for any identification; some insisted they were. Either way, another diversion was created, and with seventy reporters in the basement, Jack Ruby closed the case.

CHAPTER SIX

THE CASE AGAINST OSWALD

Fiat justitia ruat coelum. [Let justice be done though heaven should fall.]

—LUCIUS CALPURNIUS PISO, 43 B.C.

IN RETROSPECT, more and more people are coming to view Oswald as the perfect patsy, almost as if he had been delivered unto the Dallas police by central casting. Viewed in that light, it is fair to ask whether the case against him was based on evidence or props.

Virtually every piece of evidence was questionable, tainted, or destroyed for judicial purposes at the time by the local authorities, perhaps the groups most willing to appear to look foolish while in reality harboring a fear that Oswald would go public at a genuine judicial proceeding. A "Mauser" was found and a Mannlicher was produced, similar but not identical to the one Oswald ordered. Three cartridges were found near the sniper's window, and although one had a dent that would have prevented it from containing a bullet, that was no problem: That shell was a blank, fired to focus attention on the gun made obvious in the sixth-floor window while other, less conspicuous guns did their deadly work. That hypothesis goes a long way toward explaining why so many witnesses believed their first impression was hearing "firecrackers."

The bag that supposedly contained the disassembled rifle did not have any gun oil on it; for evidentiary purposes, it was not photographed on the sixth floor of the TSBD; the boxes that Oswald

163

left fingerprints on also contained the fingerprints of individuals not employed in the depository.

The story has been rehashed too many times already, and the arguments are familiar. The rifle was either a quality weapon or a rebuilt disgrace. Oswald was either a world-class marksman or an out-of-practice mediocre shot at best. He had a motive; we just never learned of it.

What is important here is to note a few inconsistencies that bring the Dallas authorities closer to being the cause of the crime than its solution. For openers, the charges against Oswald were very carelessly assembled: He was charged in the Kennedy and Connally shootings with using a *6.25* Italian rifle, and in the Tippit case, as noted, he was charged with "murder with malice aforethought." The penalty for that crime in Texas is death, but it was rarely imposed. A manslaughter charge, the more obvious one in the Tippit case, carried a maximum of five years.

The chain of possession of evidence, vital to court proceedings, was broken in virtually every instance, particularly when every scrap of evidence was handed to the FBI in the early hours of November 23. No Texas officer of jurisdiction accompanied the evidence, and with Oswald's passing, Texas never got a great deal of their evidence back.

Dallas police did not come to the assistance of Dr. Earl Rose when he insisted that JFK's death, a Texas homicide, required a Texas autopsy. That was a matter of law; police enforce the law. But not on November 22, and any attorney could have invoked Texas law to negate state charges against Oswald in the slaying of JFK. And state charges were the only ones that could have been brought based on the crime alleged on November 22, 1963.

Commission exhibit 1054 shows one group of individuals who were in the lineups on November 22 with Oswald, and they bear no resemblance to the prisoner.[1] They were two Dallas officers and a jail guard. Further, each was asked his name and occupation. The three "fakes" gave fake names and occupations. Oswald had to state his name and place of occupation; a blind man could have identified him. Oswald could have said "Hidell," but there is even uncertainty on that point. Were the "Hidell" IDs real? Why had they not been on Oswald's person when he was arrested in New Orleans? Why did Johnston exhibit 1, the arraignment document for the killing of the president, list Oswald's alias as "O. H. Lee" and not "Hidell"? Why did the testimony of Secret Service agents Lawson and Sorrels make no mention of the "Hidell" story?[2]

In his testimony, Chief Curry had a concern that Captain Fritz was showing off the evidence in an unfair way, but when Curry got the chance, he did the same thing. This caused concern for district attorney Henry Wade, who told Curry to stop the practice (after it was too late), as "there may not be a place in the United States you can try it with all the publicity you are getting."[3] Wade was right in theory but wrong in law; the case had to be tried in Texas.

Evidence was faked. The clearest indication we have of that is the photo of the Walker residence with a car in front with no license plate. Dallas detectives Rose and Stovall both testified that the hole was in the picture when they discovered it at the Paine household.[4] When Marina Oswald was shown the damaged photo, she insisted she had seen it intact, but counsel Liebeler was adamant: "The original of this picture, the actual photograph, has a hole through it."[5] That was the truth when spoken, but a photo of the evidence as revealed in Chief Curry's memoirs *The Assassination Files* shows the picture to have been intact *as discovered*. The same document that announced that the photo was found with a hole indicated that a 1957 Chevy belonged to a Charles *Kilhr*, and that he had no criminal record. The car actually belonged to Charles *Klihr*, and we do not know *his* history.[6]

The Dallas police rushed Mr. and Mrs. Paine, along with Marina Oswald, to headquarters on November 22, and took statements from Mrs. Oswald. What they expected to do with them is of interest, as they could not be used in court, but they could, of course, be released if the prisoner they implicated were deceased.

The searches, both at the Paine household and at 1026 North Beckley, were casual and amateurish, although given the limited space and belongings at 1026 North Beckley, it would be difficult to characterize that search as less than thorough. At the Paine residence, what was found the first day was virtually useless; the second day was a gold mine. It seems too coincidental that once the police knew where to look, they found treasures left behind from the day before. There are also some legal questions with respect to the jurisdiction of those searches.

Photographic evidence just disappeared. Hugh Betzner, noted earlier, had his film taken and got a thank-you. Mary Moorman took the two best photos of the TSBD during the shooting, and her photos are listed as being of the "Sexton Building." Gordon Arnold, a soldier on leave, was chased off the grassy knoll by "Secret Service" and had his film taken at gunpoint.[7] The grandchildren of Orville Nix are still trying to get his motion picture back, and for good reason—the Nix film is as vivid a portrayal of the event as the Zapruder film. Recently, a team of Japanese photo experts—and who would know better?—performed optical enhancements on a copy of the Nix film and found *two* knoll shooters.

Eventually, a survey was given to seventy-three TSBD employees by the FBI. It asked each employee where they were when the shots were fired, and if they saw Oswald at that time. It also asked if they knew Oswald, when they left, and if they saw any strangers in the building. They were not asked for their thoughts on the source of the shots, the number of shots, any random observations they might have wanted to include, and most importantly, they were not asked if they saw any police in the TSBD.

The question about "strangers" is valid, if vague. In a presidential motorcade protective situation, police would hardly be viewed as strangers, as they are expected—they are part of the gestalt. Police officers would not have been viewed as strangers, given the location and events of November 22.[8]

FBI fingerprint expert Sebastian Latona, a law and order team player, had the final say on the case put together by the Dallas police: "I don't know whether they were thinking in details as to the examination. I don't think they sat down and figured very calmly what they were going to do . . . Lord knows what went on down there."[9]

To this day, however, the American people do not.

CHAPTER SEVEN

JUSTICE DENIED

Mordre wol out, certeyn, it wol nat faille.
[Murder will out.]

—GEOFFREY CHAUCER, *The Prioress's Tale*

ON THE MORNING OF NOVEMBER 24, 1963, prisoner Lee Oswald was again interrogated by officials at Dallas police headquarters, but if the record is to be believed, nothing new was learned at that session. Persistent accounts exist, on the other hand, that Will Fritz told intimates that when Oswald's interrogation ended, Fritz was on the verge of getting Oswald to confess and name the coconspirators.

Questioning was hastily broken off in midmorning and Oswald was allowed to pick a sweater to wear for his transfer to the sheriff's department.

As Oswald was selecting that garment, a host of people already knew, or strongly suspected, that Oswald would never have his day in court. It was also true at that moment that the prisoner still did not have legal counsel and he had not been arraigned for the shooting of the governor of Texas. Perhaps that was also true because it would not matter.

The president of the United States knew. White House calls, certainly with the authorization of the new resident there, were made to Will Fritz, and the thrust of those calls, to use a recent idiom, was "case closed." Calls would subsequently be put through from the White House to Parkland Hospital to request surgeons to get a deathbed confession from Oswald.

The Dallas police knew. They had received threats during the night

167

that a vigilante group of one hundred would make an attempt to kill Oswald. The warning was issued, according to the caller, to alert the police so that none of them would be caught in the crossfire. The FBI received a similar call. The threat was taken seriously, and orders were given to notify Chief Curry, but his receiver was off the hook, so, according to Captain Talbert, the threats against the prisoner had to be relayed "the hard way."[1] Not everyone involved in Oswald's transfer, however, knew of the threats, but they should have. Further, the police arranged for two armored cars, parked on Commerce Street, to transport the prisoner; yet Fritz saw them as unwieldy, and it was decided to transfer Oswald in an unmarked police cruiser and use the armored cars as decoys.

A larger absurdity is hard to imagine. Sixty million people were viewing the transfer on live television and would have seen Oswald put into the police car. What possible assailant would fall for the decoy? Perhaps the cops had learned the fine art of posturing from their suspect.

The sheriff's department knew. Although Sheriff Bill Decker wanted to transfer the prisoner as soon as possible, and given the fact that the sheriff's department transferred 99.9 percent of all prisoners, Decker added an unfinished thought in his testimony: ". . . but as hot a piece of merchandise as this prisoner was . . ."[2] If the prisoner was as important as Decker's words indicated, it would have been incumbent on him to take charge and give the orders, and the media be damned. But he didn't. Curry and Chief Batchelor had assumed all along that Decker would be in charge of the transfer "because this is customary in moving a prisoner." But Decker wanted no part of it, and, as Lt. Woodrow Wiggins told the Warren Commission, although it was customary for the sheriff to effect the transfer, there was never a reason given in this case, and he added that not even the transfer of Oswald's property was done in the normal way—that was going to be done later.[3] Later, of course, it did not matter.

Even Captain Fritz knew, if only for a few seconds. Travis Kirk, a former Dallas attorney, told the FBI that Fritz had a "photographic memory" and certainly would have recognized Ruby, whom he walked right past.[4] In the famous photo taken as Ruby pulled the trigger, the only frontal "shield" for Oswald was Captain Will Fritz, a forty-two-year veteran of the Dallas police, who, at age sixty-eight, was hardly a "bodyguard," a full twelve to fifteen feet in front of the prisoner he was allegedly shielding.

The staff at Parkland Hospital knew. Administrator Steve Landregan gave a deposition that is startling for its predictive validity. He told of receiving a call on the morning of November 24 that indicated crowds were gathering for the transfer of Oswald, and "there was the possibility of an incident and suggested we might want to alert the emergency room." The emergency staff, who would have gone to lunch, were asked to stay at their posts until it was known that Oswald had been safely moved.[5] (No such consideration was given for JFK's motorcade; an emergency room had to be prepared for him *after* he was shot.) Registered Nurse Bertha Lozana verified Landregan story, indicating, "At 11:00 A.M. I was informed by Jill Pomeroy, the ward clerk, that we might prepare for an emergency because there was a large crowd at city hall."[6]

The telephone company apparently also knew. Parkland administrator Landregan also told that telephone servicemen were waiting at Parkland, and when word of Oswald's shooting was received, they immediately hooked up an extra twenty-five lines for the press.[7] It is hard to imagine a telephone company paying Sunday overtime unless they had reason to believe.

The staff at Dallas police headquarters also were aware. A doctor was present, stethoscope in pocket, to treat Oswald immediately after the shooting. Whether through ignorance or intent, those who treated Oswald gave him artificial respiration, which forced blood at higher speed through ruptured vessels.[8] The duty status of the Homicide and Robbery Bureau, however, reflected either a lack of concern for the prisoner's safety or a desire to close the case very quickly. Of twenty-five detectives (ten had been on duty for the motorcade), seven were on duty (28 percent), twelve were off (48 percent), three took the day off (12 percent), one was sick (4 percent), and two were on vacation (8 percent). Also, perhaps to mitigate the obviousness of an attending physician before the shooting, Sergeant Dean's Warren Commission testimony cited *Dr.* Bieberdorf as *Detective* Brederdorf.[9]

Security was again a lesser consideration than freedom of the press. As Los Angeles reporter Gladwin Hill indicated, he was present on Saturday and Sunday and never asked for identification, and "it occurred to him that it would have been possible and quite easy for anyone who desired to enter the building and kill Oswald."[10] Steven Alexander of KTAL held a camera as he entered the basement, but had no ID and was not asked for any.[11]

The Oswald family's bodyguards may also have known. In her initial testimony, Marina indicated that while she was in a police cruiser, there was an urgent need to get to a phone, so the group then went to Chief Curry's house. In an FBI interview at about the same time, Marina indicated that the stop at Curry's house was "for a period of one and one-half to two hours for the purpose of changing her children's clothes and to make a telephone call."[12] The story was subsequently enlarged by a statement of Marina's that she asked Ruth Paine to bring a few things "to her at the police chief's residence, *where she spent the night*"[13] (emphasis added). (This statement is used only to suggest police, not personal, hanky-panky. And despite the suggestion in the testimony, Mrs. Oswald did not spend the night there.)

Curry himself was nowhere to be found in the basement, and, of course, from having been notified of the threats, he knew. In fact, he was on the phone to Mayor Cabell when the one shot was fired, and was notified of the shooting while doing paperwork at his desk by Jeremiah O'Leary of the *Washington Evening Star.*[14]

With all of this prior concern, why was security so lax, and how did Ruby gain admittance?

If one fact comes through the testimony of the people involved, it is that Jack Ruby did not walk down the Main Street ramp just in time to shoot Oswald. Kenneth Croy, a reserve, testified that Rio Pierce's car went past him and up the ramp, and that nobody came down. Roy E. Vaughan, the officer singularly responsible for security on that ramp, was adamant that Ruby did not enter by passing him and using the Main Street ramp. Rio Pierce and Sergeant Putnam, a passenger in Pierce's car, were "positive" that nobody entered while they were leaving. In his testimony regarding the event, Captain Cecil Talbert indicated that Lieutenant Pierce, in today's idiom, "went ballistic" at the suggestion that Ruby went past him. Sergeant Maxey, the other passenger, was more certain, stating that given the width of the ramp, it would have been impossible for anyone to have been on the ramp while a car was using it.[15] It would not have been outside of the Warren Commission's jurisdiction to visit headquarters with a ruler and measure a police cruiser and the ramp. They just didn't. Dallas researcher Russ McLean and I, however, did, and the ramp measures a mere nine feet, eleven inches wide, which would have prevented Ruby from using it unless the squad car was so close on one side that it was endangering its paint job.

The only opposing testimony came from a reserve named Solomon, who identified William Newman as the reserve officer who noticed Ruby running down the ramp a minute before the shooting.[16] In Newman's Warren Commission appearance, counsel Burt Griffin called him a d——l—— (one presumes "damn liar") and told him to return the following evening prepared to tell the truth. In fact, the following evening, someone else (Leon Hubert) questioned Newman, and the whole issue went under the rug.

If Ruby in fact did not go down that ramp, then he had help getting in, as "Uniformed men were posted on the stairways and elevators to allow no one, with the exception of police officers, to pass."[17]

Ruby knew in advance also, or so we were led to believe when he, like Oswald, was charged with "murder with malice aforethought" for an event that was at least supposed to appear spontaneous. Ruby is the key to the events of November 24, and those events may tell us a great deal about the events of November 22 as well.

Thus the question: Who—and what—*was* Jack Ruby?

Chicago-born, Ruby had been briefly institutionalized as a youth, for, among other reasons, truancy, like his victim. He was also placed briefly with a foster family, but was reunited with his biological family, which included a mother cut from the Marguerite Oswald (Lee's mother) cookie cutter. As Ruby grew, he began to run with street gangs, and there was very little of a positive nature on his pre-1947 résumé.

The year 1947 seemed to mark a turning point. First, Ruby left the streets and associations of Chicago, eventually winding up in Dallas. That same year, a "Jack Rubenstein" provided inside information on the Chicago crime network to an eager freshman congressman named Richard Nixon, who did his best to keep his informant's name confidential.[18] From there, Ruby returned to former pursuits— but new associations, as an FBI report with Taylor Crossland is highly suggestive of Ruby's participation in a major narcotics deal in late 1947.[19] In 1951, Bryce G. Brady II, an acquaintance of Ruby's, gave him a .38 Colt snub-nosed revolver as a Christmas present.[20]

In the late 1950s there are strong suggestions of an association between Ruby and Lewis McWillie, and researchers studying mob connections to the assassination have used that association to view Ruby as a Mafia underling dealing in the vices associated with the soft underbelly of society.[21]

From May to November 1959, Ruby again jumped fences and served as a "confidential informant" for FBI special agent Charles W. Flynn. This, combined with Ruby's earlier possible involvement with Congressman Nixon, suggests that Ruby was not the total "loner" (like Oswald) that some people would have us believe. Ruby did have an awareness of what was going on around him, and he was willing to cooperate with authorities. This further suggests a weakening of his organized crime bond, if in fact it was ever anything more than a latent dream of Ruby's, who acted out his fantasies in his dealings and kissing-up to mob types. However, it must be remembered that the Cosa Nostra does not take kindly to informants within its ranks.

From 1950 to 1963 Ruby had twenty traffic violations, but there is no record that his driving privilege was ever suspended.[22] Beyond tickets, Ruby's arrest record showed nine charges lodged between February 4, 1949, and March 14, 1963. No convictions appear in the record.[23] The official record provides a most interesting hint as to Ruby's supposed spotless record. Walter C. Clewis, who occasionally booked acts for Ruby, did not particularly care for Ruby, as he "boasted not only to him but to other people in his presence that he could do anything he wanted in Dallas as he had enough information *on the Dallas Police Department and judges* [emphasis added] that he could not be convicted."[24] Here again, a key connection is made between the assassination and elements within the Dallas police— including police aide-de-camp Jack Ruby.

Although Ruby would be convicted in 1964 for Oswald's murder, the conviction was overturned, and for good reason, and Ruby died in 1967 a free man, albeit in custody, awaiting retrial for a crime for which bail was not allowed—which may explain why Ruby's "sudden" urge to kill Oswald was treated as premeditated murder.

There can be no doubt that Ruby was closely tied to the Dallas Police Department. J. L. Campbell, who testified to Ruby's homosexuality, added that he had "seen RUBY associating with Dallas police officers and riding with them in Dallas Police Department squad cars." Pete Lucas, a Dallas restaurant owner, gave virtually identical testimony.[25] There was also testimony, from Ruby's brother Sam, and Ruby's former girlfriend of ten years, Alice R. Nichols, and others, that Ruby hired off-duty officers for security purposes in his clubs.[26] This allegation was addressed to many of the Dallas officers who testified before the Warren Commission, and it was universally denied.

There was much additional testimony that Ruby was very closely linked to the Dallas police. Ruby's sister Eileen Kaminsky told that officers would always wave or yell, "Hi, Jack," as Ruby drove through Dallas.[27] Other comments included, "He seemed to know every policeman in Dallas"; Ruby "has been well known by most of the police officers in the Dallas police Department, as well as the sheriff's office."[28] Forrest Sorrels, in discussing Ruby's statements in captivity, told that "Ruby stated that he had very high regard for the Dallas Police Department and that they all knew him (or some similar remark)." Lt. George Arnett "stated that Ruby was well known among the members of the Dallas Police Department and was rather friendly with them."[29] In the Dallas police report of Oswald's transfer, however, many officers swore they never heard of Ruby.[30]

Despite the disclaimer, Ruby was known to provide officers free drinks, free meals, and even "dates" with some of his entertainers. Hugh G. Smith, a former Dallas officer, told that for three years he received whiskey from Ruby during the holiday season, and one year Ruby even delivered Smith's gift to his house.[31] James Rhodes, who worked for Ruby, told of a large dinner party Ruby gave for the force in 1960, and indicated that Ruby told him "the chief" was there. Another Ruby employee, Reagan Turman, believed Ruby knew 75 percent to 90 percent of the police officers in Dallas and that Ruby had told him that such congeniality was vital, given the nature of Ruby's business. Turman also indicated that he was familiar with the name Tippit and knew that Ruby was "acquainted with the chief of police and several other higher-ups in the police department. . . ."[32]

The best single indication of Ruby's intimacy with the police came as a result of a question put to onetime Ruby employee Nancy Perrin Rich, in which she was asked if Ruby could have gotten into the basement by posing as a reporter. Rich exploded, "Ye gods, I don't think there is a cop in Dallas that does not know Jack Ruby. He practically lived at that station. They lived in his place." She went on to add that some were higher-ups, but pointedly excluded Will Fritz.[33] Given all this, it seems odd that Chief Curry would testify before the Warren Commission that Ruby knew perhaps 25 of his 1,175 officers.

There was one additional component to the Ruby-police relationship. Harry Hall told that Ruby was involved in fraudulent betting schemes and received 40 percent of the take, "because he was supposed to have *influence with the police*"[34] (emphasis added). Convicted felon Paul Rouland Jones told the FBI, "JACK RUBY, according to JONES, must have been paying off the police department in Dallas, Texas, otherwise he could not have operated his business nor been permitted to put on the 'raw shows' that he did."[35]

The House Select Committee on Assassinations believed that Ruby was stalking Oswald and that Ruby had organized crime connections both before and after November 22, citing as evidence the presence of mob figures at his trial.[36] While he certainly was stalking Oswald, it is hard to picture someone so intimately tied—and proud of it—to the police, who is truly a member of organized crime. A punk wanna-be, perhaps, but not a full-time member. Also, mob figures at Ruby's trial are significant only in that their presence could have been a symbolic nose-thumbing at Bobby Kennedy.

Dallas Morning News employees Georgia Mayor, who believed Ruby was looking toward the TSBD when she returned to her desk after the motorcade, and Don Campbell, who left Ruby at his desk and returned to find him there, believed Ruby had no interest in attending the parade. Either way, Ruby was alibied for the critical minutes of mid-Friday,[37] and there is the suggestion there that for all his professed admiration of JFK, Ruby could have cared less about seeing him, having not bothered to vote in 1960. As Thomas Buchanan acidly noted, the only presidents Ruby cared about were pictured on U.S. currency.[38]

Nevertheless, the news of the assassination, or perhaps what Ruby saw of it, rattled him severely. Billie Rea testified that Ruby was watching television when the bulletin came on: "JACK RUBY had a very strange look on his face at that time and seemed to stare without comprehending the events." Richard Saunders returned to his news desk and described Ruby as "ashen white."[39] Ruby's rabbi, Hillel Silverman, would see Ruby later that evening "in a daze," and George Senator, Ruby's roommate, "never saw RUBY so emotionally disturbed and upset by anything during the time he knew him as RUBY was by the killing of the president."[40]

Witnesses saw and spoke with Ruby in Dallas police headquarters on November 22, and the Warren Commission printed two photos of his presence there.[41] After correcting Henry Wade regarding Cuban politics at the "midnight" press conference, Ruby met police officer Harry Olsen with Kathy Kay, one of Ruby's strippers, and there was a discussion that Oswald should be cut to ribbons. Ruby was subsequently able to get closer to Oswald on two occasions than was

Oswald's own mother, although that may have been at Oswald's choosing. Ruby's brother Earl provided two key insights into brother Jack's motivations, to be discussed further below. Earl told that Jack "heard a crowd of people say that the person who killed that Communist Oswald would be a hero." Earl Ruby also supported this author's thesis with the comment, "Everyone was outraged against Oswald. The police made little effort to dissuade anyone from attacking Oswald."[42] *"The police made little effort . . ."*

UPI photographer Pete Fisher saw Oswald pass "not more than three feet from Ruby as he was led up on the stage"[43] for the midnight press conference, suggesting that Ruby was not armed at the time. The strongest indication of that is the fact that Oswald was alive the following day. Ruby would subsequently be a presence at headquarters, although his interest would drop to zero when the transfer was announced for Sunday morning. That Saturday evening, despite the grief cited above, Ruby visited a "local Negro nightclub" in search of a replacement musician. While there, he passed out $5 bills and was "in high spirits."[44] Ruby awoke on Sunday, "very upset, with a strange look on his face, almost as if he were in shock," according to George Senator.[45]

The question of Ruby's use of the ramp to gain access to the basement on November 24 has already been discussed. The Warren Commission believed it, but the House Select Committee on Assassinations did not, suggesting *police collusion*. Detective H. B. Reynolds gave startling, if unconfirmed, information in his written deposition: "He also heard later from unrecalled sources there was a rumor to the effect that shortly before the shooting of OSWALD, JACK RUBY was seen getting out of an unattended Dallas Police squad car parked in the basement area."[46]

Alleged organized crime figure Joseph Campisi told the FBI he believed Ruby got into the basement through his friendship with and knowledge of numerous Dallas police officers.[47] Ruby, testifying months later before the chief justice while in the Dallas jail, spoke enigmatically: "If it were timed that way [his last-minute arrival after sending a telegram], then someone in the police department is guilty of giving the information as to when Lee Harvey Oswald was coming down." Ruby was also elliptical shortly after the shooting of Oswald, when, referring to police, he indicated his just-concluded actions "will save you guys a lot of trouble." That can be interpreted several ways.[48] Earlier, upon being taken into custody, Ruby indicated, "FBI and officers treating me well; I've got friends."[49] While Ruby was being interrogated he said he had "no permit to carry a gun and had no card or badge of any kind of . . ." The document then has a strikeover through the still-visible words "law enforcement officer."[50]

A most telling indictment of police procedure was provided by Gene Barnes, covering the events of Dallas for NBC. Present when Oswald was shot, he sped to Parkland and was told he would be given the identity of the assailant for a bribe. Barnes could not understand how anyone could have known so quickly.[51] Actually, it was simple: The vast majority of the officers present at the shooting knew who had done it; *a couple may have known in advance.*

Other connections are hinted at with respect to Ruby. His sudden rise in long-distance phone calls has troubled researchers. W. M. Duff, General Walker's suspect in the attempt on his life, claimed that Walker met once a month with Ruby, a concept highly doubtful when one reads Walker's testimony about *Rubenstein.*[52] Attorney Carroll Jarnigan told the FBI that he had seen Oswald and Ruby at the Carousel, plotting to kill Connally. He added a great deal of overheard dialogue to his allegation.[53] The witness, though an alcoholic, was nevertheless knowledgeable enough in his profession to know the penalty for filing a false report.

Andrew Armstrong, Joey Gerard, C. L. Crafard, and Stella Coffman, all Ruby employees, gave testimony that Ruby knew Tippit.[54] This data is only suggestive, as there were three officers named "Tippit" on the Dallas police force, and there is evidence that Ruby was best acquainted with *Gayle* Tippit.

Either way, Ruby's close association with the Dallas police, his reliance on them to beat frequent criminal charges and operate the kind of business he ran, and his willingness to bribe or hire them suggest a possible motive for killing Oswald: revenge for the killing of a police officer, whom, in the confusion of events of November 22, Ruby may have believed he knew. *And the police could have played on this emotion to use Ruby to cover their own tracks and effectively close the case.*

Other motives are available by consensus. Paul Rouland Jones, who had tied Ruby to the syndicate before 1947 and who had visited Dallas as recently as November 15, was direct: "He said from his acquaintance with RUBY he doubted that he [Ruby] would have become emotionally upset and killed OSWALD on the spur of the moment. He felt RUBY would have done it for money, but had no knowledge of who might have offered such money."[55] Jack K. Kelley scoffed at a patriotic motive in Ruby's act, choosing to believe he did it for publicity or money. Stripper "Jada" agreed, suggesting publicity as Ruby's motive, even if he got a long sentence. Jada's co-worker "Sheri Linn" agreed with the publicity motive but added that Ruby "would do anything for money."[56]

Given Ruby's debts to the IRS ($44,413.86 and possibly more), to his brother Sam ($1,300) and to Ralph Paul (several thousand), money—or the possibility of receiving it from citizens who saw the murder of Oswald as an act of patriotism—may indeed have been a motive. (Given that the Secret Service employed 526 people in 1963 at an *average* salary of $10,996.19, this puts Ruby's debts, between $60,000 and $100,000, in a "real dollars" perspective for 1963.)[57]

Ruby would admit shortly after the shooting that he "felt Oswald was a Red. Felt Oswald was alone in the assassination," a statement no doubt music to the ears of his captors. He also told that nobody else was involved with him in the shooting of Oswald, an equally musical statement.[58] Ruby would later tell that part of his motivation was to spare Jacqueline Kennedy the burden of returning for a trial, and to spare the Kennedy children any further grief. In this, like so much else he did, Ruby was a failure. Jacqueline Kennedy would not likely have been a witness at Oswald's trial, and rather than sparing an ordeal, by killing Oswald, Ruby left the question of ultimate guilt open as the Kennedy children now approach middle age. Author Buchanan put this in perspective, citing Ruby's claim of sparing the family as "the ultimate obscenity" and viewing the publicity motive with doubt: "The electric chair seems a high price for advertising."[59]

This last statement begs the question, however. Ruby clearly tried to present the killing of Oswald as spontaneous, which would have brought a manslaughter charge with a maximum of five years. This meant Ruby could have been on the streets again, reveling in his celebrity and newfound riches (if the public had bought his story), in three years. Such a scenario is not beyond the realm of possibility, either, as there were 1,080 murders reported in Texas in 1960, but only 5 death sentences.[60] Ruby subsequently received a death sentence, suggesting that *someone in an official capacity wanted him as quiet as Oswald.*

Doris Warner, who managed the apartment complex in which Ruby was living in November 1963, told that police arrived on

November 24 with a search warrant, along with Judge Joe B. Brown, who would later preside at Ruby's trial.[61] Brown's presence at the search, along with other serious judicial mistakes, would guarantee that Ruby's conviction would be overturned, as it indeed was, and would allow a new trial, perhaps for the correct charge, in a less passionate time, and perhaps Ruby would escape with "time served." It is an interesting scenario to consider. Either way, Brown's presence at the search makes the subsequent "trial" nothing more than a public-relations hoax to provide Dallas authorities with the right to keep Ruby in custody for a while—*or permanently.*

Either way, it seems apparent that the forces that prevented justice in the JFK and Tippit cases were also at work in the case in which Oswald was the victim.

In captivity, Ruby hinted a great deal about conspiracy, but rarely delivered. In one brief interview he told a reporter that events would have been very different if Adlai Stevenson had been the vice president. When the reporter, walking through a corridor with Ruby, asked for clarification about his assassination statement, he was told, "The answer is 'The man in office now.' "

Ruby's jury selection took fourteen days and his trial ten. The jury took just over two hours to return its verdict, an eternity given the number of eyewitnesses to the crime, and over four times as long as it took a jury to convict "lone nut" Leon Czolgosz of killing McKinley. Author Jim Marrs has suggested that Ruby's subsequent cancer might have been police-induced, as Ruby could have been taken to Parkland for an annual physical and left in an X-ray room *with the machinery on.*[62] A more recent work cites "Patrick Dane" (assuming a typo for P. T. Dean), seen on the knoll, and in charge of basement security when Oswald was shot, as involved in Ruby's passing.[63]

Ruby died on January 3, 1967, the seventh person to expire at Parkland Hospital in 1967. His tissue samples were put in jars and labeled "007."[64]

Henry Wade blamed the police, indirectly, for Oswald's death. The cops, Wade argued, "were at fault in Ruby killing him. There was undoubtedly a breakdown on security there in the basement."[65] Ruby's brother Hyman believed, "The police department is using Jack as a scapegoat for their mistakes."[66]

In the "Hypothesis" that will conclude this work, both Wade's and Hyman Rubenstein's theories, along with others, will be further explored. It will be shown that the police were involved in the death of Oswald, but not as Wade suggested. It will also be suggested that the police could have made excellent use of Ruby as a scapegoat—not for their mistakes, but rather *for their successes*.

CHAPTER EIGHT

SAYS WHO?

Shoot first and inquire afterward, and if you make mistakes, I will protect you.

—HERMANN GOERING, 1933, instructions to the Prussian
Police

THUS FAR WE HAVE been confronted with valid testimony that there were police in abundance in the railroad yards and elsewhere on November 22, and clearly not in postures that would put them in protection scenarios:

A photo of "the badgeman"; witnesses' testimony several minutes or hours after the shots were fired; coercion of witnesses who spoke of the knoll, or worse, avoidance of such witnesses; still worse, the ease with which official investigators dismissed such testimony as nothing more than nonsense generated by the acoustics of Dealey Plaza.

But there were witnesses, and there was testimony, and it cannot be disregarded, although if we observe the treatment of those witnesses and those people after November 22 we begin to see why and how their testimony was viewed as dangerous—or simply wrong.

GOVERNOR JOHN B. CONNALLY

The first documentable individual to suggest that a conspiracy was behind the attempt on the life of President Kennedy was the man sitting in front of him in the presidential limousine, Texas governor John Connally. In the interval between the realization that he had been wounded and the moment, a few seconds later, when he realized that brain matter on his clothing indicated a fatal wound to the president, Governor Connally was able to exclaim, "My God, *they're* going to kill us all."

When one considers that this statement was made in spite of a pneumothorax, or collapsed right lung, adjacent to which was a totally shattered rib that was never subsequently repaired, it becomes clear that this thought had a great deal of urgency for the governor to express, or he would have conserved his own energy and focused on survival.

It would be easy to dismiss the statement as just careless wording amid a grave crisis, but it was not an isolated statement. At Parkland Hospital, in the minutes before he was anesthetized prior to surgery, the governor made an additional statement, which was picked up by reporters and broadcast widely. The governor's statement was terse: "*They* also got the president."

A second such use of a specific pronoun suggests at least that the governor had premotorcade concerns regarding some lunatic fringe group, or that his hearing of events made available to his senses the immediate perception of multiple gunmen.

For years, Governor Connally's additional testimony has been grist for the mills of researchers critical of the official version of the events of November 22. Connally was initially convinced, and never wavered in his conviction, that he was wounded by the second shot. He based his conclusion on the fact that he heard a shot, had time to turn to his right, but was unable to see the president, and then turn to his left, where, when he was facing just about directly forward, he received a blow in the upper back that felt like a rolled-up fist had landed a haymaker there.

This scenario, "proven" by Gerald Posner, is, in fact, probative evidence of multiple shooters when the event is carefully examined. The official version has always said that three shots were fired and that one of them hit both elected officials in the car, one killed the president, and one missed. (This was not the initial "official" conclusion, but it best fit the Oswald lone-nut theory, so it was made "official.")

In the theory that emerged in 1993, both Kennedy and Connally were hit in frame 224 of the Zapruder film, as Connally's coat lapel, either from a bullet or from the strong north-to-south breeze there, is seen to lift up for that one movie frame. The magic-bullet claptrap is then repeated, convoluting limousine placement of individuals, basic ballistics, plus the governor's reaction. Kennedy, seen as having sustained spinal damage, *immediately* assumes "Thorburn's position," a medical anomaly introduced to assassination literature by Dr. John K. Lattimer. Thorburn's position received its name from a nineteenth-century patient who displayed a vivid tendency to splay his elbows upward and outward after sustaining spinal damage. At the same time, Connally, who lost an entire rib, had a wrist shattered, and had a bullet lodge in his femur bone in the same .00185 second, does not react until almost a full second later.

This reasoning stays within the Warren Commission's parameters even though it means that the first and nearest shot would have had to miss, yet somehow travel well over the length of a football field and wound bystander James Tague.

It also insists that the first shot was fired during Zapruder frames 160–65, when it was known that foliage obstructed the view of a gunman in the sixth-floor window of the depository. Such a gunman would have had to have been a rank amateur or worse, as he had passed up a far easier and far safer shot when the car was right beneath his place of concealment, and then waited until the car disappeared into the tree foliage to fire at an unseen target.

This could only have happened this way if that first shot, heard by many as a firecracker, was a diversionary waste of blank ammunition to focus all eyes on the sixth floor of the depository, while other, louder guns did far greater damage. This would explain the cartridge found on the sixth floor that could not have held a bullet on November 22, and it would also give other shooters the highly valuable advantage of being able to gauge the reaction to the first "shot."

What is missed in this circuitous speculative perambulation is not Connally's insistence that he was hit by a separate bullet, which he was, but rather a careful reading of the logistics of the two victims. JFK cannot tell us their respective positions; but Connally could— and did—beyond a reasonable doubt. He heard the shot, identified it as an assassination attempt, and turned to his right to see the president. *But he couldn't, so he was turning back to his left* when he was hit. This guarantees that Connally was so far to JFK's right that the magic-bullet theory should never even have been considered. Connally could not see JFK when he turned right, so he turned left to see him. What does that tell us about the relative positions of the

[Jill Brown]

[Jill Brown]

top: November 22, 1993, the 30th anniversary of the assassination: the police are still on the knoll.

bottom: EYEWITNESS TO HISTORY: Mike Robinson, center, giving an interview on November 22, 1993, with the Book Depository directly behind him. When challenged by the interviewer to take his story to the FBI, Mike said he would, if the interviewer came along with camera and microphone. His offer was not accepted. He subsequently put his story on record for me, and where it could be corroborated, it has been.

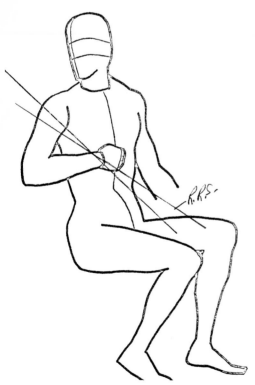

COMMISSION EXHIBIT 689

LIMOUSINE LOGISTICS: in this photo, *not* taken during the moments of the shooting sequence, Kennedy and Connally are shown in random postures in the Presidential limousine. The line with dashes and dots indicates the route of a hypothetical bullet fired from the "sniper's window," going right to left at 12 degrees; the line of dashes depicts the angles and trajectories necessary for Connally's chest wounds only—as it is highly unlikely he received the other two wounds subsequently, as noted in the text; together, they destroy whatever remaining credibility the magic bullet had. (See also CE 689, depicted.) In CE 697, Connally is once again shown well to JFK's *right*.

CE 689: Governor Connally's doctors created a scenario in which one bullet could have done all the damage sustained by the Governor; as shown, however, the angle of the bullet through the Governor is 52 degrees, while the angle depicted in the Warren Commission 385, through the President, was 11 degrees (and the angle to the sniper's window in the TSBD was 21 degrees); the willingness to go to all lengths to prove a point is shown by the Governor's wrist, which is known—and was known then—to have had a bullet enter the top and exit the bottom— a physical impossibility if you try to put your wrist to your chest as shown here.

AUTOPSY FRAUD: in a print made from the original Fox negatives, the resolution is so clear that you can see hair from the President's chest, at Point A; yet the hair on the lower rear of the head (Point B) has the appearance of a charcoal drawing; it's a fake. Its wound of entry, such as it is, is also far too high as was denounced by Humes.

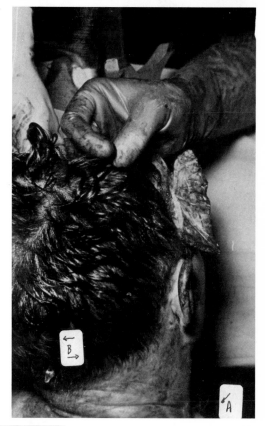

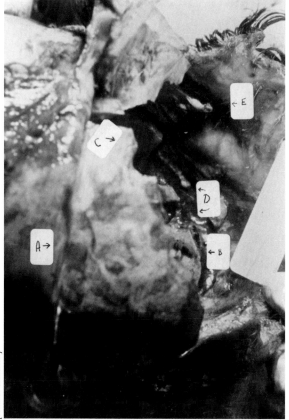

THE AUTOPSY PHOTO THAT SQUEAKED THROUGH: least publicized of all the black and white "Fox" autopsy photos, this one is the most revealing, as it proves what has long been suspected. The viewer is looking right into the right side of the head; Point A shows the external occipital protuberance, the only such structure on the head, and Humes' point of reference at autopsy. Point B shows "Humes' entry," as noted elsewhere, to the right and just above the E.O.P. (the photo is not perfectly level in alignment). This is the wound depicted in Z312; Points C and D, however, show the ominous "beveling" or "cratering" present in wounds *of exit*, in this case, in *the rear of the head*; Point E represents the entrance wound for the bullet, which, at Z313, caused the wounds of exit in the back and blew out so much additional skull with it; this wound was testified to by Roy Kellerman, present at the autopsy, as "*entry* into this man's head" being in the bottom of the hair line immediately *to the right of the ear*, with a diameter of the little finger. (From Volume 2, p. 81 of Hearings and Exhibits).

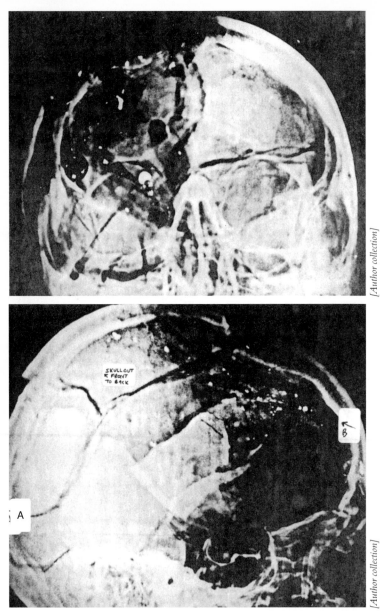

[Author collection]

[Author collection]

top: FRONTAL X-RAY: researchers have been using "incontrovertible laws of physics" regarding much of the JFK evidence, and especially the Zapruder film, to prove points; here is yet another one, thanks to the research of Randy Robertson: converging fracture lines will not cross, as even common sense dictates; yet in the JFK case, anything is possible, as shown in the X-ray that depicts fracture lines crossing; the only way it could have happened (Brown, not Robertson), is fractures caused by two simultaneous bullets, as suggested in head movements in Z312 and then Z313; it is not possible any other way.

bottom: LATERAL X-RAY: again, a series of radiating fractures; but close study shows that at Point A, an entrance wound caused fractures; this wound is at the precise spot (see Autopsy photo), described by Humes, et al: slightly to the right and just above the external occipital protuberance. Yet Point B and arrow show a trail of metal not possible from Humes' description of the wound he saw, and the trail of metal leads directly to a "cap" of skull bone which has been removed from the skull as if hit from the front to the back, another impossibility based on what the autopsy doctors testified to. Point A is the shot at Z312; point B and the arrow show the damage that occurred 1/18th of a second later, at Z313.

ROSCOE WHITE: shown in his "Marine" career, doing what he did best? Many researchers are focusing on White as a perpetrator—or at least as a prototype of the individual(s) involved in at least some of the events of November 22, 1963. In viewing this exhibit, keep in mind that it was the photo of Oswald on the cover of *Life* that convinced many people of his guilt; had White been a suspect, what impact would this photo have had?

[Jim Murray Film]

A sample of this series of photos, shot with the Hertz clock atop the Depository reading "12:40" shows an individual, believed to be an FBI agent, retrieving a stray bullet from the grassy area to the left of the recent path of the presidential limousine. Also pictured are a Dallas police officer and a Dallas sheriff's officer. All three had knowledge of the item or items pocketed by the FBI agent. All remained silent.

Driver Greer's dilemma and mass perjury by others: in this famous photo by James Altgens, Clint Hill is shown boarding the limousine several seconds after the last shot was fired. The photo shows the problem that had confronted driver Greer before the shots: the numerous individuals on the overpass who should not have been there, and the police who allowed them to stay; it also shows the white Ford, Curry's car, well short of the underpass seconds after the last shot, although most occupants of the car testified before the Warren Commission they heard the first "report" as they reached the underpass. Such testimony was either perjury, or the car was then put in reverse and backed to this location.

[Southwest Film/Video Archives]

[Southwest Film/Video Archives]

These frames from the Weigman film tell us a great deal. Taken from a vehicle well back in the motorcade, they reflect the perceptions of numerous individuals standing right in front of the Depository several seconds after the shooting ended. Yet there is no indication that any of them thought the shots came from directly over their heads. The Warren Commission would have us believe that all credible witnesses knew the source of the shots—yet these people, literally closest to the event and not confused by echoes, did not have the Warren Commission's keen perceptions.

two? Only that JFK was further inboard than Connally, making a wound in Connally's extreme right side an impossibility if the bullet had earlier gone from right to left through the president—*an impossibility*.

As it happened, there was virtually no reaction to the first "shot." Phil Willis's daughter stopped running and turned in the direction of the book depository, but that was in reaction to a cry from her mother, who feared that the child's exuberance at the event would jeopardize her. The Altgens photo, taken at Z255, clearly shows the vast majority of the crowd still looking *west,* at the president, a full five-plus seconds after the "firecracker." Many of those witnesses would give testimony that their first impression was "firecracker," but then, because of the subsequent sounds heard, they were able to posit shots being fired. Note that the second noise was frequently the key to rifle fire; the first could well have been the blank, fired at the time the president was obscured by the local fauna.

Would a lone gunman fire that shot? Very unlikely. A diversionary gunman absolutely would, as the car was far enough along that there was no turning back, but it had not yet reached the point of maximum triangulation, and the shooters needed to see the reaction of the Secret Service and/or the president, to decide in the next second or two whether to proceed or abort. We know now that had they aborted, Oswald's rifle would have been found either way, and the official scenario, absent the death of the president, would have pointed fingers of guilt at the left, Castro, and the Soviet Union, and might have thrown enough of a scare into the president that he would modify, perhaps even abandon, his policies of accommodation with the "sponsors" of the attempt on his life.

There was neither a presidential nor a Secret Service reaction between frames Z160 and Z224, except that the car began to slow down. In the ensuing five seconds, seven wounds *that we know of* killed the president and wounded the governor seriously enough that if he had been taken to any hospital besides Parkland, which had one of the nation's best trauma units in 1963, he may well have died also.

The operative pronoun in the statement "My God, they're going to kill us all" still has a great deal of validity, although media accounts at the time always seemed to stress singular pronouns such as "he," which we know to be politically, if not ballistically, incorrect, in 1993.

JEAN LOLLIS HILL

Governor John Connally was not immediately quoted on either radio or television, and his statement, "*They* also got the president," was put out on the airwaves at 1:27 P.M. CST, eight minutes before the networks had definitive word that the president had died.

Before that, however, NBC coanchor Bill Ryan indicated that a neatly dressed young man (clearly not Oswald at 1:19 P.M. CST) had been taken into custody, and then the national network cut away to Tom Whelan of WBAP, Forth Worth, who introduced the following interview between newsman James Darnell ("D") and Jean Hill ("JH").

D: What is your name, ma'am?

JH: Jean Hill.

D: Uh, from Dallas?

JH: That's right.

D: And, uh, did you see the shooting, miss?

JH: Yes, sir.

D: Can you describe what happened?

JH: Yes, sir.

D: Will you do that now?

JH: Uh, they were driving along, uh, and we were the only people in this area, on our side. A shot came from directly across the street from us. And just as the president's car became directly even with us, we, we took one look at him, and he was sitting there, he and Jackie were looking at a dog that was in the middle of the seat and about that time three shots rang out, just as he looked up. Just as the president looked up and those three shots rang out and he grabbed his chest and looked like he was in pain, and he fell over in the seat, and Jackie fell over on him and said, "My God, he's been shot." And after that, more shots rang out, and the car sped away.

D: What kind of car was it?

JH: [Incredulous] *What kind of a car was it? It was the president's car.*

D: Where did the shots come from?

JH: The shots came from the hill.

D: From the hill?

JH: Yes. Uh, it was just east of the underpass. . . .

D: Uh-huh, and uh. . . .

JH: We were on the south side. . . .

D: Could you see, did you look up there where the shots came from?

JH: Yes, sir.

D: Did you see anyone?

JH: I thought I saw this man running, but I looked at the president, and, you know, for a while, and I looked up there and thought I saw a man running, and so, I guess I didn't have any better sense, so I started running up there, too.

D: And what is your name?

JH: Jean Hill.

At that point, the interview is terminated as Jean Hill is giving her address, and Tom Whelan, who had introduced the interview, then added that information had been since received that a young man had been captured, and that there were reports of a .30-.30 rifle found at the scene.

Fourteen minutes later, the world learned that John F. Kennedy had died.

Jean Hill's credibility has been attacked early and often, but the statement quoted in full above is a treasure trove of data. She tells, without emotion or hesitation, that the shots came from the hill. She does not qualify her statement to say, "I think," or "I believe I heard"; on the contrary: *The shots came from the hill.*

Her statement, on rereading, suggests that the first shot did no damage, as it took time for the president's car to reach her position, and then more shots were fired, which hit the president, and still more shots were fired and then the car sped away. She accurately noted that the president's hands went up, although she saw chest, where throat would be accurate. Equally accurate is her recitation of Mrs. Kennedy's comment, and the fact that the president fell over.

What is missing from her narrative are two items: the horrible head impact as shown in the Zapruder film, and the arrival of Secret Service agent Clint Hill. Given Ms. Hill's location at the time of the head impact shown in Z313, she should have seen it *if it had been fired from the rear,* but she would not have seen it *if it had been fired from the right front side of the car.* With reference to Mr. Hill, it is possible that while Jean Hill searched the knoll and observed the man running, in those few seconds, Clint Hill arrived, saw to Mrs. Kennedy's safety, and the car sped away.

"The dog" has always been a fly in the ointment, and has been used by folks such as Warren Commission attorney David Belin to trash the entirety of Jean Hill's observations. However, Wallace Milam, a researcher from Tennessee, has discovered proof that there was, in fact, a dog, if only a stuffed one, that Jackie Kennedy had been presented sometime on November 22, and that she had routinely placed somewhere in the backseat during the motorcade. (If one recalls the photo in the memorialized issues of *Life,* with JFK on the cover, roses are shown in the backseat of an empty car, suggesting the tragedy of Dealey Plaza. The car shown was the one carrying LBJ; no photos were taken of the backseat of JFK's car from the Zapruder film to photos taken many hours later in the White House garage.)

David Belin's acidity to the contrary, Jean Hill was a credible on-scene witness, although not all of her recollections are accurate. Yet an interesting phenomenon occurred after her interview, which took place fifteen minutes before the world learned of JFK's death. Items began to filter in about the TSBD, and the arrest of the shabbily dressed Oswald, but not one reporter asked the obvious question: How could that lady named Hill, featured at 1:20 P.M., have told a story about shots from the hill, when we are now being told about a sixth-floor window a football field away? Nobody even hinted at the possibility of more than one assassin; rather, they quoted Malcolm Kilduff, who told that JFK had been shot *through the temple* by an *unknown assailant* (singular).

Jean Hill has maintained her story for thirty years; I was allowed to suggest questions for a broadcast to be made by Malcolm Kilduff on November 22, 1993, but he did not deign to field the obvious questions suggested in contemporary reporting. His silence is in sharp contrast to that of Miss Hill.

MIKE ROBINSON

Anyone who does not believe strongly in either irony or coincidence will have to rethink their attitudes when they hear the revelations given to me by Mike Robinson.

As it is the central thesis of this work that elements within the Dallas Police Department had a far greater involvement in the JFK assassination than heretofore considered, it seems odd that the same police department "gave" me Mike Robinson.

November 22, 1993, was the thirtieth anniversary of the tragedy in Dealey Plaza, and, as such, was the occasion for the dedication of that area as an historic landmark. I arrived there with my wife and Texas researcher Russ McLean early enough to be close enough to be able to see the goings-on. But the local blues were forcing people out of the plaza until all was ready. I was thus manhandled from the reflecting pool across the street to the TSBD, then around the corner to a point on Houston between the TSBD and the former Dal-Tex building. When I met resistance indicating I could be pushed no farther, I found myself next to Mike, who was giving an interview to a local television network.

What he had to say was incredible, and the TV anchorperson was lost for the right questions to ask. She did ask, however, if Mike was willing to take his story to the FBI, and he said he would—if the film crew would come with him to document the event. They declined.

I subsequently contacted Mike, as I had copied his name and phone number from the reporter's notes (Woodward or Bernstein I'm not). I explained that I had been standing next to him for the interview and that I had heard most of his comments, but that I just wanted to make sure I had heard them correctly. Mr. Robinson, not knowing my voice over the phone from Adam's, checked me out through people in Texas and only then shared his story.

Mike Robinson was fourteen years old the day the president was killed. Since I had been sixteen at the time, I felt I could relate to the emotions he told of.

He had watched the motorcade at Main and Harwood, the corner where Dallas police headquarters was located, with a friend whose father was a higher-up in the police. I have since been able to confirm the existence of both the friend, his father's rank, and his father's perhaps too-deep curiosity as to the events of November 22.

After the motorcade passed, the boys went to a theater, bought their tickets and popcorn, and then heard the rapidly spreading news that the president had been shot. Figuring that headquarters would be the center of subsequent action, he and his friend hastened back there in time to get to the third floor, check in with the friend's father, and then see Lee Oswald being led out of the elevator. Since this was a once-in-a-lifetime adventure for a young boy, and since the media were mobbing the area anyway, they stayed and observed the goings-on.

Mike indicated that he overheard in conversation that it was clear to anyone who was talking that the police were convinced beyond all reasonable doubt, even as early as 2:30 P.M., that Oswald was the culprit *on both counts.* He also learned that J. D. Tippit had been killed. That event, while tragic, was not overly troubling to Mike, as many neighborhood kids knew Tippit from his comings and goings at Austin's Barbeque, and Tippit had arrested Mike's brother for drinking beer in public. The local teenagers, it was noted, had no use for Tippit, whom they viewed as your garden-variety asshole.

Putting that aside, Mike and his friend saw Oswald moved from the various places he was shunted to, and also saw him inside one of the glass homicide cubicles, until such time as newspaper was taped up to keep out the curious. Mike also saw Bobby Hargis, the motorcycle officer splattered by particulate matter from the president, return to headquarters with blood and brain matter on him and his helmet, and when the realization of events hit Hargis, he violently slammed the helmet into a wall and literally went beserk, requiring a number of other officers to restrain him (an event unknown to—or unreported by—the Warren Commission).

As afternoon approached evening, a trip to the rest room became an absolute necessity, but with extra police and media on the third floor, that was impossible. So Mike was taken, by the ranking officer whose son he was with, down to the lowest level of the building, where the officers had their lockers, and told that the rest room was just past the locker room.

While in a toilet/stall, the enormity of events hit Mike hard and he became emotional about them now that he found himself literally alone with the knowledge that the president he had waved to just a few hours earlier was now in a coffin. As this emotional turmoil came upon him, the rest room serenity was broken by the arrival of three individuals. Not to appear a sissy or be embarrassed, Mike lifted his feet and "hid" in the stall so that anyone observing would think that only the three men who had just entered were present.

Their brief conversation forever changed Mike Robinson's life. Initially there were whispers, but eventually one individual—and these people were police or police-related in the officers' rest room—vented some anger through gritted teeth, with appropriate profanity, to make statements that add great credence to the thesis enunciated herein.

As Mike Robinson reconstructs the statements, their order was (angrily) "You knew you were supposed to kill Lee," followed by icy silence, then the same voice in the same nasty tone, "then, you stupid son of a bitch, you go kill a cop. . . ." At this point, another individual entered the room, and the first three fell silent. The newcomer, whom Mike could identify as wearing blue, "did his business, flushed the urinal, and left." The original three then concluded, "Lee will have to be killed before they take him to Washington."

Naturally uncomfortable with what he had heard, Mike remained in his hideout for a decent span of time after the three men left the room, then left. As he passed through the police locker room, one officer, in the process of changing his clothes, stared at Mike, as if to say, "Were you in there when we were?" Having been shown every available photo of officers on the Dallas police force at that time, Mike Robinson believes that the man who stared at him in a menacing way was *Roscoe White*.

Caveat emptor: Some of the narrative cited above came to light as a result of hypnosis. This is not uncommon police procedure, as witnessses to crimes can often be hypnotized and reveal details—from clothing to license plates—that they seemed totally unaware of in a conscious state. I was hypnotized in 1984 to begin the cure of a phobic concern, and I can personally report the success of the hypnosis. So if one chooses to see Mike as an opportunist, the obvious criticism is that he did not recall the entire story, although to this day, when he sees the ominous photo of Roscoe White in the Dallas Assassination Information Center, he admits that it scares the living hell out of him.

The hypnosis, which I asked a number of skeptical questions about and which will be well covered in Coke Buchanan's writings about Mike, was done by an expert with a Ph.D. in hypnotherapy. It revealed that it was Mike's deep-seated belief that one of the three bathroom individuals had something to do with an "agency." He also believes "100 percent" that Roscoe White killed J. D. Tippit.

I have checked with sources to see if it was in any way possible that Oswald could have been in that bathroom, or if media people had made statements that could have been confused. I was assured that Oswald did "his business" in his cell, or in the third-floor rest room, and that the one place that would have been off-limits to press, and thus private to officers, was the area in question.

I have shared the tip of the iceberg to support my theory. I am eagerly awaiting the publication of the full story of what Mike Robinson became privy [no pun intended] to that day.

BEVERLY OLIVER

In the Jean Hill interview produced in full above, the claim was made that Ms. Hill was in an area where there were very few spectators, which is true. Ms. Hill, however, was not alone.

With her was Mary Moorman, who was taking Polaroid photos one after another, and another individual known to researchers for years as "the babushka lady" based on the garment visible and the lack of other identifiable material.

For years, the world heard little from either Mary Moorman or the other, strangely attired female. To this day, Mary Moorman has for the most part maintained a very low profile, while Beverly Oliver, then a teenager who worked as an entertainer in places such as the Colony Club, adjacent to the Carousel, owned by Jack Ruby, has identified herself as the babushka lady. She was correctly played by a striking blonde (Lolita Davidovich) too scared to testify in *JFK*.

The common denominators among Hill, Moorman, and Oliver were their location with respect to the motorcade, and their influence with the local police, who allowed at least some of them to view the motorcade from that location. Both Jean Hill and Mary Moorman were in the process of trying to firm up relationships with Dallas officers, and Beverly Oliver knew many officers from their regular presence in establishments where she was employed.

We have heard Jean Hill's story; Mary Moorman, not called by the Warren Commission, has, for whatever reasons, chosen to remain for the most part largely silent. What about Beverly Oliver?

Essentially, her story corroborates Jean Hill's. The teenage Oliver had chosen to take her Yashica movie camera to the motorcade, and took the vast majority of her footage in Dealey Plaza, beginning when the president's car turned onto Elm and continuing through the fatal shot sequence. Like Jean Hill, when the dust settled and the various motorcade remnants had passed through, some at far higher speeds than the presidential car's 11.2 miles per hour, Beverly Oliver also headed due north, across Elm Street, and up the hill (although in her recent memoir, *Nightmare in Dallas,* she admits to no recollection of crossing the street). But when she got there, winded and with camera in hand, she had reason to lower her level of concern: There, on the knoll, were Dallas sergeant P. T. Dean and "Geneva's husband," which was how Beverly knew Roscoe White, mostly as a hanger-on around Geneva White, who was employed in clubs like Ruby's.

Seeing two officers on the knoll, Miss Oliver assumed that the situation was under control and that whoever had fired the shots from up there was in custody or was at least not a threat to anyone else immediately. In the next twenty-four hours, however, she was to learn that the assassin was, in fact, Lee Oswald, and that he had been in an upper window of the depository, not on the knoll. Theories like that troubled and frightened a witness who knew otherwise. Wisely, she kept silent.

By Monday, when she was about to enter the Colony Club (only Ruby's club closed for the entire weekend of the assassination), she was intercepted by FBI agents who demanded her film, which was as yet unprocessed. She had the film with her; but she also had a small quantity of marijuana (a far more serious breach of the law in 1963—the imprisonment of famed stripper and porno star Candy Barr had been for marijuana possession) with her, for the girls she worked with. Fearing that she would be searched and the grass found, she complied with the FBI's request for her film, which she has not seen since.

When she calmed down from that encounter, she had the presence of mind to take a quick mental inventory: How could the FBI have known she had a movie? She realized it was possible that another film, like Zapruder's, had caught her in it, but with her head covered, who could recognize her?

Then she realized who else had seen her with the camera: the same two individuals whom she had seen on the knoll, Dean and White. She is convinced to this day that they transmitted their knowledge of her film to the FBI, which led to its seizure. When shown a potpourri of unidentified photos by researcher Gary Shaw, she identified FBI agent Regis Kennedy, a case officer on the Marcello "case," for want of a better term, as the agent who seized the film.

She is also convinced to this day that her knowledge is the key to understanding the Kennedy assassination.

But just as Jean Hill's entire report could be discarded because it included the ridiculous notion of a dog, so, too, could Beverly Oliver's story be discounted because "experts" heard her story and, over-looking the serious parts of it, concluded that it was a complete hoax because the Yashica camera she claimed to have was not available in 1963 (I would provide more specifics, but I readily admit to not knowing an f-stop from a bus stop).

At the same assassination conference in Dallas at which it was revealed that Jean Hill could have seen a dog, albeit stuffed, a repre-sentative of the Yashica camera company indicated that while the camera in question was not widely available until 1965, such models were available in select areas throughout the United States in 1963.

Beverly Oliver had been vindicated.

As time passed, she married a somewhat shady individual who made his living by making other people offers they could not refuse. On one occasion, when they attended a dinner that included such other people as Charles Harrelson, Beverly, thinking herself to be among friends, finally raised the question about what happened in Dealey Plaza. "Hubby" whisked her from the table and told her in most ominous, threatening tones never to make such a reference again.

Today, Beverly Oliver M. is remarried and lives a life largely dedi-cated to God. She has retained much of the beauty for which people would have paid to see in 1963, and far more charm than one might male-chauvinistically expect from someone who had been employed in Dallas clubs in 1963, even as a singer.

She has also come forward with her story.

Other people will swear by all that's good and holy that Beverly Oliver was *not* "the babushka lady," and I've always listened politely to what they have to say. None, however, has told me just who the babushka lady really was, and if Beverly Oliver puts herself at risk to say so, who am I to say she is not?

There is also one more slight piece of corroborating evidence. In *Nightmare in Dallas* there is a photo taken as officers begin to charge toward the knoll. On the ground are Charles Brehm, a combat veteran of the Battle of the Bulge, his son, the Newmans and their children, Mary Moorman, and Jean Hill. The only standing witness is "the ba-bushka lady." That solitary young woman standing there, while everyone else is ducking, says "Beverly Oliver" to me very clearly. To know her is to place great credence in her story.

Everything else she has told me, as well as other researchers such as Gary Shaw, has credence and can be corroborated.

GENEVA AND RICKY DON WHITE

Roscoe White died in an explosion and fire at a welding outfit in 1971. Some people say he was killed and the event was made to look like an accident, while others say Roscoe made a stupid error that left him so badly burned that he died roughly twenty-six hours after the event.

On his deathbed, it is rumored that he implicated himself in the events of November 22, as well as in the "witness elimination program" that began shortly after the first event.

Two decades after his death, Roscoe's wife, Geneva, and son, Ricky Don (who was two in 1963), came forward with startling revelations: Roscoe had killed JFK. The facts were all made available, although a diary, which would have "proved" the scenario, had been "secretly stolen by the FBI," according to the Whites. In yet another point of interest, Roscoe's widow had been robbed in 1975, and when the stolen material was recovered in Arizona, it included one of the Oswald "backyard photos."

Much negotiating for book and movie rights followed, and at one point Ricky Don denied the whole story and seemingly went underground.

The ruse almost worked.

It is my serious suspicion that the Whites came forward only when researchers (and they were well ahead of me, so I seek no credit for this) were already on Roscoe's trail, mostly for circumstantial, but strongly circumstantial, reasons. The Whites then came forward, told their story, gained brief attention, *and then denied the whole thing,* destroying the validity of their confession and making the researchers who had done the real work independently of them look foolish. It was slick.

Either way, however, the Whites' statements of Roscoe's involvement cannot be forgotten simply because they tell us they would no longer have it believed.

Since then, the debate is not whether Roscoe was involved, but rather *could he have been involved?* It is a semantic debate; there are folks who swear Roscoe White was not a member of the Dallas Police Department on November 22, 1963, and they are right, but only in a technical sense. Roscoe "Rock" White signed on with the police on October 7, 1963, suggesting a confluence of activities, as this was the same seventy-two-hour period in which

Oswald returned to Texas, and it was within the time frame in which it would be decided that there would be a presidential motorcade through Dallas.

As of October 7, 1963, Roscoe White was a paid city employee. It would not be until January 1964 that he would attend the police academy, giving him complete "police officer" status. He did, however, have the necessary police connections well before November 22, and he would stay on the force until he resigned on October 7, 1965, two years to the day from the time he signed on. During those two years the president, as well as some interesting witnesses to the assassination, died.

So although he was not a police academy graduate, Roscoe was learning the ropes, as is customary before attending the academy, and he could very well have been on the knoll on that tragic Friday, as he would have had no specific assignment from the police command, nor would his time have to be strictly accounted for.

Subsequent revelations, by a researcher who has not yet proven his mettle to me, hint that White had serious intelligence connections both before and after his precise two-year police stint, and my own snooping has discovered that White left the Marine Corps, in which he had served with Oswald, for a period of hours, only to reenlist and get a nice, hefty bonus. That is a common intelligence method of paying operatives.

Regrettably, Roscoe White is unable to tell his side of the story. Neither is Patrick Dean, who made a major point in front of the Warren Commission by telling about a Canadian journalist who took photos of the TSBD during the shooting. Subsequent testimony caused commission counsel Bert Griffin to tell Dean to return the following day and plan to tell the truth. Dean did return the following day, but Griffin was not allowed to question him.

The two officers identified by Beverly Oliver skated through the "most intense investigation" ever held in America. That thought should make us all more careful when we use superlatives.

MRS. JOHN F. KENNEDY

Mrs. Kennedy testified before the Warren Commission *in camera* (at her residence in Georgetown) in early June 1964, with only Earl Warren, general counsel J. Lee Rankin, Robert Kennedy, and a stenographer present. The questioning could hardly be considered thorough, yet when Mrs. Kennedy volunteered information about her observations with respect to the president after the shots, the Warren Commission chose to print the phrase "reference to wounds deleted." The text of her statement has been made public through FOIA litigation, and it does not support the findings of the Warren Commission.

On November 22, however, Mrs. Kennedy was heard to say, "*They* have killed my husband," and when she refused to change out of her blood-stained outfit, she commented pointedly, "I want *them* to see what *they* have done to my husband" (all emphasis added).

But that was before the Warren Commission had the ability to delete fundamental truths.

CHAPTER NINE

VULNERABILITIES

A regime, an established order, is rarely overthrown by a revolutionary movement; usually a regime collapses of its own weakness and corruption and then a revolutionary movement enters among the ruins and takes over the powers that have become vacant.

—WALTER LIPPMANN, 1958

WALTER LIPPMANN'S APOSTROPHE to Charles de Gaulle (himself a target of assassins) is in no way meant to take a step back from any thesis advanced in this book; on the contrary, a careful reading of the ever-astute Lippmann's comments reinforces what has already been suggested about the Kennedy assassination as an act of self-preservation.

There was corruption, to be sure, but it was in the 1964 projected ticket of Kennedy and Johnson, rather than anything inherent in the thousand days of John Kennedy. Lyndon Johnson's scandals had become "a cancer in the heart of the presidency," as future presidential counsel John Dean would say, and when the Kennedy-Johnson regime was removed, a revolutionary movement, LBJ's "guns and butter" (which turned out to be more guns than butter) filled the void created in Dealey Plaza.

There were many vulnerabilities in and around Dallas, Texas, on the weekend of the tragedy under study here. No understanding of the events of that weekend can be complete without a review of how those vulnerabilities all converged in a few seconds in a pastoral part of Dallas called Dealey Plaza.

John Kennedy had four vulnerabilities: his health; the deterioration of his marriage due to numerous infidelities; his willingness to move American policy in directions that challenged those who were entrenched in the corridors of power; and the political scandals about to destroy his vice president. The last two, of course, have the most bearing on this study.

Lyndon Johnson had at least an equal number of vulnerabilities: Bobby Baker; Billy Sol Estes; the dossier his "friend" Hoover had on him; the brewing TFX scandal; his fear of losing his place on the national ticket, or worse, the fear that instead of receiving a VIP license plate, he would wind up making them; and the abilities of other powerful Texans to manipulate LBJ's vulnerabilities to suit their own interests in a situation that left him little leeway and a worst-case scenario in which he would become president.

J. Edgar Hoover, a surprise visitor to the Greater Dallas area the evening before John Kennedy's murder, had one vulnerability in addition to his sexual orientation: If JFK had returned to Washington aboard *Air Force One* alive, Hoover would be receiving a gold watch and handshakes upon his retirement within 1.16 years.

Jack Ruby had vulnerabilities that amounted to approximately $100,000, an unusually high debt for someone assumed to be a member of the most fiscally sound business conglomerate in America.

J. D. Tippit had the responsibility of taking care of a wife and three children on a police salary of $490 per month, plus what he could earn moonlighting. Tippit was also aware that he was to become a father again and that his wife was *not* pregnant. The subsequent daughter born of that liaison recently passed away; she was in her late twenties.

Lee Oswald had more vulnerabilities than could be reasonably cataloged. His marines career had been a failure, except to note that he had done sufficient posturing to be considered a died-in-the-wool "Red" in the marines, of all places, and this quite likely led to a nickel/dime black op assignment in the Soviet Union that proved of little consequence. Three years after his "defection" and the State Department's haste to get the treasonous Oswald back by paying his way and waiving regulations regarding the admission of Oswald's Soviet wife, he had little to show for a life that somehow always managed to fall well short of its owner's unrealistic fantasies. His weak black op involvement in the events in Dealey Plaza was to have changed all that, and one could argue that in a way it did. But certainly not as Oswald expected.

Vulnerabilities also abounded among a myriad of faceless persons and companies who depended on bellicosity and saber-rattling for their survival. Their vulnerability was the threat of a generation of peace envisioned following the reelection of John F. Kennedy.

The Dallas police, like most southern big-city departments a generation ago, had its own vulnerabilities. While blue-ribbon commissions are still at work to solve police corruption in a variety of cities as America has reached the mid-1990s, such a commission would have had a field day investigating the minor shakedowns and unlawful perks available to Dallas's finest in 1963. Such knowledge, in the hands of power brokers, combined with the officers' (the handful involved, not the entire department) natural politics, made them an easy target to approach for the ultimate black op.

When Americans awoke to return to their normal pursuits on Tuesday, November 26, 1963, their nation, as well as their spirit, their national pride, and their belief in their nation, had been forever altered.

John Kennedy was no longer vulnerable as he lay in quiet repose on a peaceful hillside overlooking the city he had owned only a few short days before. What remained was to convince the world that his biggest vulnerability as president was the ever-present threat of a lone nut with an agenda. Once that was accomplished, his reputation would be diminished by leaks regarding his extramarital affairs, in effect dimming the light that shone on Camelot.

Lyndon Johnson awoke in Washington on November 26 knowing that he now had the power to save his political hide, but at the price of providing a war to those operators and entrepreneurs who stalked the corridors of power; at the price of appointing a federally controlled investigating body to ratify the lone-nut theory regarding the death of his predecessor; at the price of being a hostage to the monied interests in Texas; and at the price of appointing J. Edgar Hoover FBI director for life without being too immediately obvious about it. All told, it was a high price to pay, but it proved to be cost-effective, and it yielded a handsome return.

J. Edgar Hoover, in less time than it takes to recall that his first name was John, had become a happy man, having been spared his ultimate vulnerability, retirement, and safe in the knowledge that he would never again have to deal with John Kennedy and that future dealings with Robert Kennedy would assume quite a different tone. Quicker than one could say "lone Commie assassin," the telephone line connecting the attorney general's office to Hoover's private office was removed and relocated on the desk of Helen Gandy, Hoover's secretary, where it could be ignored.

The question of Jack Ruby's debts will never fully be known, but it can be inferred that *he* never had to pay them. It is also likely that except for his sudden case of cancer, Ruby would have been a free man—and something of a celebrity—before the end of 1967. That was not to be, however, as a living, breathing Jack Ruby posed a serious vulnerability to those with other, different vulnerabilities, whom he had assisted in the events of 1963, and he could not be allowed to be loose to speak his mind. As events transpired, he wasn't and he didn't.

J. D. Tippit's vulnerabilities ended as suddenly on November 22, 1963, as did JFK's, and Tippit's family's suffering was assuaged by an immense, if unknown in terms of total or source, amount of money in 1963 dollars. As an officer slain in the line of duty, he became the hero of the piece, and his as-yet unborn child drew no attention.

Lee Oswald's vulnerabilities grew from Friday afternoon until Sunday morning, when they, too, were suddenly and swiftly taken from him by another member of the dramatis personae of this study whose vulnerabilities had demanded that he attend to Oswald's as well as his own. Through the goodness of Americans, Mrs. Oswald was briefly sustained, but has struck out on her own, to become an American citizen and to learn the truth. To date, she has accomplished one of those goals.

The power brokers lost all vulnerabilities on November 22, 1963, and benefited immensely from the elevation of a Texan who was in no position to challenge them. On the contrary, they would subsequently receive the financial largesse of an Asian genocide that cost over one million lives to no purpose—unless, of course, one considers war profiteering and national debt brokering "purposes."

The Dallas police, because of the suggested involvement of a tiny fraction of their number on November 22, stonewalled the investigation at the time, did their best to keep the awful truth within the department, and were rewarded, in circuitous ways, for their efforts on November 22.

Theirs is the remaining vulnerability, and they have kept silent.

Of the principal individuals cited in this chapter—JFK, LBJ, Hoover, Ruby, Tippit, and Oswald—three were dead before the president was lowered into the ground. Ruby survived an additional three years. Hoover was still on his throne when his end came on May 2, 1972, and his records and his home were well sanitized before the world knew of his passing. Ironically, LBJ was the last to go, in January 1973, and it is safe to assume that he took a veritable cache of secrets with him. One can only hope that he was wearing asbestos pajamas when he died in his sleep.

None of the vulnerables was alive on November 22, 1973; the full truth was not known at the dedication of Dealey Plaza on November 22, 1993.

Book Two

Red Patsy

CHAPTER ONE

LIFE BE NOT PROUD

As the free press develops, the paramount point is whether the journalist, like the scientist or scholar, puts truth in the first place or in the second.

—WALTER LIPPMAN, 1965

THERE IS A GREAT DEAL that is still neither clear nor clearly understood about the person we have come to identify as Lee Oswald. Researcher Philip Melanson, in *Spy Saga*, summed up these frustrations about Oswald with an all-encompassing sketch: ". . . disgruntled loner and muddled leftist, a Russian spy, a pro-Castroite pawn of the Castro government, a low-level Mafia pawn, and a U.S. intelligence agent."[1]

There is one thing we do know for certain: The "Lee Oswald" who was in Dallas police custody was shot by Jack Ruby, a very good friend of the police establishment, at 11:21 A.M. CST on November 24, 1963. Unshackled on the cold concrete floor, Oswald was then, despite the presence of a physician, mistakenly given artificial respiration, a deleterious medical procedure for someone bleeding internally. One of the first officers to reach the stricken prisoner indicated that he believed the wound to be grave, and asked a still-coherent Oswald if he wanted to make a statement. Oswald moved his head as if to say "no." He was then rushed to Parkland Hospital, but was treated in a different trauma-emergency bay than the one in which the president had been declared dead two days prior, as it was seen as almost sacrilegious to put the *alleged assassin* in the same emergency room as the president. Despite the oaths taken by physicians to heal the sick, there are no subparagraphs about *where* they have to heal them.

Despite valiant efforts by Dr. Malcolm Perry, who had attended the president on Friday, and who believed he had come very close to saving Oswald, the patient was pronounced dead at 1:07 P.M., two days and seven minutes after John Kennedy had been pronounced dead.[2]

Oswald was killed on television, and perhaps in part because of television, as several of the officers in the escort party indicated that once the statement "Here he comes" was made by media onlookers, banks of lights came on for the live feed telecast, and some of the officers were briefly blinded or had their visual acuity, such as it should have been in a protection scenario, impaired. In those few seconds, Ruby emerged from the crowd, fired his one shot, closed the case, and was subdued.

In those few seconds, "the tube" came of age. It has been estimated that sixty million people saw this first-ever live murder on television. The other two thirds of the American population who missed it "live" were given numerous opportunities to see reruns, and they were available on all channels. This was an event bigger, it seemed, than petty program infighting. Viewers who had been watching the transfer of the president's remains from the White House to the Capitol rotunda were switched back and forth from the Oswald shooting to the endless line of mourners hoping to get in the Capitol door before it was closed.

What should have been a day of national reflection became a day of both national horror and inward celebration. While Americans had been sharing the private grief of Mrs. Kennedy and the children, as well as their own feelings for America, they were now struck forever with the slow-motion image of Ruby lunging, Oswald recoiling, and Detective Jim Leavelle frozen in a grimace that seemed to say, "What is this all about?" Outwardly, the American penchant for violence stemming from Friday's events had been multiplied by Sunday's. We looked bad in the eyes of the world and in our own, and we knew it. Inwardly, however, many Americans, already convinced of Oswald's guilt *and politics*, were privately ecstatic that the Commie creep had been dealt swift, Texas-style justice.

So despite the many questions about Oswald's life in the 2,587 days between his enlistment in the Marine Corps six days after his seventeenth birthday and his death, 37 days after his twenty-fourth birthday, the cause of his death is not in doubt. But even in an event so cut and dried, questions are raised that beg for answers, and in a counterpoint to the thrust of the discussion so far—death—the questions surround *Life*.

Oswald's death was shown on television literally too many times to count. We all heard the auto, the horn, the shot, and Robert Huffaker announcing, "He's been shot. Oswald has been shot. . . ." It was big news. But far bigger news, so big that it would dwarf anything that ever happened to Lee Oswald, had been the death of President Kennedy, and we were *not* shown existing footage of *that*.

Why not? On November 22, Time-Life purchased the Zapruder film, 486 frames or 26.55 seconds of American tragedy, for $150,000—well over $1 million in today's spending power. That film was first aired on television *in 1975*. What were Time-Life's executives waiting for—a huge offer so they could show a sizable profit on their 1963 investment? Such a scenario hardly seems likely.

Why wasn't the Zapruder film shown? One could argue that it was not shown out of deference to the president and his family, but the other side of the argument is that whether you agree or not, the death of a president is news, and it is difficult to imagine a network programmer thinking, *Well, we've got this movie of Kennedy being shot; I wonder if it would trouble the family . . . ?* Of course it would, but that would *never* stop *anyone* in a control room.

It could also be argued that the all-too-real *tour de force* seen by Zapruder's lens would be too much for the populace, but that, too, is a specious argument. It certainly could have been preceded by an announcement suggesting that a home movie, taken in Dealey Plaza and showing in gruesome detail the death of the president, would follow. Sensitive viewers, or those who would be upset by either the basic content or the organic display, should change channels for one minute. That, too, did not happen.

The third argument is that people seeing the Zapruder film might be led to the conclusion that it showed the president being hit from the right front, and that just would not be acceptable. As it happened, the biggest "home video" ever made remained unseen by the public for a dozen years. So the question remains: Why would a news-gathering conglomerate spend $150,000 and do nothing more than print a few stills of the movie? *The movie* was the event.

Life's involvement did not end there, however. First, there are very strong suspicions within the research community that the film was quickly circulated through law-enforcement and intelligence groups and "sanitized." (This suspicion is far easier to raise than to document, however, and valid pro and con arguments have been made.) Beyond that, *Life* quickly rushed out a Kennedy issue with a full-page, black-bordered portrait of the pensive JFK on the cover. Inside were small, black-and-white frames from the film that did not suggest the front-to-back motion of the president following the fatal wound. The black-and-white photos were used, it was said, because there was an urgency to replace the already printed Roger Staubach *Life* with the JFK cover, and to create the color process would have taken too long. (Yet they waited twelve years to show the movie. . . .)

Very shortly thereafter, a "John F. Kennedy Memorial Edition" appeared, bearing a smaller version of the same portrait and including different, color frames from the Zapruder film. Of greater importance, *Life* printed the "official" version insofar as it was known at the time. In the caption for the first two photos, *Life* gave credence both to Parkland testimony and the lone-gunman theory: "FIRST TWO SHOTS. Past the book warehouse the President turned to his right to wave to someone (1). Just as his car passed behind the road sign shown in the foreground the first bullet struck him *in the neck* [emphasis added]. He clutched at his throat(2)."[3] The "magic bullet" theory, not yet necessary, was not considered, as *Life* noted, "Although some onlookers heard the shot, Governor Connally still faced ahead, unaware (3)."[4]

Pictures 4 and 5, on the same two-page layout, bear the caption "STRICKEN." *Life* noted, "With the first bullet *still lodged in him*, the President slumped forward in his seat and down toward his wife (4). At the same time the second shot struck Governor Connally. . . . Then the assassin fired a third time."[5] In larger type at the top of the page, Lee Oswald was identified as the assassin and the reader was told he fired three times. By this time, of course, the assassin was dead, and the word "alleged" was not necessary. Of equal import, that issue is today a collector's item—particularly a copy from the *initial* press run, quickly aborted, which indicated that frame Z313 showed a *frontal* shot.

Having made these gaffes, some of which the Warren Commission would have to deal with, *Life* recouped some of its standing with officialdom in Washington by printing its February 21, 1964, issue with Oswald on the cover. Shown in a "backyard photo" admittedly retouched, Oswald was portrayed in the cover story as *the assassin*, a decision the Warren Commission had reached in private but would not publish for another seven months.[6] It is hard to accept as coincidence that *Life* published that cover and story at the same time that the Warren Commission would take testimony from its first three witnesses: Marina *Oswald,* Marguerite *Oswald,* and Robert L. *Oswald.* How could those people, especially Marina, who grew up in Stalinist Russia, and Robert, who had somehow to go on with his life despite the stigma suddenly attached to his name, be expected to give honest and objective testimony when the person they are testifying about has his picture and assumed guilt trumpeted on the cover of *Life*? In the same issue, *Life*'s readers were told "On the rifle range, 'he was excellent,' " based on accounts by Garland Slack and Malcolm Price, who we now know were viewing impostors. *Life* should have seen Price's Warren Commission testimony, which, under oath, indicated that he had seen Oswald at the rifle range on the Sunday *after Thanksgiving, exactly one week after Lee Oswald died.*

Life magazine, it should also be noted, gave a resounding endorsement of the Warren Commission in its first issue after the release of the Report, an issue that would also include stills from the Zapruder film. Those stills, it should be added, were clear, and nothing like the grainy, pasty stills that appear in Volume XVIII of the Warren Commission exhibits. Did the commission work from a good print of the film, or the kind of poor, bootleg copy that was circulating in the 1970s? That issue is as yet unresolved.

It would not be until the third anniversary of the president's death, in November 1966, that *Life* would have a cover showing Z230, with Connally seemingly not wounded, and would have a title saying simply, "A Matter of Reasonable Doubt."[7] Had anyone at *Life* read their captions of the JFK memorial issue, the question would have been a matter of reasonable doubt *in 1963.*

Later, in 1967, *Life* printed additional photographic materials— many of great value—but as set pieces in a narrative by John Connally. He explained why Kennedy went to Texas (against Connally's advice, we are told), and that it was "Kennedy's advance men" who planned the motorcade route. Like the Warren Commission, *Life* showed no curiosity about pursuing Mr. Connally's concerns for JFK's safety, his comments about some wrangling over seating arrangements in the motorcade, or his knowledge of which advance men picked the route.[8]

Why did Oswald's death, but not Kennedy's, get lengthy television coverage? Why did *Life* pay so much money for something that gave them such little return? Was the February issue, which further convicted Oswald, just a coincidence? Why, suddenly, in 1966, did *Life* get religion? And finally, why, when they commissioned Josiah Thompson to study the assassination and he did so with thoroughness and deep insight, did *Life* then pull the rug out from underneath him and force him to use artist's renderings of the various Zapruder frames and not the clear originals? Although the worth of *Six Seconds in Dallas* was not in this way diminished, the proof—the drawings—were watered down. *Why?*

The sudden, shocking, and televised death of Oswald seemed to certify all that had been suspected of him, although in truth, to be shot on television does not make one guilty as charged. Both Kennedy, in a hero's funeral, and Oswald, in a very private ceremony from which his half brother was excluded, were laid to rest the following day. Temporarily, thanks to *Life*'s silence, so were the doubts.

CHAPTER TWO

OF MARINES AND MEN

And when he goes to heaven, to St. Peter he will tell,
Another marine reporting, sir;
I've served my time in hell!

— GRAVE EPITAPH, GUADALCANAL, 1942

IN HIS FORMATIVE YEARS, Oswald drifted in and out of several schools, succeeded at nothing, and gave no indication of any professed desire on his part to enlist in the marines and be taught to destroy human lives. His brother Robert and half brother John Pic believed then, and testified later, that their brother's wish to enter the service stemmed from a desire to separate himself from his mother, Marguerite. Thus we find Oswald trying, and failing, to enter the Marine Corps before his seventeenth birthday. We must also suggest that Oswald could have separated himself from his mother by walking out the front door and getting a job, but that does not seem to be the course that history was to take.

Told he must wait until reaching age seventeen, Oswald began to display a duality of behavior that would raise many subsequent questions. On October 3, 1956, three weeks before he succeeded in joining the marines, he wrote to *The Socialist Call* to tell them, "I am a marxist and have been studying socialist principles for well over fifteen months. . . ."[1]

The labyrinth is thus entered. While we know that Oswald was learning the Marine Corps manual by heart and reading Karl Marx at the same time, he was also writing for socialist literature, which would arrive at just about the same time that Oswald swore to die, if necessary, for his country. Weeding the genuine Oswald out of the proliferating personalities continues to pose a challenge for anyone who would subsequently meet—or study—Lee Oswald.

The paradox began in basic training. Allen R. Felde, who was also a marine recruit in 1956, recalled Oswald constantly talking politics, and criticizing Truman's and Eisenhower's handling of the Korean situation. Felde also remembered that Oswald kept up a regular correspondence with American politicians, Strom Thurmond among them, to complain of existing conditions in the United States. Felde also recalled Oswald riding with other recruits on leave time, but that Oswald always went his own way when the destination was reached. Felde couldn't recall if Oswald was a good shot or not, suggesting he was not noteworthy for being either expert or very poor.[2] Edward J. Epstein, who has made the most detailed study of Oswald's marine acquaintances (a far more thorough look than the Warren Commission provided), indicated that there was a clear consensus among other marines that Oswald was the nonviolent type, and was not one to fight back.[3]

As Oswald's marine "career" continued, the duality of personality was enlarged by the emergence of a "Red" in the U.S. Marine Corps, one of the least likely places one would expect to find an individual openly practicing and espousing such beliefs. Henry Hurt, in *Reasonable Doubt,* titled a chapter "PFC Oswaldskovitch: The Oddest Leatherneck," and researcher Philip Melanson titled a chapter "The Pinko Marine."[4]

The outlines of the story are familiar: Oswald was receiving literature printed in the Soviet Union, playing Russian music in the barracks, calling fellow marines "comrade," and when the other marines complained to superiors, nothing was done. In spite of this attitude, Oswald wound up being assigned to one of the most sensitive marine posts on the planet. As researcher Melanson concluded, "The Marine Corps is not renowned as a bastion of liberal tolerance and free thinking, but it acted in Oswald's case as if it were."[5] In 1995 it was front-page controversy to consider allowing a "gay" to join the marines; in 1957, a matter of months after the cessation of McCarthyism, it would have been extremely difficult to imagine a possible "Red" openly flaunting his political persuasion and being given sensitive work and a top security clearance. "Red was as bad as it got in the early 1960s," Mark Lane would later write.[6]

Parallel concerns are Oswald's finances and behavior while in Japan. Fellow marines recall Oswald, while stationed at the Atsugi U-2 staging area, dating women whose social needs would be well beyond the reach of Oswald's finances. On October 27, 1957, Oswald received a self-inflicted wound from a toylike weapon more suited for a lady's handbag than for a fighting leatherneck who had access to all kinds of weapons and would not need a smallish spy weapon. Yet Oswald was detained in the hospital for three weeks because of the flesh wound, and was later court-martialed for having the weapon in his possession. He would subsequently be court-martialed a second time, and "serve time" on that occasion, yet other marines claimed they saw Oswald out and about in civilian clothes during the time of his supposed confinement.[7]

These events raise serious questions. Did Oswald's dating habits financially compromise him? How would Oswald later finance his defection in light of these spending sprees? Were the three-week hospital stay and the court-martial sentence just excuses to separate him from his unit for other activities? "Whatever Oswald's security clearance," Philip Melanson has written, "his presence in the bubble ensured that he would possess information 'useful' to the Soviets."[8] In the Soviet Union of 1959, a dishwasher was "useful"; what Oswald knew about the U-2 would have been pure gold to the Soviets.

Yet somehow the Marine Corps never quite viewed it that way. J. Edgar Hoover would later tell the Warren Commission that the FBI checked with the Marine Corps in November 1959 when Oswald's defection became known: "No derogatory information was contained in the USMC files concerning Oswald. . . ."[9] We can infer from that datum that either courts-martial were not considered derogatory, or they were straw men to cover other events occurring in the career of Lee Oswald.

In an in-house document, the Marine Corps used even more circumspect, and therefore *suspect*, language regarding Oswald's access and clearance priorities:

There is no evidence contained in the personnel file that OSWALD'S security clearance was ever terminated, nor is there evidence that he was granted access to any information of higher than confidential characterization. It was, however, the practice of the Marine Corps, that on occasions where assignments, similar to OSWALD'S, required a higher clearance than confidential in order to perform specific classified electronic duties, personnel with clearance commensurate with the duties to be performed were assigned thereto.[10]

Researchers, however, have drawn their own conclusions. Dick Russell insists that Oswald had "CIA connections in Japan,"[11] and this should not be at all surprising, since the U-2, which Oswald tracked, was a CIA operation. Former CIA operative Victor Marchetti wrote of an Office of Naval Intelligence program, contemporary with the marine career of Oswald, to recruit a few dozen "loner types" to go to the Soviet Union and see communism up close. Researcher Jim Marrs carried Marchetti's theory one step farther, showing how the U.S. servicemen defecting to Russia showed a sudden increase at about the time of Oswald's departure.[12]

We have already seen that the Marine Corps purchased four million rounds of Mannlicher-Carcano ammunition in the 1950s, and since it was unusable in any American-produced or -issued weapons, we can only attach a sinister, covert purpose to that consignment.

James A. Wilcott, a reputed CIA finance officer, told the House select committee that Oswald had been recruited from the military for a Soviet penetration (with the military possibly using the otherwise unexplained death of marine Martin Schrand as a "hook" into Oswald), and that he, Wilcott, had handled some of the finances involved in the Oswald recruitment. Although the scenario is plausible, this author is dubious of Wilcott's bona fides, in the absence of documentation to support the allegation. Of course, given its CIA origin, such absence should not be considered shocking.

Oswald's marine records, as reported to the Warren Commission, contained a couple of curious anomalies. From Allison G. Folsom exhibit 1, we learned that at the time of induction, Oswald's eyes were hazel. Subsequently, under "testing and special qualifications" appeared the simple listing "Russian." In a March 1959 physical exam, Oswald was measured at seventy-one inches, or five feet, eleven inches, with gray eyes.[13] This suggests that the Marine Corps was willing to recognize Oswald's Russian skills, and a skill unused is a skill abused. Also of note is the fact that Oswald's eye color changed during his marine service (five different eye colors would be noted in various documents), and the Oswald killed in the basement of police headquarters was two inches shorter, at autopsy, than the Oswald discharged from the marines (a testament, perhaps, to the severity of Russian winters).

In an elliptical reference, we learn that "On June 28, 1961 [while Oswald was in Russia], Dallas confidential informant T-1 advised that subject [Oswald] had special educational training while in the U.S. Marine Corps. . . ."[14] This suggests two possibilities: Oswald was getting more "education" than the Marine Corps was admitting to, perhaps in the area of Russian language and customs, or else the FBI was paying informants for information they could have had for free from Oswald's Marine Corps file, if it was honest.

Well before that document came to light, however, Warren Commission chief counsel J. Lee Rankin wanted to know what languages Oswald had studied at the language school at Monterey.[15] Whatever was learned as a result of their curiosity was not published, as we are still left to believe that Oswald was self-taught in Russian, an astounding ability for someone with a history of truancy, horrendous spelling, and no high school diploma.

Having completed what many believe to be his "sheepdipping" (preparation of a cover story—including his "Red" posturing and his courts-martial, proving disenchantment), Oswald asked the American government for a premature discharge from the marines, on the unchecked pretext that his mother needed him. In addition to a discharge, he requested a passport, and forces within the American government provided the twice court-martialed marine with both the discharge and the passport, and in haste. It was apparently never thought through—or was it?—*but why would someone requesting a hardship discharge to help his mother in New Orleans want or need a passport?* This constitutes a further strong indication that Oswald's "defection" had "Made in U.S.A." stamped on it.

In taking his leave from the Marine Corps, Oswald signed the traditional statement that he could be recalled to duty and again court-martialed if he disclosed information that should remain secret. Apparently this was overlooked when Lee Oswald, the former U-2 radar plotter, returned from the Soviet Union approximately two years after the Soviets downed Gary Powers' U-2, wrecking the Paris summit conference and preventing peace from breaking out. Perhaps Oswald was not court-martialed because the marines felt sorry for him because his eye coloration kept changing and he had shrunk two inches.

As researcher Epstein has demonstrated, Oswald's marine buddies were asked many questions by unidentified investigators after Oswald's defection.[16] What is interesting in this episode is that we do *not* know the thrust of their investigation. Were they checking up on security violations of a genuine defection, or were they making sure that Oswald's cover had not been blown in the marines? And if so, were they, by their mere presence, reinforcing it?

The Warren Commission believed that Oswald had been plan-

ning to defect for at least two years prior to the event, but this
somewhat defies logic, for if Oswald truly was considering such a
betrayal, he would have been of much greater value to the Soviets
by staying in the marines.[17] The group that therefore benefited most
from his trip to Russia was the U.S. intelligence community, not
the Soviets.

Warren Commission exhibit 1150 informed us that Oswald's bank
balance at the time of his leave-taking from the marines was $203.
His USMC separation pay was $219.20, but some of those funds
were needed to return to Texas, and while there he spared his mother
a pittance.[18] Where and how he got the $1500 to finance his Russian
sojourn is as yet unsolved but lends itself to some obvious
speculations.

After his discharge, Oswald's "honorable discharge" was downgraded to a "less than honorable" discharge *from the Marine Corps
Reserve*. The reasons were clear and cogent: As a resident of Minsk,
USSR, Oswald was unable to attend the monthly reserve meetings,
and his status was changed. This is not to be confused, however,
with the standard interpretation of a dishonorable discharge from
the marines; they are not the same. Nevertheless, the change in
discharge may also have been a boost to his bona fides, and the
charade was no doubt continued when he returned home and
made a constant stink about having his discharge upgraded, although surprisingly, there is no hint whatsoever that Oswald, once
back in the United States, ever took notice of, or attended any
meetings of, the Marine Corps Reserve. He simply postured about
the semantics of one document.[19]

The enigma was almost complete. In a report of an FBI interview,
Marina Oswald was quoted as saying, "In his [Oswald's] brief recollections to her of his military service, he left the impression that he
had enjoyed that service."[20] Marina would not be asked about this
by the Warren Commission.

A gung-ho teenager joined the marines with his head full of
Karl Marx; he then became the nonviolent political spokesman of
discontent in America, all from a marine barracks. He openly
flaunted all things Russian. He was assigned to a top-secret intelligence unit, where he learned of the most secret espionage weapon
in the American arsenal. A series of events seemed to compromise
him and weaken his finances. He was removed from his unit on
two occasions, and the Russian language showed up on his marine

records. He asked for and received a quick discharge with no questions asked, and then made straight for Mother Russia on somebody else's bankroll.

A profile such as that would suggest serious criminal charges should the "subject" ever return to the United States. But Oswald had not yet completed his "betrayal," and the charges were never brought.

CHAPTER THREE

TO RUSSIA, WITH LOVE

A riddle wrapped in a mystery cloaked in an enigma.

—WINSTON CHURCHILL, commenting on Russia

HAVING OBTAINED A FRAUDULENT DISCHARGE from the Marine Corps based on his mother's medical infirmities, which simply did not exist in September 1959, Oswald returned to Texas, paid his family a brief visit, and departed for the Soviet Union. To this day, however, both his means and motives for the Soviet sojourn remain shrouded in mystery.

The possibilities are narrow. He may have been a genuine defector, gone to find happiness in the workers' paradise. If this were true, however, there would have been no need for the subsequent noisy posturing that occurred at the U.S. embassy in Moscow, or for Oswald's return to America.

A second possibility is that his defection, along with his secrets, would help him rise above the radio manufacturer in Minsk that he was to become. The question then arises, "What secrets?" The Russians already knew about the U-2 and its successful history of over-flights; they also were painfully aware that they could not shoot it down. Oswald's knowledge, while vital, had little or no practical application to them. But make no mistake about it: Oswald was questioned, and intensely, Yuri Nosenko's disclaimers to the contrary notwithstanding.

Given that, what could Lee Oswald have told them? "If you can just get the pilot to keep it under sixty thousand feet, you'll have a chance"? Not likely. Beyond his awareness of the U-2, there was very little in Oswald's ken that would have been of life-and-death interest to the Soviets (although it must be noted that the Soviets were always looking), as what codes or radio frequencies Oswald knew would be subject to regular changes, particularly if, in fact, someone who knew them "defected" to America's most serious and deadly Cold War enemy.

So much for being on the Russian side. The other possibility is that we sent him, perhaps as nothing more than espionage cannon fodder, with the assumption that while the Russians were busy figuring Oswald out, a real spy could avoid their dragnet. Or he was sent to see how a defector would be treated. Or he was sent to tell the Russians the God's honest truth, which they already knew, but it would generate much mirth in the United States intelligence community to rub the Soviets' noses in manure. Simply put, the U-2 at ninety thousand feet was untouchable. Oswald could have told the Soviets all he knew and, as noted, it would not have helped them.

An examination of the events subsequent to his arrival may tell us a great deal about which side of the fence "Comrade Oswald" was sitting on.

Upon his arrival in the Soviet Union on a temporary visa, he was given an instructive gift by his Russian hosts, a copy of Dostoevsky's *The Idiot,* a symbolic gesture suggesting that the Soviets knew exactly who—and what—Oswald was.[1]

While awaiting word of his acceptance into Russian society, Oswald gave two interviews to American journalists in Moscow. Priscilla Johnson would later testify that her interview with Oswald left her with the feeling that "the plight of the U.S. Negro brought him to the USSR."[2] This is a difficult thesis to reconcile, given Oswald's later relationships with Guy Banister et al. (hardly civil rights fanatics), Oswald's seeming absence of civil rights concerns in the United States (the "Clinton, Louisiana" posturing aside), and finally, what could Oswald possibly do about the plight of the U.S. Negro from far-off Russia?

When Aline Mosby interviewed him, she indicated, "Beyond his *brown eyes* [emphasis added], I felt a certain coldness." She also indicated that some of Oswald's statements sounded rehearsed (a claim that others would make), and she told of Oswald's boast that he saved the $1,500 necessary for the trip. She concluded that she considered defectors to fall generally within one of two categories, but "Oswald appeared to be a one-man third category."[3] Indeed . . .

Both journalists tended to agree that Oswald was overplaying his "defector" role and that the Soviets wouldn't buy it.[4] Oswald, however, had to go through the ritual, as he had to know, or have been taught, that the Soviets were listening.

To reinforce his credentials, Oswald staged a performance for the benefit of consuls Snyder and McVickar at the U.S. embassy in Moscow, conveniently attempting to renounce his citizenship at a time when the embassy was closed. Documents from this event suggest Oswald would offer secrets, or "has offered"[5] secrets to the Russians, but his knowledge, as suggested above, was of little immediate, practical value, as well as causing some embarrassment to the Russians, who once again, however, were listening. Oswald would later deny such offers, and readily admit that he was interviewed upon arrival and before departure by the MVD, whom Oswald termed "the secret police."[6] Oswald may have known the Russian language and its complicated Cyrillic alphabet, but there is a world of difference between "MVD" and "KGB."

Author (and self-confessed coconspirator) Robert Morrow has postulated that Oswald was sent to Russia to marry Marina in order to get her uncle to defect.[7] This defies credibility, as it suggests a search that makes the needle in the haystack seem easy, and it also flies in the face of an admission from Marina that the only marital difficulties the Oswalds had in Russia revolved around Lee's unwillingness to inform Marina's relatives that the newlyweds were returning to the United States.[8]

Of equal interest would be subsequent comment by Yuri Nosenko, who suddenly decided to defect to America after the president's assassination, that the Soviets had no interest in Oswald, and the sworn affidavit of CIA director McCone, dated May 18, 1964 (shortly after Nosenko's arrival), that the CIA had never heard of Oswald.[9] Both denials beg the issue: Both countries, by the very nature of their respective intelligence apparatuses, *had to know about Oswald*. What they are telling us is that *they did not want to know about Oswald*. Warren Commission Exhibit 917 demonstrates this "ostrich" approach to the Oswald dilemma, as it mentions "defection of LEE HARVEY OSWALD, former Marine and [deleted]."[10] Former marine and *what*? There is no reason to delete something innocent; it is only the sinister that must remain hidden.

Oswald was giving it his best shot, but the Soviets were not buying, so he had to up the ante, filling a bathtub with water and slitting his wrist after leaving a poetic suicide note. This raises the most obvious question: How can someone who was unable to kill himself at a distance of *two inches* subsequently be far more successful when dealing with a moving target at 265 feet?

Once Oswald was accepted on a temporary basis by the Soviets, he was shipped off to Minsk (which, according to Consul Snyder, was punishment enough), where he would make radios and become weary of a regular diet of cabbage. In subsequent ruminations, Oswald would write much that was far more anti-Soviet than anti-American.[11]

Marina Oswald would later testify that Oswald did not take a liking to "Russian Communists" and that Oswald *refused* to become a Soviet citizen, although she did admit that Oswald made a radio appearance in the USSR providing "propaganda in favor of the Soviet Union."[12]

Six months after Oswald's arrival in Russia, a U-2 spy plane was shot down, but unless someone can prove that Oswald was responsible for the plane being at sixty-five thousand feet altitude instead of the usual ninety thousand feet, it is nothing more than grist for the "Red patsy" mill. The critical timing in the loss of the U-2, combined with America's unwillingness to be forthcoming with respect to it, rendered the upcoming Paris summit conference stillborn and guaranteed the continuance of the Cold War, with all its inherent bellicosity, rhetoric, and defense spending. Much the same conclusion could be drawn with respect to the events of November 22, 1963.

In a letter to brother Robert (with whom Lee had broken off communications at the time of the defection), Oswald wrote on February 15, 1962, that he had seen Gary Powers, the pilot of the U-2. The letter also expressed curiosity about Oswald's press clippings back home.[13] Since Oswald could not know for sure, but had to assume that his mail was being read at both ends, this particular letter served two eloquent public relations functions: tying himself to the U-2, and noting a desire for fame or publicity. The same letter chided Robert for not answering an earlier letter, raising the question of whether that first letter was detoured by U.S. or Soviet intelligence. Inasmuch as the Russians had Oswald making radios and eating cabbage, and the United States would soon pay Oswald's way back, it seems clear that the lost letter became inadvertently misplaced on their side of the Iron Curtain.

Author Edward Epstein cited reports that the CIA was in regular contact with an ex-marine working in a radio factory in Minsk,[14] suggesting either that Oswald was, in fact, a low-grade "intelligence" operative capable of providing the CIA with everything they wanted to know about the state of the art in cheap commercial Russian radios, or that someone else was reporting to the CIA and that the Marine Corps had become a training station for future Russian radio workers.

While Oswald was busily engaged in his electronics career, the CIA was becoming involved in the debriefing of thousands of tourists who visited the Soviet Union every year. When "defector" Robert Webster returned from his sojourn in the USSR, he was extensively debriefed by the CIA.[15] Why wasn't Oswald?

Or was he?

Amid the radios and the cabbage, a lovely young woman named Marina Prussokova entered Lee Oswald's life, and her story is also instructive. While her testimony regarding Oswald and his rifle would subsequently go far to certify his guilt in the eyes of the American public, she also told of his ownership of a rifle in Russia, adding that he was "unsuccessful in bagging any game."[16] Marina also indicated that if she had known of any desire by Lee to return to the United States, she would not have married him.[17] But the Russian émigré community would later be unanimous about two things, and one was that Marina married Lee to get out of Russia.

Researcher Jim Marrs discovered that Marina's "identity" seemed to change at the time of the marriage, as her documents suggested she was born in a city that did not exist at the time of her birth, and her birth certificate was issued after her marriage, although she would have needed it to get married.[18] When documents were needed for her to leave the USSR, no police, prison, or military records were made available. The Soviets simply could have said that none existed, but instead they remained silent on the issue.[19]

State Department functionary Virginia James, the caseworker for Marina Oswald, indicated that by law, Marina was required to get a third-country visa (i.e., Belgium) to leave the USSR, but Ms. James urged a waiver of that requirement [Rule 243 (g)], as it was hoped that Lee Oswald would be able to leave the Soviet Union quickly, as he was seen as "an unstable character, whose actions are entirely unpredictable."[20] If that is an honest appraisal of Lee Oswald's character, why would *any nation* be in a hurry to get him back? A subsequent memo from Ms. James indicated regret that the waiver of 243 (g) still had not been issued, and she theorized that it meant that

Marina and her infant "are being punished for Mr. Oswald's earlier indiscretions." *What indiscretions?*

Ms. James concluded this subsequent memo even more obliquely: "It is in the best interests of the United States to have Mr. Oswald depart from the Soviet Union as soon as possible."[21] Translation: Oswald is an unstable nut who has possibly committed treason, but gosh, we'd love to welcome him back.

At the same time, Robert Oswald, who had little if any stake in the matter, was contacted by agents of the Immigration and Naturalization Service about the "routine case" of allowing Marina to enter the United States. He testified before the Warren Commission: "The gentleman advised me he assumed that Lee was employed *by the government* [emphasis added] in some capacity in Russia."[22] Needless to say, the Warren Commission demonstrated no curiosity whatsoever as to just which government it was assumed was then employing Oswald. Jim Martin, Marina's bodyguard-*cum*-attorney in early 1964, asked her how she got out of Russia: "She said that Lee arranged it, and that is all she would say."[23]

The second thing that the Russian émigré community in Texas agreed on was their unanimous disbelief that the Soviets would let Marina leave as casually as they did. Peter Paul Gregory called her release "more than extraordinary"; George Bouhe viewed it as "almost incredible"; many others agreed.[24] There may be a more simple explanation than the miraculous: The loss of Marina Oswald (née Prussokova) was a small price for the Soviets to pay to be rid of Lee Oswald, given what the *U.S. State Department* was saying about him.

Lee Oswald's departure from the Soviet Union is as much a curiosity as Marina's—and his unnoticed arrival back in America even more so. One odd State Department document discussed the handling of the Oswald matter, saying, "This was in line with the practice followed throughout the Oswald case, as in other 'defector' cases."[25] Why is the word "defector" in quotation marks in this document? It would be logical for it to read, "as in other defector cases," and stop there. But to add those extra punctuation marks is to allow for the suspicion that Oswald was only a "defector," not *a defector*.

Oswald, of course, had written to the embassy, insisting on a guarantee of an "agreement concernig [sic] the dropping of any legal proceedings against me."[26] Even though Oswald was asking that charges be dropped before they were even brought, and despite the State Department's low estimate of Oswald, he got his wish, as no charges were brought. There is also no evidence in the official records that any charges were ever considered.

In preparing a self-questionnaire requested by his Soviet hosts, Oswald prepared two dissimilar versions, so as to straddle the fence if needed. In one, prepared just before the birth of the first child, Oswald indicated he had one child, a son, David Lee. He was obviously expecting a boy.

America clearly wanted him back, regardless of his pedigree. In a State Department document signed "Rusk," it is noted, "The Embassy's careful attention to the *involved case* [emphasis added] of Mr. Oswald is appreciated."[27]

"Involved"? How so? And by what possible yardstick is Lee Oswald important enough to merit the attention of the U.S. secretary of state?

A State Department memo of March 31, 1961, that expressed concern about returning Oswald's passport to him, concluded, "However, it is believed that whatever risk might be involved in transmitting the passport by mail under the above conditions would be more than offset by the opportunity provided the United States to obtain information from Mr. Oswald concerning his activities in the Soviet Union."[28] Agreed; *but to "obtain information from Mr. Oswald," it might have been necessary to ask him some questions. Perhaps many questions.*

Virginia James indicated the FBI had told the State Department that Oswald had no known connections with American communists "and had shown no proclivities for communism. . . ."[29] This was the same FBI that would later tar Oswald with the reddest of brushes. Warren Commission member Allen Dulles would later ask State Department legal adviser Abram Chayes, "You made a very strong case that his [Oswald's] continued residence in the Soviet Union was harmful to the foreign policy of the United States?" Chayes answered (missing the point of the question), "Well, we were very anxious to get him back. . . ."[30] Chayes was not asked the obvious question: Why?

There are still unanswered questions about the Oswalds' strange and somewhat luxurious layover in Amsterdam, especially since his profile was so negative and his finances were worse. Those questions will likely remain unanswered until the vaults at Langley spill forth their treasures.

Finally, we have the comment from Marguerite Oswald, who told the Warren Commission that Lee told her that not even Marina knew why he had returned to America.[31]

And neither do the rest of us know.

CHAPTER FOUR

THE SPY WHO CAME
BACK FROM THE COLD

So it's home, home again—America for me.

—Henry Van Dyke, 1908

The man (with wife and daughter in tow) who arrived back in the
United States in June 1962 *was* the same man who had been born
on October 18, 1939, *was* the same man who served in the Marine
Corps and "defected" to the Soviet Union in 1959, and *was* the same
man who would be charged and killed in connection with the death
of President Kennedy.

If one studies the available documentation, it becomes clear that
there are discrepancies—far too many for coincidence—in the history
of Lee Harvey Oswald. His scars, most notably the mastoidectomy
he underwent in youth, and the botched suicide, come and go in the
official record. His hair is reported as irregularly as it was growing—or
disappearing—at the end of his life. His English was anywhere from
atrocious to reasonably articulate, and his Russian ranged, in various
reports, from middling to exceptional.

He had six different eye colors: hazel[1] on his USMC fingerprint
card; gray[2] on his Selective Service classification, a July 1962 FBI
report by special agent Fain, on his 1959 and 1963 passport applications, and on his Selective Service card; blue[3] on a subsequent Selective Service card, on a May 1962 FBI report by the same special
agent Fain, on an Immigration and Naturalization Service document,
and a State Department Security Office memorandum; blue-hazel[4]

224

on an FBI report by Milton Kaack in October 1963; blue-gray[5] on a USMC health record; and his eyes were noted as *brown* in the previously cited interview with Aline Mosby in a Moscow hotel.

His height also seemed to undergo similar biological mood swings. He is listed as five feet, eleven inches on his application to Albert Schweitzer College in 1959, in the July 1962 FBI interview, on his 1963 passport application, on his USMC health record, and on his Selective Service Card.[6] He was listed as five feet, nine inches by the Texas Employment Commission *and at autopsy*.[7] There are also a few photos of Lee that show him barely taller than the five-foot, three-inch Marina.

The thesis put forth for this is "substitution," and the problem with it is that it is impossible to determine when it occurred, or if it occurred, as the discrepancies occur throughout the entire time continuum from Oswald's Marine Corps enlistment to his death in Dallas. The numerous available documents, and there are no doubt more awaiting future scrutiny, virtually guarantee a plausible counter-argument that a "substitution" occurred in the marines, in Russia, or after Oswald's return. Evidence, yes; conclusive, no.

Of greater import was the nature of Oswald's contacts once he returned to the United States. Although J. Edgar Hoover's anti-communist diatribes would occasionally make his erstwhile friend Joe McCarthy seem timid, and although Hoover had knowledge of Oswald virtually from defection, there was no FBI "welcoming committee" when the Oswalds reached the United States.[8] It is as inconceivable in hindsight to imagine a scenario in which a self-proclaimed treasonous defector arrived home without a law enforcement presence as it would be if the ongoing O. J. Simpson soap opera were to be interrupted by a confession from the defendant that went unnoticed.

Instead, the Oswalds were met by one person, Spas T. Raikin, a representative for a Welcome Wagon-type outfit that fronted for intelligence connections. Oswald grew quickly tired of his company and headed to Texas, making a stopover in Atlanta that has prompted sinister questions, as the Oswalds had met a Captain Davidson in the USSR who had family in Atlanta and had been in contact with espionage agent Oleg Penkovskiy prior to his execution by the Soviets.[9] Upon arrival in Texas, Oswald sought out Pauline Bates, a stenographer, to type the manuscript of his Russian adventure. The ever-furtive Oswald, who even kept the carbons, told Ms. Bates that a friend, an oil geologist of Russian origin, was going to help him get the book published. While there are many such geologists in the Dallas-Fort Worth area, one comes more readily to mind than all the rest: George DeMohrenschildt. The others would always remain skeptical of Oswald, as they were loyal Russians and he was seen as traitorous by them. But not DeMohrenschildt; although there may be no two less similar people on the planet than Oswald and DeMohrenschildt, there he was within days of Oswald's return to the United States, eager to help him get out the story of his time in Russia. *Some people might call such an activity a "debriefing."*

Richard Case Nagell confirmed such a scenario to writer and researcher Dick Russell,[10] but that unfortunately raises the question of why the Oswalds were treated to special accommodations in Holland if they were to be debriefed in the United States. Often, however, the intelligence community insists on hearing the story more than once, with the hopes that subsequent tellings match.

DeMohrenschildt would later elliptically suggest to the Warren Commission that Oswald was receiving some outside, covert funding, a fact also confirmed by Nagell.[11] Of all the oil geologists who figure in the Kennedy narrative, even marginally, DeMohrenschildt was always the best connected to intelligence circles. Others are now making their way onto the suspect list, as recent document releases point to some strange connections between the heretofore simplistically viewed "Russian émigrés" and some high-power cartels that suggest "deep politics."

Although the CIA remained aloof or even distant during the Warren Commission's lifetime, once the galleys of the Report were circulating, the CIA answered a few of the commission's months-old questions. Author Anthony Summers told of the CIA possessing 1,196 documents on Lee Oswald, "some of them many hundreds of pages long."[12] A veteran CIA paper shuffler told this author that the above-cited estimate may be well short of reality. At the same time that the CIA was denying all knowledge of Oswald despite massive documentation of *something*, it has also been suggested that Oswald was a natural for FBI street work, as his varying political persuasions made him the perfect subject to gather all kinds of people around him. His disdain for Hoover and the FBI, although possibly posturing, also suggests that Oswald would be an unlikely assassin of JFK, the person most likely to remove Hoover.

Contradictions abound. At the time he was entering on his leftist pamphleteering career, he gained employment at the William B. Reily Coffee Company, whose owner was known to support right-wing causes and would never have knowingly hired the local major-domo of the Fair Play for Cuba Committee. Oswald's application listed Sgt. Robert Hidell, USMC, as a reference, and listed himself as five feet, nine inches.[13] Oswald would subsequently be fired for absenteeism from the Reily Company, the only such employment where his absenteeism was ever a factor. It was also the only employment he ever had in close proximity to Guy Banister Associates and the New Orleans intelligence community.[14]

While at Reily, Oswald constantly talked guns with Adrian Alba next door at the Crescent Garage, where FBI and other government vehicles were serviced and housed. At no other time, however, did anyone else from Reily or any other of Oswald's jobs ever recall Oswald discussing guns.[15] Oswald would apply for a job at the S. K. Manson Marble and Granite Company in New Orleans and list *Charles Harrison* as a reference.[16] (Charles *Harrelson* is a frequent suspect in assassination literature.)

Oswald's pamphleteering posturing has been well documented, but some details have received only scant attention. Vincent T. Lee, nominal head of the FPCC until it collapsed following negative publicity in the wake of the assassination, wrote to Oswald, "I definitely would not recommend an office [in New Orleans], at least not one that will be easily identifiable to the lunatic fringe in your community." Oswald wrote back, in character, "I want it to attract attention, even if it's the attention of the lunatic fringe."[17]

Oswald accomplished that objective by using space provided by Guy Banister, a familiar character in the New Orleans scenario, who had the distinction of being so far to the right he would make your garden-variety Klansman look like a bleeding-heart liberal. The Secret Service would later conclude that Oswald's FPCC never had offices at 544 Camp Street and that nobody could be found who recalled Oswald there.[18] This suggests careful use of language ("offices") as well as either a failure to look for witnesses or an unwillingness to consider the possibility that Guy Banister gave marching orders of silence after Dallas. It is also instructive that in CE 1412, a sample of Oswald's FPCC literature, the location has been obliterated. It is equally instructive, as author James DiEugenio has noted, that Oswald's copies of *The Crime Against Cuba* were from the original printing, which would not have been available to Oswald after his return from the Soviet Union; however, the CIA had bought up a quantity of the first printing.[19]

Even the "Hands Off Cuba" leaflets themselves have a dubious pedigree. Myra Silver, employed by the Jones Printing Company, which is opposite the side entrance to Reily Coffee, told the FBI that someone using the name "Osborne" ordered one thousand FPCC leaflets on May 29, 1963 (another irony, inasmuch as it was JFK's last birthday). Ms. Silver could not, however, identify Oswald as the purchaser, and while the handwriting does look like Oswald's, the spelling is perfect, including words that Oswald would usually fall over, such as "committee," "literature," "lectures," and "everyone." It also strikes one as odd that Oswald's original order form for such a meager purchase would still be available months later.[20] Douglas Jones, the owner of the printing company, believed it was not Oswald but rather a "husky type person" who ordered the handbills, while employee J. I. Anderton identified Oswald but claimed the order was for five hundred handbills.[21]

FBI assistant director Alan H. Belmont would later conclude about Oswald, ". . . his activities in New Orleans were of his own making, and not as a part of the organized activities of the Fair Play for Cuba Committee." Marina Oswald had an even better insight: "I think that Lee was engaged in this activity primarily for purposes of self-advertising. He wanted to be arrested."[22]

In handing out his leaflets at the dock where sailors were coming off the USS Wasp, Oswald seemed to have a death wish. When the Office of Naval Intelligence was questioned about this event, they checked their records on "subject" and had no report of the incident, concluding that this *lack of information* comprises "about ninety-eight per cent of *available* [emphasis added] ONI information pertaining to the subject."[23] More semantics.

Not long after his attempt to win converts to the Cuban side from among American sailors, Oswald struck up an extremely brief friendship with Carlos Bringuier, whom he even offered to loan money, a suggestion of deep conviction on Oswald's part, since he was not only niggardly but also perpetually broke.[24] Shortly thereafter, Celso Hernandez noticed Oswald with pro-Cuban handbills and reported this to Bringuier, who went to the location and started a fracas. Hernandez noted, "Many persons had gathered on the street and were encouraging the three men to kill OSWALD."[25] Oswald's posturing was now working so well that he was being noticed by the crowds and was the one who wound up being fined in the brief incident.

Patrolman Warren N. Roberts, Jr., interviewed Oswald and his three assailants *together* after the disturbance, and "did recall OSWALD answering questions in a mechanical manner, much like a machine that could be turned on and off."[26] In addition to the well-publicized interview with FBI agent Quigley, Oswald was also interviewed by Lt. Francis L. Martello, making three interviews for an event just slightly more significant than possession of an overdue library book. Martello indicated that Oswald showed him much identification, but all in the name Oswald—not Hidell. He also indicated that Oswald told him he had become interested in the FPCC while in the Marine Corps, and that had caused him some trouble (although calling other marines "comrade" did not), and when Martello asked the prisoner if he was a communist, Oswald answered in the negative. When asked if he was a socialist, Oswald replied, "Guilty."[27]

Oswald had drawn more than just the curiosity of New Orleans authorities. On the day after the Oswalds departed New Orleans, their landlady, Mrs. Jesse Garner, was interviewed by the FBI about their behavior and the company they kept.[28] Does the FBI do this every time someone moves?

An individual named Jerry Buchanan told the FBI that Oswald, acting in an FPCC capacity, had been involved in fights in October 1962, and *in Miami* in March 1963.[29] General Walker would later tell the Warren Commission that he believed that Oswald's FPCC activities were events "that can be viewed from many different ways."[30] Inasmuch as Oswald's total leaflet time was measurable in minutes, that he regularly left the scene after the photos had been taken, and that his total leaflet order could be measured in hundreds, it seems rather obvious that Oswald was posturing in such a way as to discredit pro-Castro forces down the road. It should also not escape our notice that Oswald got an enormous amount of publicity out of his meager leaflet campaign. There have always been oddballs on city street corners handing out all kinds of garbage that would have been better off remaining in the forest, yet oddball Oswald managed to get photographed at virtually every (however brief) stop on his leaflet tour. Odd.

Pamphleteering to discredit the left in the summer of 1963, even at U.S. warships or among hostile street crowds, was still safer than the events of April 10, 1963, in Dallas, where a person or persons unknown fired a shot at right-wing general Edwin Walker, U.S. Army resigned. If Marina Oswald's account is accurate (and it had a tendency to metamorphose with successive tellings, or perhaps through variations in translation), Oswald admitted firing the shot, and hid the rifle in the ground or amid foliage. Oswald told his wife he walked back and forth, as "the police thought the would-be assassin had an automobile."[31] The irony in that confession is that on November 22, 1963, when any police officer with any intelligence would have been looking for the fleeing assassin or assassins in motorized transport of some sort, Oswald got bagged precisely because he was walking. Again, very odd.

The weaknesses in the Walker story, however, are many. Marina could not recall Oswald leaving with the gun on that occasion, yet insisted in repeated interviews that he retrieved it within days and returned with it wrapped in a raincoat.[32] She could not recall whether she took the famous backyard photos before or after the Walker shooting, but logic dictates that if she knew of the event at the time, she would not take quickly to the suggestion that she photograph a suspected attempted murderer. She also indicated that Lee burned certain materials two or three days after the event, but this, like Oswald's retrieval of the rifle days later, does not square well with the family's departure for New Orleans shortly after the shooting.[33] The Warren Commission would show a characteristic lack of curiosity about the condition of an old wooden gun supposedly buried in the ground.

Witness Kirk Coleman, not called by the Warren Commission, also gave detailed descriptions of the Walker assailants he saw leaving in an automobile, which would rule out Marina's stories of Oswald's perambulations, and finally there is the delicate matter that the Walker bullet, when subjected to neutron activation analysis, did not match up to any of the Mannlicher JFK bullets.[34]

Mrs. Igor Voshinin told author Dick Russell that she heard about Oswald and the Walker assault from George DeMohrenschildt and that she forwarded the information to the FBI;[35] yet the case was still open and unsolved until after the events of Dealey Plaza. Could it be that the FBI and/or the Dallas police did not want to arrest Oswald for an April event when they knew they could really get the goods on him in November?

Oswald would later write to Communist Party, U.S.A., leader Arnold Johnson, calmly telling of attending a meeting hosted by General

Walker, "who lives in Dallas." The letter is so matter-of-fact that it is hard to imagine that Oswald fired the shot; or else he knew his—and/or Johnson's—mail was being read.[36]

Oswald supposedly left behind a note that Marina discovered after Lee had left on the criminal Walker mission. As Sylvia Meagher has astutely pointed out, the note does not overlap at all well with the Walker shooting and may have been related to some other contemporary event about which we are still uninformed.[37] Two last thoughts occur here: Oswald, according to Marina, was nervous before the Walker incident, and left a note. There was no such note left on November 21 or 22, and when asked if Oswald was as nervous in November as in April, Marina told the Warren Commission the two time frames had "absolutely nothing in common."[38]

Both the leaflet and the Walker events did, however, discredit the left, as did Oswald's attempt to register to vote in Clinton, Louisiana, during the summer of 1963. Oswald waited in line for several hours amid a sea of downtrodden black faces, while two other white males, one David Ferrie (few people would mistakenly identify *him*) and either Guy Banister or Clay Shaw, waited in a nearby Cadillac.[39] Part of his motivation for voter registration, aside from drawing notice to a liberal cause, was to be registered in that parish so he could gain employment at a nearby mental institution. Imagine the headlines on November 23 if that career move had come to pass: Oswald would have then been the Commie-defector-sharpshooter from the mental ward, and none of the images would have been correct as printed.

When not pamphleteering, supporting the black cause, or shooting at overzealous generals, Oswald, we are asked to believe, was also stalking former vice president Nixon but was prevented from making the attack when Marina, a ninety-eight-pound pregnant woman, overpowered him and locked him in a bathroom. The attack also did not occur because Nixon was not in Dallas, nor had he received an invitation to Dallas, at the time suggested.[40]

Other details arrest our attention. Oswald may or may not have "practiced" with the rifle, again depending on the precision of the translations from Marina's statements to various investigating groups. In CE 1401, a deposition given in December 1963, she twice denied that Oswald ever practiced with the gun; by February 22 she told how Oswald cleaned the gun regularly (with what we do not know, as nothing was ever found) and mentioned he told her he had been practicing with it. He took the gun out in a raincoat, but Marina had no personal knowledge of where he went or if he practiced. This is later clarified to have been an evening in March, which soon became the time period during which one or two backyard pictures were taken.[41]

Oswald, who earned an average of $215.64 a month (that we know of) from his return to the United States to his death, and who was unaccounted-for during seventeen days in the fall of 1962, nevertheless applied for another passport, in June 1963, and again government haste blessed him, as the document was issued the next day. The list of passport applicants that included Oswald's name had the notation "no" next to his name, but that was explained as "New Orleans"; inexplicably, no other applicant had any city listed.

It is interesting to note the comparisons between Oswald's two passport applications. The first, executed while he was still in the service, indicated his father had been born on December 8, 1908, and his mother on July 3, 1909. It also indicated that he wanted to travel to Cuba (legal then), Finland, and Russia. The second application listed his father's birth date simply as "1895" and the mother's as "1907" and listed his marriage date as April 31, 1961. (Most Americans know both the date of their wedding *and* the number of days in April.) The second passport application also lists USSR and "Findland," but makes *no mention* of Cuba, as has been widely reported.[42] It probably is a moot point, however, as the issuing officials obviously did not read *or compare* Oswald's passport applications with his comical parental asides; the job of the passport officials was to give Oswald a passport on demand, even if he had listed his parents as Neanderthals.

Oswald was also writing to Arnold Johnson, a Communist Party, U.S.A., official at the same time, hinting that he would be moving either to the Baltimore-D.C. area in the fall of 1963, or to New York, and that he wanted information as to how to keep in touch.[43] This is clearly posturing, as by the simple act of mailing the letter, *he was obviously already in touch.*

Was this stranger who came back from a "defection" in the Soviet Union really a communist? If we depend on government sources *prior to November 22*, the answer is an overwhelming "no."

In CE 1070 we learn that "Investigation conducted by the Federal Bureau of Investigation likewise did not establish Communist Party membership of petitioner [for passport]."[44] The FBI, which according to passport office chairperson Frances Knight "was reviewing his [Oswald's] file at regular intervals," was perplexed: "We did not know definitely whether or not he had any intelligence assignments at that time,"[45] so they did not flag Oswald's passport requests. The suggestion is clearly there, however, that Oswald was a U.S. agent of some sort, as the request would have been flagged just on the *suspicion* that Oswald had been an *enemy* intelligence operative.

FBI special agent Fain, in an August 30, 1962, report, would write "OSWALD and wife unknown to confidential informants," yet Oswald was known to at least four informants in a report by Fain on July 10, fifty-one days earlier.[46] In CE 3037 it is revealed that confidential informants in New Orleans never heard of Oswald in anything communist-related, and Dallas informants report the same conclusion with respect to the Dallas-Fort Worth area.[47]

Whenever Ruth Paine was asked about Oswald and communism, she regularly corrected the interrogator and used the term "Marxist" and once went on to characterize Oswald as a "Trotskyite." Her husband, Michael, told the Warren Commission that Oswald "told me he had become a Marxist in this country without ever having met a Communist . . ." and Michael had a familiarity with such politics, as his father, George Lyman Paine, had been a leader of the Trotskyite movement in the United States[48] (proving that lineage has nothing to do with security clearances in the case of creative genius).

The oddest Oswald reference appeared in an FBI report dated October 31, 1963, by special agent Milton Kaack. Basing his conclusions on confidential informant T-7, "who is familiar with Cuban activities in the New Orleans area," Kaack concluded that as of September 9, T-7 indicated that "Oswald was unknown to him."[49] Again, given Oswald's activities that summer in New Orleans, which involved pamphlet distribution, a fracas, an arrest, and radio interviews and debates, the data suggest that the FBI was making every effort *not* to bury Oswald *until they could once and for all bury him.*

For all his posturing and willingness to manipulate the truth for his own ends—whatever those ends were—it seems clear that if Oswald had wanted to have communist affiliations, it would have been a very simple matter to arrange. After all, he had made himself a defector, a pro-Cuban fanatic, and a black-vote activist. Why not a communist? The answer may well be that his odd behavior had to point directly, like a weather vane in a hurricane, at Fidel Castro, a more manageable enemy to the U.S. intelligence community than

Castro's master, Nikita Khrushchev. But Oswald did not embrace communism.

And so, as events brought Oswald back to his rendezvous with destiny in Dallas, a clear pattern of intrigue emerged, and intrigue, regardless of whether you are wearing a white or a black hat, still guarantees that you are intriguing with others. After Dallas, of course, Oswald's intrigues would paint him as a dedicated Red, or died-in-the-wool communist, as Hoover told the Warren Commission on May 14, 1964. It just seems odd that the same people who blamed Oswald as a "Red" were the ones who distrusted JFK and saw him as a "Red."

There is an obvious contradiction there.

CHAPTER FIVE

THE MAN WITH THE WOODEN GUN

*The impostor employs force instead of argument, imposes silence
where he cannot convince, and propagates his character by
the sword.*

—"THE LETTERS OF JUNIUS" (pseud.), 1770

UPON HIS RETURN to the United States, Oswald was not job-motivated, according to his widow.[1] The reasons for this are not wholly
clear. The Dallas-Fort Worth Russian émigré community, already
suspicious of Oswald for his defection, his often ambivalent stance
on issues, and his at best sophomoric and at worst argumentative and
abrasive personality, wondered how he was able to leave the Soviet
Union with such ease and take a pair of Soviet citizens with him.
The answer to that is easy: The Soviets were happy to rid themselves
of foreign agents, no matter how trivial their presence might be.
After all, the KGB must live within a budget, like every other bureau-
cracy, and following Oswald around was an expensive nuisance. Marina and the baby thus became expendable.

Émigré leader George Bouhe reinforced Marina's "not job-motivated"
testimony when he told how Oswald would apply for a job, and
when asked where he worked last, he would answer, "Minsk, Russia."[2] From such answers are built poor résumés for employment in
Texas. The émigrés also entertained strong suspicions that Oswald
was a Soviet agent.[3] A further concern was that Oswald's Russian
was far too good for someone so poor in English expression. The

misunderstanding there stems partly from reading Oswald's writings, which at times seem dysgraphic; in speaking, he was reasonably articulate on occasion, albeit in mostly unsolicited political rhetoric.

After nine months of reacquainting himself with American customs that were abhorrent enough in 1959 to cause his "defection," Oswald ordered two weapons, a war surplus rifle and a better, but still inexpensive, .38 caliber pistol. They were shipped to "A. J. Hidell" at a post office box clearly rented by Oswald. Oddly enough, in CE 2585, the FBI would insist that *at no time* during the rental of P.O. Box 2915 in Dallas (October 9, 1962, to May 14, 1963) did Oswald ever indicate that anyone else was entitled to collect mail there. A similar confusion is noted, posthumously in Oswald's case, when Ruth Paine indicated that Russian magazines were delivered to her home but for Oswald. If true—and there was the usual cross section of Soviet literary flotsam at the Paine residence—the enigma is deepened, as Oswald had a post office box also. The standard interpretation is that the box was a mail drop for the kind of literature he enjoyed, and it would give him enough privacy that neighbors or coworkers would not know his reading habits and begin to suspect him. Yet if his reading material was arriving at Ruth Paine's, *exactly what* was he receiving at his post office box? It is highly likely he was receiving something, as the frugal Oswald would not have rented a post office box destined to collect dust and/or junk mail. So just as we do not yet fully know or understand who or what "Hidell" really was, we are equally uninformed about the real reasons for Oswald's postal habits. And we may never have the answers to these riddles.

It is instructive that at this time the Oswald family budget could hardly afford to have the breadwinner spend the equivalent of a good week's salary on two totally unnecessary weapons, but there was clearly a purpose—and perhaps an urgency to them. As noted, the choice of the Mannlicher is curious, as it immediately separated its owner from anyone who would fall into the category of hired gun, just as no musician would stand onstage at the Grand Ole Opry in 1963 and attempt to impress an audience while playing a $19 guitar.

Oswald would then pose in the backyard of the Neely Street residence, dressed in black, the color always worn by "the bad guys" in Hollywood productions, demonstrating to the world his ownership of the two weapons, as well as his literary tastes. Oddly, the two papers, *The Worker* and *The Militant,* profess starkly divergent ideologies, and a believer in one would have serious reservations, if not contempt, for the other. Nevertheless, it was an impact statement: Oswald owned guns, and he read *leftist* literature. As someone intent on merely creating an image, he may not even have been sophisticated enough to realize how foolish this posture would look to someone who understood the contents of the papers in question.

Marina has admitted taking the photos. They have been questioned for a variety of good reasons: the shadows, the size of the rifle compared to Oswald, the flowering shrubbery at a time when it should not have been in bloom, and the square jaw on the head of the subject in the picture. On November 21, 1993, I had my own photo taken in the backyard of that now-grubby tenement. It was a beautiful, sunny day; I stood near the staircase at midday, and my body shadow was virtually identical to Oswald's in the questioned photos. Facially, however, there was no "Hitler mustache" shadow under my nose; the shadow went to the camera's left, across my right cheek— oddly, in the same direction as the body shadow.

The rifle-to-Oswald proportions problem can be put to rest if we recall the great amount of retouching done to that series of photos. The most famous of them, which appeared on the cover of *Life,* was widely circulated elsewhere, and editors took license to retouch whatever part of the photo they thought needed better resolution. The shrubbery can also be explained: The year 1963, meteorologically, was the hottest year of the 1960s, and it is entirely possible that the higher temperatures began early, causing some local flora to be slightly out of sync. The jaw, too, can be explained, as CE 1797, taken on November 22, and published in Volume XXIII, p. 417, of the *Hearings,* shows a very distinct square jaw protruding at a time when prisoner Oswald seemed under stress.

The shadows in the photos, as well as the fact that the body proportions vary throughout the series of photos, can only have sinister implications. I can only agree with the assessment made by Anthony Summers, who believed that Oswald doctored the photos himself while still employed at Jaggers-Chiles-Stovall. If the pictures were later needed for some conspiratorial scenario, they would be available, as it is hard to imagine Oswald leaving for work on November 22 with a gun and the intent to kill the president *and* intentionally leaving behind such incriminating photos (or carrying "Hidell" identification), unless they were intended to serve a temporary purpose. Once served, Oswald could, as he did, claim he could prove they were fakes, and photographic inspection would certify his claim. Nobody would be likely to suspect that he had doctored them himself. Oddly, the photos that most convinced the world of Oswald's guilt have always been spoken of as having been discovered on Saturday, when the police searched the Paine residence while Mrs. Paine bought groceries, suggesting her appetite had not suffered although her houseguest had been accused of murdering the president. Yet Michael Paine, in an unguarded moment, told the Warren Commission that he was asked to identify at least one of the poses *on Friday night,* which, if true, calls into question the veracity of the story of their discovery, and, by extension, their veracity in general. It also gives authorities countless extra hours to use the photos for their own purposes before officially "discovering" them.[4]

In addition, Robert A. Taylor claimed he bought an unfired .30-06 rifle in March 1963, from two men, one of whom *was* Oswald, for the bargain price of $12.[5] If false, this suggests imposture, placing "Oswald" with weapons; if true, it reinforces the theory that Oswald's gun ownership had to be restricted to the worthless Mannlichers, so there would be no possible confusion involving real guns down the road.

Our attention is next focused on the events of the summer and fall, especially the month of November 1963, when "Oswalds" seem to appear and make a point of drawing notice—usually unfavorable. While much of this has been studied and well documented by other researchers, I would like to focus on a few events and bring some new conclusions to light.

The first 1963 imposture that we know of is documented in *The Man Who Knew Too Much,* as someone went to a great deal of trouble on July 26, 1963 (another irony: the anniversary of Castro's revolution), to sign in to the Atomic Energy Museum in Oak Ridge, Tennessee, where Oswald's paraffin casts would later be tested. The signature read, "Lee H. Oswald, USSR, Dallas Road, Dallas, Texas."[6] There are several anomalies here: The handwriting is not Oswald's, nor could it have been, as he was in New Orleans; secondly, someone went to a lot of trouble to write such a ridiculous entry, clearly one that would stick out from the usual entry of "Mabel Jones, 224 Maple Avenue, Sticksville, Indiana." Whoever that someone was knew a great deal about a supposed loner and clearly wanted that loner to receive Soviet-related notice. Also, the choice of site is instructive. If this entry were made in a bed-and-breakfast in Wyoming, it would be significant. But at the Oak Ridge Atomic Energy Museum? Lastly, it would appear that the forces behind this signature had already decided on an Oswald-Dallas connection, to be used in the future, because at the time the spurious entry was made, *Oswald did not live in Dallas.*

The month of August would not require impostures, as Oswald was his own publicist, busy getting roughed up and fined in New Orleans. He was also trying to register to vote so he could secure a job in a Jackson, Louisiana, mental hospital (had he obtained such employment, even for a week, it would have been one more knot in the noose around his neck. Sidebar, November 23: "Oswald, who is known to have spent time in a mental institution in Louisiana . . ."). Finally, Oswald was busy debating Carlos Bringuier and Ed Butler, who taught Oswald a lesson in one-upmanship when they revealed during the "debate" that Oswald had been a defector. The only known imposture at this time came from a report from Mrs. Opal Robertson, who saw someone, in late August or early September, target-shooting in the Trinity River in Dallas, at a time when Oswald was still in New Orleans and was weeks away from returning to Dallas. She told investigators that the shooter "looked like Oswald" and was in the company of a small boy, approximately age four. Nearby was a dark, old vehicle. Five days later, Mrs. Robertson would see the person again, and she indicated he gave Irving, Texas, as his residence.[7]

Early September was equally uneventful, but the second half of the month was hectic. On the very same day, Oswald was in Mexico posturing as an American who wanted to get to Cuba and eventually the Soviet Union, *and* was visiting Sylvia Odio in Dallas, from which would come conversations between Miss Odio and the Cubans accompanying "Oswald" that he was a nut, a sharpshooter, and an extreme malcontent with respect to JFK (the only such anti-JFK rhetoric we are aware of, in contrast to a host of pro-JFK statements by Oswald). Unable to resolve the obvious discrepancy, the Warren Commission first decided that Miss Odio was simply mistaken, and later produced testimony, on September 21, 1964, the week the Report was issued, from Loran Hall, that he and two confederates staged the Odio visit. Days later, with the Report serialized in paperback all over America, Hall and his friends changed their minds and denied the whole story. Eventually the HSCA believed both Sylvia Odio and her sister Annie, who had witnessed part of the encounter.[8] The

Odio incident presented the Warren Commission with one of its most serious problems, and is instructive as such. If Sylvia Odio is correct, then someone was impersonating Oswald in Mexico, positively to invigorate his pro-Castro, pro-communist résumé; if the imposture occurred at Miss Odio's residence, then someone, knowing Oswald to be hundreds of miles away, went to a lot of difficulty to stage a charade just to plant the seed that a former marine sharpshooter thought Kennedy should have been shot for his failure at the Bay of Pigs, an event that undoubtedly drew a lot of the real Oswald's attention while he was producing radios and eating cabbage in Minsk. To resolve the dilemma, the Warren Commission decided first that Miss Odio was mistaken, and that nobody had ever come to her residence, and then they did an about-face and admitted that Loran Hall et al. were the jolly pranksters and the event was a confusion by Miss Odio. In one of those coincidences that never seem to go away, Sylvia Odio received psychiatric treatment for the trauma induced by this event, and one of her therapists was a Dr. Stubblefield, hardly a common name, yet one that would resurface in the early months of 1964, as he was a consultant for the defense team of Jack Ruby.

If there is one sidebar to the Kennedy assassination that may never be satisfactorily resolved, it is the supposed trip of Oswald to Mexico in late September and early October of 1963. As in other posturings, he made himself too well known to bus passengers, and to people in Mexico, and he staged a scene in the Cuban embassy reminiscent of his tantrum at the U.S. embassy in Moscow at the time of his "defection."

He had applied for his Mexican tourist card listing his occupation as a photographer for a New Orleans Negro newspaper, again aligning himself with the left politically. Silvia Duran, the consul he berated, could not identify "Oswald" before the HSCA, and the CIA photos taken of him entering and leaving the embassy show a much heavier man with a crew cut, who is later seen as the assassin "Saul"; he is pictured in CE 237 and Bardwell Odum exhibit 1 in the *Hearings*. The CIA eavesdroppers reportedly heard poor Russian spoken, and they supposedly routinely destroyed the tapes, yet some of them remained for a few months at least. Recall that all this transpired well before the CIA issued its blanket denial of any connection to, or knowledge of, Lee Oswald.

The name "Oswald" and the destination "Lared" [Laredo] are

listed on a Mexican bus manifest; Mexican officials, however, told the FBI that no such person bought a ticket or made such a trip.[9] The Warren Commission also published a hoax letter that told that Oswald, while in Mexico, received $7,000 from a Cuban to kill President Kennedy.[10] If Oswald was indeed in Mexico, the bus bringing him back to America had Dallas as its destination, as Marina, expecting her second child, had accepted the gracious offer of Ruth Paine to share her residence in Irving, a suburb of Dallas.

The remainder of October would be quiet, while the month of November, which saw a veritable proliferation of Oswalds, and a tragedy in Dealey Plaza, would be the zenith of "Oswald" sightings.

Grocery store owner Leonard Hutchinson insisted that Oswald tried to cash a $189 check, an impossibility for Oswald on a $1.25-per-hour salary, paid weekly, from the TSBD. The Oswald who appeared at Hutchinson's market did so regularly, at times for which Oswald was clearly alibied, and the individual always needed a haircut.[11] This, too, suggests further imposture, as Clifford Shasteen, a local barber, claimed to have cut Oswald's hair every ten to fourteen days, an unlikely possibility given Oswald's lack of hair and funds.

On November 1, an Oswald drew attention to himself while purchasing ammunition in Morgan's gun shop in Fort Worth. This occurred after a "check cashing" event at an Irving A&P, recalled on April 13, 1964, by the cashier, in which Oswald signed and cashed a $33 Texas unemployment check dated October 1, 1963; alarm bells should sound based on that scenario, as "Oswald" supposedly left New Orleans in late September and only arrived back in Dallas on October 3. Were Texas Employment Commission officials so concerned about the welfare of a former defector that they cut him a check for unemployment while he was busy in Mexico trying to betray his country? And who could imagine that the tightfisted Oswald would hold an October 1 check for a full thirty days?[12] This October 31 Irving event was a Thursday, although Ruth Paine would tell the Warren Commission that November 21 was Oswald's only Thursday visit; the November 1 ammunition purchase happened on a day when Oswald was busy at the TSBD, and would later hitch a ride home from Wesley Frazier. On the same day, and this would have been possible on his lunch hour, Oswald opened his last post office box, listing both FPCC and ACLU (again, both leftist) as affiliations. Yet three weeks later, when Oswald was visited in custody by ACLU officials eager to help him, Oswald told them he did not feel he was in need of their legal services. His post office boxes may have had an occasional sinister purpose, but "as advertised," they were posturing, pure and simple.

The following week, "Oswald" and family *drove* up to a furniture store that once housed a gunsmith. The two ladies in the store, Mrs. Hunter and Mrs. Whitworth, were convincing in their testimony that the customers they saw were Oswald, Marina, and two appropriately aged children. Marina strongly denied ever being in any used-furniture outlet, or that Oswald was home to shop during the week, or that he drove a car to the shop.[13] A day or so later, an "Oswald" left a gun for repair at the Irving Gun Shop, although employee Dial Ryder denied ever seeing Oswald, and denied having ever worked on a Mannlicher or the Japanese scope in question.[14]

The furniture store/gunsmith week ended with a hectic flourish over the weekend. Although Ruth Paine would testify that she and the Oswalds were together for the weekend that comprised Saturday, November 9, Sunday, November 10, and Monday, November 11 (Veterans' Day), *someone* was quite busy.

On Saturday, November 9, "Oswald" took his much-publicized test drive with car salesman Albert Bogard. Following the assassination, Bogard took and passed a polygraph examination about the driving event, suggesting at least that he believed in his own testimony.[15] Oswald was also reported to have been at the Sports Drome Rifle Range on November 9.[16]

On Sunday, November 10, Oswald was back at the rifle range and was subsequently seen at 11:00 P.M. by Harvey L. Wade at Ruby's Carousel Club. Wade would make the statement based on the recollection that Oswald had taken part in the emcee (Billy DeMar's) "memory act."[17] DeMar, the man who performed the "memory act," would make the same allegation, only to be debunked by other Ruby employees who would claim that the lighting in Ruby's club, particularly the spotlights on the stage, would make it impossible to identify anyone positively.[18] Therein, however, lies the crux of the assertion. While DeMar perhaps could not positively identify "Oswald" because of the lights, he still could see enough of the individual to recognize enough similarity to *think* it had been Oswald.

The following weekdays were quiet, but Oswald did not visit the Paine residence on his last full weekend alive, and there were sightings. He was again seen at the Sports Drome Rifle Range, although three gun club members disagreed about the event. E. P. Bass was sure it was Oswald, although H. Hunter would disagree, insisting that he would have recalled such a "junky" gun.[19] Such theorizing nevertheless overlooks a vital point. For Oswald to have been at a rifle range on November 17 means he would either have had to be firing a gun other than the TSBD Mannlicher, which would serve only publicity and not target-practice purposes, or he would some-how have had to make his way to the Paine residence, get the Mann-licher from the garage, get to the range, then reenter the Paine garage unseen and replace the gun.

Even then it is difficult, as November 17 was the date of the "Abilene incident," in which an individual left a message containing two phone numbers and signed "Lee Oswald" with the neighbor of a well-known violently anti-Kennedy Cuban in Abilene, Texas. Abi-lene is roughly two hundred miles west-southwest of Dallas, a rather long walk for someone who could neither drive nor afford alternate transportation.[20]

Oswald, not observed to be footsore, worked at the TSBD on Monday through Thursday of the week of the presidential motorcade, and went to the Paines' on Thursday evening either to patch up an earlier quarrel with Marina, to secure curtain rods, or to get Hi-dell's rifle.

Either way, the suspected impostor would take a curtain call a few minutes after the shots and the Kennedy presidency ended.

While Oswald was using a bus and taxi to return to the neighbor-hood of 1026 North Beckley, Sheriff's Deputy Roger Craig reported seeing an individual leave the TSBD in haste and enter a Rambler station wagon. Craig would later see Oswald in custody and admit to being "positive that OSWALD is identical with the same individ-ual he observed getting into the Rambler station wagon as men-tioned above."[21]

Alcohol, Tobacco, and Firearms special agent Frank Ellsworth would also view the suspect on November 22, and come to the conclusion, for a terrifying instant, that Oswald was an individual he had arrested earlier on a weapons charge. Ellsworth then realized Oswald was a very close look-alike to John Thomas Masen, a local gun shop operator. Researchers since that time have focused on Masen as the Oswald look-alike portrayed in the events cited in this chapter and others, although Jim Garrison harbored suspicions that Kerry Thornley might have filled that role. The only evidence for the Thornley impersonation would be grocer Hutchison's testimony about "Oswald" always needing a haircut.

In rereading the testimony of the witnesses who were privy to the "second Oswald," a strong degree of conviction is evident in their statements. They are very convincing that Oswald was the person they saw at the event they described, although other testimony puts Oswald at work or at one of his two ad hoc residences. The Warren Commission certainly would have liked its readers to believe the presence of Oswald at rifle ranges, or test-driving sports cars that he could soon afford, but the evidence, even as they were capable of stretching it, denied them the chance. It becomes obvious that someone, possibly Masen, did impersonate Oswald, and the story is well told in George Michael Evica's *And We Are All Mortal*. The work involves cross-checking among Special Agent Ellsworth, researchers Dick Russell and George Michael Evica, and Masen himself. Such corroboration as exists is located in Warren Commission *documents* (which, unlike commission "exhibits," were not published). Nevertheless, the story is tantalizing and may unlock much of the "second Oswald" riddle.

The problem, to assume devil's advocacy briefly, with the Masen theory is that many of these impostures involved guns, and the gun-owning community in and around Dallas should have recognized Masen from his associations in the business, if, as Ellsworth, Evica, and Russell insist, Masen was literally Oswald's twin. Also, although I have no idea what Masen looked like in 1963, it seems odd that after the assassination not one of his customers ever reported making a purchase from a gun dealer who could have passed for Oswald's twin. Also, Masen was interrogated to see if Oswald bought ammunition from him, and apparently no one in police circles took note of the resemblance—or dared to. . . .

Having made those observations, however, is not to discredit or ridicule the Oswald-impersonator theory. The Warren Commission did that and looked foolish in the process. The key to understanding the imposture is to note that which is common throughout the series of events. They all generally point to Oswald, guns, politics, and finances beyond his reach. They all come in handy as temporary allegations or negative résumé entries in the forty-seven hours that Oswald lived after his arrest, or beyond that to cement a hideously pathetic life and legal case.

More important, however, is the fact that they all occurred in relative isolation and with very small and mutually exclusive audiences: a car dealer; a few rifle buffs; a barber; a stranger in Abilene; Sylvia Odio; a few "gringos" on a bus; a customer or two in the

Carousel. There was never an event where an impostor stood publicly at some very well attended meeting, identified himself as Lee Harvey Oswald, and said something politically revealing, personally abrasive, or otherwise obnoxious in order to be remembered as part of a scenario. Had this happened, and dozens of people from the meeting denied it was Oswald and insisted it was someone else, the Warren Commission, its presidential sponsor, and its sources—in Dallas and D.C.—would have collapsed like a house of cards.

Lastly, with the possible exception of confusion in the testimony of Malcolm Price, there is no trace of any "Oswald impostors" on the scene after November 22. The damage had been done; although Oswald had alibis for virtually all the events from either Roy Truly, Marina, or Ruth Paine, they went for naught. Truly was viewed with skepticism as the man who ran the TSBD, and had let Oswald get away when encountered by Dallas officer Marrion Baker. Marina's credibility was never all that high with the American public, even if they could not understand her. Ruth Paine was suspect for her Good Samaritan behavior in taking in Marina, seen as a sinister act, and for helping Oswald get the job at the TSBD—perhaps a plotter after all, and a current focus of much research.[22]

The evidence regarding a "second Oswald" is clear and undeniable. We know "Why?" "How?" "When?" and "Where?" We can also make the obvious conjecture as to why the Warren Commission went out of its way to bury the whole scenario in its Speculations and Rumors section. What has not yet been proven convincingly (someone in the Ellsworth/Russell/Evica network must have been able to secure a photo of Masen) is the "Who?" Because if the Oswald impersonator was not Masen, it is likely that he, like Oswald and the truth, was buried.

And possibly even before the real Oswald, as the impersonator's job ended at midday on November 22; the real Oswald had to live a few hours at least, so the public could see him in his shabby clothes and with his bruised face, and collectively convict him *before* Ruby was given his cue.

CHAPTER SIX

THE HUNT FOR
RED OSWALD

Even the clumsiest assassin, before going off to shoot the president,
would have burned the pictures showing him with the murder
weapon; checked the contents of his wallet to see that no card
bearing the name A. Hidell was kept; and thought for five
minutes about what he would do after firing the last shot.

—LEO SAUVAGE, *The Oswald Affair,* p. 267

Would a man intent on murdering the president of the United
States embark on his mission carrying such a comprehensive
collection of personal documents?

—JOHN DAVIS, *Mafia Kingfish,* p. 244

THE QUOTATIONS CITED ABOVE epitomize the obvious illogic in the
events that surrounded the apprehension of the "suspected assassin,"
Lee Oswald. On the other hand, they forcibly demonstrate the logic
that argues that Oswald was possibly a tangential coconspirator and,
as such, also possibly the unwitting patsy.

No genuine assassin (lone or otherwise) would leave behind such
incriminating photos, and it should strike the reader as odd that except for police, gun-related, or leaflet-related photos, there were very
few if any (excluding surveillance) photos of Oswald taken after his
return to the United States. So he had to be quite aware of the few
that did exist.

Nor would an assassin carry identification, albeit fake and possibly homemade, tying him under the name "Hidell" to the purchase of the weapon and to a one-man radical Cuban group in New Orleans.

It is equally illogical and unlikely that someone able to be a successful presidential assassin would not have prepared a better escape than to hop aboard a local bus headed *into* the maelstrom of Dealey Plaza and from there into a large loop around the downtown area, and failing in that, would count on a taxicab to get home. Lee Oswald has made the history books, but he is also deserving of an entry in *The Book of Lists* under the category "only famous assassin to make getaway on public transportation."

However, as noted, it is a very logical scenario for a patsy to find himself in, and given that the photos, documents, and escape routes may not have been considered as urgent or incriminating by someone not having presidential assassination on his mind, *patsy* Oswald improvised rather well. Sensing that something very unexpected had happened to the motorcade, Oswald exited the TSBD, pointing out the location of a pay telephone to a "Secret Service agent" in front of the TSBD (this person is alternatively seen as journalist Robert McNeil of current television fame, but if it was, the timing of the event is destroyed, as McNeil performed a search of the overpass area and the knoll before approaching the TSBD; by the time he got there, the "Oswald" of Warren Commission fame would already be bored with a bus ride to nowhere). Regardless, the Warren Report Oswald then sauntered a few blocks east, and sought refuge on Cecil McWatters' bus, the last place anyone would look for the villain in a crime that usually suggested extremely special talents and meticulous planning. As the bus became bogged down in traffic, a motorist got out of his car to tell McWatters and his passengers of the shooting of the president.[1]

It may well have been at that instant that Oswald himself learned how deeply he was involved in something that he had not had full knowledge of even an hour before. Realizing this, he exited the bus and headed for a taxi parked adjacent to a bus terminal. Logic would have dictated taking the first out-of-town bus, but logic also would have told Oswald that the police would have sealed such exits, which they had not. So he chose the taxi, offering it to a woman (nice touch), and then sitting in the *front* seat, which might cause the casual onlooker (or police, who already knew whom to arrest) to doubt that he was a passenger, but perhaps another cabbie getting a ride home from a coworker. Still with his wits about him, he exited the cab several blocks from the rooming house at 1026 North Beckley Street, paying the 95-cent fare and allowing for a nickel tip. (Mistake: Cabbies never forget big spenders or cheapskates.)

The question must be asked why Oswald exited the cab far enough away that he still had a few minutes' walk. Was he suspicious of walking into a trap or ambush? If so, by whom, and how would they know, unless Oswald was in reality *part* of something, and he had just realized the exact nature of his role? He would, of course, later announce his patsy status to the press and the police. The press took notice of it.

Notwithstanding, Oswald's actions in the twenty-five minutes after departing the TSBD suggest, if not shout, "patsy" rather than assassin, particularly the "distant" exit from the cab. Who would have known about the North Beckley Street address? It was rented in the name "O. H. Lee," although the police were there to search it by midafternoon with no clear indication in the documentation *how* they became aware of it. Nobody at the TSBD knew exactly, although Wesley Frazier knew about a place in "Oak Cliff"; the Paines and the Oswalds were ignorant of its location, although Ruth Paine had the phone number, which could have been cross-checked. There's just no record that it was done that way.

Yet Oswald feared to go directly there.

Neither Oswald's fears nor his wits deserted him upon arrival at the 1026 North Beckley Street address, as he uncharacteristically changed clothes in midday.[2] This action suggests that he did not want to be recognized in the clothing he had worn that morning, a hint that person or persons unknown would have a way to recognize him and Oswald preferred to meet them, if at all, with surprise on his side. In an interesting sidebar to the wardrobe change, Officer Marrion Baker, who had gotten a good look at Oswald in the TSBD lunchroom, testified that Oswald was wearing a different shirt when arrested. This testimony does more than just change the image of Oswald from that of a slob to that of a fashion plate. First, it dictates that Oswald could tell the truth on occasion, as he told his captors that he had changed. More importantly, however, it gives the lie to the FBI, which took both the "arrested" shirt and the Mannlicher to Washington in the early morning hours of November 23 and discovered a tuft of fibers from the "arrested" shirt on the weapon. Baker's testimony demonstrates that either Oswald had had the weapon and that shirt together at some previous time, proving nothing, or that the FBI was trying to introduce fraudulent, posthumous evidence.[3]

By the time Oswald was changing, a description bland enough to fit any number of individuals had already been broadcast. We do not know its precise source. A few minutes after Oswald's departure from the rooming house, officer 221 had a description for the suspect in the Tippit slaying: white male, 27, 5'11", 165 pounds, black wavy hair, fair complexted [sic] wearing light gray Eisenhower jacket, dark trousers, and white shirt; "armed with a .32, dark finish, automatic pistol."[4] The gender, age, complexion, jacket, and trousers are reasonably accurate; the height and weight suggest a different person, as does the hair; the shirt could not be more wrong, and two out of three parts of the gun description are way off the mark. A .32 is quite different from a .38, and an automatic is to a revolver what a convertible is to a station wagon. In a subsequent transmission, the gun changes slightly, but is based on more definite data: "The shell at the scene indicates that the suspect is armed with an automatic .38 *rather than a pistol*" (emphasis added).[5]

If it was in fact Oswald who committed the murder of Officer Tippit, and there is evidence to argue both sides of that question, it must still be asked how the encounter and the shooting came to be. As noted, why would Tippit stop Oswald, a bland creature on foot a good distance from the scene of the crime? Does this sound like the behavior of an assassin? Why would Tippit be so careless? He would not have stopped Oswald for anything less than suspicion of murdering the president;* such being the case, could he have believed an assassin would be unarmed or not feel threatened as a policeman approached to take him into custody? How could he let his guard down so thoroughly? There's not a hint anywhere of Oswald being a quick-draw artist, yet the officer took four bullets while unholstering his service revolver, although we must allow for the possibility that the first shot was fatal.

Even then, it does not all add up, and it still suggests patsy rather than assassin: Tippit stopped the person he knew to stop, expecting no resistance.

The next known stop on the journey of the peripatetic defector-*cum*-assassin was at Johnny Brewer's shoe store window, where Os-

---

*Another possibility does exist. Several sources have told this author that J. D. Tippit had a reputation for rousting anybody and everybody, and usually just for the hell of it; some of them remember Tippit as "the neighborhood ——hole."

wald's lack of thespian skills betrayed him, and Brewer sensed in Oswald's behavior a seriousness of purpose with respect to avoiding the police vehicles going up and down the block with sirens screaming.

From there, Oswald traveled part of a block to the Texas Theater, which he entered without buying a ticket. Whether his wits, nerve, or both had deserted him in so entering would be a valid question. On the other hand, because the ticket booth was empty, with ticket seller Julia Postal at the curb to view the manhunt in progress, perhaps Oswald was acting wisely in not going to the curb to ask to buy a ticket. It is also possible that he did not plan to stay in the theater any longer than it would take to make a prearranged contact, a suggestion often hinted at in the literature and supported by theater patron Jack Davis. Oswald, according to Davis, came and sat next to him, in a theater with nine hundred seats and only fifteen to twenty patrons. Staying only briefly, Oswald left Davis and went and sat next to others.[6] Oswald's search for a contact is also supported by logic, for if he were *not* looking for someone, wisdom would have suggested he enter the front of the theater and exit the back, then leave the area in haste. By the time the police, who heard from Julia Postal, alerted by Brewer, arrived, and searched the theater, Oswald could have been a good distance away.

When the police did arrive, in quantity, Captain Westbrook testified, "A male employee said, 'The man in the fourth row from the back in the middle aisle is the man.' "[7] While Westbrook might have confused Brewer with a theater employee, the statement as it appears in the quotation allows for sinister possibilities—that Oswald was "fingered" in the theater, not contacted—or else the "Brewer" confusion should have been cleared up. It would have been easy enough to do.

Once identified, Oswald was slowly and cautiously approached by police, and did nothing with respect to his weapon until the police were on top of him. Had he drawn it sooner, theater or no theater, patrons or no patrons, he would have been shot dead on the spot. Perhaps he thought briefly that these police were on his side of the fence, but when that possibility did not materialize, he took alternative action, pulling his gun, but close-in, so there was no shooting, yet he had resisted, giving himself an explanation for his arrest, and pistol possession, which he would claim in confinement, is obviously far less serious than murder of a policeman or a president.

Within seconds he was subdued and immediately began shouting, "I am not resisting arrest!" He still had his wits and apparently he still placed a value on his own life.

Once he was in custody, Oswald's billfold identification indicated he was "Oswald" and "Hidell," and Oswald did nothing to cooperate with the authorities in clearing up the confusion, a seemingly odd decision, since the Mannlicher-Carcano had been shipped to "Hidell" at the post office box rented by Oswald. This again suggests a patsy scenario, for "assassin" Oswald would have identified himself by his birth name and simply denied the existence of "Hidell." But "Hidell" was essential to the tangential role Oswald had fallen into, and he was unwisely carrying the "Hidell" documents, so for reasons known perhaps only to him and those who contrived the event, he continued the charade.

In focusing his intelligence on staying alive, Oswald was unknowingly already in a trap from which he would never emerge. Several individuals who were at headquarters when Oswald was brought in have insisted that the police were openly saying, as early as 2:00 P.M., that Oswald was the defendant for both murders.

Although it is not possible to document all of the agencies that *were* contacted after the arrest of Oswald, it is odd that the 112th Military Intelligence Group in San Antonio was contacted to see if they had anything about a "Hidell," and they were able to check their files and conveniently learn that "Hidell" cross-referenced to a Harvey Lee or Henry Lee Oswald. (The file was "routinely destroyed," so it cannot be checked for precision.) This, too, is unusual, as the CIA had taken photos of a heavyset man, Henry Lee Oswald, in Mexico, and also, and perhaps of equal or greater merit, was the concern that "Hidell," prior to November 22, had only appeared as the name that ordered the Mannlicher-Carcano.

What it all amounts to is that somehow military intelligence knew a great deal about Oswald/"Hidell" but did nothing about it and what they admitted to knowing should either have caused serious concern, which it did not, in spite of Oswald's "defection," or it should have been ignored, which it also was not. People rent post office boxes and purchase mail-order rifles far too regularly and routinely for this to be a serious concern of *military intelligence*.

Oswald should have had counsel at all times during questioning, but he never had any such legal assistance. Given the nature of the charges that authorities were readying against him, they, too, should have insisted that his rights be protected. The suspect himself seemed to have done some homework on the issue of legal counsel, requesting assistance from John Abt, a New York lawyer who had represented *communist* defendants in conspiracy cases involving violation of the Smith Act, which made it a crime to belong to an organization advocating the violent overthrow of the U.S. government. This again suggests patsy status, as Oswald had a prepared defense, but it was for belonging to a group of which he was not a member, as opposed to being the only suspect in the murder of a president, hardly within the legal realm of even John Abt.

In his brief Warren Commission testimony (nine questions), Abt indicated he had never heard of Oswald. Abt spent far more time with the Warren Commission, however, as the legal counsel present during the testimony of witnesses active in communist-related organizations or publications.

The closest Oswald got to legal counsel was a visit from local ACLU attorneys, whom Oswald spurned although he had listed the ACLU only three weeks earlier on his final post office box rental. The other legal opportunity that passed him by involved a telephone call to flamboyant New Orleans attorney Dean Andrews on November 23. The call, purporting to come from a "Clay Bertrand," requested Andrews to defend Oswald in Dallas. Andrews was in the hospital at the time, and by the time he was released, Oswald was beyond hospitalization.[8]

Dallas police and FBI efforts at interrogation of the unrepresented high-school dropout yielded precious little data, yet raised further sinister concerns. In a February 6, 1964, affidavit (he usually communicated by letter), J. Edgar Hoover deposed that Oswald had been interviewed by FBI agents on November 22 "to obtain any information he might have been able to furnish *of a security nature.*"[9] The same affidavit that spoke of the Oswald FBI security debriefing went to great lengths to deny that the FBI ever had any mutually beneficial contacts with the prisoner. There's an odd contradiction there: The FBI claimed to have no connection to Oswald, yet they wanted to debrief the accused presidential assassin for reasons of security?

Locally, Captain Fritz, seen as the consummate interrogator, pointedly asked Oswald during one questioning session if he had had any interrogation training.[10] This was hardly a throwaway question, and my fascination with statistics inclines me to be skeptical that such a question would have been posed to 1 percent or fewer of Fritz's previous criminal contacts, although that is not provable. Yet the question remains: Why was such a question put to Oswald? Notice has been taken in the past of similar thoughts expressed by various officials, and here the head of the Dallas Homicide Bureau ratified the suspicion. The marines certainly offer no such training to the average recruit. The Soviets would hardly offer interrogation resistance to a "defector" whose brains they desired to pick clean. So what was Fritz's suspicion based on, and where could the Warren Commission's Oswald have picked up such expertise?

Needless to say, Fritz's suspicions were not broadcast at the time, as officialdom, and the media, and as a result the majority of the population, were focusing on Oswald's guilt and politics. The ever-curious Seth Kantor added an odd scribble on his notepad: "poss[ibility] of Commie plot—[Oswald] questioned by FBI in recent days."[11] Did "recent days" mean the forty-odd hours of Oswald's custody, or did the FBI's questions to Oswald occur before 12:30 P.M. of November 22? If so, we have been duped once again.

FBI informant and erstwhile postal inspector Harry Holmes told of repeated questions put to Oswald regarding communist affiliations, and of Oswald's stock answer that he was a Marxist, not a communist.[12] Assistant District Attorney William Alexander, whose instincts had earlier told him that the murderer of Officer Tippit was also the presidential assassin, followed in the Hoover school of thought, offhandedly branding Oswald "a Goddamn Communist."[13] Henry Wade, Alexander's boss, was more forthcoming. Admitting he had won death penalty convictions on less evidence than he had against Oswald, he added, "I have absolutely no evidence that he was a Communist."[14]

Statements like Alexander's, made in a crowded hallway, as opposed to Wade's statement, made in a Warren Commission hearing room well after the event, certainly helped shape a Gallup poll that indicated that many Americans believed communists were involved in a JFK plot.[15]

After Jack Ruby temporarily put the issue to rest, permanently putting Oswald to rest, the nation suddenly began to become queasy about events in Dallas, but they never lost their perspective, formed quickly, about Oswald's guilt or politics. Ruby's action only ratified the theory that something about the event was becoming offensive to the nostrils.

Oswald was posthumously fingerprinted by the FBI, for reasons unknown, and even then his image was tarnished, as the card bears the intransigent suggestion, "refused to sign." Elsewhere the issue is clarified, as it notes that the subject was "deceased."[16] Equally moribund was a package addressed to "Lee Oswald" that was discovered in the dead-letter office of the Irving Post Office. The package contained a paper bag similar to the one allegedly used to transport the Mannlicher into the TSBD.[17] Someone was going to extreme lengths to convince the world of Oswald's guilt in a situation where either the valid evidence did not or there was no case. As it turned out, the "valid evidence" was never challenged in a court of law.

Other forces were also in motion that weekend. Marina Oswald understandably did very little to aid the investigation while her husband remained alive, and after his death, her stoicism was pierced by governmental suggestions that amounted to alternating threats and promises. Despite these, she maintained that Oswald harbored no hostility against JFK or Connally (although she would later hedge on Connally), she denied seeing Lee with a gun, yet she admitted that based on what she had heard, she was satisfied "that Lee Oswald had killed President JOHN F. KENNEDY," putting her in agreement with the vast majority of a stunned population as of November 28, 1963.[18]

In a tasteless and erroneous display of just how far the "Red patsy" syndrome had gone, Secret Service agent William H. Patterson filed a report dated November 25, 1963, coincidentally the date of the funerals of President Kennedy and his alleged assailant. To understand fully the public-relations-like campaign at work, the brief report must be quoted almost in its entirety. The opening paragraph indicated that Marina had been contacted about ten days before the assassination, "and she had told them that her husband worked in the building from which the president was killed." As written, this was ridiculous, since the president was clearly alive ten days before the assassination.

The second paragraph tells how Patterson spoke to an FBI agent "on the subversive desk" who told him that Oswald had contacts with "two known subversive agents about fifteen days before the shooting." He added, "The entire information was top secret and he could not tell us any more, but he felt sure that the file would be turned over to our chief." Two questions are obvious here: First, why didn't the public, through the Warren Commission, ever see this report, which was mentioned in the commission's own working papers? *And secondly, why didn't this information reach the head of the Secret Service while John Kennedy was still alive?*

Regarding Marina, her bona fides were also questioned, as Agent Patterson wrote, "She advised that she was a Castro supporter and from the interview it was felt that she is still a hard core communist." (Arguably, it is difficult "still" to be something you never were in the first place.)

A statement containing less truth would be hard to imagine, unless it contained the timeworn phrase "lone assassin."

Mrs. Oswald was also seen to be oblique: "She stated he had never mentioned killing the president but would not mention anything about shooting Connally." The report concluded, "It was felt by the interviewer that she was not telling the truth and still believed in communism."[19]

A few days later, the Secret Service introduced their Russian translator, Special Agent Leon Gopadze, to Mrs. Oswald as "Mr. Lee," the same name Oswald had used when rooming at the boardinghouse.[20]

In a final, little-known tangential event, an eighteen-year-old self-styled Virginia Nazi arrived at Dallas Police headquarters with a near-life-size effigy of Castro. "A sign affixed to the Castro effigy blamed the Cuban dictator for President John F. Kennedy's assassination and urged an invasion of the Communist-controlled island."[21] That was, after all, the purpose of the exercise from the very beginning.

The deception had succeeded. Oswald had been painted as a "Red" to the exclusion of all other political hues, and this despite constant disclaimers from him, as well as from people who had enough knowledge to form a judgment. Oswald also confessed to being a patsy, but since no corroborative evidence was sought with regard to that confession, nor was the suspect questioned about the only probative confession he made, that part of the story became a curious footnote, not a cause for action.

It strikes me as unusual that that which Oswald vehemently denied, after having avoided communism for so long in his posturing era, would be so easily believed, while that which he confessed to ("patsy") could be so easily ignored.

Truth had now assumed a political and subjective nature, and from this event many Americans dated their loss of faith in government pronouncements.

Book Three

White Lies

CHAPTER ONE

HOOVER TO WARREN TO CHANCE

Hoover was *the FBI.*

—J. GARY SHAW, *Cover-Up,* p. 183

FORMER FBI SPECIAL AGENT HENRY WADE, district attorney for Dallas County on November 22, 1963, was quoted early on in the investigation into the assassination of the president as saying, ". . . preliminary [i.e., pre-Hoover] reports indicated that more than one person was involved in the shooting."[1]

An FBI document not made public until 1977 showed that thirteen hundred miles away, at approximately 3:30 P.M. *Eastern time,* eight minutes before Lyndon Johnson was even sworn in aboard *Air Force One* and a mere thirty-nine minutes after Oswald's arrest, J. Edgar Hoover called Robert Kennedy to report that the killer was an ex-marine who defected to the Soviet Union and was also known to be a procommunist nut.[2]

The import of these two events cannot be overlooked. Wade would not subsequently repeat any conspiratorial statements, although Chief Curry would refuse to deny such a possibility. Hoover's statement, on the other hand, flew directly into the face of all previous *known or admitted* activity by the FBI with respect to Oswald, assuming Oswald was the ex-marine defector Commie nut that Hoover was referring to.

We have already seen how there was absolutely no documentation, not even based on Oswald's at times bizarre posturing habits, of

Oswald as a *communist*. He had been reissued a passport in haste, according to testimony by the head of the Passport Office, specifically because FBI reports indicated that Oswald had no communist affiliations, or that there existed the possibility that Oswald was somehow in the employ of the U.S. government.

We have also seen several FBI reports that showed that the bureau's web of confidential informants had no awareness whatsoever of Oswald in local communist or Cuban cells. It was also noted that Oswald was interrogated by bureau agents on November 22 "to obtain any information he might have been able to furnish of a security nature."[3] More curious wording and more ambiguous, inexplicable meaning are hard to imagine. What could Lee Oswald, in custody, possibly have told the FBI with respect to security?

But suddenly, on November 22, Oswald blossomed into a full-tilt, murdering Bolshevik demon, known, well before November 22, according to Agent Patterson's report cited in "The Hunt for Red Oswald," to the FBI subversive desk because of recent (and presumed) subversive activities.

As suggested in passages cited above, which pointed toward Hoover's pre- and postassassination complicity, his statements were holy writ with respect to the actions of every subordinate in the bureau, be they upper-level management personnel, journeymen agents, or fledgling rookies. In that sense, the FBI investigation was concluded before Lyndon Johnson raised his right hand, and at a time when the Dallas police were still not sure if they had arrested a Hidell or an Oswald (although, as noted in "Red Patsy," the police knew that their suspect, whoever he was, had committed both murders). All that was required was for the FBI to flesh out the details of Oswald's guilt, and this, of course, was made easier by his all-too-brief custody in Dallas, as well as by the willingness of Dallas authorities *not* to have the case too closely examined. Or ever *cross*-examined.

Another curious and yet–unexplained anomaly then emerged. While the FBI was concluding its investigation in December, the Secret Service was investigating the crime. They had been involved in its investigation well before that time, and they would continue to do so well after. Yet the Secret Service manual is very clear in that the service's responsibilities do *not* include investigation or apprehension with respect to assassins.[4] This raises an obvious concern: Why were they investigating? Did they suspect that Hoover had made his decision about the case, which was binding on every bureau

employee, and had then lifted the rug to sweep everything else underneath it? Did the Secret Service have reason to suspect that they
would emerge from Hoover's "investigation" with a black eye, and
forfeit some of their responsibilities and/or budgetary privileges?

Did the Secret Service, dedicated to the protection of the president
(and, since then, others) and the American currency, smell something
very rotten?

The evidence is clear that something was very wrong, and it only
got worse when Jack Ruby, former confidential FBI informant for
Special Agent Charles Flynn, murdered Oswald. If there is a scintilla
of truth to the bevy of allegations that Oswald had some minor role
in Hoover's FBI, we arrive at a scenario in which a bureau "asset"
was charged with killing the president, was then killed by a second
bureau "asset," and the FBI itself was put in charge of the case.

The FBI was therefore possibly investigating the killing of one of
its employees by yet another of its employees. "Extreme justice,"
according to Racine, "is often injustice."[5]

The problems with our understanding of the FBI case did not begin
on November 22, 1963. The FBI interviewed Robert Oswald on
June 26, 1962, and he was asked to inform the bureau when his
brother Lee returned to Texas. As it happened, Lee was already back
in the Lone Star State, prompting Robert to conclude, "If they did
not know that Lee Harvey Oswald had returned in June, until June
26, 1962 [when he told them], somebody was asleep on the job."[6]

The following April, when someone took a shot at the Walker
residence, the key witness was Walter Kirk Coleman, a young man
who saw automobiles, and gave descriptions to Dallas authorities that
did not delineate Oswald but that did include weapons and automobiles. Although *not* called before the subsequent Warren Commission,
Coleman did give a statement to the FBI repeating what he had
told local authorities (which had no mention whatsoever of Oswald).
Coleman's FBI report is curiously titled *Lee Harvey Oswald*.[7]

Two weeks before the motorcade, Oswald delivered a note to
Dallas FBI headquarters. This would be the same day he wrote the
curious "Dear Mr. Hunt" letter that asked for clarification of Oswald's position before any further action was taken. The "Hunt"
letter remains a mystery, although there have never been more than
two considerations as to who "Hunt" was: E. Howard Hunt or

H. L. Hunt, or, by extension, his progeny. The FBI letter is equally important, as its intended recipient, Special Agent James Hosty, was ordered by Gordon Shanklin, special agent in charge of the Dallas office, to destroy the document—hardly bureau procedure. Hosty would subsequently be censured and transferred, along with sixteen other agents. The record is not clear why. It would not make sense, however, to assume that Hosty was punished only because he followed Shanklin's order, as Shanklin was not punished.

On November 22, we have already seen Hoover act in haste over the telephone, but this was reinforced on paper by a memo involving Hoover and Nicholas deB. Katzenbach, standing in for the grief-stricken RFK at the Department of Justice. The memo suggested that everything possible must be done "to convince the public that Oswald is the real assassin."[8] While there are many key words in that terse statement, the most significant one would seem to be "real." Had the memo suggested "to convince the public that Oswald is the assassin," it would seem extremely hasty prejudgment; but to go to such lengths to make him the "real" assassin strongly suggests that there were well-founded suspicions that he was not. Katzenbach would later commit to paper the notion that "speculation about Oswald's motive ought to be cut off."[9] This campaign was obviously successful, as to this day we have no motive for Oswald, and not even the otherwise omniscient Warren Commission could offer one.

During the night of November 22–23, under intense pressure from officials in Washington, the Dallas police high command inexplicably gave the FBI literally all the evidence they had *against Oswald*. It is understandable that Dallas authorities might have needed laboratory analysis or expertise on a piece-by-piece basis from the FBI laboratory, but to surrender the entire corpus of the case against a still-living Lee Oswald and send no officers to protect that evidence was to guarantee that it would not be seen again. Much of the material never made it back to Dallas, although it never needed to be produced as "evidence" in any federal or any other kind of case. In a case involving thousands of unresolved "coincidences," one of the strangest would seem to be that the FBI possessed the key evidence against a defendant who was killed by an FBI informant, thus relieving them of the obligation to return such evidence. Further, it allowed them to bury or confuse much of the evidence, for, strange as it may seem, Dallas police authorities never "officially" saw the magic bullet, the set piece in the emerging lone-assassin theory. They also never saw the home movie taken by Abraham Zapruder, the airing of which in the mid-1970s caused enough national concern that a new investigation—with a new conclusion—was launched into the assassination of the president.

And while the Dallas authorities gave the FBI all they had on Oswald, there is not even a hint that they requested FBI follow-up on any of the several other individuals detained or suspected, howsoever briefly, on November 22.

Ignored at this point were the statements of undercover FBI operative Edward Becker, who had knowledge of the activities of Carlos Marcello, described by his FBI case officer as "a tomato salesman."[10] Does the FBI assign a senior agent like Regis Kennedy to every Louisiana "tomato salesman"? Information regarding Marcello's intense dislike for the Kennedy brothers was also available to Eugene DeLaparra, another FBI informant, but this data also was overlooked.[11]

"Buried" would also describe what happened to information provided to the FBI by Dallas police officers who saw weapons practice on the knoll on Wednesday, November 20, the same day that a Mauser was casually brought into the TSBD, a multistory building overlooking the presidential motorcade route. Equally interred were the reports that Oswald had been seen in Clinton, Louisiana, in the company of David Ferrie and either Guy Banister or Clay Shaw, as well as other reports from Louisiana officials indicating serious allegations being made about the president's safety by an individual named Rose Cheramie.[12] Author Mark North, who has thoroughly researched the FBI's chicanery, also noted that the page from Oswald's notebook that contained data with respect to Agent Hosty also contained the name "Gandy." A "Helen Gandy" was Hoover's private secretary; Oswald may thus have been important enough to have direct access to Hoover's office. Failing that, we must believe that Oswald may have been making incorrectly spelled notes about a deceased Indian believer in nonviolence.[13]

Equally buried is the truth of the whereabouts of J. Edgar Hoover on the evening of November 21, 1963. It has always been hinted that Hoover, along with a handful of other power brokers, attended a gathering at the Dallas home of Clint Murchison. Hard evidence is not lacking: Hoover's private driver, a black "gofer" later given an FBI badge to make it appear that the bureau had decided to become an equal opportunity employer, gave compelling evidence that his employer had been in Dallas on November 21, as did Madeline Brown, longtime LBJ paramour. If Hoover was in that metropolitan area, it is highly likely that his presence would have been demanded at the Murchison event, which was not held to raise funds for the 1964 reelection of John Kennedy. It is also to be remembered that if Hoover was at the Murchisons' home late into the evening of November 21–22, there must have been an urgency to it, as Hoover was back at his desk in Washington as if nothing had happened, and Hoover did not like to fly. That, however, is the only form of conveyance that could have returned him from Dallas to D.C. in time.

FBI agents told gunsmith Dial Ryder to keep the "Oswald repair tag," promising they would return to get it. This requires the question to be asked as to exactly when it became bureau policy to allow witnesses to keep valuable pieces of evidence.[14] The government showed a willingness to seize Oswald's shower shoes, his pay stubs, and Mrs. Paine's slide projector and 78rpm record collection, yet they showed considerably less interest in a repair tag for a high-powered rifle. This is selectivity honed to its finest edge.

Simultaneous to their maintenance of the lone-nut story, the FBI did everything possible to hinder the operation of the Warren Commission. J. Lee Rankin, who would become general counsel to the commission, was a compromise choice, as the original choice, Warren Olney III, had been an FBI agent and was critical of Hoover. At the same time, Hoover, subsequently referred to by FBI assistant director William Sullivan as "the greatest blackmailer of all time," gave marching orders to agents to find derogatory material on Warren Commission members and staff, a clear indication that he may have had to resort to his usual blackmail to preserve their silence on some of the issues they would subsequently be exploring. His directive to gather data on the commission and its staff is clearly beyond the category of patriotic curiosity, particularly when there are strong suggestions that Hoover already possessed some kind of handle on the commission's venerable chairman.[15]

The previous orders to those agents—and hundreds were involved—amounted to finding out everything that possibly pointed in the direction of both Oswald and Ruby being portrayed as lone assassins. By the date of the creation of the Warren Commission, November 29, literally hundreds, if not thousands (including many not published), of FBI reports were submitted, detailing both Oswald's and Ruby's formative years, and interviews were conducted with thousands of individuals, most of whom had nothing to offer, as they had known Ruby in the 1930s but knew of no connection between him and the as yet unborn Oswald.

FBI agents did considerable spadework; the results, however, suggest that their chief intended their shoveling efforts focused more to inter than to uncover.

Jean Hill's friendly motorcycle officer "J. B." told her at the time, "It looks to me like they've [FBI] already decided the case they want to make, and they'll do their damndest to discredit any witness whose testimony might weaken their case."[16] If one Dallas officer could tumble to the FBI's scam, why not the venerable Warren Commission?

As events would prove, they did also.

To undercut the formation of the commission, the FBI released its report on the assassination on December 5, the date of the first meeting of the commission. To underscore the "thoroughness" of this document, also known as the Gemberling Report, it should be noted that it even contained testimony about dreams people had regarding the Kennedy assassination.[17] (The last known use of dreams as items of evidence had occurred in Salem in 1692.)

The commission would be assigned quarters in the Veterans Building, at 200 Maryland Avenue, N.E., in Washington. To aid the commission's work, the FBI installed a scale model of Dealey Plaza, and movie projectors. Although not a gambler at heart, I would wager heavily that scale models and projectors were not *all* they installed.

The commission would constantly be frustrated by Hoover's preconceived notions of Oswald's—and only Oswald's—guilt. Staff members were upset at the lack of FBI cooperation, or by the bureau's willingness to forward five thousand documents when asked for five, guaranteeing that quality would be sacrificed to quantity for the understaffed commission. J. Lee Rankin, who had passed Hoover's muster for general counsel, summed up the commission's concern in late January: "Part of our difficulty ... They [FBI] have decided that it is Oswald who committed the assassination; they have decided that no one else is involved."[18] Hoover also made sure there were frequent "lone assassin" leaks, and, as noted, was made director for life on May 8, six days before his commission testimony. The permanence of his tenure amounted to a guarantee of freedom from prosecution, and for good reason, as Hoover perjured himself on several occasions during his brief appearance before the commission.[19] He also demonstrated an appalling ignorance of events while trying to flaunt expertise; he referred to the depository at one point as "The Texas Book House." (For his perjury, as well as other un-American and illegal acts committed during his tenure, Hoover nevertheless had the new FBI headquarters in Washington named after him. The only other nominees must have been Hermann Goering and Lavrenti Beria.)

The commission, lacking the documentation as well as insight into 1963 FBI mentality, had no idea of—or no willingness to admit to— the massive FBI wiretap efforts of the bureau prior to 1963, nor the volume or tone of the anti-Kennedy rhetoric recorded for FBI posterity from those wiretaps.

Equally troubling was the commission's widely divergent, compartmentalized staff. The seven senior members were too busy elsewhere to devote much time to their responsibilities, and had to rely on the FBI's honesty, which would cause disappointment. When the FBI interviewed Dr. Earl Rose, the topic was *Oswald's* autopsy (and there is very little that is unclear about how *he* died), with not a word about the treatment accorded Dr. Rose when trying to perform his duties with respect to the murder of the president.[20] When federal agents interviewed Mrs. Lovell Penn, whose pasture had been invaded by shooters with 6.5mm rifles shortly before the assassination, she was not asked to identify Oswald from among those she saw (as she could not); she was not asked for details, or even about the 6.5mm cartridge she found. The entire report, Commission Exhibit 2448, runs to forty-four words, fewer than the previous *sentence*.[21] Commission exhibit 1416, an FBI interview with railroad worker James L. Simmons, is arguably the most contrived FBI report to that point in the published record. Try to follow the exact wording, which is an adaptation of Simmons' assertion that he saw smoke on the knoll:

> SIMMONS said he recalled that a motorcycle policeman drove up the grassy slope toward the Texas School Book Depository Building, jumped off his motorcycle and then ran up the hill toward the Memorial Arches. SIMMONS said he thought he saw exhaust fumes of smoke near the embankment in front of the Texas School Book Depository Building. SIMMONS then ran toward the Texas School Book Depository Building with a policeman. He stopped at a fence near the Memorial Arches and could not find anyone.[22]

Abounding with geographical impossibilities and slick wording to suggest that Simmons was saying something he was not, this document was nothing short of obstruction of justice by the agents who signed it, Thomas A. Trettis, Jr., and E. J. Robertson, and it was also an instructive sample, as the depositions of virtually all the railroad workers (one out of ten of whom was heard by the commission) were similarly hatcheted by the FBI.

Nor was this the last FBI semantic nightmare. Attempts were made to change the wording of the Dallas police inventory of Oswald's possessions to read "Minox light meter" rather than "Minox [spy] camera," a device recently admitted to be a Minox *camera,* but by its real owner, Michael Paine. Thus the FBI faced—or solved—two dilemmas with their "light meter" scenario: It was not a camera, and it kept Michael Paine out of the loop, which was just as well, since he could not have taken the photos developed from the film in the "light meter."

In addition, all references to Guy Banister spoke of his office at 531 Lafayette Street, although the office was equally accessible through the 544 Camp Street entrance, the address that happened to appear on some of Oswald's pro-Castro, "Hands Off Cuba" leaflets.[23]

By mid-1964, all remaining TSBD employees had been fingerprinted, but the report that provided this information was silent as to whether any of those prints matched the many non-Oswald prints in the "sniper's nest," or if not, whether the FBI looked into its millions of prints to find out whom they did match.[24] That report, like so many others that had nothing to do with him, was labeled "Lee Harvey Oswald" eight months after he was put into the earth, preventing further fingerprinting of him.

The FBI also took an interesting survey. They contacted all seventy-three known TSBD employees and asked them to reply to a series of questions. They were asked (1) Where were they when the shots were fired? (2) Did they see Oswald as the shots were being fired? (3) Did they know Oswald? (4) When did they leave? and (5) Did they see any strangers in the building?

Interestingly, this brief survey did *not* ask (1) the source of the shots, as many employees testified to a variety of locations for the shots they believed did not emanate from the depository, and that they quickly reentered the building, a behavior not likely if they had any inkling the killer was in there; (2) the number of shots, as the FBI had already decided that; (3) any observations the seventy-three individuals would care to add to the record; and (4) whether anyone saw any police officers, as opposed to "strangers," in the TSBD."[25]

Ultimately, the political survival of J. Edgar Hoover, as well as the survival of the FBI *as Hoover had molded it for thirty-nine years,* depended on the acceptance of the Oswald-lone-nut theory. If it had been a conspiracy, clearly the public perception would have been that the FBI missed it before the event, and covered it up after the fact. Likewise, Oswald had to be not just a lone assassin, for even then, his résumé/bona fides should have made him an FBI concern. He also had to be a "nut" who decided to do something different for lunch on Friday, November 22, 1963.

Years after the event and Hoover's passing, the House Select Committee on Assassinations concluded that the FBI investigation was so flawed that they probably would not have discovered a conspiracy if one had existed. The reasoning, which they did not include, was fundamental: The FBI was never looking for a conspiracy. In their Report, the House select committee concluded, "FBI generally exhausted its resources in confirming the case against Lee Harvey Oswald as the lone assassin, a case that Director J. Edgar Hoover, at least, seemed determined to make within twenty-four hours of the assassination."[26]

Interestingly, we have excellent evidence that such an agenda was not exclusively Hoover's. In tape recordings aired on ABC's *Nightline* on December 1, 1993, Lyndon Johnson is heard, prior to the appointment of the Warren Commission, telling columnist (and close friend of JFK's) Joseph Alsop that the FBI should investigate the case fully and then pass its results to the state of Texas. Alsop argued for a blue-ribbon commission (instead, we got Earl Warren et al.); Johnson wanted to know why the FBI should not handle the matter; Alsop indicated they would not be believed.[27]

Now, there is a scenario: Lyndon Johnson hoping that the combined resources of the FBI, handed as gospel to Texas authorities, would satisfy the public. Had that occurred, the loose ends convicting Oswald would have been completed well before Christmas 1963, much less the 1964 election.

★   ★   ★

The title of this chapter was not accidental. A couple of generations back, there emerged on the baseball scene an infield combination known as "Tinker to Evers [rhymes with 'Beavers'] to Chance." They received this acclaim as they were able to turn a dozen or so double plays in one season, a feat hitherto unknown. Their title was also a sign of respect for their baseball ability in such deft sleight of hand that spectators were left wondering how it was done. Since their time, any such sleight of hand that is deft enough to leave the public curious has received the "Tinker to Evers to Chance" acclamation.

In 1963, J. Edgar *Hoover* covered up many events related to the assassination of President John F. Kennedy. Hoover passed along what he saw fit, usually worthless, sanitized, or misworded voluminous garbage, to Earl *Warren*, whose understaffed fact-finding body could neither wade through the mass nor understand it.

The truth was left *to chance*.

CHAPTER TWO

THE WARREN COMMISSION

A lot of people are talking in terms of, well, you know, maybe there is more to this than just the case of one man and one act. But it is going to take a long time before we ever know for sure, if we ever do.

—DAN RATHER, KRLD, November 23, 1963

But nobody reads. . . . There will be a few professors who will read the record. . . . The public will read very little.

—ALLEN DULLES, member of the Warren Commission

I can't lie because I didn't bring a lawyer with me.

—a curious comment by Ruby's roommate George Senator to Warren Commission counsel Leon Hubert, after Senator was reminded, as testimony resumed, that he was still under oath (14H 186)

As WE ARE ALL PAINFULLY AWARE, John Kennedy was killed by a brief flurry of gunfire in Dealey Plaza, in downtown Dallas, Texas, shortly after noon on November 22, 1963. We also know that it has become a point of commonality among Americans living at the time to recall, usually without difficulty, exactly where they were at the moment they heard the news.

The weekend became a blur. Family members returned home at the end of the workday, some of which were cut short, and opted

270

to open a "can of something" because the usually simple chore of preparing a meal seemed overwhelming. We remained in close touch with media accounts, although there really was a dearth of "news," since there was only one event that day, and the official verdict of that one event already seemed a foregone conclusion.

Our faith, shattered by the tragedy, was somehow given a boost because we knew that the FBI and the Secret Service, in addition to local authorities, would leave no stone unturned in their pursuit of justice. Little did we know that the stones left unturned could fill a quarry that the totality of Egyptian pyramid builders would have rebelled at.

Saturday was a relatively slow news day, inasmuch as America was drained from the adrenaline shock of Friday's events and probably had not gotten the usual night's sleep. Somehow, we wanted things back to normal, yet knew they never again could *be* normal. We were even ambivalent about football, as some colleges played their Saturday games and others canceled, out of respect for the slain president. The NFL went on with business as usual on Sunday, while the fledgling AFL canceled. Sports touts would at least have something with which to grab a headline.

Many Americans knew that Monday would not be a workday, which took some of the usual edge off of Sunday. Yet in our still unclear mental states, we thirsted for more news, and we waited near the television for that one additional opportunity to view this *monster,* this *Oswald* who had killed our president, and for many of us, our dreams.

We did get a glimpse of him. He took a few steps, a horn honked, a shot was fired, and suddenly the comfort that was ever so slowly returning to our individual private worlds was again shattered. *Something really was wrong—very wrong.* America and Americans might have tolerated one "lone nut" killer, but now it strained credibility to be told that Friday's "lone nut" had been killed by Sunday's "lone nut."

All over America, cash registers rang up "NO SALE."

In Texas, investigations were demanded now for the totality of the event at virtually the same time that phone calls from the White House were dictating to Chief of Homicide Fritz that he should shut the investigation down and leave it to the world to make the obvious conclusion that it was Oswald and Oswald alone. This was hardly a new concern for Dallas authorities, as they had been told by a White House caller on Friday night how to word Oswald's indictment for the murder of the president.

Other phones, however, were also being utilized in Washington, as leaders of both the House of Representatives and the Senate, appalled by events of both Friday and Sunday, as well as Dallas police investigative ineptitude, were giving strong consideration to launching investigations into the events of the tragic weekend. It is a sad irony to note, but researchers have found it odd that the same people who criticized the performance of the Dallas police later loudly applauded the work of the Warren Commission, and many conclusions were identical.[1]

The New York Times put the issue before the American people in the broadest possible perspective: "The full story of the assassination and its stunning sequel must be placed before the American people and the world in a responsible way by a responsible source of the U.S. government."[2] Unfortunately, the wording of the Times comment allowed for the possibility that there were, in fact, irresponsible sources in our government.

The die, however, had been cast. J. Edgar Hoover had submitted his absentee ballot, and FBI agents knew gospel when they heard it being sung. Lyndon Johnson, concerned that the tragedies had taken place in his home state, also had personal concerns, since the assassins' bullets had quieted the hounds of political scandal that were baying under the windows of the then vice president, who now sat in the Oval Office, redecorated for JFK during the Texas trip, but instantly transformed by Johnson, who ordered JFK's effects, plus some of his staff, removed immediately, if not sooner.

Local authorities in Texas were also satisfied with the Oswald case, as it has also been suggested elsewhere in this book that to have looked closer would have been to invite disaster.

In his eulogy to the slain president, Chief Justice Earl Warren lamented, "What moved some misguided wretch to do this horrible deed may never be known to us . . ." and in those sixteen words he virtually guaranteed that the constitutional separation of powers would be defied and he would be put in charge of the federal probe. After all, he had identified the killer as one individual, tending to rule out conspiracy, and he had raised the possibility that the truth would never be known. In yet another irony, his efforts over the next ten months would point toward a "misguided wretch," and for at least thirty-one years after the completion of his labors, the truth would not be fully available.

With public confidence ebbing and governmental pressure mounting, Lyndon Johnson decided to appoint a blue-ribbon presidential commission to investigate fully the slaying of John Kennedy, to determine who committed the crime, and to discover why the assassin, Lee Harvey Oswald, could be so easily killed in the custody of seventy Dallas police officers. If one studies the stated priorities carefully, it would seem that question number two provides a clear answer to question number one.

Deception, however, even preceded the creation of the commission. For reasons not specifically documented, although it can be inferred that he would want the highest law-enforcement officer in the land (and Hoover had already shown his colors), Johnson cajoled Earl Warren to take the chairmanship of the commission. Warren, who had run for vice president in 1948 under Thomas E. Dewey on the Republican ticket, but who had voted in 1960 for Kennedy, was told that if the Cuban/Soviet allegations tied to the assassination continued unabated, the public might clamor for war.

Such a thesis is ludicrous. The only time in our history we have clamored for war was on December 8, 1941, and not even the wildest assassination theorist has blamed the Kennedy tragedy on the Japanese air force.

Johnson failed to convince Warren in round one. His second hole card was that he had already spoken to his other six nominees, and told Warren that they were all agreeable, but only if Warren would accept the chair. Warren relented, despite his constitutional objections, which were wholly valid. What would happen, he would later ask, if Jack Ruby's appeal reached the U.S. Supreme Court after a commission presided over by the chief justice had found Ruby guilty in the eyes of the whole world? Regardless, Johnson's gambit was fraudulent, as John McCloy's biographer has written that McCloy was not even *approached* until after Warren had accepted.[3] Also, recently released Johnson tapes portrayed an equal aversion to commission membership by Richard Russell, which may in part explain why he heard the testimony of only 6 of the commission's 488 witnesses.

The commission was quickly fleshed out after the appointment of Earl Warren. John Sherman Cooper of Kentucky, Hale Boggs of Louisiana, and John McCloy, literally of the world, due to his lengthy career in American affairs overseas, had relatively close ties to JFK, although the first two would occasionally differ on regional issues. Richard Russell, a staunch Democrat, had been vocally critical of JFK for his civil rights initiatives. To represent "intelligence interests"

5 Allen Dulles, fired by Kennedy in the wake of the Bay of Pigs, was added, and a poorer appointment could hardly be imagined, as Dulles sat through much of the commission's work (being retired, he was the only one with the time) and never even hinted at CIA assassination initiatives aimed at one of Oswald's theoretical heroes, Fidel Castro. Finally, at the possible urging of J. Edgar Hoover, Republican congressman Gerald Ford rounded out the seven-man commission. Ford, who had led the pre-1963 call to "impeach Earl Warren," would later be the direct pipeline to the FBI, so that when the commission received material that caused them concern, Hoover and his top assistants were aware of it long before they received anything in writing from the commission, and could conduct a damage assessment and then either ship thousands of contrary materials or erect a stone wall. It should also be noted that Gerry "Impeach Warren" Ford's mere presence on the commission gives the lie to LBJ's plea to Warren that the other members demanded Warren to chair the commission. Lastly, Ford would later use secret materials not published by the commission in a book titled *Portrait of the Assassin*, and when questioned about this in his 1973 vice presidential confirmation hearings, would deny it.[4]

In one often unnoticed aspect, the president's commission was unique. Throughout America's history, going back as far as the squabbles between the Federalists and the Democratic-Republicans, it has been an axiom of the two-party system that the party in power "deals the cards." If appointments are to be made, they are made by and for the best interests of the party in power. Thus, if a seven-man group were to be empowered by Lyndon Johnson, it would be a foregone certainty that at least four of the members would be from Johnson's party. The other three might have been Republicans, out of courtesy, or for log-rolling purposes (and who knew and understood log-rolling better than LBJ?). Yet this axiom of party politics was ignored in the case of the Warren Commission, which was comprised of five Republicans and only two Democrats. Was the composition of the commission dictated by the possibility that it would fail, and that the Republican majority it contained, a former chief spy and a less than universally popular chief justice included, would take the heat? Was there a possibility that down the road, sometime just short of the 1964 election, Americans would not swallow the lone-assassin fantasy? Before hastily answering either of these questions, do two things: Discover how many other such presidential creations were so populated by the *other* party, and recall who made the appointments. The Warren Commission further emasculated itself early on by choosing not to insist on the services of independent investigators, relying instead on the FBI and the Secret Service.

The resolution creating the commission gave them subpoena powers, which they used to alert witnesses of their imminent appearance before the commission. Surprisingly, the subpoena power was poorly used, a clear demonstration of the lack of cohesion of the commission, as many "preliminary" questions to witnesses asked if they had received at least three days' notice prior to the appearance, and many had not. They were then given the opportunity to return, or stay and give their testimony. All but one stayed. Beyond that, they never used their granted subpoena power. The witnesses they invited, of little probative value, arrived. But what of Guy Banister, David Ferrie, Joseph Milteer, or Sergio Arcacha Smith? *They* would have required a subpoena. None received one.

The commission also had the power to deal with perjury, which they mentioned to a few, but by no means the majority, of the witnesses, as well as the power to grant immunity. Although perjury was regularly committed, and the commissioners, and to a greater extent the counsel hearing the testimony, knew it was perjury, nothing was done. Immunity might have been useful in some cases, but the power to grant it, like the authority to deal with perjury, was never used. The perjury power was self-defeating, of course, as how could the commission publish findings that were based on anything but the God's honest truth? Therefore, no perjury was found. With respect to immunity, one witness, Robert Alan Surrey, a follower of General Walker, invoked his Fifth Amendment right not to testify thirty-one times in Volume V, pages 420 ff, and it did not even raise an eyebrow from the commissioners present. If he had been a "major suspect" in the death of the president, then the commission was correct to allow him to invoke his rights, and they could build their case against him without his own testimony. But he was *not* a suspect. He was there to testify about the Walker incident, and his sponsorship of right-wing publications. Clearly, immunity should have been granted, and he should have been forced to answer the commission's questions. Why it did not happen that way is left to the reader.

The commissioners, save Dulles, were busy men at the heart of government. As a result, they were supervisory personnel, as even in the cases of witnesses who appeared before commission members, the counsel, not the commissioners, did the bulk of the questioning. John McCloy would later comment, 7"The commissioners themselves regarded their commitment to the investigation as a part-time responsibility," adding, "There was neither the time *nor the political will* [emphasis added] to conduct a thorough investigation."[5]

Researcher Edward Epstein, who had the first "outsider" look at the commission's working papers, has provided the best insights as to how the commission was fleshed out. As it was known that the commissioners would have a very limited role,[6] staff attorneys were hired. Senior attorneys were hired at $100 per diem, though most of them could not afford to work for such a pittance, so "Some of the senior council worked for the commission for only a few days and lent their reputations but not their time."[7] Junior attorneys were hired at $75 per diem and were glad to get the work and wound up doing much of it, often in such incredible bursts that they could never have been adequately prepared, nor could they have adequately digested the vast amount of material they were supplied with in testimony.

At a very early meeting, prior to the calling of any witnesses, the commission received from former CIA chief Dulles copies of a monograph that suggested that assassinations followed a pattern of lone nuts acting out their hostilities. This was reinforced by former Secret Service chief U. E. Baughman, who put the same thoughts in his *Memoirs*. John McCloy, a man familiar with conspiracies, was quick to point out that Lincoln had been killed as a result of a plot.

That same early meeting was the opportunity to create a division of labor among the staff, and that division presumed the outcome of the investigation. Out of the six areas created, "Area II" of the investigation would focus on identifying the *assassin* [singular]; "Area III" would study *Oswald's* background, in essence confirming the identity of the person sought in "Area II."

The Warren Commission asked 109,930 questions to 488 witnesses, from February 3, 1964, to September 15, 1964. It is a clear indication of the uselessness of the commission's work that they were "created" on November 29, 1963, but heard no witnesses for sixty-six days. Finally, on February 3, 1964, they took testimony from Marina Oswald, a non-English-speaking boarder at the Paine house who was hanging laundry when the assassination occurred. It is almost impossible to believe that given such a delay, the Warren Commission had anything on its agenda but the ratification of Oswald's guilt. Imagine: A political murder is committed in a major American city in 1995; a spokesperson for the investigating authorities steps before a bank of microphones and announces, "We plan to begin a thorough investigation sixty-six days from now." The thesis is ludicrous, as evidentiary trails can chill in far fewer than ten weeks; on the other hand, they had Oswald, so they did not see the need for other trails.

The commissioners themselves were only present at the questioning of 93 witnesses, with the other 395 witnesses being deposed by counsel in various parts of the country. The published accounts indicate which commissioners were present at the 93 hearings, but "present" is defined as *there at some time during the proceedings.* "Present" did not mean they stayed for the entire session, or even beyond a few questions. No witness testified before all seven members of the commission, nor were all seven ever "present" at one time or another during the testimony of any witness. Edward Epstein, in asking counsel Norman Redlich how they did it, was told, "Very simply, they didn't." Epstein also inquired of counsel Wesley Liebeler what the seven commissioners did, and Liebeler replied, "In one word, 'nothing'."[8]

Wesley Liebeler's "nothing" can be quantified statistically, and will be done so here for the first time in any publication. What is known is that of the 93 witnesses heard by the commission members, Earl Warren was listed as present at all sessions, usually, however, to handle the preliminary questions, such as "Will you state your name?" or "Will you raise your right hand and be sworn?" Only in a few instances did he ask substantive questions. There are times, however, when Warren was cited as "present" for the testimony of a group of three, four, or five witnesses, and he had a few words with the first of them, then left for the Supreme Court and did not return. Thus there are twenty-two witness sessions where the commission would like us to believe its chairman was present, when in fact he was not.

The two government "insiders," Gerald Ford and Allen Dulles, attended 70 and 60 hearings, respectively. Congressman Ford's efforts could best be described as obfuscation, as there were just too many instances when testimony was actually heading somewhere only to have Mr. Ford interrupt with a question such as "What time did this happen?" or something equally probative. Dulles, on the other hand, was far more shrewd, as well as active, and asked far better questions, but he, too, often changed the subject. In *The Warren Omission,* a companion volume to this which deals strictly with what the commission did and did not do, it will be demonstrated that the group under current scrutiny would have been more accurately labeled the "Dulles Commission."

John Sherman Cooper attended 50 hearings and asked some reasonable questions, but did not always get reasonable answers. Like John McCloy, who attended 35 meetings, Cooper would often find a witness's testimony confusing or contradictory. Yet when either tried to clear the record, the testimony remained confusing and/or contradictory, and both Cooper and McCloy were never seconded by anyone in their curiosity.

Hale Boggs attended only 20 meetings, and often arrived after they began, so his questions, pertinent as they might have been, were often repetitive. Richard Russell, as noted, attended 6 of the 93 hearings. He did not make himself vocal until more than 23,000 questions had already been asked, and did not ask his final question until several thousand more had been asked. In the first ten months, he asked a total of three questions to witnesses with knowledge of the crime, and one question, of a budgetary nature, to Secretary of the Treasury Douglas Dillon. On September 6 he led the last-minute requestioning of Marina Oswald, to glean vital data regarding Mexican bus ticket stubs found in an old TV listing.

A statistical breakdown of the commission's labor is even more instructive: Of the 93 witnesses who testified before one or more members of the Warren Commission, a total of 37,097 questions were asked. Of the 37,097 questions asked with commissioners present, 6,964, or a mere 18.77 percent of the questions, were asked by the commissioners, and it must be recalled that they asked the majority of the 805 preliminary questions.

Not surprisingly, Allen Dulles, who had the most to lose of the seven commissioners, asked the most questions: 2,154. Gerald Ford, the FBI's man on the commission, was second, with 1,772. Their total of 3,926 exceeded that of the other five commissioners combined. John Sherman Cooper asked 926, John McCloy 795, Earl Warren 608, Hale Boggs 460, and Richard Russell 249. Their combined 6,964 questions amounted to 6.33 percent of the questions asked by the group that came to be known as the Warren Commission. Such limited participation prompted researcher Gary Shaw to write, "It is a fact that even in an ordinary case involving a chicken theft, *all* of the jury is required to hear *all* of the testimony before delivering a verdict."[9]

Equally instructive are the *kinds of questions* asked before the commissioners. For the purpose of this study, I broke them down into eight categories:

1. Preliminaries—introductory questions to the witnesses, usually to determine education, background, nature of employment, or family. While common in courtroom practice, they add nothing to the record.

2. To the point—questions that would materially add to the investigation, or have the potential to add such value. In calculating such questions, I tried to be generous even in some odd situations. Example: Abraham Kleinman was asked if he had any knowledge of how Jack Ruby got into the basement to shoot Oswald; ridiculous as this question may seem *as posed to Ruby's accountant,* it would have counted as "to the point." The question was valid; it was just asked to someone who was in no possible position to give a valid answer to it.

3. Not vital—questions that simply added nothing to the record, and led to nothing being added to the record. They generally started nowhere and went nowhere.

4. Clarification—questions that clarified earlier answers. In noting tallies, one would suspect that questions of this type are proportionate in the sense that if a witness was asked 10 questions "to the point" and 200 "not vital," the 78 clarification questions would be clarifying far more "not vital" material than "to the point" material.

5. Leading/hearsay—the Warren Commission shattered the rules of evidence, frequently telling the witnesses the answers to the questions and then having the witnesses harmlessly—and meaninglessly—rattle off a string of "yeses" or "nos". The reader should take into account that a decent number of these questions were of value; they were just posed in such a way as to seriously undermine their validity. Occasionally the counsel even admitted to their chicanery. Also, "hearsay," unless it was flagrant, was usually counted in the more appropriate category where the question belonged, so these totals are really leading questions and blatant hearsay.

6. Conclusionary—questions that called for the witness to draw a conclusion. An expert witness—a doctor, a ballistics expert, or a fingerprint expert—can give opinions. A casual tourist

who stumbled into Dealey Plaza during six key seconds cannot, and should not, be asked, unless the record notes that
the question is an opinion.

7. Foregone conclusion—questions that reflected the official verdict yet could not be substantiated by the witness. Example:
A gun dealer was shown the Mannlicher, which he believed
his company shipped through the mail to "A. Hidell." When
he was asked in so many words whether he sold the gun that
killed the president, that is a foregone conclusion, as all the
witness can say is that he sold the gun—he has absolutely no
knowledge of what happened to it thereafter.

8. Nonsense—just what the name implies.

In terms of the 37,097 questions posed to commission witnesses,
the breakdown and percent totals are as follows:

1. Preliminaries—805 (2.10%)
2. To the point—1,537 (4.10%)
3. Not vital—16,073 (43.30%)
4. Clarification—7,354 (19.80%)
5. Leading/hearsay—9,676 (26.00%)
6. Conclusionary—922 (2.40%)
7. Foregone conclusion—323 (0.80%)
8. Nonsense—407 (1.09%)

Total 37,097 (100.00%)

If it comes as a surprise to the reader that only 4.1% of the questions were truly probative, and a combined 69.3% were either not
vital or of a leading nature, bear in mind that the commission, and
certainly the FBI from which it received its source material, had
already made certain decisions. The questioning, then, served to reinforce those decisions and prevent deviation from them. The "to the
point" questions almost invariably invoked the first commandment
of the legal profession: *Thou shalt not ask a question to which thou dost
not know the answer.* The "not vital" questions, if constant at 43.30%
for *all* witnesses, would have taken up the same percentage of the
7,909 pages of published testimony. This totals 3,424.5 pages, or
roughly three readings of the unabridged *War and Peace.* This gives
bulk and therefore credibility to the commission's conclusions, as its
defenders always point to the 26 volumes of published material and

focus on the quantity, *not the quality.* The "leading/hearsay" material gave the commission the opportunity to put words into the mouths of witnesses, and make no mistake about it: They were exclusively "lone-nut assassin" words.

It must then be asked if the *total* statistical breakdown of all witnesses is a reflection of the numbers generated by studying just those witnesses who appeared with a commissioner present, and the answer, sadly, is a resounding yes.

All told, the commission, be it the magnificent seven or staff counsel, asked 109,930 questions. A comparison of statistics indicates the similarity in styles between those hearings involving the commissioners and those depositions where counsel were on their own:

COMMISSION	TOTAL
Preliminaries—805 (2.10%)	6,200 (5.60%)
To the point—1,537 (4.10%)	4,928 (4.40%)
Not vital—16,073 (43.30%)	48,164 (43.80%)
Clarification—7,354 (19.80%)	15,233 (13.80%)
Leading/hearsay—9,676 (26.00%)	30,796 (28.00%)
Conclusionary—922 (2.40%)	2,580 (2.30%)
Foregone conclusion—323 (0.80%)	610 (0.005%)
Nonsense—407 (1.09%)	1,419 (1.20%)
["Off the record"—185]	[342]
Totals 37,097 (100.00%)	*109,930 (100.00%)*

The data suggest a nearly perfect correlation between commission activities and counsel methods in five of eight areas. The difference in "preliminaries" can be explained by counsel's lack of familiarity with some of the witnesses they dealt with. After all, the commission heard Marina Oswald, Clint Hill, Mrs. Kennedy, and Commander Humes. Counsel heard such luminaries as Alfreadia Riggs, Huey Reeves, and Herbert B. Kravitz. The "preliminary" tally is also slightly skewed because Curtis Crafard was asked 223 prelims, George Senator 103, Hyman Rubenstein 268, and George W. Fehrenbach 105. The other 484 witnesses were asked an average of only 11.36 preliminary questions, about what would have been expected.

The "clarification" percentage decreased in counsel depositions as it seemed that the staff attorneys had a tendency to be satisfied with the first response more often and did not push harder. Much of this may have to do with the rush of witnesses and inadequate preparation.

The "foregone conclusion" percentage dropped for obvious reasons: The staff attorneys were not dealing, for the most part, with witnesses capable of making such decisions, although that factor did not always prevent the commissioners from pursuing such a line of questioning.

If it seems unsettling that of 109,930 questions posed, only 4,928 were "to the point" (although a decent number of the 30,796 leading questions were abruptly to the point), even those figures belie the real truth of the Warren Commission. The commission, it must be recalled, had several foci: the killing of the president; the killing of Officer Tippit; the killing of suspect Oswald; the background of suspect Oswald; and certain Secret Service concerns with respect to improved presidential protection. Because of this multiplicity of concerns, the commission called witnesses who fell essentially into the following ten areas, with the number of witnesses in parentheses; the total number of questions relative to that issue and the average number of questions per witness are in brackets:

AREAS	QUESTIONS	AVERAGE NUMBER OF QUESTIONS PER WITNESS
JFK killing (177)	[30,530]	[172.48]
Tippit killing (19)	[3,258]	[171.47]
Oswald killing (93)	[16,836]	[181.03]
Administrative (1)	[73]	[73.00]
Experts (2)	[99]	[49.50]
Unrelated (5)	[641]	[128.20]
Security (3)	[652]	[217.30]
General Walker (1)	[513]	[513.00]
Diplomacy (2)	[104]	[52.00]
Character (185)	[57,254]	[309.48]
Totals 488	*109,930*	*225.26*

With respect to the nature of the categories, the first three are self-explanatory; "administrative" involved questions put to Charles J. Price, Parkland Hospital administrator, who was merely testifying to the verification of Parkland records that had been subpoenaed. "Experts" involved two witnesses, Maj. Eugene Anderson and Sgt. James

A. Zahm, who testified about the Mannlicher and its scope, respectively, but with no knowledge whatsoever of the crime. "Unrelated" and "security" were just that, dealing with future Secret Service budget concerns, FBI-Secret Service liaison, and the burning issue of whether Speaker of the House McCormack was now receiving Secret Service protection as the constitutional successor to Lyndon Johnson. "General Walker" refers to the testimony of Robert Surrey, who was questioned with commissioners present, but only with respect to the attempt on the life of Maj. Gen. Edwin A. Walker, U.S. Army resigned. "Diplomacy" involved the testimony of Dean Rusk and Llewellyn Thompson, neither of whom had knowledge of any of the three killings, but who had knowledge of the diplomatic reactions and ramifications of the events.

"Character" witnesses were the remainder. This category included witnesses who had no provable knowledge of the crime (or who gave no testimony that they had knowledge of the crime) yet knew, either well or barely, Oswald, Ruby, or Tippit. This category would include the members of Oswald's family; the members of the Russian émigré community; Ruby's employees; Ruth and Michael Paine; and attorneys who entered the issue after November, such as James Martin and Mark Lane.

During the course of this research, I have asked many members of the assassination research community whom they would most like to question regarding the events of November 1963. Leading answers range from David Ferrie, to George DeMohrenschildt, to Clay Shaw, to J. Edgar Hoover, to CIA director McCone (and surprisingly, to former CIA boss Allen Dulles—imagine the commission questioning itself), to David Atlee Phillips, and to Yuri Nosenko. A good number surveyed shared my own bias that the key piece of evidence in the case was the president's body at autopsy, and the questioning there would be on Humes, Finck, and Boswell. Humes, as it turned out, was asked only 215 questions, fewer than the average witness, and fewer than such key witnesses as Myrtle Evans, an acquaintance of the Oswald family *during the Great Depression;* Mrs. Mahlon Tobias, who had information with respect to where the Oswalds lived; and Mrs. Tobias's husband, who was in an admittedly weakened mental state but who was nevertheless asked 229 questions.

Autopsist Dr. Boswell was asked 14 questions; his colleague, Dr. Finck, was asked 75.

The autopsy doctors were asked a combined total of 304 questions, fewer than the 342 asked William D. Crowe, Jr., the emcee at Ruby's strip joint.

It seems odd that 57,224 questions, 52.05 percent of the total, were asked to people with no direct knowledge of the crime, and of the ten biggest totals per witness, nine were for character witnesses. Ruth Paine, surprisingly, was asked 5,236 questions, the most of any witness. In descending order, the top ten are rounded out by Curtis LaVerne Crafard (3,972), George Senator (2,792), Marina Oswald (2,615), Robert Oswald (2,351), George DeMohrenschildt (1,628), Andrew Armstrong (1,592), John Edward Pic (1,325), Michael Paine (1,019), and Jesse Curry (1,002). These ten witnesses were asked 23,532 questions, or 21.40% of the total.

To put that in perspective, neither Robert Oswald nor John Edward Pic had seen Lee Oswald in the year before the assassination, and Curtis LaVerne Crafard, Andrew Armstrong, and George Senator (Ruby employees or acquaintances) added virtually nothing to the record, even about Jack Ruby. For the curious, those ten witnesses were asked only 554 questions "to the point," and Marina was asked more than 200 of those 554.

In terms of the real case, the numbers do not improve. The popular conception is that the Warren Commission, as well as its subsequent Report, are about the assassination of John F. Kennedy. Yet, as noted, the Kennedy questions totalled 30,530, or 27.77% of all questions asked, but only 2,065 of them were "to the point," so we come to the point where, in statistical quantification that has the possibility to be subjective, 2,065 questions of 109,930 dealt with valuable data with regard to the killing of the president. *This amounts to 1.87 percent of the Warren Commission's "work."*

If the reader therefore finds the 7,909 pages of published testimony to be wanting, what of the remaining 9,831 pages of exhibits?

Regrettably, in this venue also, the emphasis was on quantity as opposed to quality.

Within those 9,831 pages, which comprise Volumes XVI through XXVI, 3912 exhibits were published. Some were given simple numerical designations, such as commission exhibit 1 (CE 1), and these numbers run to commission exhibit 3154. Some of the numerical exhibits have multiple parts, so a letter would follow the number, as in CE 453 A. The remainder bear the names of individuals, such as the series of backyard photos that appeared in periodicals around the United States. Each was discussed by FBI expert Lyndal Shaneyfelt, and those exhibits became Shaneyfelt ex. 1, and so on. Occasionally, however, there is serious confusion, and one again wonders why. A prime example of this phenomenon is a series of photos taken of Oswald passing out leaflets amid a crowd of people who were either curious onlookers or sympathetic followers. Many witnesses were asked to identify Oswald in the photos, and it is not at all difficult, although several witnesses did not believe that the person they saw (an impostor?) looked like the obvious Oswald in the photos. Nevertheless, these photos are labeled "Pizzo Exhibits A, B, and C." The problem is that Frank Pizzo, who was Albert Bogard's superior at the Lincoln-Mercury dealership where an "Oswald" test-drove a car while the real Lee Oswald was sitting at the Paine residence in Irving, had nothing to do with those photos. He looked at them and made such comments as were truthful. His name on the exhibits, however, tells us nothing of their origins. One, Pizzo C, was taken in police custody. But Pizzo A and B remain enigmas, and the commission, in so naming them, condemned them to enigma status. They also allow the reader to draw the inference that Pizzo identified Oswald, which he did not.

A subjective criterion was again used as a yardstick to measure the worth of the material published as exhibits. Using a one-to-five scale, a one was "useless"; two was "of little value"; three was "of some value"; four was "of interest"; and five was "of serious interest."

Using those criteria, the following results were generated. The left-hand column represents the number of exhibits for each category, with the percentage of the total exhibits in brackets. The right-hand column gives the page totals devoted to the five categories, again with percentages listed in brackets. The fractional parts of pages noted are a result of putting multiple exhibits on the same page, and often of differing value qualities.

NUMBER OF EXHIBITS	PAGES OF EXHIBITS
Useless—2,668 [68.20%]	5,492.33 [55.86%]
Of little value—437 [11.10%]	1,583.33 [16.10%]
Of some value—458 [11.70%]	1,473.91 [15.00%]
Of interest—270 [6.90%]	1,191.58 [12.12%]
Of serious interest—79 [2.00%]	89.83 [0.90%]
Totals *3,912 [100.00%]*	*9,831 [100.00%]*

A complete breakdown of the statistics is available in the Appendices, in Table 4 ("Dates of Witnesses' Appearances") and Table 5

("Witness Totals by Category"). The totally useless exhibits that were published are cited in an Appendices supplement titled "Nonsense." The purpose in making these exhibits public is more serious than humorous, as the Warren Commission's conclusions must be understood in terms of sources they were drawn from. If the sources are mostly nonsense . . . Lastly, the author does *not* recommend that anyone attempt a similar count unless you are on good terms with an eye doctor.

Despite the lack of desire for a probing, no-holds-barred investigation, which the intransigence, for personal or conspiratorial reasons, of J. Edgar Hoover would have prevented, the commission plodded along in its attempts at least to reach a verdict. Their methods, however, are still suspect.

The first three commission witnesses, who took up the commission's full attention from February 3 to 22, were Marina, Marguerite, and Robert *Oswald,* two of whom had not seen the accused assassin for a year prior to November 22, 1963, and would not have had any knowledge with respect to a rifle purchased in March, or to the accused's state of mind eighteen months after his return to America.

Marina Oswald was asked to identify a rifle, presumably C2766, but she indicated that rifles were all pretty much the same to her. The problem here is that no witness (obviously, since she was first) had testified that the weapon shown to Marina had any bona fides. It was up to her to identify the rifle as Oswald's, and eventually the commission would round up witnesses to link it to the assassination.

The family may also have been called first, particularly the outspoken and oft-spoken Marguerite, to blunt bad publicity. Commission witnesses' testimony was frequently leaked, and if Oswald's mother had testified in July instead of February, particularly with the help of her attorney, Mark Lane, who had an instant grasp of what was wrong with the commission and the case, she might well have soured the public on the Warren Report. Her testimony in February prevented that.

Marina Oswald provided the commission with an instant identity crisis. They found themselves believing some of what she said, but not all of it, a dilemma that usually causes attorneys to forgo entirely the use of such a witness. The commission believed Marina's allegation that Oswald had been the man who tried to kill General Walker, but they did not believe Marina's story with respect to Nixon, since he was not in Dallas at the time.

Their ultimate problem, however, was that Marina Oswald was the best witness the commission had against Lee Oswald, so they could not very well impeach her testimony, a sad comment on the way "justice" was arrived at.

Marina testified from February 3 to 6. Interestingly, it was on February 4, after one day of one witness's testimony, that Chief Justice Warren told the world that there were materials available to the commission that would not be seen "in your lifetime." This prompted Murray Kempton to write in *The New Republic,* "There is something uncomfortably petty about a man who locks up a document and then complains about the ignorance of another man who hasn't read it."[10]

With such methodology for their guide, the commission plodded through months of self-serving hearings and exhibit-collecting, eventually publishing about 4 cubic feet of material and sequestering 357 cubic feet of material. As their June 30 deadline came and went, drafts were hastily rewritten, and the collection of the material in the 26 volumes, which Allen Dulles noted would never be read, was begun. It has been asserted that the final draft of the Report was written by Otto Winnaker, a member of the Army Historical Division, who had previously been one of Hitler's official Nazi historians.[11]

Such was the corpus of what the Warren Commission did. What they did *not* do is equally, if not more, instructive.

CHAPTER THREE

THE "WARREN OMISSION"

> *The CHAIRMAN. Senator Cooper, at this time I am obliged to leave for our all-day conference on Friday at the Supreme Court, and I may be back later in the day, but if I don't, you continue, of course.*
>
> *Senator COOPER. I will this morning. If I can't be here this afternoon, whom do you want to preside?*
>
> *The CHAIRMAN. Congressman Ford, would you be here this afternoon at all?*
>
> *Representative FORD. Unfortunately, Mr. McCloy and I have to go to a conference out of town.*
>
> *The CHAIRMAN. You are both going out of town, aren't you?*
>
> *Senator COOPER. I can go and come back if it is necessary.*
>
> *The CHAIRMAN. I will try to be here myself. Will Mr. Dulles be here?*
>
> *Mr. McCLOY. He is out of town.*
>
> *The CHAIRMAN. If you should not finish, Mr. Jenner, will you phone me at the Court and I will try to suspend my own conference over there and come over.*
>
> *Senator COOPER. I will be here anyway all morning and will try to come back this afternoon.*
>
> *The CHAIRMAN. Thank you very much.*
>
> —A CURIOUS COMMISSION EXCHANGE IN THE MIDST OF
> THE TESTIMONY OF RUTH PAINE.[1]

IT SEEMS ODD, to say the least, that a blue-ribbon presidential commission charged with finding all the facts in an investigation of the broad-daylight murder of the president of the United States could feature an exchange such as the one above. Such an exchange would seem far more likely coming from a costumed group of performers about to squeeze into a tiny car and then emerge in the center ring and pile out, to the delight of the audience.

It also seems odd that as Earl Warren ("The CHAIRMAN") and Senator John Sherman Cooper were casting about for someone to run the show, they made no mention whatsoever of two of the commissioners, Hale Boggs and Richard Russell. It was as if they did not exist.

The commission, in fact, overlooked, or treated with curious methodology, many, many things. Part of their problem was the time constraints imposed on their labors, the compartmentalization of the investigation, and their lack of independent investigators. After all, it is difficult to conduct an investigation without investigators. Also, it is very easy to suspect that the commission and its staff knew they were being toyed with by the FBI and had no choice but to labor under that handicap as well.

Another constraint may have been that the commission was simply not allowed to think, although Dr. Malcolm Perry, in a knock against assassination critics, indicated, ". . . I have yet to meet one who has read the entire twenty-six volumes of the Warren Commission report [sic]." Well, Doc, I've read all twenty-six *four times*, and I can tell you how it played. The commissioners or counsel read the FBI reports *as given,* then wrote a short series of questions for each witness. The more the FBI probed, the more questions that would be asked. So while the FBI was draped all over Ruth Paine and threatening Marina Oswald, they took very short reports from you Dallas doctors.

The bottom line, Dr. Perry, et al., is that there is not one witness in those famed twenty-six volumes who was simply asked, "Please tell us what you know about the events of November 22." Instead, the Warren Commission went through its script, as folks like Dr. Perry, who have been on both sides of the fence in this case, should know.

It's simple: Just tell us what you know. We'll listen carefully, and if anything you say sparks an interest, *then* we'll ask the necessary follow-up questions. (There's a term for it in legal circles: "cross-examination"; but how many members of the commission were trial lawyers?) *But it never happened; not once.*

Scripts were created and read to witnesses, whose answers were limited to the scope of the questions asked. Forrest Sorrels, in one answer the commission must have disliked, asked if the question could be reread. Harold Norman told this author that his questioning was also laid out in front of the people asking the questions.

Primarily, however, we must recall that their goal was to prevent a nuclear war, and in such a noble cause, occasional sacrifices must be made. In this case, the occasional sacrifice was *the truth*.

At least six witnesses, all members of the Russian émigré community, considered Marina's departure from the Soviet Union highly unusual, but the issue was never pursued.[2]

There are many instances of witnesses making statements that make reference to testimony taken much earlier in time—the previous day or week, which appeared nowhere in the record and suggested "rehearsed." FBI expert Paul Stombaugh, giving an answer, was corrected by counsel Eisenberg based on an earlier conversation that does not appear in the official record.[3] Commander Humes, on his only day of testimony, told that he had first seen the president's clothing "yesterday."[4] Howard Brennan, a witness who committed perjury and the commission knew it (only to stretch even the perjury in his memoir of the event), was repeatedly asked if he had been "coached."[5] At least a dozen other witnesses' testimony would seem out of sync timewise.

Carolyn Walther, Robert Hill Jackson, Amos Lee Euins, and Howard Brennan, literally the "Who's Who" of TSBD eyewitnesses, all denied in their testimony that they saw a scope.[6] The rifle ultimately blamed for the assassination, it was concluded, had one.

It was usually commission policy to ask a witness if he or she would read written documents previously submitted by investigative bodies and make corrections as needed. Most needed a few changes. But at least ten witnesses literally disavowed the content of the report as given, and had serious reservations about the process. Captain W. B. Frazier did so, and his testimony ended very quickly.[7] G. E. Worley offered the unsolicited remark, "I would have to say, after reading that report now, that report from the FBI is not very good."[8] Ira J. "Jack" Beers, whom we now know to be the photographer who exposed the film that captured the "tramps" for posterity, although he was not asked about any pictures he took, was more kind: "The agent must have misunderstood me or misread his notes or something."[9]

Or something.

Officer M. L. Baker, as well as Secret Service agents Lawson,

Sorrels, and Hill, all commented on the vast number of open windows on the motorcade route, with Agent Lawson suggesting the number of twenty thousand.[10] He obviously didn't count them, but with that kind of awareness, why was nothing done, and why wasn't Chief Curry asked about the obvious absence of local precautions?

The commission paid no attention to the various documents that listed Oswald's height from five feet, nine inches to five feet, eleven inches, but not necessarily in that order. The same amount of attention was paid to documents and testimony that attributed six different eye colors to Oswald.

In terms of quantity, the biggest single effort made by the Warren Commission was their attempt to place as many individuals as possible at the scene of the crime at the time of the shooting *of Oswald*. At least thirty-two witnesses, most of whom were police, or reservists, plus journalists Jack Beers, Ike Pappas, Seth Kantor, Robert Huffaker, and physician Fred Bieberdorf, were given identical diagrams of the police basement and asked to locate themselves on the diagram provided. This is not to fault the commission; this effort was proper procedure. The question then becomes, why did they not do the same thing for all Dealey Plaza witnesses? It would have required no more architectural skills than the basement layout, and could have potentially provided a wealth of information regarding the as yet unsolved killing of the president. Yet when it came to witnesses' locations in Dealey Plaza, either the witness was asked to draw a clumsy sketch and put an "X," as Jean Hill did (and it was then stamped "Top Secret"), or their verbal description sufficed.

In terms of quality, one of the key overlooked items of evidence was a conversation among Secret Service agent Mike Howard, his brother Pat Howard, and journalist Thayer Waldo. The gist of the conversation, according to an FBI memo of May 27, 1964, was that a "Negro" janitor, who had a criminal record, had been detained by police and questioned. It was also suggested that he was being kept in a safe place until he could testify before the Warren Commission. Based on what he heard, Waldo filed a story. The Howard brothers then denied that they had any awareness that Waldo was a journalist, raising the question that if they didn't know who he was, what was he doing riding in their backseat, and they also denied the part of Waldo's story that indicated "that the Negro janitor was a witness to the shooting of the president."[11] Neither of the Howard brothers was called to testify before the commission; Thayer Waldo was, but was not asked anything about the substance of the May 27, 1964, memo, although he gave testimony on June 27.

We learn in Commission Exhibit 768 that photos of the people involved in the "Stevenson incident" of October 1963 were distributed to security people at the Trade Mart. "A number of individuals who resembled those in these photographs were placed under surveillance at the Trade Mart."[12] This was good police procedure. But after the fact, were those photos made available to the Warren Commission? Were the photos shown to Dealey Plaza witnesses to see if any of the earlier demonstrators showed up in the kill zone? Were they compared with photos taken in Dealey Plaza? The answer, of course, is no.

Other suspects were, of course, ignored. A radio transmission spoke of a suspect in a '63 Chevy Impala, with Georgia license 52J 1033.[13] It would have been relatively simple to discover the owner of that vehicle, but there is no such record—just a transmission of a suspect. The same is true of the report of Secret Service agent Roger Warner, who left his post at Air Force One to deal with a suspect, Donald Wayne House, in Ranger, Texas.[14] Agent Warner was not called by the commission, and there is not a word of testimony, nor a photo, nor even an identification check of suspect "House" in the official record. A subsequent transmission told of the need for a wrecker in the parking lot of Cobb Stadium "for suspect's car."[15] The car, and with it, the "suspect," then vanish into the limbo of history. The Secret Service had information on November 15, 1963, of a plot involving militants to assassinate the president and other government officials.[16] The subject, a Klan member, was not named, and was certainly not called before the commission to answer any questions.

George DeMohrenschildt told of Oswald "getting some regular checks from somewhere."[17] He was not asked how regularly, from whom, or the source of his information. It was as if he had said that Oswald had pimples as a teenager. State Department legal adviser Abram Chayes, speaking of Oswald, told the commission, ". . . we were very anxious to get him back."[18] The obvious—and unasked—question was, Why? I am certain a lot of people would like to know why the State Department was anxious to get Oswald back; it seems odd that a presidential commission was not curious.

Many witnesses were asked about the contents of notebooks. Curtis LaVerne Crafard went through page after soporific page of being unable to identify names or numbers in Ruby's various small spiral notebooks. Yet the entry in Seth Kantor's book, "7:55 'I'm just a patsy,' "[19] went unnoticed in Kantor's testimony, where the focus was on disproving Kantor's statement that he shook hands and spoke briefly with Jack Ruby at Parkland Hospital early on the afternoon of November 22. Even though the "patsy" notation could be viewed as a denial, it could also be viewed as a limited confession. It was not pursued. Instead, the commission treated Kantor as an insidious liar, and when they could not break his story, they simply denied it.

Gunsmith Dial Ryder's FBI report is at odds with his commission testimony. In commission exhibit 1325, Ryder indicated he thought he recognized Oswald (but not a positive ID) as an individual who had brought in an Argentine rifle to have a scope mounted.[20] The event was not even raised in his subsequent testimony. Too many rifles?

In an earlier document, the rifle was again a problem. Marina Oswald was interviewed, and indicated that she was aware that Ruth Paine maintained a very thoroughly annotated calendar. Either the calendar had a very unusual entry, or an agent was playing games with Marina's head, as the report indicated, "She stated that she knows nothing about Mrs. Paine making a notation on her calendar such as 'Oct. 23—LHO purchase of rifle.' "[21]

Equally baffling is the commission's unwillingness to have witnesses make a fair identification of the rifle. There is no indication anywhere that any witness made an identification of the Mannlicher-Carcano after being shown *several* guns. Equally baffling is the commission's unwillingness to show the world at large a Mauser. It is all too well known that a Mauser was prominently mentioned over the assassination weekend. It would have been easy for the commission to acquire one, and print a photo of it for comparison purposes with the Mannlicher. But they did not. William Waldman and Mitchell Scibor of Klein's Sporting Goods were not asked the most simple of questions: Was the Mannlicher sent to "Hidell" with a clip? Without an answer to that question, we have to discover where—and if—Oswald obtained a clip. A curious FBI agent purchased a Mannlicher in the same manner as "Hidell" and did *not* receive a clip. It may seem like a small point, but large cases are made of small points, and the Warren Commission, in this case, made neither the small point nor the large case.

Much of the remaining errors of "omission" can be treated chronologically, to kaleidoscope the process that led from hints of a series of plots, to a lone assassin subsequently killed by a police informant in police headquarters.

The Warren Commission, in its diligence, found and took testimony from *three* of Oswald's fellow marines. A few others were reached and submitted signed affidavits, but you cannot question an affidavit. You can only read it and believe it or deny it. Edward J. Epstein, however, located *seventy-three* of Oswald's marines acquaintances.[22]

After his prematurely terminated marine service, Oswald went to Russia, and was believed to have lived quite well there, giving rise to a theory that he was being remunerated for something beyond the production of Russian radios. The Russian émigrés questioned by the commission, however, told a different story of Oswald's financial status in the USSR, and the commission's questions constantly pointed toward Oswald's financial resources. This was fine, but no serious conclusion was drawn.

Although thousands of questions would be asked, and literally hundreds of documents published "proving" that Oswald went to Mexico, the commission is strangely silent with respect to the unusual "layover" of the Oswald family in Holland. This attracts the researcher's curiosity, as the Oswald family was provided virtually luxury accommodations in Holland, at a time when they had to scrounge as well as borrow money to make the trip home. It clearly suggests an intelligence, not a tourist, scenario.

With respect to the Mexico trip, it was alleged that Oswald sat next to an elderly white male, identified as "ALBERT OSBORNE who is also known as JOHN HOWARD BOWEN." When interviewed by the FBI on January 7, Osborne admitted Bowen was an acquaintance. When "Bowen" was interviewed by a different agent on February 8, he told that Osborne was an acquaintance, but he denied sitting next to Oswald.[23] Finally, on March 5, either Osborne or Bowen (the record is unclear) admitted to being both.[24] This absurdity is offered only to suggest either the gullibility or the nonchalance of the investigating officers, and considering that they were investigating events connected to the murder of the president of the United States, they should have been neither gullible nor nonchalant. They are, in fact, strenuously trained otherwise. There are, unfortunately, far too many cases of witnesses being believed at face value when they were telling absurd stories.

The motorcade route itself has always been a source of confusion,

and a November 19 memo by advance agent Winston Lawson provided no specifics regarding the motorcade, and it did not suggest
any familiarity with the final route. Interestingly, it did mention,
"Agents will wear their red and white permanent lapel pin."[25] This
contradicts the theory often floated that someone had insider knowledge of the pins to be worn by the Secret Service that day; the
memo proves they wore the ones they usually wore.

Two days later, Jesse Curry indicated in an interview that a few
people would be under observation during the president's stay in
Dallas.[26] He was never asked who they were, or why they were being
put under observation. The answer to the second concern might
seem obvious, but it still should have been asked.

The *Dallas Morning News* of November 22, 1963, was included in
the exhibits of the Warren Commission, but with the motorcade
route *cropped*.[27] The commission faced a quandary in that it could not
prove that Oswald knew the motorcade route, particularly when the
Secret Service seemed unsure of it.

Many questions were left unasked and unanswered about Dealey
Plaza events. Officer Harkness immediately smelled a rat with respect
to the epileptic seizure, but it was never pursued, although the individual was identified, but not called by the commission.[28] The commission also never came to grips with the bullet fragments, although
they did squeeze them into the "magic bullet" scenario. The problem, most simply put, is that two fragments lost so much velocity
that they remained inside the limousine. Yet another somehow went
almost the length of a football field to strike pedestrian James Tague.
Further, Commission Exhibits 697 and 698, in addition to pictures
published since the commission ceased its labors, cast doubt on the
fact that Governor Connally was "inboard" of JFK in the limousine,
another contention vital to the "magic bullet" theory, which, in turn,
is vital to the commission's conclusion of Oswald as the lone assassin
(although the Report said it was not vital).[29]

Several Dealey Plaza eyewitnesses were interviewed, but in the
suddenness of the tragedy that occurred there, many simply walked
away, unknown to authorities and ignored by history. At the same
time, however, there were a number of witnesses in the jail on the
southeastern corner of Houston and Elm streets who had an excellent
vantage point with respect to the TSBD. None of these people was
called, and their names were available—the city of Dallas had to
maintain records of the daily log of prisoners.

Shortly after the shooting, Officer J. M. Smith smelled gunpowder around the hedges in the parking lot behind the picket fence area. Smith has made this information available to researchers, although he was not asked about it by the commission.

It has never been resolved whether Jean Hill was rudely hustled to the sheriff's office, as she has contended for thirty years, or if she was escorted there by Mr. Featherstone of the *Dallas Times Herald*. The latter theory is the commission's view, although Featherstone was not called to confirm it.[30] Of equal concern is the media's (and, by extension, the commission's) willingness to ignore Jean Hill. Before the networks had the news that the president had died, Jean Hill gave an interview indicating that shots came from "the hill over there." Before long, the depository was singled out as the location of the assassin, and no curious journalist ever asked, nor did the commission, "What about that lady who spoke about shots from the hill?" Apparently even idle curiosity is not allowed when presidents are ambushed in broad daylight.

Parkland nurse Diana Bowron (who forfeited much credibility by telling that Parkland doctors "tried massaging his heart manually" in Livingstone, *Killing the Truth,* p. 180) confirmed what the vast majority of the Parkland staff indicated, that there was a gaping hole in the *back* of the president's head, adding, "There was blood all over his neck and shoulders."[31] Given the circumstances, this should not seem out of place. What is odd, however, is that the autopsy photos portrayed Kennedy's scalp as intact, and gave it a just-washed look. The nurses who washed Kennedy's body of lingering bloodstains to prepare it for the casket were not asked if they saw a back wound, and they should have seen the wound, and they should have been asked about it.[32] Some were not asked because they were not called.

While the late president was being readied for his unscheduled return to Washington, investigators at the book depository finally got around to looking in the corner window where witnesses had seen a rifle. They found empty cartridges, a bag (which, although never photographed, could have contained a rifle), plus fried chicken remains, a soda bottle, and a cigarette pack. The curious part of the sniper's nest was the *cigarette pack.* Oswald was not a smoker, although the commission asked a number of character witnesses if Oswald smoked. This still missed the point. Logic dictates that given the TSBD as a book warehouse, there would certainly be at least the suggestion that smoking would be off-limits in certain areas containing vast amounts of flammable paper. Such being the case, the presence of the cigarette pack would almost guarantee that it was placed there by a smoker *not aware of depository regulations regarding smoking*. The least the commission could have done was consider this question.

While that evidence was being found so it could later be ignored, the Protective Research Section of the Secret Service was still totally in the dark about Lee Oswald. In a subsequent memo, Robert Bouck, head of Protective Research, would indicate that Oswald was unknown to them as of 1:30 P.M. EST, but "Other government agencies were contacted and by midafternoon we began receiving information from these sources."[33] Bouck, who did testify before the commission, was not asked what the information was *or who the other agencies were*. Perhaps it did not matter to the commission, since Oswald was dead.

At roughly the same time, Curtis LaVerne Crafard would later testify, he awoke, and it was his recollection that the shooting had been at noon and that Ruby returned to the Carousel Club by 1:30 P.M.[34] Crafard, whose character may be questionable, as he served fourteen months in the army and was given a "general discharge under honorable conditions, not eligible for reenlistment,"[35] was believed with respect to Ruby's whereabouts, while respected journalist Seth Kantor and bystander Wilma Tice were considered mistaken.

Slightly later in the afternoon, Officer Tippit received the autopsy demanded by Texas law, although there are questions regarding the autopsy in the published materials. Four bullets were allegedly recovered from Tippit's body, yet the ambulance driver, not called by the commission, has told researchers that one bullet hit a button on Tippit's uniform and did not penetrate.[36] The possibility of a fifth shot was never cleared up.

A fifth-bullet scenario also became a possibility in Dealey Plaza, as Carl Day made references to a bullet striking in the grass in the open part of the plaza.[37] No questions of this nature were put to Day when he testified before the Warren Commission. Day's reference had been published in a local paper the weekend of the assassination. Failure to follow it up suggests research so shallow by the commission that their final product would not have passed muster as a senior thesis in college, and for many additional reasons.

Mary Moorman took photos of the motorcade that included the TSBD in the background. One of the two pictures has surfaced since the original submission of this manuscript, yet the other remains a mystery. Either way, the commission should have had them so there would be no mystery. However, Bill Wiseman did admit to seeing the photos in a deposition at the sheriff's office, adding that they showed "the window where the gunman sat when doing the shooting."[38] Neither Mary Moorman nor Bill Wiseman were called to give testimony.

The tapes and press conference materials from Parkland Hospital were also seized at the time and have not yet reappeared.

At the other end of the medical chain, the president received a pathological exam that would probably not constitute a legal autopsy, at Bethesda Naval Hospital, a government-controlled facility in the northern suburbs of Washington. Two "autopsy face sheets" exist, with identical contents, except one contains the notation, "Verified, G. Burkley." Dr. Burkley, the president's physician and the only doctor present at both Parkland and Bethesda, was "verifying" observations committed to paper that the autopsy doctors would later deny. Dr. Burkley was not called to testify.

Dr. Humes, the pathologist of record, would later deny, before the House Select Committee on Assassinations, the authenticity of a photo of the back of the president's head.[39] Nevertheless, Humes's loyalty was never called into question, as he was considered by the Warren Commission as the man most qualified to exhume *Oswald's* body. This suggests not only an unreasonable faith in Humes, but also an unreasonable lack of faith in private Texas pathologists as well as the legitimacy of the individual buried in Oswald's grave.[40]

In another case of two virtually identical documents, Commission Exhibit 1536, as originally written, indicated that Jack Ruby had mob connections. The same document, when published, had three paragraphs exised, and the mob connection was sanitized.[41] One can only wonder how many such documents were treated with such cavalier disdain for the truth.

Reserve officer William Newman believed he saw a white male run down the Main Street ramp about one minute before the shooting of Oswald on Sunday, November 24, an allegation mentioned in two separate exhibits[42] without any identification of the individual. The Warren Commission chose to believe that Newman had identified Ruby, and chose not to believe those who insisted Ruby could not have come down the ramp. (The House Select Committee on Assassinations would later dismiss the ramp theory also.)

Oswald's mother would be told by Dr. Malcolm Perry on that

Sunday that "the Texas law is that we have to have an autopsy on a body."[43] It's strange that nobody besides Dr. Earl Rose thought of that on Friday, November 22, when a different, far more famous patient expired in Parkland Hospital from multiple gunshot wounds of less obvious origin. Perhaps Dr. Perry, with his concern for assassination critics who had not read the twenty-six volumes, overlooked the need for an autopsy on the late president.

On November 28, in an interview with the FBI, Sheriff Decker had nothing further to say about the transfer and the shooting, basically declining to discuss the matter. The Warren Commission chose not to ask him about this, or about his seeing a bullet hit the pavement behind the lead car, or about the totality of Decker Exhibit 5323, which, when taken together, shouts "conspiracy!"[44]

Shortly after Decker took up his pose of silence, Dallas police press officer Glen King admitted that the police had virtually been gagged: "It has been indicated to the police department in Dallas the Warren Commission prefers that we not comment on certain areas of this investigation and on certain aspects of the evidence we have."[45]

The *Houston Post,* in its January 1, 1964, issue, reported Oswald as an FBI agent. Henry Wade commented, "It may be true, but I don't think it will ever be made public."[46] Wade may not have realized it, but just by the fact that it was in the newspaper meant it had been made public; what he meant was, the government would never admit it. The Warren Commission accepted J. Edgar Hoover's sworn assurances that Oswald was not on his payroll, and that was that. This, of course, was *after* the famous exchange between commissioners Allen Dulles and Hale Boggs in which Dulles insisted that an agent would lie if necessary to protect a source, and the theory gave Dulles (and, by implication, Boggs and everyone listening) no problems.[47]

Mark Lane, a very early witness, told the Warren Commission that he had sought out expert advice with respect to the ammunition available for the Mannlicher-Carcano, and had been told that it did not fire perfectly all the time because of its age.[48] While this may be true or not, it is noteworthy that the commission called experts about the rifle and the scope—but not about the ammunition. Thereafter, Lane got the runaround, to the point where it would make a chapter in itself, but nobody could tell it better than Lane.

Jean Hill fared no better. Although her testimony is published as if from the downtown Dallas post office, Miss Hill has made a series

of counterclaims: that she was interviewed on an upper floor at Parkland (and borne out by counsel Specter's schedule that day, as Specter
took a deposition at Parkland at 2:06 P.M., then the alleged post office
deposition at 2:30 P.M., and was then back at Parkland for Dr. Peters
at 4:00 P.M.; perhaps Specter was the "magic counsel" working at
the behest of a "lone commission"); that Specter browbeat her before
they went on the record; and that her testimony, as published, was
a "total travesty, giving it equal value to the Report as published."[49]
The only answer to this resides ultimately with the stenographer, and
their names were not part of the record unless they were addressed
by counsel.

Similar treatment to that reported by Miss Hill was visited upon
Arnold Rowland, who had the misfortune to observe a rifleman at
the opposite end of the TSBD at 12:15 P.M., a time Oswald could
not have been either on the sixth floor or in possession of a weapon.
An FBI report of March 25 came perilously close to character assassination, as the FBI went out of their way to discredit Rowland's
testimony.[50] Did they treat star witness Howard Brennan this way?
Of course not; he saw what he was supposed to.

The commission did not call Soviet defector Yuri Nosenko, as the
CIA was picturing him at that time as uncertain with respect to his
bona fides, a euphemism for "fake." If he was fake, that should have
been up to the Warren Commission, not the CIA, to decide, and
they perhaps could have learned much from Nosenko's fakery, if
true. Further, if the CIA took years to figure Nosenko out, it's no
wonder we haven't heard their Oswald story yet.

The commissioners were as selective in whom they believed as
they were in what they believed. In Commission Exhibit 1288, Bar-
ney Ross told the FBI that Jack Ruby "might have run innocuous
errands for Capone." Yet the commission concluded, "There is no
evidence that he [Ruby] ever participated in organized criminal activity."[51] One wonders what would constitute an "innocuous errand"
for Al Capone, and if Ruby ever participated in any *disorganized*
criminal activity.

Ultimately, selective credence was given to the testimony of Marina
Oswald and Helen Markham, yet the commission chose *not* to believe
Seth Kantor, Wesley Frazier and his sister Linnie May Randle (regarding
the size of the package Oswald had on November 22), W. W. Litch-
field, Wanda Helmick, Gertrude Hunter, Edith Whitworth, Roger
Craig, Arnold Rowland, Victoria Adams, William Whaley, Albert
Bogard, Dial Ryder, C. A. Hamblen, Earlene Roberts, and Wilma

Tice, to name a few. At the same time, they took, at face value, the FBI interview with TSBD employee O. V. Campbell. Campbell, unsure of where the shots originated, rushed back into the TSBD and indicated that Oswald was immediately known to be missing. The report continued: "Mr. CAMPBELL observed a photograph of LEE HARVEY OSWALD . . . and stated that he is sure that this is a photograph of the employee named above, but added that he is not personally acquainted with him *and has never seen him*" (emphasis added).[52]

Howard Brennan, who would make the claim that he could have identified Oswald in a lineup as the man in the TSBD sixth-floor window, but did not do so because he feared possible reprisals from coconspirators, told of being interviewed by all seven commissioners (four were present), and going over old times with "Governor Warren." Brennan added, "A recorder was at his fingertips that he could start and stop at his discretion."[53] If true, Brennan's assertion is the indiscretion of the case, as tape recordings of the meetings and hearings would prove invaluable.

The House Select Committee on Assassinations would later discredit Brennan's testimony, and his personal memoir, published posthumously, would forever shatter his credibility.[54]

Researcher Gary Shaw has written that only three of the seven commissioners viewed the Zapruder film.[55] Beyond that, the commission flatly refused to view the autopsy photos of the president, first, because the one he was shown caused Earl Warren some sleepless nights (what did he expect after the Zapruder film?), and secondly on the basis that if the commission saw the photos, they would have to publish them. This was a sound policy, but it was hardly followed. *They saw a great deal that remained unpublished.*

When 158 frames of the Zapruder film were published in Volume XVIII, the two key frames, Z314 and Z315, were reversed, creating the impression that the president's head went *forward*, not *backward*, after the bullet impact depicted in Z313. It again seems odd that what J. Edgar Hoover would later call a "printer's error" happened just at the key segment of film. It is equally odd, of course, that the single most important home movie before Rodney King would be butchered in processing and lose four key frames: Z208, 209, 210, and 211. (They do exist, just not usually as part of the film.)

John Connally's X rays were published in Commission Exhibit 691, although *the president's* X rays were omitted for reasons of taste. In a similar vein, FBI associate director Alan Belmont offered the commission Oswald's FBI file, but it was refused on the "if we see it, we must publish it" theory.[56] If the FBI's Oswald file had contained only one sheet of paper, with only one sentence, "Oswald killed JFK," it would have been on the front cover of the Warren Report. So one can only wonder what *was* in that file that the commission did not want published.

In a key conclusion, the commission found that the Mannlicher-Carcano rifle fired high and to the right, a finding consistent with the photos that were published of sample targets.[57] But the commission then went on to assert that this was an aid to the shooter, although the car was going *down and to the left*. To someone who never took a course in physics, this would only seem to double the chance for error, not increase the marksman's ability.

The commission used virtually identical logic to suggest that on November 21, Oswald retrieved his rifle from the blanket in the Paine garage, secreted it in a bag (of totally unknown origin), and sealed it, all because Ruth Paine found a light on in the garage.

Documents did not fare much differently. Helen Markham Exhibit 1 is titled "COPY OF A TRANSCRIPT of a tape recording of an alleged telephone conversation between H. L. Markham and Mark Lane."[58] The tape recording was played in Mrs. Markham's presence, and counsel noted for the record that the female voice was clearly that of Mrs. Markham. So why is the exhibit "alleged"? From there, the witness denied it was her voice, or that she had the cited conversation, and then indicated she may have had the conversation, but it was with Captain Fritz of the Dallas police, not Marguerite Oswald's lawyer, Mark Lane. Markham, a witness the commission counted on, to the exclusion of perhaps better witnesses, was seen by counsel Joseph Ball as "utterly unreliable" and an "utter screwball."[59] Oddly, Mrs. Markham was not asked about her place of employment, the Eat Well Cafe. Ordinarily, such a line of questioning would have no value; in this case, it was a greasy spoon frequented by Ruby, George Senator, and Larry Crafard, among others. George Senator was able, amid selective memory, to recall a waitress named Helen.

The Warren Commission routinely dispatched questions to a variety of agencies. Many responded promptly, and with answers to the point. In Commission Exhibit 948, the State Department responded to questions, and their response to "question 5" regarding a "secret document" was instructive. The page in question, the State Department replied, "Was at one time accompanied by a one-page message from the CIA . . . the copy in Oswald's passport file was accidently destroyed on November 23, 1963, while it was being thermofaxed."[60]

J. Edgar Hoover, in a letter dated June 9, 1964, notified the commission that Ruby had been a confidential bureau informant. The letter was not published, but Hoover was not to blame for this oversight. Hoover also wrote to the commission, at the end of April, of the very real possibility that serial number C2766 could have appeared on more than one Mannlicher, since all Italian arms factories were producing them. It was, however, but one sentence in a long exhibit.[61]

In a different editorial sleight of hand, the commission noted that Ruby's bank accounts, post office boxes, and safe-deposit boxes were empty. But the statement regarding Ruby's depositories belied the fact that there had to have been a reason for having them in the first place, and this was ignored.

Price Exhibits 2 through 35 also raise serious inferential concerns. The testimony by O. P. Wright, to whom Darrell Tomlinson had handed what might have been the most famous bullet of the twentieth century, devoted three paragraphs to President Kennedy's watch *but made no mention of the bullet.*[62] The remainder of the Price exhibits were quite thorough, referencing events involving Kennedy, Connally, Mrs. Kennedy, the protection scenario at the hospital for LBJ, the hearse, the coffin, the stretchers, the presence of the Secret Service, FBI, press, and priests, but there is no mention of the magic bullet, Commission Exhibit 399. Why not, and why did no member of the president's commission become curious?

Commission Exhibit 2003 featured, among other things, thirty-nine telegrams of congratulations to Jack Ruby, which had nothing whatsoever to do with the investigation, but were instructive of the popular state of mind at the time. Farther along, they published an additional sixty-five telegrams.[63] An equally fascinating exhibit is CE 949, which the State Department supplied to the commission to demonstrate whose passports had been revoked and why. The whys are left in the document; all five pages of names, however, became the victims of whiteout.[64] CE 1910 and 1911 are lists of places where Oswald *did not* apply for jobs.[65] A misprint no doubt caused commission exhibits 1059 and 1060 to appear as they do. Each is a one-page extract of a longer document involving the departure from the USSR and the arrival in the United States of Oswald; both documents begin in midsentence.[66]

FBI agent John Gallagher, the last witness to testify before Warren Commission counsel, had given an earlier deposition showing that Oswald would test positive for nitrates regardless of whether or not he handled or fired a gun, as the printed boxes and paper used in the TSBD contained barium and antimony, two substances vital in the process of the paraffin test. Gallagher also indicated that there were no traces of copper found on either the front of Kennedy's shirt or his tie, suggesting that the damage done to them (since revealed to have been done by a scalpel) could not have been done by the pristine, copper-jacketed "magic bullet." If that bullet exited JFK above the shirt collar, it further strains our credulity to accept that it was fired from above and behind and entered *his back*.[67]

Such samples as are cited, along with the many others detected by previous researchers and writers, begin to suggest why, by October 19, 1964, less than a month after its publication, the Warren Report's lone-assassin conclusion was doubted by 31 percent of the American population.[68] This statistic may also be an index of literacy in the United States in late 1964.

There was, however, one more serious "omission."

The largest, most ominous of the Warren "omissions" was the commission's willingness, if not desire, to accept the results of the pathology examination performed on the remains of the president at Bethesda Naval Hospital as proven fact.

Nothing, in fact, could have been farther from the truth.

Researchers who have preceded me in this quest have also focused on the question of the "autopsy" (which it was not in the legal sense). David Lifton, more than a decade ago, published *Best Evidence*, which, when matched up against the Warren Commission's meager efforts on the subject, could have been titled *Best Indictment*. Mr. Lifton did yeoman service in raising questions about the timing of the event, the nature of the wounds, the people present (whom Commander Humes was unable to name before the commission, suggesting either an unfamiliarity with the pathology staff due to lack of time with them, or a "you there, hand me that metal gadget" approach to medicine, or both), and generally cast serious doubts about the entire event, including the findings. Subsequently, researcher Harrison Edward Livingstone gathered together many of the individuals whom Mr. Lifton had discovered for a face-to-face roundtable, and the total was clearly more than the sum of the parts. This material, along with much else, was published in 1992 in *High Treason 2*.

It is not my intent to rehash the arguments these gentlemen have put forward; they speak eloquently for themselves. I would, however, like to add my own findings to the growing concerns regarding the "autopsy."

The House Select Committee on Assassinations had difficulties with the autopsy results because the pathologists had not inspected the president's clothing, specimens had not been properly maintained, a thorough procedure was *not* performed, and the pathologists were hardly the most qualified. The latter concern will be the focus here, as they missed something at autopsy that would not of necessity alter the nature of the crime but would certainly suggest that they were not the people to perform the autopsy, and if one finding is so obviously incorrect, how much faith can be lodged in the others?

Paul O'Connor, a technician at the autopsy and a key witness in both works cited above, has indicated that Admiral Burkley was giving a lot of orders at the autopsy, and in the name of the "Kennedy family."[69]

Perhaps the Kennedy family had a right to some sensitivity, but not at the expense of suspending justice for the sake of privilege. Next to the death of an individual, the most gut-wrenching experience the survivors may have to deal with is the thought of their loved one being literally taken apart on an impersonal stainless steel table filled with holes that collect body fluids. Internal organs are removed for examination and replaced like giblets in a Thanksgiving turkey, and the skull is severed to remove the brain. It certainly is not pretty, and it is unlikely that most of us would like to pursue such a career.

But those who do are supposed to know what they are doing, and Humes, Boswell, and Finck may not have. In the Sibert/O'Neill Report which provided the impetus for *Best Evidence,* it is written, "During the latter stages of the autopsy, Dr. Humes located an opening which appeared to be a single bullet hole which was below the shoulders and two inches to the right of the middle line of the spinal column."

During the latter stages? If a pathologist who has made observations of the body, placed it for the purpose of having numerous photos exposed, and further placed it to have X rays made ostensibly to locate metal still within the body cannot detect a bullet wound until the "latter stages" of the autopsy, he should not be performing it.

It is a matter of equal concern that the most fundamental autopsy procedure, that of recording observations, seemed to have been totally ignored. We have all seen crime dramas where the autopsist is examining the body in question and a microphone is hanging to record every verbal observation made by the pathologist. America must have been a poor country indeed in 1963 if the Dallas police could not afford a tape recorder and Bethesda Naval Hospital could not afford a microphone hookup for its morgue—or its commander in chief.

Yet it was Commander Humes's inability to understand what was right in front of him that calls into question the totality of conclusions regarding the wounds of the president, or, to stand alongside the two works cited in this section, to suggest that something very sinister was occurring with respect to the president's body.

In his testimony before five members of the Warren Commission on March 16, 1964, Commander Humes gave his interpretations of the bullet wounds found on the president. He also commented about other markings on the body, including two "cutdowns" performed at Parkland. (These were, according to the Parkland doctors, incisions, 2 cm in length, in the upper chest region, to place drainage tubes when it was believed by the Parkland staff that there had been some violation of the chest cavity by a missile, an admittedly unlikely possibility in an "official" scenario that involved a bullet that went in the back of the neck and came out the front of the neck.)

The thinking at Parkland at that time was that a bullet had entered the front of the president's throat and had ranged downward into the chest cavity; the presence of oxygenated blood during the Parkland inspection of the trachea seemed to the doctors, who did not have time on their side, to confirm their initial diagnosis. The Parkland doctors, it should be noted, never saw JFK's "back" wound. If there had been such a violation of the chest cavity, the magic bullet would lose much of its magical quality, and without the magic bullet, the Warren Report becomes just another 1964 best-selling work of *fiction*.

The Parkland measures also tend to reinforce the initial FBI report of a bullet entering JFK's back, penetrating briefly, and not exiting. That could certainly account for oxygenated blood in the pleural cavity as well as the need for—and placement of—chest tubes.

Humes testified, "We examined those wounds very carefully, and found that they, however, did not enter the chest cavity. They only went through the skin. I presume that as they [the Dallas doctors] were performing the procedure it was obvious that the president had died, and they didn't pursue this."[70]

Oh, but they did, sir, and you missed it. Price exhibits 2 through

35, the summation of the medical treatment afforded the wounded men at Parkland, indicated that "chest tubes *were placed* [emphasis added] and connected to sealed underwater drainage."[71] Dr. Paul Peters testified that chest tubes were placed.[72] This goes far beyond saying that the cutdowns were made and then abandoned. Dr. Gene C. Akin, Dr. Marion Jenkins, and Dr. R. N. McClelland agreed.[73] Dr. Ronald Coy Jones told both the FBI and the Warren Commission that he in fact placed one of the chest tubes and assisted Dr. C. R. Baxter with the other one, a statement corroborated by the latter.[74] Dr. William Kemp Clark, who along with Dr. Malcolm Perry were the senior physicians attending the president, told routinely, "There were chest tubes being inserted" by the time he reached the emergency room.[75]

Seven *civilian* Parkland doctors, in the performance of normal resuscitative duties in a very abnormal trauma situation, spoke of the *placement* of chest tubes. Approximately eight hours later, *government* pathologists viewed incisions that did not broach the chest cavity. This suggests that either the Parkland doctors, all seven, were incompetent, or lying, or both; or that Humes was incompetent, or lying, or both; or that the two separate sets of medical personnel were viewing a different body.

If the error was made in Dallas—and it is difficult to believe that seven qualified trauma specialists would simultaneously forget everything they had been taught in medical school—there should have been a housecleaning at Parkland Hospital.

If, on the other hand, the error was made at Bethesda *Naval Hospital,* the possibilities cited above all strongly imply conspiracy. If Humes was not competent, as the chest-tube question suggests, why was he put in charge of such a vital procedure, or was he put in charge of the autopsy so that nothing would be found? If he was reporting inaccurately, that, too, suggests conspiracy, because the reporting raises the possibility that the Dallas doctors saw, and treated, suspected chest damage that the autopsy doctors did not want to deal with, as it would destroy the official version. This concept gains credibility when we recall that Humes's autopsy report is open to speculation as to when it was submitted and dated. It gains further credibility when we discover that there were at least two autopsy reports. Dr. Alfred Olivier, a veterinarian stationed at Edgewood Arsenal to shoot animals and measure wound damage, told of re-creating the president's skull wound and test-firing at gelatin-filled skulls to verify Humes's work. In recounting his tests, he told the commission: "We placed a mark on the skull at that point, according to the autopsy the bullet emerged through the superorbital process. . . . "[76] Dr. Olivier may indeed have been working from "the autopsy," but he just wasn't working from the autopsy report made public. According to Olivier, he was able to re-create the entrance wound, low in the back of the head, and the exit, in the vicinity of the right eye.

The question of the chest tubes would not have had any effect whatsoever on the survival of President Kennedy. For all intents and purposes he was killed in the middle of Elm Street, five minutes before he was wheeled into the emergency room. An autopsy, however, was and is the ultimate blueprint of a crime, and the chest-tube concerns noted here are one more extremely strong indication that something was very wrong with the proceedings at Bethesda on the evening of November 22, 1963.

Certainly, the Warren Commission should have gone to the trouble to discover an answer to a question as fundamental as that.

Thirty years later, however, we are still asking it.

And there are thousands of other concerns not addressed.

HYPOTHESIS

President Kennedy's assassination was the work of magicians. It was a stage trick, complete with accessories and false mirrors, and when the curtain fell the actors, and even the scenery, disappeared.

—"JAMES HEPBURN," *Farewell America*, p. 281

THE ASSASSINATION OF PRESIDENT JOHN F. KENNEDY on November 22, 1963, was a long time in the making. So, too, has been the search for its solution.

The crime was not initiated with Lee Oswald making a fateful decision on November 21 to bring his rifle to work the following day. Nor did it end with a pair of lucky shots from a war-surplus rifle.

The odyssey that led Oswald to the point of being the sole individual charged in Dallas for the assassination of John Kennedy began in 1955, not 1963. In 1955, the youthful, slightly effeminate Oswald, who had been forever deprived of a father and had been dominated by a shrewish mother, joined the New Orleans Civil Air Patrol, a paramilitary recruiting ground.

There he was introduced to Capt. David W. Ferrie, known to have a proclivity to seek the affection of young boys, who was immediately drawn to the new cadet. Oswald, however, resentful of his maternally dominated childhood, rejected Ferrie's advances with a show of bravado that included the truthful boast that he was going to join the U.S. Marine Corps as soon as he was old enough, or sooner if he could fake it.

The rebuffed Ferrie changed tack, exchanged his pedophile hat for his intelligence garb, and proceeded to give Oswald the advice typical of that provided to future gung-ho marine types: Know your job and know your enemy. Ferrie would also file Oswald's name away in his vast intellect for future reference, and would learn in the following year that Oswald had, in fact, kept his promise to join the Marine Corps.

Oswald, meanwhile, took Ferrie's advice to heart. Believing in 1955 that the Marine Corps was his ticket out of the life of Marguerite Oswald, he gave it his best effort, alternately studying the Marine Corps manual that had been provided by his older brother Robert or reading the works of Karl Marx.

When not reading such mutually exclusive works, Oswald would occasionally try to appear pedantic, to gloss over past academic and personality shortcomings, and since there is not much from the Marine Corps manual that can be entertainingly quoted in mixed company, he fell back on his readings of Marx.

Once Oswald made such pronouncements, however inconsequential their origins, his personality was such that he had to defend his statements, and in so doing he created an image that followed him to the grave—in part because he never gained the maturity to step back from his quoting of Marx and admit that he was just showing off what little knowledge he possessed.

In 1956, at a time when John Kennedy was fortunate to be alive after back surgery that caused him to receive the last rites of the Roman Catholic Church twice, Oswald joined the Marine Corps. Two things then happened: One, Ferrie, who had not forgotten Oswald, notified his superiors in the intelligence community, who contacted Oswald's superiors in the marines and suggested that he was a possible future "asset," an individual who can be used for purposes outside of the normal job description—in this case, of the Marine Corps; and secondly, in his routine personnel evaluation, the corps recognized that he was not the typical leatherneck, as most of them would have identified "Marx" as a television quiz-show host, not the author of a radical, if unsuccessful, political theory. As a result, forces within and without the marines came to view Oswald as a potential "asset."

Oswald had the same basic training as other marines, but he was quickly segregated thereafter from the vast majority of his fellow trainees, who would be further taught how to storm whatever beaches needed storming. Oswald was given aviation and radar training, hardly typical for the branch of service that had fought "from the halls of Montezuma to the shores of Tripoli" and that fought their battles "on land and on the sea." There's just nothing in there about marine radar or aviation, although obviously it did exist—in this case, for covert purposes. After all, it is much cheaper, as well as far more inconspicuous, to pay a marine private to watch a radarscope for a spy plane than to pay the salary of a journeyman government intelligence operative.

Despite his occasional Marxist eloquence, or perhaps because of it, Oswald was assigned to a top secret CIA installation at Atsugi, Japan, from which some, but not all, U-2 flights over the Soviet Union were launched. Curious about the plane whose pilots requested air currents at "ninety angels" (ninety thousand feet), Oswald once went to view the unusual craft, only to find its hangar sealed tight and guarded by submachine-gun-toting sentries.

At the same time, Oswald's past Marxist self-education made him a "natural" for further training in all things Soviet, and since he never had "the right stuff" for combat, the Marine Corps got what they could out of Oswald, increasing his "asset" status by assisting him in his inclination to learn the Russian language, and by looking the other way when Oswald foolishly flaunted his newly taught skills in the barracks. For Oswald, it was natural: Since he could not make friends, he could at least get noticed. Much the same would happen later during Oswald's acquaintance with Guy Banister.

Oswald had almost carte blanche in the marines, as his unit often went in one direction, but Oswald always seemed to get detached from them and wind up back at Atsugi. His three-week stay in the hospital for a self-inflicted flesh wound was hardly characteristic of either Marine Corps toughness or standard medical procedure, but was rather suggestive of time spent segregated from others to broaden his Soviet résumé. Much the same could be said of his time spent in the brig following his second court-martial, which itself followed what appeared to be a trumped-up incident in which Oswald poured a drink on a sergeant.

When Oswald left Atsugi, he was transferred to El Toro Naval Air Station in California, one of hundreds of marine installations around the world, but oddly one in close proximity to the Monterey Language School, which had a world-class reputation for quick and efficient tutelage in foreign languages. People whose paths later crossed Oswald's would remark upon the amazing fluency of his Russian, while a few others, perhaps not enchanted with his personality, were more critical of his language skills, including his English.

Somewhere in the helter-skelter that would characterize America's desperation for Soviet intelligence in the late 1950s, Oswald was approached either by marine superiors or by intelligence operatives, and his status was upgraded from "asset" to "junior agent," a promotion that suited Oswald just fine, as it had the possibility to confirm his sought-after freedom from his mother, and it gave him the opportunity to flaunt his "skills," a possibility that had been rare in his formative years.

Oswald was going to be somebody after all. Unbeknownst to him, his marine career had just reached a plateau. Also unknown to him, as well as his sponsors, was the portent that he would be world-famous for three days in November 1963.

In 1959, Oswald's marine job description varied from radar specialist to "gofer," in which capacity he was part janitor, part landscaper, and part jack-of-all-trades at El Toro. This was no doubt a result of U.S. concerns that Soviet agents would keep careful watch on such bases in America, where access was far more free than at Atsugi. Oswald also requested, and was granted, a "hardship" discharge from the corps, a signal to anyone watching that Oswald was no longer interested in the U.S. military, and they were no longer interested in him. In sum, it was a good career move. Highly valued FBI man Guy Banister would create a scenario with similar underpinnings, which caused his "separation" from the bureau. The key word in both separations is "scenario."

In late summer 1959, with 422 documentable dollars to his name, Oswald left California to journey home to Texas, a trip that depleted at least some of his capital. His finances would be enhanced by small increments from the intelligence community, most likely the Office of Naval Intelligence, as Oswald was not in the big leagues yet. By the time he departed for Russia, his net worth had reached $1,500, a figure that Oswald could *not* have saved during his marine tenure, given his expensive dating habits during his Japanese service, and knowing that he did go on leave while in California.

The trip itself has caused much speculation, as it involved a less-than-cruiselike boat passage, and then a mysterious flight to Helsinki, Finland, at a time when no such flights existed. There were also matching irregularities in Oswald's passport records. Another oddity of the midpassage was Oswald's habit of keeping to himself aboard ship, on the pretext of seasickness, an unlikely malady for someone who had traveled so much at sea with the marines (although more probable than average for someone with a history of mastoid and other ear problems). Equally odd was the fact that Oswald knew to go to Helsinki, the easiest covert entrepôt to the USSR.

Upon entering the Soviet Union at a time when, not coincidentally, numerous other disaffected former U.S. soldiers were also arriving there, he was given a quick entry visa by the Soviets, but not permanent permission to stay. He was also given Dostoevsky's *The Idiot* as a welcoming present by the Intourist service, an extension of Soviet intelligence, and there is hardly a more suggestive gift imaginable than *The Idiot*. Of note, there are no editorial references to this gift by Oswald in any of his subsequent handwritten ruminations, suggestive of an intelligence role in the visit; for if he truly were a defector loyally dedicated to the Soviet Union, he would have been badly wounded by the choice of gift; his silence suggests otherwise.

Oswald was interviewed by American journalists in Moscow, and his answers to their questions suggested a circumspection based on the realization by Oswald that his Soviet hosts were also listening carefully. For the same reason, he staged a loud and bellicose performance at the U.S. embassy in which he denounced his American past and yearned for a Soviet future in the ultimate workers' paradise. He also *promised* he would commit treason.

We may never know, but Oswald may have overplayed his hand, and had to fall back on a fake suicide to impress whoever was deciding whether he would stay or be asked to leave, since his visa had expired. On a gut-level hunch, I doubt the Soviets truly bought the botched suicide.

Oswald was nevertheless debriefed, and extensively so. He told his Soviet interrogators a great deal of truth that they already knew, but he had no doubt been programmed to provide some disinformation as well, shortening the range of the U-2 and altering the "blind spots" in the U.S. West Coast radar apparatus to prime target spots. If the Soviets had ever tried to exploit the "blind spots" Oswald provided, they would have found themselves on prime-time American radar.

Defector Oswald would subsequently appear on Soviet radio in a brief propaganda spot, but would never be treated like the major defectors of the past, simply because he was not on their level, and there was no earthshaking U.S. intelligence flap at his defection. The absence of such intelligence concern tends to prove Oswald's "agent" status, as he did possess much knowledge for a "defector." Having provided the Soviets what he knew, or had been told to repeat, he was shipped off to Minsk, where he would be given a gratuitous financial "thank you" by the Soviet Red Cross, and a job making radios. This was to prove his mettle as a true believer in the Soviet state, but Oswald quickly tired of it.

Oswald's whirlwind courtship and marriage to Marina can be viewed either as an enigmatic act of a disenchanted genuine defector, an act of love sponsored by the loneliness of cold Russian winters, or an ingenious attempt to maintain his agent status, regardless of where the future took him. Upon his return, with a Russian wife who had been raised by an officer in Soviet intelligence, questions were whispered: Is he an agent, and if so, is he one of ours or one of theirs? And therein lies the safety valve: When confronted with such questions, most people threw up their hands in despair and moved on to more answerable concerns. The charade, if it was one, had succeeded.

It has been documented throughout the course of this work, and especially in "Red Patsy," that despite the public perception of Lee Oswald as a defector who would give top secret information to the Soviets, our government seemed to operate in inordinate haste to get Oswald and family back to the United States, and generally to strike a pose of avoiding contact with him. The entire scenario screamed "American agent!" and was a concern to those Oswald came in contact with socially. The government was willing to waive the normal circumstances that would have applied to permit Marina to enter the United States, a fact those same Russian émigrés found just as difficult to believe. The government gave the Oswald family financial aid of $435.71 to make the return trip. And when Oswald arrived home, he was avoided by investigative agencies as if he were carrying a deadly bacillus, when logic would dictate that once we had him back on our side of the Atlantic, many questions should have been asked, or handcuffs should have been produced.

Or both.

Oswald's arrival back in the United States amounted to a classic case of mixed signals. No law enforcement or serious intelligence operatives were there to meet him, a clear indication that they did not want his cover shattered. Some of the Oswald baggage from the Soviet Union went astray. Finally, in late June, Robert Oswald was contacted by the FBI and told to alert them when Lee returned. As it happened, Lee and family were already back, suggesting that American intelligence sources had either duped the FBI regarding Oswald's return, or the FBI was part of the charade.

It would be equally foolish to suggest that Oswald somehow slipped through the cracks. A more reasonable suggestion would be that doors were opened wide for him, and the intelligence avoidance of him was clearly intentional.

Ultimately Oswald would be questioned by the FBI on a couple of occasions, but would "bristle" at questions about why he went to Russia. This is nothing short of ludicrous; if "defector" Oswald had bristled at anything during a *genuine* FBI interview after his return from Russia, he would have been placed in custody for a series of felonies, up to and including treason, and those charges would have stayed on the books until Oswald ceased his bristling. But that did not happen either, as the FBI very uncharacteristically took Oswald's anger in stride. The worst that happened to Oswald in the entire period of his defection (besides having to live in Minsk) was his downgraded discharge from the Marine Corps Reserve, and that may have been done to enrich his defector bona fides.

The FBI interviews, however, are moot, for long before the bureau got to Oswald, the CIA did. Through the intervention of the ever-gracious George DeMohrenschildt, Oswald was debriefed, told that he was still a valued member of "the team," and also was told that he should neither be overly concerned with his income nor live too lavishly with any private funding that came his way. He was also told that his covert role would involve frequent changes of employment and residence. Oswald accepted the tutelge and would henceforth follow DeMohrenschildt like a puppy, until Oswald was ordered to New Orleans and Clay Shaw/Bertrand would take DeMohrenschildt's place.

There are hints in Oswald's conversations to his mother and brother that he was more than he appeared to be, and it is also known that the FBI, *army* intelligence (for a marine?), and other agencies kept close tabs on an individual that the CIA was claiming they never heard of.

To this point, however, we must recall that Oswald was an asset or a low-end contract agent. He would continue to be carried on American intelligence ledgers but would never be promoted to assassin. Anyone even remotely aware of Oswald's Marine Corps shooting ability would immediately rule out this possibility, for although Oswald qualified once as a sharpshooter and once as marksman, assassins are cut from the "expert" class, and only from the best of that select group.

Mid-1962 provided the crossroads in Oswald's covert career. His mission to the Soviet Union had at best received mixed reviews, as it was difficult to posit that he successfully completed any imaginable mission save for some possible disinformation about the U-2's range, which would have been meaningless after Gary Powers' flight. With Oswald back in the United States, the Office of Naval Intelligence (ONI), his original sponsor, would have to keep a distant eye on him and make a judgment on his readjustment to American society and his acceptance by that society. If he were totally shunned as a traitor, his usefulness to the intelligence community was at an end. If his past was forgiven or overlooked, it would forever remain on his résumé and might have value in the future. In the meantime, the CIA had stepped in, in the person of George DeMohrenschildt, but this would ruffle no feathers in the intelligence community, as the CIA could hardly be accused of muscling in on a top ONI operative.

The second half of 1962 held extremely significant portents for John Kennedy, however. His emerging liberalism, his unwillingness to confront either the Cubans or the Soviets forcefully, his drive for civil rights, his willingness to close oil-profit loopholes, his disdain for further intervention in Laos or Vietnam, and his willingness to prosecute those who misused the American system, added to his prospects for a reelection that could truly provoke change, alarmed those in the corridors of power.

Because of that, the subsequent sponsors of Kennedy's murder decided to send Kennedy a very personal warning, one that would tell him that he was vulnerable for his sexual peccadilloes as well as for his life: On August 4, 1962, Marilyn Monroe was found dead in her California dwelling, coincidently at a time that RFK was nearby in San Francisco to make an address. While other researchers have seen Miss Monroe's death as either the suicide that it was officially ruled, or something more sinister, I would like to suggest, particularly for those who have seen *The Godfather,* that the death of Marilyn Monroe was *the horse's head. It was the ultimate step this side of Dallas,* and it was meant as a dire threat to the Kennedy brothers, even though it solved, temporarily at least, one of their problems.

For a while, "the horse's head gambit" worked. Kennedy talked tough on Cuba a few weeks later, and without firing a shot, forced the Soviet missiles and IL-28 bombers home, and left Khrushchev with egg on his face. Americans also learned that we had a decided superiority in the arms race over the Soviets, and that superiority could be traced directly to Kennedy's promises during the 1960 campaign to bring an end to the "missile/bomber gap." Kennedy was speaking softly but carrying a very big stick.

As events subsequent to the Cuban Missile Crisis were to prove, however, it was not the all-encompassing American victory that had been perceived at the end of the terrifying "thirteen days" in October. Kennedy had pledged *not* to invade Cuba, and he would not only keep that pledge, but also begin a campaign to make sure that disaffected elements within the United States did not stir up any further problems. The military chieftains looked on in horror as our Jupiter missile bases in Turkey and Italy were dismantled, giving rise to the suspicion that perhaps a trade had been agreed to between Kennedy and Khrushchev, and that we had not scared the Soviets out of Cuba, but rather traded missiles for missiles.

The last straw was the beginning of the "thaw" in the Cold War, with the corollary that relations with Russia and Cuba might be improved and that Vietnam would have to defend itself with the indigenous population and with no largesse for American defense contractors. The hopes for the continuation of that "thaw" would die in Dallas.

"The horse's head gambit" had failed; now it was a matter of going after the head (not the tail) of the dog, as the Mafia metaphor would portray the event.

Those who stalked the corridors of power were seething at both Castro and Kennedy in the early months of 1963: Castro, for being allowed to get away with an attempt at nuclear blackmail; Kennedy, for letting him off with a slap on the wrist.

In the first few months of 1963, the divergent interests cited in "Preliminary Conclusions" began to come together. The CIA was becoming more disenchanted day by day with JFK, for although the agency had played a serious role in the Cuban Missile Crisis, they were easily able to recognize that Kennedy's reelection was rapidly approaching, and with it, the transfer of RFK from the Justice Department to directorship of the CIA. Organized crime, the CIA's willing partner in the anti-Castro drive, could easily envision further prosecutions by the Kennedy administration in the second term, and could also imagine unpleasant scenarios in their fiefdom once the pliant J. Edgar Hoover was pensioned off and a real lawman took over the FBI. The "southern tier" of conservatives, segregationists, and oilmen were becoming less and less enchanted by Kennedy every day. Members of Brigade 2506, who had been unsuccessful on the beaches at the Bay of Pigs, and whose return Kennedy had negotiated in late 1962, were quick to demonstrate their ingratitude for the gesture and their hatred of Kennedy for what they saw as a 1961 act of cowardice and betrayal. J. Edgar Hoover and Lyndon Johnson heard the clock ticking on their political careers. "Big money" interests in the United States took serious notice of the fact that Kennedy saw to the beginning of the issuance of "U.S. Notes," currency that was introduced into our economy as need arose by, of all groups, the U.S. Treasury, the group constitutionally obligated to do so. Other monies were "brokered" into the system by the Federal Reserve, of which there is no mention in the Constitution, which is silent on private corporations controlling the issuance of American currency.

Although it is highly unlikely that there ever occurred anything like a conference among these various elements, the intelligence elements, which had so recently spearheaded the planning, were willing (and who wouldn't be?) to transfer the ownership of the project to Texas interests that were both financially powerful and politically connected. They would look for an assassination site far from Washington, and one that had a history of being conservative. It would also be helpful if that city had a police establishment of an equally conservative, anti-Kennedy bent, and one that could be purchased with petrodollars or related perquisites such as oil leases or franchises. All of this pointed to the South, where Kennedy had had some electoral successes in 1960, and would no doubt have more in 1964, because of the black vote. That, however, did not trouble the plotters; there were no black police officers in many places in 1963.

The official concern in early 1963, however, was still Castro and Cuba, and it was at this point that Oswald was reactivated and told to secure both a pistol and a rifle—nothing fancy—and do so in the name of someone *pro-Cuban*. It may well have been that the ONI was willing to loan Oswald to the CIA to go after Castro, as Oswald could hardly be *suspected* of being a potential Castro assassin after having defected to the Soviet Union and then returned to the United States in a decidedly pro-Castro frame of mind. If such a mission failed, Oswald could easily be portrayed by the world press as the ultimate nut, dividing his time between supporting and stalking the bearded Cuban leader.

An alternate scenario revolves around what is today referred to as the issue of "gun control." In the early 1960s, key individuals on Capitol Hill were becoming increasingly concerned about the prolif- eration of weapons on American streets and the resulting crime. Nar- cotics imported by groups cited above had much to do with these problems, and the weapons proliferation was a way to protect their unique cottage industry. It has been argued that someone able to give Oswald orders told him to purchase both the rifle and the pistol, and be obvious about the purchases to the point of leaving a massive paper trail and being quickly photographed with both weapons and pinko literature. Somewhere down the road, those legislators who were using Oswald would reveal his nickel-and-dime antics and show how a returned, treasonous defector could openly purchase deadly weapons through the mail, and flaunt the practice.

Regardless of which scenario one follows, Oswald complied with the requests of his "handlers," using the fictitious "Hidell" identity along with *his own handwriting* in ordering the weapons. It would be this mistake, the ability to link the "Hidell" who owned the weapons to the "Oswald" who had defected to Russia, that would cause intel- ligence planners to have Oswald posture as pro-Cuban, but they could no longer use him to assassinate Castro. If he had rented the box as "Hidell" and not "Oswald" and bought the weapons the same way, history might be different. (Because he did it as both names, he came in very handy immediately after the president was killed.) But as far as Cuba was concerned, such an attempted deception would have been seen as translucent, particularly when "the late Fidel Castro's" Soviet allies revealed what they knew of "Oswald." Ken- nedy, however, was also a target, and Oswald's posturing, in either postulated scenario, made him the perfect patsy.

Once Oswald received the weapons and was photographed with them, events began to accelerate. Oswald lost his job at Jaggers- Chiles-Stovall, a firm that worked with the intelligence community. Several reasons were cited for Oswald's termination, but the most important, if unstated, reason was that J-C-S could not be involved with an employee who might within days be arrested for attempted murder or worse: Elements within the intelligence community had reached Oswald and included him in a "scenario" involving the firing of a rifle at the residence of General Walker.

This event, which would occur on April 10, 1963, would have a number of powerful ramifications. First, it would signal an end of Oswald's Dallas stay, and he would move on to New Orleans. Second, it would give him a propensity for violence that would have great value after November 22. Third, it would portray the radical right as the victim, not the aggressor, and no one would subsequently suspect that the Walker event had been *staged* to draw attention *away* from events in the fall. The right-wing element in Dallas was almost vitiated as future suspects because of the events of April 10, as they now had the ultimate plausible deniability. Fourth, those events would give police authorities a permanent stranglehold on Oswald, simply by keeping the Walker case open and unsolved.

As noted, it is possible that Walker was not even in the room at the time a bullet was fired into it. As events would later prove, a bolt-action rifle could be operated in 2.3 seconds; is there any proof that General Walker could realize what had happened, react to the event, and get out of the line of fire in 2.3 seconds? Absent such proof, the event seems staged, with Oswald again a bit player, but it was another great résumé entry.

Prospects for work seemed better in New Orleans than in the Dallas climate that knew Oswald the defector. At the same time, George DeMohrenschildt's duties took him to Haiti, so Clay Shaw, in New Orleans, became Oswald's ultimate overseer.

In New Orleans, Oswald found employment as a coffee machine greaser at the William B. Reily Coffee Company, and this employment was no doubt sponsored by Clay Shaw or a go-between. And the benefits were good: The company was owned by a dedicated anti-Castro fanatic, it was located in the heart of the New Orleans intelligence establishment, it was close to the offices of Guy Banister, and for a long time there were no questions asked when Oswald was regularly absent from that place of employment. Ultimately, as the plotters' focus shifted to Dallas, Oswald would be terminated for the very absences that had been tolerated when needed, and the Reily Company would be "sanitized," as several employees would fall into jobs at the National Aeronautics and Space Administration.

While in New Orleans, Oswald would fall into the clutches of Banister, whose patron was also Clay Shaw, and David Ferrie, Oswald's tutor from his premarine days. Their plans, as revealed to Oswald, were for him to create a serious pro-Castro, strongly leftist posture, while they, along with the exiles being trained north of Lake Pontchartrain, were readying themselves to take "executive action" against Castro. Castro was the target as Oswald understood the scenario; Kennedy, however, had already replaced Castro among those creating the scenario. Castro, after all, could no longer be removed until Kennedy had been.

Oswald did what he was told, carrying out a simplistic pro-Cuban leaflet campaign in a city with only loathing for Castro. Oswald was always photographed in these brief leaflet adventures, and it is difficult to believe that news sources in New Orleans gave repeated free publicity to a street corner nut with pro-Castro leaflets. On the contrary, the photos were intelligence-oriented, and would come in handy in late November, as well as for a commission appointed by the newly installed president *from Texas*.

In an equally leftist posturing effort, Oswald visited Clinton, Louisiana, to be part of a black-voter registration drive, a solitary and unmistakable white face in a long line of people who had already waited too long for fundamental American rights. Ferrie was also along on this trip, and was accompanied by either Banister or Shaw. The latter identification is not urgent: They were virtually interchangeable.

Fate intervened in that summer of 1963. After Kennedy's much-publicized American University speech on June 10, followed by a civil-rights message the next day, his direction for America was more clearly revealed and lost him some remaining support in the corridors of power. At the same time, a Kennedy-ordered raid on the exile camps destroyed what little threat the exiles posed to Castro, and as a result, Oswald's—and only Oswald's—focus remained on the elimination of Castro, while Banister, and to a greater extent Ferrie, maneuvered Oswald into the rendezvous in Dallas.

The August 1963 fight in which Oswald received both the blows and the conviction almost completed his patsy résumé, and it began the winding down of his New Orleans efforts. It also came at the same time that the president's trip to Texas in the fall was announced.

One more ingredient was necessary to flesh out Oswald's "Cuban" background, and that objective was met when Oswald was dispatched to Mexico City on the pretext of attempting to get back to the Soviet Union via Cuba. If the Soviets had tired of him in 1962, they clearly had no use whatsoever for him in 1963, but those planning to kill Kennedy needed Oswald to appear in this additional act of the farce. The CIA erred when they photographed the wrong "Oswald" coming out of one of the embassies in Mexico City, but no matter: The FBI and the Warren Commission would bury this inconsistency, just as they would take no notice of the "Oswald" appearance at Oak Ridge, Tennessee, in July, or the deadly serious visit to Sylvia Odio during the real Oswald's Mexican sojourn.

Unbeknownst to the real Oswald, an imitator or imitators would begin laying false trails that would all point in his direction after November 22. Of equal interest was the thrust of Oswald's intention to "return" to the Soviet Union. On one hand, he did not possess even the down payment for such a venture, suggesting the necessity of outside funding if the venture were real. Second, his efforts came to naught when his reentry into the Soviet Union was vetoed *by the Soviets*. It may well have been at exactly this time that elements within the KGB ordered unknowing double agent Richard Case Nagell to eliminate Oswald, as the Soviets feared that he was up to something very serious, and given his thirty-one-month residence in the Soviet Union, they wanted no part of it.

Oswald was told to return to Dallas, where he would be an instrumental member of a group that would rid the world of Fidel Castro. This scenario assumed the usually nonemployment-motivated Oswald, but it overlooked the fact that Mrs. Oswald was expecting a second child, as well as her desire for common consumer goods such as a washing machine and someday an automobile. Oswald was propelled back into the job market, and fortuitously for everyone except JFK, found employment near Main Street in downtown Dallas.

What remained was to sell Oswald the final bill of goods and then guarantee that somehow the president's car could be placed in relative proximity to the book warehouse where Oswald was exercising his intellect for $1.25 per hour. Once it was learned that a Dallas motorcade would be included in the fall presidential Texas trip, the plan moved a giant step closer to fruition.

In the meantime, if Oswald was to be implicated fully, more evidence of violent or pro-Soviet behavior was necessary, so a fake Oswald or Oswalds—or a very busy John Thomas Masen—began appearing in and around Dallas in the fall of 1963, usually in gun-related or "I'll soon be coming into money" scenarios. The one failure in all of this was the plotters' unawareness of Oswald's inability to operate a motor vehicle. After all, every twenty-three-year-old drives; it's an integral part of the rites of passage. *Every twenty-three-year-old except Oswald, that is.*

The Dallas scenario would be highly complicated in its planning and equally simplistic in its execution—which was also its purpose. As suggested earlier, at least three or four groups were brought within the orbit of the event, possibly but not positively including a Cuban exile group, an organized crime group, a southern right-wing crew, and a "Dallas police"—or imitator group, which had Dealey Plaza for their prime site. The first three groups were never more than stage props or backups, while the primary group, "Blue Death," was comprised of a small group of rogue police elements or those who could give the appearance of police, to avoid the immediate dragnet at the time of the shooting.

This thesis is reinforced by too many odd occurences in Dallas law-enforcement circles: the selection of the Trade Mart as the luncheon site, which diverted precious police and Secret Service manpower, leaving the motorcade route guarded in many places by unarmed reserves; the total unwillingness of the sheriff's department to have an involvement in motorcade security (or later, in Oswald's transfer), as if they possessed a clairvoyance uncommon in police circles; the small police presence in Dealey Plaza, with no officers posted between the corner of Elm and Houston and the triple underpass (a distance of five hundred feet), with the possible exception of those involved in the assassination; the failure of the police to clear the triple underpass of civilians, as those civilians would have gone to the next best vantage point to view the parade, putting them *behind the picket fence;* the unwillingness to hear of, or investigate, fake Secret Service men in Dealey Plaza; and the failure to react to witnesses' observations regarding the Texas School Book Depository, at a time when the police—and civilian—surge was toward the knoll, where only railroad people *or police* would be found.

Subsequently the police would self-destruct their own case so that Oswald could never have come to trial for murdering the president, as police at Parkland, among other suspected activities, did not come to the coroner's aid in demanding a Texas autopsy for the president. They also handled the evidence against Oswald—as well as Oswald himself—so poorly that the ultimate result, had Oswald survived, would have been a trial for Oswald's participation in the murder of Officer Tippit. While that event was also on the "Blue Death" agenda, it reinforces that thesis because most police killers, particularly those linked to communism in the early sixties and those who might be accused of other serious crimes, would stand no chance whatsover. Oswald would have received the death penalty, and the world would have easily concluded that he was equally guilty of killing the president.

Thus was born Oswald the patsy, while a shooter atop the jail, as well as at least one on the knoll, had either police connections or police uniforms. The shooter in the TSBD could only have escaped by posing as an officer or a journalist, and there was no guarantee to that sniper that journalists would be admitted to the crime scene as quickly as they were. A possible shooter high up in the Dal-Tex Building might easily have chosen the same ruse as his coconspirators, and it is noteworthy that two suspects were roused from that location, again allowing a large police presence in which uniformed officers could easily come and go. All of the above shooters could easily have slipped into place during the six-minute diversion created when an individual had a seizure fewer than one hundred fifty feet from the spot where the president would be shot. In a several-mile-long motorcade with no other such seizures, that is a strange coincidence indeed.

The key to the plan was the three patsies ultimately chosen: Lee Harvey Oswald; J. D. Tippit; and, as a backup if necessary, Jack Ruby. It is highly unlikely that the trio ever met, as Oswald was operating under the control of a "Mr. Hunt," most likely E. Howard or H. L. It was this "Mr. Hunt" whom Oswald would write to on November 8: "Dear Mr. Hunt, I would like information concerning [sic] my position. I am asking only for information. I am suggesting that we discuss the matter fully before any steps are taken by me or anyone else. Thank you, Lee Harvey Oswald."*

It is hard to imagine such a letter being written in any context outside of "executive action." It is hardly the kind of document that would emanate from a $1.25-per-hour stockboy in a warehouse, as it sounds far more like an in-house corporate memo that would ordinarily have included the notation, "Let's do lunch."

Of equal importance was the other document penned by Oswald on November 8. This one was hand-delivered to the Dallas FBI office, and was subsequently destroyed by Special Agent Hosty, on the orders of Dallas special agent in charge Gordon Shanklin, within hours of Oswald's death. The FBI would like us to believe that the letter was a threat against the FBI because Oswald did not like agents of the bureau rattling Marina's cage; if this story had a shred of truth to it, the letter would have been kept and used for the dust jacket on the Warren Report. The destruction of the letter strongly suggests

---

*Letter shown and quoted in full in Marrs, *Crossfire.*

that it contained a message that the FBI never wanted the public to be aware of, perhaps a warning of ominous events later in the month that either the bureau did not take seriously or its director preferred to ignore. Recall that the previously referenced FBI telex regarding an assassination threat all but bore the signature of Oswald, as it was written in his dysgraphic idiom.

Oswald was given a simple mission by "Mr. Hunt" but failed to understand its simplicity, hence the letter of November 8. Oswald was told that a *fake assassination attempt* would be staged, in Dallas, with John Kennedy as the target. Oswald's role was to deliver the Mannlicher, which had been purchased by FPCC member "Hidell" and was therefore traceable to pro-Castro elements, to an individual who would later use it, or a substitute, in a most obvious way in the sixth-floor window of the book depository, making sure to leave the Mannlicher-Carcano behind.

As it happened, the gun was fired only once, and contained blank ammunition—this was the firecracker sound heard by many witnesses. The remainder of the time the gun was "posed" in the depository window by someone who knew he would neither be caught nor identified, and it created the gestalt that the weapon *seen* created the gunfire *heard,* and distracted possible witnesses from seeing other shooters. No ground-level witness who saw a sixth-floor book depository weapon saw it fired more than once, and none reported a telescopic sight.

As it happened, the well-triangulated shooting occurred in volleys—so what witnesses reported as three shots was essentially three volleys, and some of the weapons might have been sound-suppressed (silencers), which tends to lower the velocity of the subsequent bullet, explaining some wounds that are better understood at lower velocities. The first volley involved a coordinated effort from the TSBD and the knoll. Within a period of just over one second, the TSBD sixth-floor impostor fired his blank, and the knoll shooter hit Kennedy in the front of his throat just prior to photographer Zapruder losing Kennedy in his image finder because of a road sign. This shot from the front, unlike the later Z313, did not strike enough bony tissue to alter the president's posture greatly; we also don't know what exactly that posture was, because of Zapruder's noted problems with the highway sign. Confirmation of such a shot was provided by Secret Service agent Warren Taylor, who told researcher Vince Palamara that he saw what may have been a shot hit the street behind the vice president's follow-up car (see Palamara, *Third Alternative,* p. 41). What Special Agent Taylor was seeing was the bullet that entered Kennedy from the front and exited from the rear, impacting well behind the presidential vehicle.

The second volley would occur a second and a half later, involving shots from the west end of the TSBD (but not, as previously suggested by researchers, a "low-angle shot" from the Dal-Tex, because the downward slope of Elm Street and the presence of Secret Service agents on the rear seats and running boards of the follow-up vehicle would have prevented such a shot) and the roof of the jail. The jail shot hit the president in the upper back in Zapruder frames 231–32 and did not transit his body. The west-end depository shot ripped through the governor's chest about one-sixth second later, between Zapruder frames 234 and 236, and ricocheted into the limousine windshield or exited the vehicle after shattering and "riding" a rib.

The final volley again involved the west-end TSBD shooter, the jail, and the knoll. The jail shooter hit the president in the back of his head, in the location indicated by Humes, in Zapruder 312; the knoll shooter had his aim compromised slightly by the Z312 shot from behind, which pushed JFK slightly forward. Thus the knoll shot impacted on the right temple, well in front of the ear, when it had been sighted in, literally, "right between the eyes." The head bullets were explosive, and despite the massive damage done by them, little trace remained, except the Mannlicher-like fragments thrown into the limousine by police elements at Parkland. The west-end TSBD shot was late, and did the remaining damage to Governor Connally (wrist and thigh wounds—note Connally's movements *after* the fatal head impact on Kennedy) within one-half second of the fatal shots to the president. This portion-of-a-second delay may account for many witnesses' perceptions that the final shot sounded like a "double bang."

Oswald had been told that the purpose of the fake attempt was that once a bullet or a blank was fired over the limousine into the expanse of lawn in the plaza, the Secret Service would swarm over the president, law-enforcement people would find the Mannlicher as planned, trace it to "Hidell" and hence to pro-Cuban forces, and the United States would clean out Castro's rats' nest once and for all. Oswald, who would have to leave town until the noise cleared down, was told that when all was said and done, he would be the hero of the piece, and no blame could attach to him as long as he stayed away from the sixth floor during the motorcade. He may also have naively believed that it was not a crime to be a coconspirator in the firing of a blank as the president was passing, so even if he were linked to the rifle, what could he be charged with?

A previously unpublished key to this riddle is so simple that it has never been considered before, yet has always been right in front of us for our consideration. *The weather forecast, as well as Friday morning's weather, was not good.* If the weather had lived up to the forecast, and rained beyond the midmorning hours in Dallas, the motorcade would have included the bubble top on the presidential limousine. While not bulletproof, its mere presence would diminish the zeal and success possibilities of any genuine assassin, as it would make a challenging rifle shot far more difficult. Yet in spite of the inclement weather, Oswald duly delivered his rifle to its subsequent user, as the scenario that Oswald had been taught, involving a fake attempt, was still possible with the bubble top on the car. Only when the weather cleared and the bubble top was removed did the other Dealey Plaza "kill" teams begin to move into place, as noted by witnesses Julia Mercer, Lee Bowers, and Julius Hardee.

Oswald thus delivered his package to someone in either plain clothes or a uniform, near the rear door of the TSBD, which explained how Wesley Frazier saw the package leave his car after delivering Oswald, but no one in the TSBD saw it enter. The choice of the sixth floor could only have been made by a nonemployee, as that area was the busiest in the building because it was being refloored. Fortunately, this individual had a ready-made "sniper's nest" created when boxes were moved to allow for the flooring work. The presence of the flooring work and crew suggests that if Oswald were the assassin, he would have intentionally avoided the sixth floor and used the seventh, a storage area, but that would have made the weapon, outside the window for display purposes, slightly less obvious to the nearby pedestrians. The soon-to-be "sniper," in a police uniform by 12:20 P.M., could chase the onlookers away on security grounds and indicate to them that silence was valuable to their safety. He then removed his shirt, leaving the light-colored T-shirt seen by witnesses, and fired the blank or blanks, left the stage-prop cartridges and rifle, redonned his police shirt, and blended into the police presence in the TSBD. Eyewitnesses and films confirm a second person in the sniper's nest, and although that accomplice is as yet unaccounted for, it is unlikely that his identity strays far from the projected scenario.

Tippit and Ruby were told stories that were variations of the theme told to Oswald. Tippit, under great pressure because he had impregnated a girlfriend with a female child, was told by police higher-ups (Tippit's bosses and Ruby's friends) that while Kennedy was in Texas, *Castro would be killed,* and the resulting wave of patriotism demonstrated by conservative Texans would convince Kennedy that the time was again ripe for U.S. intervention in Cuba. Tippit was shown a photo or photos of Oswald and told he was the Castro sniper, and that his escape, if successful, would bring him back to Dallas on November 22. Tippit was to be on the lookout in Oswald's neighborhood and render any assistance Oswald might need.

However, by 1:00 P.M. on November 22, Tippit realized (as had Oswald) that the scenario had changed quite radically from what he had been told. Although we know very little about Tippit, we can assume that he was not opposed to financial help, since he had to support a family of five (plus a potentially talkative girlfriend and daughter) on $490 a month. Tippit, however, was not going to have anything to do with a *presidential assassination,* and confronted Oswald, taking four bullets in the exchange. Whether these bullets were fired by Oswald, whose pistol would not be suitable for ballistic comparison, or by a second officer in the squad car, which had just visited the 1026 North Beckley address, may never be known. Tippit, however, would be the first patsy to die. Of equal significance, just as the April 10 "attempt" on General Walker would serve to divert suspicion away from right-wing elements, so the death of Tippit would divert suspicion away from the Dallas police. This put "Oswald" in deeper, and took the heat away from the police, who became heroes, if only briefly, for the loss of one of their own, and for their swift apprehension of Oswald.

Ruby was told an even more fanciful tale, although with debts that were astronomical in 1963, he may have been gullible enough to believe it. He was told of the *fake* assassination plot, and it was added that the sponsor, a Lee Oswald, would be captured quickly within city limits. Ruby would then use his police connections to gain access to headquarters and silence Oswald. If made to appear a spontaneous act, as suggested by Ruby's presence at Western Union at 11:17 A.M., or four minutes before the shooting of Oswald, it would tend to mitigate the charge of "with malice *aforethought,*" and Ruby would be charged with manslaughter, which carried a maximum five-year sentence, and with preprogrammed judicial errors in the trial, he would get a new trial and ultimately serve a couple of years, for which he would be well paid, and would reenter society with celebrity status. He bought it at the time of its telling, and took it in stride.

At 12:30 P.M. on November 22, all three patsies got wake-up calls they did not expect. Oswald may or may not have heard the shots, but he certainly heard the sirens, and learned either from Roy Truly, or from a citizen who informed McWatters' bus passengers, that the president had been seriously wounded. In this sense, Oswald was the first to realize his patsy status. He escaped the TSBD, got his pistol, but oddly returned to Dallas, behavior highly uncharacteristic of a fleeing assassin. Perhaps he intended to pay "Mr. Hunt" a visit and request even further clarification.

Tippit, who had been unusually active on pay telephones on the twenty-second, perhaps to find out if there had been an attempt on Castro, knew by 12:30 P.M. that there had not been, and then suddenly learned that JFK had been the target. Tippit's change of status from anti-Castro conspirator to American patriot cost him his life.

Ruby, often wrongly believed to be pictured in front of the TSBD within seconds of the shooting, was at the *Dallas Morning News,* from where he could view Dealey Plaza, while placing his ads for the weekend. He, too, became aware of the change in the scenario shortly after 12:30 P.M. and also realized that his part in the scheme was not as previously indicated, but would still involve the elimination of the suspect and subsequent notoriety. Nevertheless, the change in plans accounted for Ruby's sudden shock (as he undoubtedly had some contact with Oswald), as noted by numerous employees of the *Dallas Morning News,* as well as by other acquaintances during the weekend.

Oswald was taken into custody, and although the official wheels of justice would not charge him for hours, it was quickly understood that he was the only suspect in both crimes, a fact passed from Chief Curry to Mayor Cabell while both were still at Love Field. This in itself was odd, as Curry would later tell the Warren Commission that it took until well into the evening for his department to put together a case strong enough to bring charges against Oswald for the shooting of the president. If that is true, the obvious question then becomes: Why was access out of Dallas not sealed, or other suspects sought in the hours between the shooting and the time charges were brought against Oswald? Strange as it sounds decades later, the crime committed against JFK never took one step past Oswald, even when he was not positively seen as guilty by some police higher-ups not in the know.

Oswald remained remarkably unflappable in custody, except when Agent Hosty was ushered into the interrogation (perhaps because Oswald's assassination warning note to him had "gone astray"), when he was put in a lineup that was ridiculous, and when confronted with pictures of himself and the weapons. Oswald nevertheless believed that somehow his intelligence connections would come to his rescue, so he played the police game during the interrogation, including making pleas for an attorney who had never heard of him, but one who had defended *Communists* in *conspiracy* cases. Attorney Abt never met Oswald, who was to be silenced by copatsy Ruby before the mass of unresolved contradictions could reach public attention in anything as formal as a public trial or in any conversations between defendant Oswald and *any attorney*.

The Dallas police would be overly accommodating to Ruby for the rest of the weekend, but would then charge him with first-degree murder and help win a conviction that would earn him a death sentence. This, of course, was reversed in time, but Ruby would be diagnosed with cancer in December 1966 and would die on January 3, 1967, the last of the patsies to die.

The circle was almost complete. Simple details remained. The Secret Service's behavior at Parkland, including the brandishing of weapons and the very real threat that they would have shot coroner Earl Rose to get the president's body out of Dallas, was the beginning of a code of terrifying silence maintained by the doctors, who would make statements that contradicted the official version, only to retract them when the official version changed slightly. That silence would last until the publication of Dr. Charles Crenshaw's book *in 1991*.

J. Edgar Hoover would announce Oswald's guilt in absurdly premature haste, and that pronouncement would define the entire remainder of the FBI's focus. When subsequent witnesses were deposed by the bureau, the reportage was often at odds with what the witness had said, but the Warren Commission based their questions on the FBI raw data, so the questions by the commission were essentially tailored by the FBI's interpretations of the witnesses' statements.

The president's body was then taken on a government airplane, put in a government ambulance, and taken to a government hospital, where shoddy pathological procedures were performed by government employees, partly due to lack of experience of the pathologists, and partly due, if one believes in the Easter Bunny, to the Kennedy family's reluctance to have JFK's body violated any farther. If he had died of suspected heart failure, that would have been understandable; but with part of his head in the limousine, and other parts on the floor of a Dallas hospital, this theory is untenable. Further, the president's body was not fixed prior to the "autopsy"; rather, the autopsy results, as well as the photographs and X rays that were not seen by anybody for years, were the items fixed. JFK was then honored in a succession of government buildings and buried in a government cemetery.

The president's limousine, as well as the follow-up car, were removed from Parkland Hospital in unseeming haste, to be flown on a government airplane back to Washington, where they were taken to the White House garage and searched by government officials. Very quickly, perhaps too quickly, after the death of Oswald, the president's car was driven by an employee of the Ford Motor Company to Hess and Eisenhardt in Cincinnati, with a helicopter escort the whole way, where it was rebuilt from the wheels up. Had Oswald lived, would the car have been returned to Dallas? Not likely, and even if it had, it would have been useless as evidence.

A handful of individuals in Dealey Plaza were detained briefly, to create the appearance that the Dallas Police Department was investigating the case when in fact they knew whom to arrest in advance. The three tramps taken into custody were diversions: street characters (but not tramps) hired for a few bucks to run in every which direction at the time of the shooting and catch possible onlookers' attention. They would then meet at a prearranged site in the railroad yards and leave town on the first freight out, only to be prevented by towerman Lee Bowers. In one photo of the tramps, the eldest tramp did, in fact, bear a striking resemblance to E. Howard Hunt; in the remaining photos, however, he looks more like a Cro-Magnon man. The tall tramp may resemble Charles Harrelson, aged twenty-five at the time, but until someone can produce either a 1963 photo of the subject, or Harrelson's high-school yearbook and age-regress Harrelson to age twenty-five, the man in the photo remains unknown. The third "tramp" has been linked to the killing of Martin Luther King, Jr., and also has been "identified" as Charles Rogers, seen as a CIA knoll shooter. What is lacking is proof.

Expert pilot David Ferrie would take a highly mysterious 364-mile drive on the afternoon of November 22, and it seems clear that the purpose was not to ice-skate, as Ferrie would later confess, but rather to make constant use of an innocuous, untraceable pay telephone. It is also clear that he was not in the process of helping Oswald, who had been arrested before Ferrie's departure. This, too, shouts "conspiracy!" particularly when one recalls that Ferrie was taken into custody by the late Jim Garrison, turned over to the FBI, and then almost immediately released with an apology and a clean bill of health from the bureau. The FBI, it should be noted, is not in the habit of apologizing for questioning suspects, particularly those with histories of losing jobs for bizarre sexual proclivities. It is their job to deal with such people.

In spite of a weak case against Oswald before his execution, FBI special agent Richard Harrison arrived at Miller's Funeral Home with a rifle (type unknown to the funeral personnel) and fingerprint ink. Funeral director Paul Groody would tell researchers that he could not understand the event and that he had a very difficult time getting the black ink off of Oswald's corpse. What remains unexplained is the need for posthumous prints of Oswald, and all the explanations seem sinister: His prints were put *on* the accompanying rifle; the Dallas police never printed him, knowing his fate in advance; or something very odd turned up when those prints went into the computer and another set was needed. After all, "Lee Oswald" was a marine; that person's fingerprints were readily available. The presence of the rifle in a funeral home in any honest investigation is totally inexplicable.

Americans, who in 1963 (but not lately, alas) would believe what their government told them, would swallow the lone-assassin theory whole, until such time as the first researcher took a critical look at the evidence upon which it was based and exposed it for the farce it was. Since 1964, public support of the official version has dwindled to nil.

Marina Oswald was neutralized by her alien status, by threats of deportation, by her inability to speak English, and by the "men in suits" (Dr. Charles Crenshaw's phrase) assigned to "protect" her. Mrs. Oswald was, in fact, very thankful for Secret Service protection at a time when her safety was threatened; it was FBI tactics that she found quite un-American.

Many key witnesses would die in the weeks and months to come, but some of the deaths were legitimate, while a few served as a warning to the many witnesses who *"thought"* they saw or heard something other than the official version as it was quickly defined.

Newly installed President Johnson, already scandal-plagued, would be greatly concerned by the fact that Oswald's "Mr. Hunt" was either an oil baron to whom LBJ owed fealty, or a government employee. He would also have to be concerned that the event had happened in his own backyard and that many of the key suspects had been in LBJ's presence the evening before. The Warren Commission was his way of dealing with these concerns, as well as guaranteeing that the original FBI version would become gospel *before* the election of 1964. As we have seen in "White Lies," the "Warren" efforts were as much of *commission* as they were of *omission*. Oddly, as it would turn out, the Warren Report was virtually identical to the Dallas investigation, which overlapped very closely with FBI conclusions drawn on November 22.

Mrs. Tippit would receive a documentable $657,000 in donations from sympathetic Americans. One wonders how much additional *cash* would be delivered to Dallas police headquarters to be divided among the handful of "blue death" participants—the officers, a couple of higher-ups, and the fake Secret Service agents used to create an immediate damage assessment—although they were most likely on loan from a federal agency and had nothing to do with the Dallas blues, and certainly had no connection to the real Secret Service.

An additional sidebar would reinforce the event. From the time of the assassination to the death of J. Edgar Hoover in May 1972, no Dallas officers were ever allowed the use of FBI training facilities, an offer otherwise available to any accredited law-enforcement agency. This was perceived at the time as Hoover's way of punishing the Dallas police for suggesting the FBI knew about Oswald prior to the tragic weekend. It may just as well have been a straw man to make the Dallas police look bad, when in fact they had succeeded in their task. Either way, the public learned of Hoover's decision and accepted the former explanation.

The Oswald family (Marguerite excepted), as well as the Kennedy family, would by and large accept the ultimate "official verdict." Oswald's family preferred to think of Lee as a loner who wrought vengeance on an authority figure, *not* as the patsy of a high-level conspiracy. Even if the Oswald family had believed the "patsy" scenario, *who would have believed them?*

The Kennedys accepted it because it was the politic thing to do.

Before that tragic weekend ended, thirty-eight-year-old Robert Kennedy had donned the mantle of the Kennedy legacy, and as soon as there was an opening at 1600 Pennsylvania Avenue, he would put in an application. But that application would have been largely invalid if his brother was known to have been killed by a conspiracy. Why would Americans go to the trouble of voting for another Kennedy if the same conspirators could remove him with the ease demonstrated in Dallas? Nevertheless, we can posit that RFK had independent pathology tests conducted on JFK's brain, and when those results became known to him, Robert Kennedy had the brain destroyed, and took his unrevealed knowledge of JFK's death to a grave in Arlington that adjoined his brother's.

Shortly before that, however, on June 3, 1968, Bobby Kennedy would tell a cheering California college crowd, "I now fully realize that only the powers of the presidency will reveal the secrets of my brother's death." The following day, Bobby Kennedy was mortally wounded, and twenty-seven years later, America is still waiting for the full story of his—and John Kennedy's—deaths.

Allow yourself a brief moment to consider what Robert Kennedy would have said at his January 20, 1969, inaugural. After removing his hand from the Bible, but prior to launching into Sorensen's and Schlesinger's stirring rhetoric, he would no doubt have announced the immediate firing of J. Edgar Hoover, named a successor who would have won confirmation, and indicated that the first task assigned to the new FBI director would be to launch a full investigation into the activities of both Hoover and LBJ, two men who hated Robert Kennedy more than they had despised John Kennedy.

As we know, however, a lone nut prevented that. Several ironies have been suggested throughout this book, and this will be the last: JFK, officially, was shot from behind, although there is very strong evidence of shots from the front. RFK was officially shot from the front, yet the coroner's report indicated the fatal bullet entered the rear portion of his head and travelled forward, after having been fired from so close in that it left soot in RFK's hair and a powder-burn tattoo on his right ear. Is it possible that the Johnson-Hoover axis played a curtain call in Los Angeles?

The penultimate fictional chapter had been written by Earl Warren et al., and the remaining cast of characters was put on hold until the House Select Committee on Assassinations would hear them and almost reratify the Warren Commission's conclusions, while being very critical of their methods. This second Kennedy assassination investigation would suggest conspiracy, and request the Justice Department to reopen the case. Instead, they never lifted a finger, but officially closed it in 1988.

America and Americans had been through a tragedy. The death of a president is in itself a terrible event for the nation, and it is only magnified when it occurs by unnatural causes and unseen forces. The tragedy becomes unbearable, however, when the truth of the event is put beyond the reach of the public.

John Kennedy was our president; we elected him. The truth of his death should have been public domain from 12:30 P.M. CST, November 22, 1963. That truth, however shocking it might have been then, would have been far less painful than more than three decades of uncertainty and governmental interference.

Blue death fired the shots that killed the president. "Dallas's finest" then released all suspects except Oswald and made a mockery of the investigation that could not be allowed to reveal the killers in uniform.

The *Red patsy* took the blame and a police accomplice's bullet. His presumed guilt, combined with the change in government leadership, effectively ended the existing thaw in the Cold War.

White lies began the process of American citizens distrusting government pronouncements and robbed us of the truth.

Until now.

EPILOGUE

THE THESIS AND SUPPORTING CONCEPTS you have read in "Blue Death," "Red Patsy," and "White Lies" are the culmination of many years of work on an event that was once seen as "6 seconds in Dallas" but that has been expanded to be "Treachery in Dallas," and by recent efforts to be perhaps 8.36 seconds, and the difference is not suggested for the purpose of demeaning or making little of the additional 2.36 seconds. They may add to our understanding of the event, and if so, all the better.

The point is, the ambush of President Kennedy happened with incredible swiftness, and the time it took to read this book is an eternity when compared with the few seconds necessary to propel the popular president of 1963 into eternity.

It is hoped that this book has answered many concerns over which the reader has wavered, as I suspect most readers have at least a passing acquaintance with the events contained herein.

As a historian, I have no intention of standing before a bank of microphones and trumpeting to the world that it is the only answer, the final answer, and that all other research should be suspended because I have closed the case. On the contrary, I will say that you have read here the best logical deductions to be made from available source material.

It goes without saying that the key word in the previous sentence was "available."

And it is a word that troubles me, and other members of the research community, deeply.

If, in fact, a lone nut, for no clear purpose, single-handedly took the life of President Kennedy, and then was dispatched by a local publicity-seeking thug forty-eight hours later, why have we faced a stone wall of secrecy, hidden materials, destroyed documents, and government prevarication for more than thirty years?

The question was put in the clearest possible perspective on November 22, 1993, when, in a noted irony, the Dallas police brushed me and the crowd back to a point where I found myself face to face with a witness who gave key testimony against the Dallas police.

But an hour later, with Dealey Plaza filled with onlookers and security, the site where John Kennedy was killed was dedicated as a national historic landmark. The guest of honor, if you will, was the widow of John Connally, who had passed away on June 15, 1993.

And therein exists the concern for the ongoing stonewall: Mrs. Connally was gracious enough to be in attendance for this ceremonial observation of grief, yet when her husband died, there was no thought whatsoever given to having the metal still in him removed. Such an action could have answered many questions, but it was not taken. Instead, Nellie Connally helped dedicate Dealey Plaza, and I must tell you, if an English-speaking visitor from a foreign country had wandered into that plaza on November 22, 1993, he or she would have had a great deal of difficulty understanding the ceremony.

It certainly was not focused on either the life, death, or unfulfilled promise of John F. Kennedy. Instead, it was about the generosity of local folks who stood to lose a few precious square feet of land that the plaza might live.

The event typified the frustration of the research community. Throughout this and other books they are called "buffs," "critics," or in the case of Vince Palamara trying to speak with William Manchester, Vince was called "ilk" before Manchester even knew which stripe of "ilk" Vince was. It would not be unreasonable to call all those who are concerned "the research community." There's no law that says you have to purchase, read, or accept their material, but fairness suggests a certain sense of decency toward all.

Having earlier vented my spleen that Gerald Posner was given governmental carte blanche to have a sit-down with Yuri Nosenko, I would suggest that such an event is a similar symptom of the problem of getting the truth, just as Mrs. Connally's ambivalence proved to be a roadblock. Nosenko has now been spoken to, and by a member of the "research community." But would the people (read:

CIA) who gave Posner access to Nosenko give similar access to Dick Russell, John Newman, Peter Dale Scott, Jim DiEugenio, or Philip Melanson, and let them ask the questions that Mr. Posner did not? *Like hell.*

Files dribble out, but they are just as much nonsense as was published thirty years ago. Files are gone, never to be seen again. Whatever was of value and sequestered has had plenty of time for critical government scrutiny, to ensure that neither a name nor an inappropriate semicolon escapes scrutiny.

A "recently released file" from the archives of the FBI makes it quite plain that a second gun, a pistol, was found in a paper bag in the area between the book depository and the knoll within hours of the president's assassination. What does that document do to the central thesis of this work?

It only reinforces it. Note has already been taken of the obviousness of Oswald's rifle *and* pistol purchases, as well as his eagerness to be photographed with both while not being concerned about those photographs on the morning of November 22. It is entirely possible that the "bag pistol" was just another prop, like the Mannlicher-Carcano, put in place to be used as needed. Inasmuch as Oswald pulled one pistol on the police in the Texas Theater, and one is all he announced to the world he bought, then the "bag gun" had to be buried. However, if Oswald had not been captured armed—a thought that allows for the possibility that he would have been executed on the spot and had the "bag gun" planted—the subsequent second gun could have been brought forward by authorities as proof that Oswald had had it with him as he exited the TSBD in obvious haste and tossed it aside, wrapped, like the curtain rods/rifle, in brown paper. It also would have further proved his guilt in the assassination, as it would clearly prove, as did the actual Tippit killing, that the accused assassin had a penchant for violence. Also, if we can even allow ourselves to speculate about the potential uses of that gun to perpetuate a fraud, what does that tell us about the official version? If nothing else, it suggests that there were already two pistols, and the one that killed Tippit, whether it belonged to a former defector or not, became his, and the gun he was "toting" in the theater disappeared into the void of history from which this "paper bag gun" emerged in the 1990s.

The reality, of course, is that we'll never really know, because for some reason obviously *not* related to the lone assassin, the FBI decided it was not in the national interest, or perhaps it was in the matter of national security to, well, let's say, keep the gun private a while. More than three decades.

The full truth will never be known until *all* source material has been made available to all researchers, not just Posner.

And it should be done before JFK is a footnote to ancient history, remembered as people today perceive James Buchanan.

TABLES

TABLE 1

SUSPECTED "SHOOTERS" IN KENNEDY ASSASSINATION

Shooters	Likely Affiliation, if Available
Charles V. Harrelson	Contract killer
Jean Soutre Michael Roux Michael Mertz	Foreign contract killers*
Sauvier Pironti Lucien Sarti ("badgeman") [FNU] Bocognoni	Organized crime
Roscoe White	Dallas Police Department
Harry Weatherford	Dallas Police Department
Patrick T. Dean	Dallas Police Department
Charles Rogers	CIA
"Saul" [CE 237]	Contract killer
Loran Hall Elaido del Valle	Cuban exile
William Greer	Secret Service
George Hickey	Secret Service
Umbrella man	CIA

*It is not perfectly clear whether Mertz and Roux are real people or were aliases used by Soutre. Highly respected researcher Jim Marrs, in *Crossfire*, p. 204, insists that they exist.

Shooters	Likely Affiliation, if Available
"Man in black"†	KGB
Harold Doyle	Tramps
John Forrester Gedney	
Gus W. Abrams	
Charles Nicoletti	Texas oil money
John Roselli	
Malcolm Wallace	Lyndon Johnson
Jack Ruby‡	Mob fixer
David Ferrie§	Right/JFK hater
Tom Files	Unknown; still selling story
Lee Harvey Oswald	Lone nut

†The "man in black" may be the least-known suspect. When viewing the Zapruder film, the man in black is seen near the curb on the southwest corner of Elm and Houston, facing in Zapruder's direction and not far from Phil Willis and his daughter. It is alleged that he was holding and firing two silenced Russian machine pistols, and that he killed Kennedy and wounded well a dozen people—the ones shown "prone" on the landscape after the shooting sequence was over. This theory is the brainchild of George C. Thompson.

‡Ruby is seen as a motorcade shooter in Buchanan's *Who Killed Kennedy?*

§Ferrie is seen as a knoll shooter in a British documentary, *The Day the Dream Died*. This is based on an enhancement of the Nix film, which purports to show Ferrie atop a bumper, with a rifle, as the limousine creeps through the kill zone. Available through "The Warren Retort," 11435 Kleberg Road, No. 210, Dallas, TX 75253. There is much of interest on the video, but Ferrie is not on the knoll; I nevertheless thank Dallas researcher Russ McLean for unearthing the video.

TABLE 2

SUSPECTS CONSIDERED FOR ALL THREE PHASES OF THE ASSASSINATION

Suspect	Conceive Assassination?	Carry It Out?	Cover It Up?
CIA	Yes	Yes	No
Hoover/FBI	*Yes*	*Yes*	*Yes*
Right	Yes	Yes	No
LBJ	*Yes*	*Yes*	*Yes*
Nixon	Yes	No	No
Oil	Yes	Yes	No
Mob	Yes	Yes	No
Secret Service	No	No	No
Castro & Co.	Yes	Yes	No
Anti-Castro	Yes	Yes	No
KGB	Yes	Yes	No

TABLE 3

CORRELATION OF
SUSPECTS WITH OSWALD

Group	Was Oswald Part?
CIA	Yes
Right	Yes
Hoover/FBI	No
Nixon	No
LBJ	No
Oil	Yes*
Mob	Yes†
Secret Service (1)	Yes
Secret Service (2)	Yes‡
Secret Service (3)	No
White supremacists	Yes
Castro & Co.	Yes
Anti-Castro	Yes
KGB	Yes

*Oswald's oil involvement stems largely from his possible associations with right-wing groups in New Orleans, plus the "Dear Mr. Hunt" letter, discussed elsewhere, that some see as addressed to H. L. Hunt.

†Unlikely as Oswald might seem in a sharkskin suit lighting cigars with $100 bills, there is a weak association with his uncle, Dutz Murret, who had some mob connections. Interestingly, Murret is the only employed individual who was *not* asked his occupation by the Warren Commission. Also, the standard theory, challenged here, is that there was a connection between "mobster" Ruby and Oswald.

‡Howard Donohue, prime mover in Secret Service 2, continues to "stick to his guns." He told me, almost offhandedly, "Of course, Oswald fired a couple of shots, but the result was the accident involving Hickey. Oswald could not have fired that shot."

TABLE 4

DATES OF WITNESSES' APPEARANCES*

2/3[1]	3/4[1]	4/1[38]	5/1[3]	6/2[3]	7/2[1]	8/5[2]	9/1[1]
2/4[1]	3/9[4]	4/2[18]	5/5[4]	6/3[2]	7/7[1]	8/6[2]	9/2[1]
2/5[1]	3/10[4]	4/3[13]	5/6[2]	6/4[4]	7/13[12]	8/24[5]	9/4[1]
2/6[1]	3/11[3]	4/6[13]	5/7[1]	6/5[2]	7/14[7]	——	9/9[1]
2/10[1]	3/12[2]	4/7[21]	5/11[1]	6/6[1]	7/18[1]	——	9/15[1]
2/11[1]	3/13[3]	4/7–8[10]†	5/13[5]	6/7[1]	7/21[6]	——	——
2/12[1]	3/16[3]	4/8[30]	5/14[8]	6/8[3]	7/22[12]	——	——
2/20[1]	3/17[1]	4/9[17]	5/15[1]	6/9[4]	7/23[12]	——	——
2/21[1]	3/18[2]	4/10[1]	5/17[2]	6/10[4]	7/24[19]	——	——
2/22[1]	3/19[1]	4/14[6]	5/18[2]	6/11[3]	7/25[5]	——	——
2/27[1]	3/20[4]	4/15[7]	5/19[1]	6/16[1]	7/28[2]	——	——
——	3/21[7]	4/16[11]	5/20[2]	6/17[3]	7/29[2]	——	——
——	3/23[7]	4/17[7]	5/26[1]	6/18[3]	——	——	——
——	3/24[28]	4/21[5]	5/28[5]	6/22[1]	——	——	——
——	3/25[42]	4/22[6]	——	6/23[6]	——	——	——
——	3/26[18]	4/23[6]	——	6/26[10]	——	——	——
——	3/27[1]	4/24[1]	——	6/27[5]	——	——	——
——	3/30[6]	4/29[1]	——	——	——	——	——
——	3/31[16]	4/30[2]	——	——	——	——	——

*The witness total presented here, 566, is indicative of the fact that many witnesses made more than one appearance.

†The dates noted here are as they appear in the testimony.

TABLE 5

WITNESS TOTALS BY CATEGORY

Witness Type	Witnesses	Total Questions	Percent of Total
Oswald as victim	93	16,836	15.31
Tippit as victim	19	3,258	2.96
Kennedy as victim	177	30,530	27.77
Unrelated	5	641	0.58
Administrative	1	73	0.06
Experts	2	99	0.09
Security	3	652	0.59
Diplomacy	2	104	0.09
Walker	1	513	0.46
Character	185	57,224	52.05
TOTALS	*488*	*109,930*	*100.00*

APPENDICES

Appendix 1 shows the chronological (*as printed*) testimony of the 488 witnesses who gave testimony. The key here is the groupings—the Oswalds are called first, to neutralize them and to prevent them from countering leaks that occur after their testimony. Others, like the "imposter" witnesses—Slack, Bogard, Wood, et al, are grouped together as if to give their false impressions credibility. Study the groupings carefully, and note how an occasional critical witness is grouped among "safe" witnesses, thereby vitiating the contrary testimony.

Appendix 2 demonstrates the number of questions asked, from the most to the least. Note carefully which individuals were asked the most questions, and, further down, the numbers of questions asked to virtual unknowns who had little to add. Eventually, you will get to the testimony of the medical people, who had the most to offer, but were given short shrift.

Appendix 3 demonstrates questions "to the point" in descending order, and does not need much clarification. The star witness, a terrified alien from Soviet Russia who was facing deporation, was asked the most relevant questions. The numbers plummet quickly thereafter.

KEY TO ABBREVIATIONS

PRE=Preliminary questions. Name, job, education, etc.
TP=To the point; a valid question.
NU=Not valid; a wasted or useless question.
CL=Clarification; Usually proportionate to TP or NU;
LH=Leading or hearsay; some are valid, but the witness should not be told the answer, nor would such nonsense be allowed in court.
C=Conclusionary; the witness is asked an opinion; this is only valid if the witness would qualify in law as an expert, ie. medicine, guns.
FC=Foregone conclusion; Questions that put words into the mouths of witnesses that L H Oswald was involved, period.
N=Nonsense; absurd, ridiculous, funny, as well as the title.
OTR=the # of times the witness was taken "off the record." If the Warren Comm. was seeking full disclosure, this total should be zero.

TYPE
CHAR=a character witness, who had no direct knowledge of the crimes which killed either JFK, Tippit, or Oswald.
JFK=Witnesses with knowledge of events regarding the death of JFK.
JDT=Witnesses re: death of J D Tippit
LHO=Witnesses re: death of L H Oswald

WITNESS	PRE	TP	NV	CL	LH	C	FC	N	OTR	TOTAL	TYPE
OSWALD, MARINA	22	217	1411	444	361	46	56	58	5	2615	CHAR
OSWALD, MARG.	9	48	169	317	39	8	3	22	1	615	CHAR
OSWALD,ROBT	15	33	1179	560	400	124	8	32	15	2351	CHAR
MARTIN,JAMES	10	6	562	196	168	35	0	2	10	979	CHAR
LANE, MARK	8	7	81	98	40	7	0	7	0	248	CHAR
KELLERMAN,ROY	9	67	271	168	154	32	8	15	1	724	JFK
GREER,WM.	6	12	156	31	46	17	1	3	1	272	JFK
HILL,CLINT	6	13	102	25	18	5	3	3	0	175	JFK
YOUNGBLOOD,R.	7	5	54	17	9	3	1	2	0	98	JFK
JACKSON,ROBT.H.	14	12	55	32	21	6	1	1	0	142	JFK
ROWLAND,ARNOLD	20	14	210	78	48	14	0	5	0	389	JFK
WORRELL,JAMES R.	13	12	90	45	23	3	0	2	0	188	JFK
EUINS,AMOS LEE	11	20	48	37	23	5	0	2	0	146	JFK
FRAZIER,BUELL W.	16	12	218	127	180	3	5	5	0	566	JFK
RANDLE,LINNIE M.	3	2	28	19	55	6	1	2	0	116	JFK
CUNNINGHAM,CORT.	8	15	152	142	129	24	7	11	1	488	JFK
WHALEY,WILLIAM	7	9	87	68	110	2	0	1	0	284	JFK
McWATTERS, C.	13	81	198	68	50	3	35	29	1	477	JFK
FORD,KATHERINE	5	4	178	75	100	14	1	1	0	378	CHAR
FORD,DECLAN	11	4	68	30	52	14	0	1	0	180	CHAR
GREGORY,PETER P.	5	1	43	21	36	15	0	2	0	123	CHAR
HUMES,JAMES J.	7	30	17	79	41	21	13	7	1	215	JFK
BOSWELL, J.T.	5	3	0	2	3	1	0	0	0	14	JFK
FINCK,PIERRE	10	7	6	26	8	12	5	1	0	75	JFK
PAINE,MICHAEL	8	13	482	161	297	37	7	14	1	1019	CHAR
PAINE,RUTH	10	25	2181	801	1995	155	31	38	15	5236	CHAR
BRENNAN,HOWARD	15	72	47	143	27	1	1	1	1	307	JFK
WILLIAMS,BONNIE	10	22	172	44	131	1	4	4	0	388	JFK
NORMAN,HAROLD	11	8	123	18	83	2	1	1	2	247	JFK
JARMIN,JAMES	8	11	158	23	107	4	1	0	0	312	JFK
TRULY,ROY	12	10	214	74	150	12	8	2	2	482	JFK
BAKER,MARRION	8	21	199	64	144	6	5	7	5	454	JFK
REID,MRS.ROBT	10	2	79	19	82	3	3	2	0	200	JFK
MOONEY,LUKE	9	10	57	17	49	0	0	1	0	143	JFK
BOONE,EUGENE	7	9	17	8	29	0	0	0	0	70	JFK
McDONALD,M.N.	9	12	74	8	62	2	2	0	0	169	JDT
MARKHAM,HELEN	4	16	165	79	176	0	2	0	0	442	JDT
SCOGGINS, WM.	11	9	150	37	114	3	0	2	2	326	JDT
DAVIS,MRS.B.J.	1	6	95	31	64	2	0	0	1	199	JDT
CALLAWAY,TED	8	11	49	11	48	0	0	0	1	127	JDT
CARRICO,CHARLES	13	25	105	24	20	5	9	2	1	203	JFK
PERRY,MALCOLM	13	10	204	42	51	11	10	3	2	344	JFK
FRAZIER,ROBT.	11	26	392	130	213	21	7	4	8	804	JFK
SIMMONS,RONALD	7	5	47	31	26	6	2	1	0	125	JFK
NICOL,JOSEPH	2	10	58	50	78	3	3	1	2	205	JFK
LATONA,SEBASTIAN	7	27	192	99	225	16	4	1	9	571	JFK
MANDELLA,ARTHUR	5	3	30	34	40	3	2	1	0	118	JFK
STOMBAUGH,PAUL	6	9	169	69	113	5	3	5	1	379	JFK
CADIGAN,JAMES	12	22	145	69	106	5	1	1	4	361	JFK
SHAW,ROBERT	12	13	142	60	58	5	3	0	6	293	JFK
GREGORY,CHARLES	11	8	112	40	16	4	1	2	1	194	JFK

WITNESS	PRE	TP	NV	CL	LH	C	FC	N	OTR	TOTAL	TYPE
CONNALLY,JOHN	3	17	94	24	21	0	3	2	0	164	JFK
CONNALLY,MRS.J.	2	3	11	3	4	1	0	0	0	24	JFK
CURRY,JESSE E.	14	34	458	158	323	5	6	4	8	1002	LHO
FRITZ, WILL	9	11	268	130	412	10	2	1	1	843	JFK
BAKER,T.L.	3	0	1	1	3	0	0	0	0	8	JFK
DAY, J.C.	8	10	248	87	120	2	3	0	0	478	JFK
SHANEYFELT, L.	14	30	259	160	217	17	1	1	4	699	JFK
BOUCK,ROBERT	6	9	83	46	87	3	3	2	5	239	JFK
CARSWELL,ROBERT	2	0	2	1	0	0	0	0	0	·5	UNR
LAWSON,WINSTON	9	18	173	89	124	4	5	2	7	424	JFK
COLE,ALWYN	13	25	263	65	86	9	1	0	8	462	JFK
FAIN,JOHN W.	7	5	178	82	65	2	6	1	2	346	CHAR
QUIGLEY,JOHN L.	8	5	63	29	19	5	0	1	2	130	CHAR
HOSTY,JAMES P.	9	17	235	118	94	3	5	3	4	484	JFK
BELMONT,ALAN H.	7	10	74	76	51	7	2	2	1	229	SEC
REVILL,JACK	25	11	187	103	155	3	0	4	1	488	LHO
BRIAN.V.J.	6	2	69	42	41	0	0	4	0	164	CHAR
OLIVIER, ALFRED	7	20	76	55	27	23	0	0	2	208	JFK
DZEMIAN, ARTHUR	11	3	5	7	7	8	0	0	0	41	JFK
LIGHT,FREDERICK	11	2	17	5	13	4	0	1	1	53	JFK
HOOVER,J.EDGAR	5	3	31	26	28	3	0	4	3	100	JFK
HELMS/McCONE	6	7	28	15	16	2	0	2	1	76	JFK
KELLY.THOMAS J.	6	4	35	15	9	2	2	1	0	74	JFK
GAUTHIER,LEO	3	0	17	11	2	0	0	1	0	34	JFK
KENNEDY,MRS.JOHN	2	2	10	8	8	1	0	0	0	31	JFK
RUBY,JACK	10	79	277	322	67	5	0	0	4	760	LHO
WADE, HENRY	5	18	175	64	52	4	2	11	4	331	JFK
DEAN,PATRICK	22	23	308	131	66	2	0	2	6	554	LHO
CARR,WAGGONER	2	2	3	2	2	0	0	0	0	11	JFK
SNYDER,RICHARD	7	20	141	71	110	13	2	3	1	367	CHAR
McVICKAR,JOHN	7	4	33	24	54	4	2	0	1	128	CHAR
CHAYES,ABRAM	5	15	46	60	98	6	1	3	6	234	CHAR
WATERMAN,BERNICE	4	3	49	54	78	2	2	2	2	194	CHAR
RUSK,DEAN	4	4	19	12	9	0	0	0	2	48	DIPL
KNIGHT,FRANCES	7	2	33	24	61	3	1	6	0	137	CHAR
COULTER.HARRIS	11	0	5	2	5	0	0	0	0	23	UNR
SURREY.ROBERT A.	17	15	188	126	142	8	7	10	0	513	WALKE
ROWLEY,JAMES	7	23	145	67	75	15	5	8	8	345	SEC
WEISMAN,BERNARD	12	18	368	107	208	7	0	18	0	738	JFK
KLAUSE,ROBERT	2	7	100	18	70	1	0	0	0	198	JFK
THOMPSON, LLEWEL	3	3	28	5	11	5	1	0	1	56	DIPL
DILLON,DOUGLAS	4	4	29	18	18	1	3	1	0	78	SEC
CLARK,WILLIAM K.	8	20	71	19	22	4	6	2	0	152	JFK
McCLELLAND,ROBER	11	14	36	16	5	7	2	1	0	92	JFK
BAXTER,CHARLES	10	8	24	6	5	6	4	0	0	63	JFK
JENKINS,MARION	9	6	21	7	8	4	1	1	2	57	JFK
JONES,RONALD	6	8	38	7	7	2	0	0	0	68	JFK
CURTIS,DONALD	10	3	30	6	6	1	0	0	0	56	JFK
BASHOUR,FOUAD	7	2	18	7	8	0	1	0	0	43	JFK
AKIN,GENE	11	3	16	11	6	3	3	1	0	54	JFK
PETERS, PAUL	6	4	26	7	10	1	1	4	0	59	JFK

WITNESS	PRE	TP	NV	CL	LH	C	FC	N	OTR	TOTAL	TYPE
GIESECKE,ADOLPH	8	4	17	6	7	0	3	0	0	45	JFK
HUNT,JACKIE	9	7	34	5	6	0	0	0	0	61	JFK
SALYER, KENNETH	9	4	13	4	1	0	0	0	0	31	JFK
WHITE,MARTIN	10	2	13	1	3	0	0	0	0	29	JFK
SHIRES,GEORGE	9	19	44	17	21	6	2	0	1	118	JFK
DULANY,RICHARD	9	1	10	1	2	0	0	0	0	23	JFK
STANDRIDGE,RUTH	8	4	48	10	16	0	3	6	0	95	JFK
WESTER,AJANE	11	0	37	6	4	0	0	1	0	59	JFK
ROSS, HENRIETTA	5	0	14	1	3	0	0	1	0	24	JFK
JIMISON,R.J.	11	1	35	2	13	0	0	0	0	62	JFK
TOMLINSON,D.	17	3	32	19	31	0	2	0	1	104	JFK
BOWRON,DIANA	11	7	56	3	11	0	1	1	0	90	JFK
HENCHCLIFFE,M.	7	6	47	6	10	0	2	0	0	78	JFK
NELSON, DORIS	11	0	36	6	7	0	0	1	1	61	JFK
PRICE,CHARLES	5	0	55	7	6	0	0	0	0	73	ADM
COUCH,MALCOLM	14	19	43	13	50	1	4	0	0	144	JFK
DILLARD,TOM	9	8	19	13	37	0	1	0	2	87	JFK
UNDERWOOD,JAMES	4	1	10	2	13	0	0	1	0	31	JFK
CRAWFORD,JAMES	8	5	25	3	19	0	0	0	0	60	JFK
MITCHELL,MARYANN	5	2	13	7	9	0	0	0	0	36	JFK
ROWLAND,BARBARA	24	14	116	23	80	3	3	11	0	274	JFK
FISCHER,RONALD	21	20	46	28	19	0	1	0	0	135	JFK
EDWARDS,ROBERT	13	14	33	24	18	0	0	3	0	105	JFK
HILL, JEAN L.	6	44	107	65	65	2	1	2	1	292	JFK
MILLER,AUSTIN	12	7	21	8	14	0	0	0	0	62	JFK
REILLY,FRANK	8	6	29	19	25	0	0	2	0	89	JFK
BROWN, EARLE	7	11	35	18	32	0	0	1	0	104	JFK
SKELTON,ROYCE	9	6	18	7	16	0	0	1	0	57	JFK
HOLLAND,S.M.	5	9	33	35	53	2	1	0	2	138	JFK
FOSTER,J.W.	14	13	31	19	37	0	0	0	2	114	JFK
WHITE,J.C.	17	2	16	6	22	0	0	1	0	64	JFK
MURPHY,JOE	6	8	29	13	23	0	0	0	0	79	JFK
CRAIG, ROGER	21	29	82	29	56	2	4	3	0	226	JFK
RACKLEY,GEORGE	19	5	29	10	23	0	5	3	0	94	JFK
ROMACK,JAMES E.	31	7	47	14	20	2	1	2	0	124	JFK
BOWERS,LEE	5	14	26	13	20	1	0	2	0	81	JFK
MARTIN,B.J.	8	12	36	9	23	0	0	2	0	90	JFK
HARGIS,BOBBY W.	4	5	10	6	9	0	0	0	1	34	JFK
HAYGOOD,CLYDE	16	8	55	18	29	0	1	3	0	130	JFK
BREWER, E.D.	9	4	65	11	24	0	2	2	0	117	JFK
HARKNESS,D.V.	18	10	62	19	31	2	0	0	0	142	JFK
SAWYER, J.H.	15	13	51	24	52	1	2	3	0	161	JFK
HENSLEE, GERALD	9	0	16	5	9	0	0	1	0	40	JFK
SHELLEY, WILLIAM	10	10	93	25	85	2	3	5	0	233	JFK
PINKSTON,NAT	9	0	17	1	11	0	0	0	0	38	JFK
LOVELADY, BILLY	6	4	42	18	32	1	2	1	0	106	JFK
KAISER,FRANKIE	14	2	41	18	21	0	0	0	0	96	JFK
GIVENS,CHARLES	33	10	100	18	54	3	0	7	0	225	JFK
WEST, TROY	17	5	67	10	27	0	0	0	0	126	JFK
ARCE, DANNY	13	7	50	13	24	0	1	1	0	109	JFK
MOLINA, JOE	8	3	41	8	16	0	0	0	0	76	JFK

WITNESS	PRE	TP	NV	CL	LH	C	FC	N	OTR	TOTAL	TYPE
DOUGHERTY.JACK	22	7	89	14	68	0	2	2	0	204	JFK
PIPER, EDDIE	12	7	50	14	37	0	1	1	0	122	JFK
ADAMS,VICTORIA	13	8	59	13	22	0	1	1	0	117	JFK
HINE, GENEVA	7	7	41	7	16	2	0	1	0	81	JFK
BURNS, DORIS	13	4	8	7	12	0	0	0	0	44	JFK
BLEDSOE,MARY	6	7	212	77	190	7	10	13	1	522	CHAR
ROBERTS,EARLENE	13	13	89	21	63	0	2	2	0	203	JFK
BENAVIDES,DOMING	22	14	77	25	47	0	0	1	0	186	JDT
DAVIS, C.V.	13	22	145	44	95	0	2	2	0	323	JDT
BREWER,JOHNNY	17	10	69	9	40	1	0	1	0	147	JDT
POSTAL.JULIA	14	3	36	9	39	0	0	1	0	102	JDT
BURROUGHS,W.	7	2	31	3	19	0	0	1	0	63	JDT
CARROLL,BOB K.	12	21	70	8	29	0	4	0	0	144	JFK
HUTSON,THOMAS	20	9	54	17	27	0	4	4	0	135	JFK
WALKER, C.T.	21	12	67	17	34	5	1	3	0	160	JFK
HILL,GERALD	9	21	88	35	66	2	0	2	0	223	JFK
POE,J.M.	19	9	29	9	17	0	1	0	1	84	JDT
GIBSON,JOHN	8	7	33	12	17	1	0	0	0	78	JDT
PUTNAM,JAMES	17	6	30	17	47	2	0	3	0	122	JDT
PIERCE,RIO S.	15	6	32	12	13	3	0	1	0	82	LHO
OWENS,CALVIN	9	5	12	9	12	4	0	0	1	51	JDT
SMITH,WILLIAM	13	6	36	7	23	0	0	0	0	85	JDT
APPLIN, GEORGE	12	11	40	24	46	0	0	3	0	136	JFK
HAWKINS, RAY	6	8	25	12	13	0	1	8	0	73	JFK
MONTGOMERY,L.D.	22	23	165	72	63	4	0	3	2	352	LHO
JOHNSON, MARVIN	18	10	16	18	29	3	6	1	0	101	JFK
WEITZMAN,SEYMOUR	11	8	18	20	20	0	1	0	2	78	JFK
WESTBROOK, W.R.	7	6	57	36	43	0	0	1	0	150	JFK
BOYD, ELMER	5	40	187	26	94	6	0	12	0	370	JFK
STUDEBAKER,ROBT.	5	15	78	42	102	6	1	3	0	252	JFK
DHORITY, C.N.	7	15	79	18	51	2	0	1	0	173	JFK
SIMS,RICHARD	6	48	294	51	199	16	3	16	0	633	JFK
STOVALL,RICHARD	9	9	50	20	49	0	1	2	1	140	JFK
POTTS,WALTER	7	5	35	14	32	0	1	5	0	99	JFK
ADAMCIK, JOHN	21	18	74	11	28	3	0	1	0	156	JFK
MOORE, HENRY	21	7	44	5	29	0	2	2	0	110	JFK
TURNER,F.M.	18	22	93	15	43	1	0	2	0	194	JFK
ROSE. GUY F.	8	7	29	4	30	0	0	1	0	79	JFK
PERRY, W.E.	8	2	40	2	19	0	0	0	1	71	JFK
CLARK,RICHARD	10	3	53	7	31	0	0	2	1	106	JFK
ABLES,DON R.	13	5	43	4	25	0	0	1	1	91	JFK
LUJAN, DANIEL	18	2	33	7	38	0	0	0	1	98	JFK
BROWN, C.W.	18	9	24	6	20	0	0	2	0	79	JFK
GRAVES, L.C.	29	45	152	33	76	6	0	5	3	346	LHO
LEAVELLE,JAMES	20	24	103	19	84	2	0	2	1	254	JFK
BARNES, W.E.	15	36	152	26	74	10	5	7	1	325	JDT
HICKS,J.B.	8	5	18	5	15	2	0	0	0	53	JFK
HOLMES,HARRY D.	11	30	103	41	97	3	3	11	2	299	JFK
BOOKHOUT,JAMES	5	20	64	10	35	4	2	2	1	142	JFK
CLEMENTS,MANNING	5	11	28	1	8	3	0	0	0	56	JFK
OLDS,GREGORY L.	6	2	14	4	2	0	0	0	0	28	CHAR

WITNESS	PRE	TP	NV	CL	LH	C	FC	N	OTR	TOTAL	TYPE
NICHOLS,H.LOUIS	7	1	8	4	8	0	0	0	0	28	CHAR
SORRELS,FORREST	19	57	251	54	194	12	4	7	0	598	JFK
WALDMAN,WILLIAM	8	23	48	16	30	1	4	4	1	134	JFK
SCIBOR,MITCHELL	6	8	13	1	8	0	0	1	0	37	JFK
MICHAELIS,HEINZ	17	16	41	14	55	0	0	2	1	145	JDT
CASTER,WARREN	7	6	13	0	4	0	0	0	0	30	CHAR
SHIELDS,EDWARD	7	2	20	0	7	0	0	1	0	37	JFK
GUINYARD,SAM	12	21	46	5	58	1	1	1	0	145	JDT
ROBERTSON,MARY J	7	2	20	5	31	1	0	0	0	66	JFK
O'DONNELL,KENNET	3	17	129	3	23	3	3	5	0	186	JFK
O'BRIEN,LAWRENCE	1	8	100	4	46	0	1	3	0	163	JFK
CABELL,EARLE	6	10	48	3	50	0	1	2	0	120	JFK
CABELL,MRS.E.	3	9	25	7	33	2	0	3	0	82	JFK
WILLIS,PHILLIP	9	11	12	5	33	2	1	1	1	74	JFK
WILLIS,LINDA	3	4	4	1	6	0	0	0	1	18	JFK
BAKER,MRS.DON	3	18	22	29	59	4	2	5	0	142	JFK
ALTGENS,JAMES	9	9	22	21	48	0	0	3	0	112	JFK
SMITH,JOE M.	9	12	48	4	50	1	1	1	0	126	JFK
BARNETT,WELCOME	4	9	16	7	37	5	2	2	0	82	JFK
WALTHERS, EDDY	6	7	17	11	34	5	1	2	0	83	JFK
TAGUE, JAMES	5	11	17	18	34	1	2	1	0	89	JFK
HUDSON, EMMETT	6	11	47	9	48	4	0	1	0	126	JFK
SMITH,EDGAR	4	3	14	5	21	0	1	0	0	48	JFK
ZAPRUDER,ABRAHAM	8	7	39	7	34	0	0	2	0	97	JFK
LAWRENCE, PERDUE	16	4	74	9	3	1	2	0	0	109	JFK
VOEBEL,EDWARD	5	5	106	10	66	15	1	8	0	216	CHAR
WULF,WILLIAM E.	14	2	19	2	25	4	0	0	0	66	CHAR
SMITH,BENNIERITA	9	0	51	10	19	1	0	0	1	90	CHAR
O'SULLIVAN,FREDE	12	8	13	2	20	0	0	0	1	55	CHAR
SAWYER,MILDRED	6	2	12	0	13	0	0	1	0	34	CHAR
BOUDREAUX,ANNE	9	0	30	10	24	5	0	1	0	79	CHAR
PETERMAN,VIOLA	6	0	31	15	41	7	0	25	0	125	CHAR
EVANS,MYRTLE	2	4	96	40	85	18	6	6	0	257	CHAR
EVANS,JULIAN	5	3	38	11	71	13	2	0	0	143	CHAR
VINSON,PHILIP E.	16	0	39	10	28	2	1	5	0	101	CHAR
CONWAY,HIRAM	8	0	55	13	27	5	0	6	1	114	CHAR
MURRET,LILLIAN	7	19	272	122	364	42	10	45	0	881	CHAR
MURRET,MARILYN	23	12	151	41	119	22	7	8	0	383	CHAR
MURRET,C.DUTZ	11	6	65	10	77	4	1	2	0	176	CHAR
MURRET,JOHN	12	5	52	7	38	8	1	1	0	124	CHAR
PIC,EDWARD	10	0	44	8	38	1	0	3	0	104	CHAR
CARRO,JOHN	13	3	12	13	21	3	0	0	0	65	CHAR
HARTOGS,RENATUS	9	1	46	16	34	2	0	1	0	109	CHAR
SIEGEL,EVELYN	13	1	11	7	26	0	1	1	0	60	CHAR
DELGADO,NELSON	25	14	219	72	200	24	5	4	1	563	CHAR
POWERS,DANIEL P.	3	10	136	57	87	19	5	3	1	320	CHAR
DONOVAN, JOHN E.	6	13	89	10	28	14	3	3	0	166	CHAR
FOLSON,ALLISON G	6	7	37	11	32	0	0	0	0	93	CHAR
DONABEDIAN,GEORG	4	0	11	7	10	0	0	0	0	32	CHAR
ISAACS,MARTIN	10	3	18	7	21	0	1	0	0	60	CHAR
BATES,PAULINE V.	12	5	68	55	58	3	0	3	0	204	CHAR

WITNESS	PRE	TP	NV	CL	LH	C	FC	N	OTR	TOTAL	TYPE
CLARK,MAX	8	12	68	10	27	7	2	0	1	134	CHAR
BOUHE,GEORGE	17	22	128	23	90	20	3	3	0	306	CHAR
MELLER,ANNA	13	8	69	20	31	10	1	4	1	156	CHAR
HALL,ELENA	14	13	114	16	61	14	1	6	0	239	CHAR
HALL,JOHN R.	15	10	41	6	28	13	0	1	0	114	CHAR
RAY,MRS.FRANK H.	16	6	55	9	28	12	2	0	0	128	CHAR
VOSHININ,MRS.IGO	30	0	96	66	120	13	1	8	1	334	CHAR
VOSHININ, IGOR	30	2	89	93	106	6	0	5	0	331	CHAR
RAIGORODSKY,P.	8	2	182	43	85	16	1	5	8	342	CHAR
RAY,MRS.THOMAS	12	9	56	14	29	3	3	1	0	127	CHAR
RAY,THOMAS M.	11	4	37	10	30	6	1	1	0	100	CHAR
BALLEN,SAMUEL B.	10	11	101	6	31	7	2	1	0	169	CHAR
DYMITRUK,LYDIA	34	0	60	36	92	3	2	17	0	244	CHAR
TAYLOR,GARY E.	21	5	225	42	131	17	4	27	3	472	CHAR
MAMANTOV,ILYA	29	32	156	45	146	15	6	15	4	444	JFK
GRAVITIS,DOROTHY	26	2	75	18	28	7	4	1	0	161	CHAR
GREGORY,PAUL R.	11	16	120	8	66	14	3	6	0	244	CHAR
LESLIE,HELEN	10	0	19	7	13	1	0	1	0	51	CHAR
DEMOHRENSCHILDT,	18	43	585	239	649	38	6	50	0	1628	CHAR
DEMOHRENSCHILDT,	23	18	176	66	241	15	1	15	1	555	CHAR
HOWLETT,JOHN JOE	2	1	3	4	6	0	0	0	1	16	JFK
KRYSTINIK,RAYMON	11	3	66	8	45	13	3	0	0	149	CHAR
GLOVER,EVERETT	32	7	180	53	131	11	1	9	1	424	CHAR
BRINGUIER,CARLOS	10	3	59	42	65	2	0	2	5	183	CHAR
MARTELLO,FRANCIS	5	4	42	3	35	6	0	0	2	95	CHAR
STEELE,CHAS JR.	7	3	83	9	63	1	0	5	0	171	CHAR
STEELE,CHAS.SR.	8	0	5	0	8	0	0	1	0	22	CHAR
GERACI,PHILIP	6	0	37	13	28	3	0	0	0	87	CHAR
BLALOCK,VANCE	9	2	50	1	22	1	1	0	0	86	CHAR
LEE,VINCENT T.	1	5	35	19	14	0	0	1	0	75	CHAR
JOHNSON,ARNOLD S	2	5	109	21	27	9	0	3	0	176	CHAR
TORMEY,JAMES J.	1	2	16	3	5	0	0	0	0	27	CHAR
DOBBS, FARRELL	3	2	49	30	24	1	0	0	1	109	CHAR
ABT, JOHN J.	3	0	2	1	3	0	0	0	0	9	CHAR
CUNNINGHAM,HELEN	10	1	105	44	72	1	0	10	1	243	CHAR
ADAMS,R.L.	5	0	36	7	28	0	0	0	1	76	CHAR
BROOKS,DONALD	9	0	36	8	28	0	0	0	0	81	CHAR
STATMAN,IRVING	4	0	37	27	50	2	0	4	0	124	CHAR
BARGAS,TOMMY	6	0	52	5	50	3	1	6	0	123	CHAR
STOVALL,ROBERT	10	6	27	9	46	1	1	3	1	103	CHAR
GRAEF,JOHN	5	2	76	22	85	5	5	10	1	210	CHAR
OFSTEIN,DENNIS	12	18	162	13	106	11	0	3	0	325	CHAR
LEBLANC,CHARLES	11	1	33	2	35	2	1	5	0	90	CHAR
ALBA,ADRIAN	8	14	61	6	55	7	1	1	0	153	CHAR
TOBIAS,MRS.MAHLO	4	4	108	47	187	4	2	28	0	384	CHAR
TOBIAS,MAHLON	3	3	79	18	110	4	4	8	1	229	CHAR
GARNER,MRS.JESSE	7	3	77	6	88	2	1	6	0	190	CHAR
HULEN,RICHARD L.	7	2	29	3	53	2	0	7	1	103	CHAR
BARNHORST,COLIN	8	0	27	15	46	0	0	0	0	96	CHAR
JOHNSON,GLADYS	6	6	82	4	74	2	0	1	0	175	CHAR
JOHNSON,A.C.	13	3	101	1	46	1	0	0	0	165	CHAR

WITNESS	PRE	TP	NV	CL	LH	C	FC	N	OTR	TOTAL	TYPE
SHASTEEN,CLIFTON	4	1	68	22	106	1	0	3	0	205	CHAR
HUTCHISON, L.E.	9	5	87	22	131	5	1	1	0	261	CHAR
PIZZO,FRANK	8	6	27	20	95	0	0	9	1	165	CHAR
BOGARD,ALBERT G.	15	7	34	4	31	3	0	2	0	96	CHAR
DAVIS,FLOYD G.	7	11	30	6	45	7	2	1	0	109	CHAR
DAVIS, V.L.	6	3	31	4	29	0	0	2	0	75	CHAR
PRICE,MALCOLM	11	9	58	8	72	2	0	1	0	161	CHAR
SLACK,GARLAND	8	7	25	4	26	0	0	0	0	70	CHAR
WOOD,DR.HOMER	7	8	20	4	27	2	0	2	0	70	CHAR
WOOD,STERLING	8	9	70	5	53	3	0	1	0	149	CHAR
WOOD,THERESA	3	0	7	0	5	0	0	1	0	16	CHAR
SMITH,GLENN E.	15	2	52	1	40	3	0	0	0	113	CHAR
SEMIGSEN,W.W.	7	0	35	5	52	0	0	0	1	99	CHAR
WILCOX,LAURANCE	5	1	54	15	82	2	0	0	0	159	CHAR
PIC,JOHN E.	18	13	509	147	569	38	1	30	2	1325	CHAR
THORNLEY,KERRY	10	8	157	42	161	32	1	6	0	417	CHAR
GIBSON,MRS.DON	8	6	215	33	261	22	2	13	0	560	CHAR
STUCKEY,WILLIAM	5	2	108	46	108	8	0	5	0	282	CHAR
JAMES,VIRGINIA	6	3	65	15	52	1	0	0	0	142	CHAR
RITCHIE,JAMES	8	1	14	1	15	1	0	0	0	40	CHAR
SEELEY,CARROLL	15	11	69	13	69	0	0	1	0	178	CHAR
MUMFORD,PAMELA	6	2	79	4	54	3	0	0	0	148	CHAR
RYDER,DIAL D.	26	12	59	11	82	9	0	0	0	199	CHAR
SCHMIDT,HUNTER	7	1	22	6	23	1	0	0	0	60	CHAR
GREENER,CHARLES	2	8	43	7	42	5	0	1	0	108	CHAR
HUNTER,GERTRUDE	8	6	53	2	51	4	0	1	0	125	CHAR
WHITWORTH,EDITH	10	8	77	8	50	5	1	7	0	166	CHAR
ANDERSON,MAJ.E.	11	3	35	0	5	5	0	0	2	59	EXP
ZAHM.SGT.JAMES	12	2	13	0	6	7	0	0	1	40	EXP
HAMBLEN,C.A.	3	4	10	2	18	0	0	1	0	38	CHAR
FENLEY,ROBERT	10	0	27	2	27	0	0	0	0	66	CHAR
LEWIS.AUBREY L.	16	4	68	5	49	0	0	0	0	142	CHAR
ANDREWS,DEAN A.	3	8	89	8	95	1	0	0	1	204	CHAR
RODRIGUEZ,EVARIS	12	6	46	5	23	1	0	3	3	96	CHAR
PENA,OREST	8	25	93	19	125	1	0	5	0	276	CHAR
PENA,RUPERTO	4	3	19	2	15	1	0	4	0	48	CHAR
ODIO,SYLVIA	14	27	121	15	127	8	0	4	1	316	CHAR
WALKER,GEN.EDWIN	7	19	123	37	116	5	2	6	6	315	CHAR
REYNOLDS, WARREN	11	8	48	4	58	8	0	2	0	139	JDT
JOHNSON,PRISCILL	5	4	44	27	27	7	0	2	2	116	CHAR
ROGERS.ERIC	3	4	28	0	24	2	0	3	0	64	CHAR
LEHRER,JAMES	12	0	11	1	18	2	0	0	0	44	CHAR
BATCHELOR,CHARLE	10	26	230	50	94	9	0	3	3	422	LHO
DECKER,BILL	12	5	32	20	47	0	0	0	0	116	LHO
FRAZIER,CAPT.W.	11	4	42	13	32	0	0	0	0	102	LHO
JONES,O.A.	9	11	67	33	61	0	0	3	4	184	LHO
SOLOMON,JAMES M.	8	1	21	4	27	1	0	0	0	62	LHO
STEVENSON,M.W.	12	15	112	24	78	8	1	3	1	253	LHO
TALBERT,CECIL	15	14	161	41	110	4	0	0	9	345	LHO
ARNETT,CHARLES	25	19	301	97	88	5	0	0	3	535	LHO
BEATY,BUFORD L.	14	11	112	47	30	3	0	0	0	217	LHO

WITNESS	PRE	TP	NV	CL	LH	C	FC	N	OTR	TOTAL	TYPE
BROCK,ALVIN R.	13	2	52	7	35	0	0	3	0	112	LHO
COMBEST, B.H.	10	16	52	8	54	5	0	0	0	145	LHO
CROY,KENNETH	17	13	265	42	54	5	2	2	0	400	LHO
CUTCHSHAW,WILBUR	13	15	178	26	54	10	0	0	2	296	LHO
DANIELS,NAPOLEON	10	9	40	21	79	1	0	2	0	162	LHO
HARRISON,WILLIAM	19	27	260	52	84	8	1	1	4	452	LHO
HOLLY, HAROLD	11	5	29	9	22	0	0	1	1	77	LHO
KRISS,HARRY	8	1	24	14	37	0	0	0	0	84	LHO
LOWERY, ROY LEE	11	6	29	12	27	0	0	0	0	85	LHO
MARTIN,FRANK M.	11	5	43	12	33	8	1	1	0	114	LHO
MAXEY,BILLY JOE	10	2	30	19	28	2	0	2	0	93	LHO
MAYO,LOGAN W.	13	10	52	8	25	0	0	1	1	109	LHO
MILLER,LOUIS D.	16	17	192	18	14	2	0	2	1	261	LHO
NEWMAN,WILLIAM	34	23	183	33	55	6	0	0	0	334	LHO
PATTERSON,BOBBY	15	4	17	2	22	0	0	0	0	60	LHO
SLACK,WILLIE	11	5	42	9	31	1	0	4	0	103	LHO
STEELE,DON F.	8	1	31	6	7	1	0	1	0	55	LHO
VAUGHAN,ROY	9	23	110	13	68	7	1	3	0	234	LHO
WATSON,JAMES C.	8	4	26	13	35	3	0	2	0	91	LHO
WORLEY, G.E.	14	5	101	22	14	0	0	0	0	156	LHO
WIGGINS,WOODROW	16	10	36	10	32	2	0	2	0	108	LHO
ARCHER,DON RAY	10	10	45	13	41	3	0	0	0	122	LHO
CLARDY,BARNARD	10	8	61	16	67	8	0	1	1	171	LHO
McMILLON,THOMAS	18	14	172	38	43	2	0	1	1	288	LHO
BIEBERDORF,FRED	7	5	28	5	20	0	0	0	0	65	LHO
CASON,FRANCES	8	0	28	2	18	0	0	2	0	58	LHO
HARDIN,MICHAEL	12	2	43	5	27	0	1	0	0	90	LHO
HULSE,C.E.	11	0	19	0	17	0	0	0	0	47	LHO
BEERS,IRA J.	11	6	62	12	10	3	0	0	0	104	LHO
HANKAL,ROBERT	7	3	25	6	29	1	0	1	0	72	LHO
HUFFAKER,ROBERT	12	2	45	14	21	2	0	0	0	96	LHO
PHENIX,GEORGE	12	5	31	11	41	3	0	1	0	104	LHO
TURNER,JIMMY	12	10	60	22	59	6	0	0	2	169	LHO
FUQUA,HAROLD	8	.2	30	5	33	0	0	0	0	78	LHO
KELLY,EDWARD	9	0	9	1	8	0	0	0	0	27	LHO
McKINZIE,LOUIS	15	2	53	7	92	0	0	1	0	170	LHO
PIERCE,EDWARD E.	9	4	50	6	54	1	0	0	0	124	LHO
RIGGS,ALFREADIA	18	0	62	8	73	0	0	0	0	161	LHO
SERVANCE, JOHN	7	2	33	5	50	1	0	0	0	98	LHO
EBERHARDT,A.M.	12	6	126	24	27	9	0	0	2	204	CHAR
EVANS,SIDNEY	12	5	38	5	44	0	0	2	0	106	LHO
CARLIN,BRUCE RAY	22	9	120	26	98	3	0	2	0	280	LHO
CARLIN,KAREN B.	10	14	182	13	162	7	0	6	1	394	LHO
LANE,DOYLE E.	9	7	66	3	47	0	0	2	0	134	LHO
PITTS,ELNORA	8	15	75	19	69	2	0	2	0	190	LHO
PRIDDY, HAL	6	1	28	9	25	0	0	0	0	69	LHO
REEVES, HUEY	14	14	99	17	63	4	0	1	0	212	LHO
RICHEY,WARREN E.	9	10	46	11	38	1	0	0	0	115	LHO
SLAUGHTER,MALCOL	8	9	34	7	23	3	0	0	0	84	LHO
SMART,VERNON	14	8	109	25	23	3	0	0	2	182	LHO
SMITH,JOHN ALLIS	8	13	34	8	39	0	0	0	0	102	LHO

WITNESS	PRE	TP	NV	CL	LH	C	FC	N	OTR	TOTAL	TYPE
STRONG, JESSE	8	7	29	7	15	1	0	1	0	68	LHO
WALKER, IRA N.	10	10	38	7	43	2	0	1	0	111	LHO
DANIELS, JOHN	8	4	20	2	17	1	0	1	0	53	LHO
JACKSON, THEODORE	10	3	31	5	20	1	0	1	0	71	LHO
ARMSTRONG, ANDREW	42	53	790	121	547	19	3	17	1	1592	CHAR
CHEEK, BERTHA	11	5	197	40	52	5	0	0	0	310	CHAR
CRAFARD, CURTIS L	223	83	2296	270	985	67	4	44	2	3972	CHAR
LITCHFIELD, W.W.	33	18	58	16	89	6	1	1	0	222	CHAR
NICHOLS, ALICE R.	18	18	215	24	27	5	0	0	0	307	CHAR
PATTERSON, R.C.	16	3	85	13	21	0	0	0	0	138	CHAR
PAUL, RALPH	14	30	411	118	360	15	1	7	0	956	CHAR
SENATOR, GEORGE	131	87	1282	540	656	81	2	13	2	2792	CHAR
RICH, NANCY PERRI	103	31	228	77	159	1	0	2	0	601	CHAR
RUBY, EARL	28	7	585	124	182	13	0	8	0	947	CHAR
GRANT, EVA	11	26	442	132	201	96	1	9	8	918	CHAR
RUBY, SAM	9	3	136	17	51	5	0	0	0	221	CHAR
BEAVERS, WILLIAM	8	5	6	8	5	8	0	0	0	40	CHAR
HERNDON, BELL	13	25	57	36	10	7	0	0	1	148	LHO
WALL, BRECK	40	14	178	16	27	4	0	5	0	284	CHAR
PETERSON, JOSEPH	29	6	118	15	21	4	1	2	0	196	LHO
OLSEN, HARRY N.	34	27	273	16	11	12	0	4	2	377	LHO
OLSEN, KAY HELEN	31	16	236	25	19	5	0	8	0	340	LHO
RUBENSTEIN, HYMAN	268	22	190	99	91	12	0	2	0	684	CHAR
BIGGIO, WILLIAM	3	1	4	2	10	0	0	0	0	20	LHO
KING, GLEN D.	12	10	41	12	43	4	0	0	0	122	UNR
HALL, C.RAY	9	4	36	13	52	3	0	2	0	119	LHO
KANTOR, SETH	14	18	154	54	44	3	0	0	1	287	CHAR
CROWE, WILLIAM	30	19	159	27	97	8	0	2	0	342	CHAR
CRULL, ELGIN	11	7	33	12	27	1	0	1	0	92	UNR
COX, ROLAND A.	8	5	57	8	40	1	0	0	0	119	LHO
FLEMING, HAROLD	11	5	50	10	42	1	0	0	0	119	LHO
GOIN, DON E.	12	4	72	10	31	0	0	3	0	132	LHO
HALL, MARVIN E.	10	3	75	7	35	2	1	5	0	138	LHO
RICHEY, MARJORIE	31	5	88	20	12	4	0	0	0	160	LHO
AYCOX, JAMES	6	1	30	7	5	1	0	0	0	50	CHAR
PALMER, THOMAS	14	6	85	8	11	8	0	0	0	132	CHAR
JOHNSON, JOSEPH	29	2	27	4	5	4	0	0	0	71	CHAR
PULLMAN, EDWARD	14	2	81	14	15	1	0	0	0	127	CHAR
KRAVITZ, HERBERT	13	2	21	3	6	4	0	0	0	49	CHAR
ROSSI, JOSEPH	11	4	31	6	6	1	0	0	0	59	CHAR
WRIGHT, NORMAN E.	11	2	72	4	7	4	0	1	0	101	CHAR
MOORE, RUSSELL L.	23	10	152	21	22	10	0	1	0	239	CHAR
DIETRICH, EDWARD	20	1	35	11	31	0	0	1	0	99	LHO
KAMINSKY, EILEEN	48	3	71	25	25	3	1	3	0	179	CHAR
FEHRENBACH, GEORG	105	14	135	32	83	9	0	5	0	383	CHAR
ROBERTSON, VICTOR	11	9	79	3	8	7	0	0	0	117	LHO
RHEINSTEIN, FRED	7	1	29	8	33	0	0	1	0	79	LHO
PAPPAS, ICARUS	9	17	108	26	17	4	0	1	0	182	LHO
McCULLOUGH, JOHN	6	7	57	20	11	5	0	1	0	107	LHO
KLEINMAN, ABRAHAM	15	2	41	4	4	2	0	0	0	68	CHAR
TICE, WILMA	20	6	40	18	25	3	1	1	0	114	CHAR

WITNESS	PRE	TP	NV	CL	LH	C	FC	N	OTR	TOTAL	TYPE
HELMICK,WANDA	18	2	84	17	15	4	0	0	0	140	LHO
POWELL,NANCY M.	22	6	226	42	60	12	0	1	0	369	CHAR
DOWE,KENNETH	23	1	41	13	4	3	0	0	0	85	CHAR
HANSEN,T.M.	14	5	59	26	7	3	0	0	0	114	CHAR
MILLER,DAVE L.	12	1	70	5	5	0	0	0	0	93	CHAR
BENTON,NELSON	7	8	91	16	46	0	0	1	0	169	LHO
BELLOCCHIO,FRANK	5	2	58	7	40	4	0	1	0	117	CHAR
BRANCH,JOHN	14	2	85	15	76	4	2	3	0	201	CHAR
DUNCAN,WILLIAM	2	4	35	5	27	3	0	0	0	76	CHAR
HALLMARK,GARNETT	8	4	25	6	38	3	0	0	0	84	CHAR
HODGE,ALFRED	12	3	42	9	54	2	0	0	0	122	CHAR
JOHNSTON,DAVID L	15	6	42	6	43	3	0	1	0	116	JFK
KAUFMAN,STANLEY	7	4	30	14	20	5	0	0	0	80	CHAR
McCURDY,DANNY	4	0	29	6	26	3	0	0	0	68	CHAR
NEWMAN,JOHN	11	6	107	13	66	3	0	0	0	206	CHAR
NORTON,ROBERT	26	1	47	8	55	0	0	0	0	137	CHAR
PRYOR,ROY	11	6	60	9	72	10	0	2	0	170	CHAR
WATHERWAX,ARTHUR	13	9	58	7	54	7	0	1	0	149	CHAR
REA,BILLY	19	0	38	7	28	2	1	0	0	95	CHAR
SANDERS,RICHARD	4	4	56	13	38	1	0	1	0	117	CHAR
WALDO,THAYER	10	3	37	7	46	2	0	1	0	106	LHO
GOODSON,CLYDE	7	1	40	4	27	0	0	0	0	79	LHO
JENKINS,RONALD L	12	3	44	4	27	0	0	4	0	94	LHO
JOHNSON,SPEEDY	14	1	55	14	43	10	0	2	0	139	CHAR
STANDIFER,ROY	8	1	40	0	28	1	0	0	0	78	LHO
MEYERS,LAWRENCE	22	16	117	27	12	5	0	1	1	200	CHAR
TASKER, HARRY	5	6	65	22	50	3	0	1	0	152	LHO
OLIVER,REVILO	17	3	169	105	104	0	0	1	4	399	UNR
GALLAGHER,JOHN	7	9	27	5	14	4	0	1	0	67	JFK

WITNESS	PRE	TP	NV	CL	LH	C	FC	N	OTR	TOTAL	TYPE
PAINE,RUTH	10	25	2181	801	1995	155	31	38	15	5236	CHAR
CRAFARD,CURTIS L	223	83	2296	270	985	67	4	44	2	3972	CHAR
SENATOR,GEORGE	131	87	1282	540	656	81	2	13	2	2792	CHAR
OSWALD, MARINA	22	217	1411	444	361	46	56	58	5	2615	CHAR
OSWALD,ROBT	15	33	1179	560	400	124	8	32	15	2351	CHAR
DEMOHRENSCHILDT,	18	43	585	239	649	38	6	50	0	1628	CHAR
ARMSTRONG,ANDREW	42	53	790	121	547	19	3	17	1	1592	CHAR
PIC,JOHN E.	18	13	509	147	569	38	1	30	2	1325	CHAR
PAINE,MICHAEL	8	13	482	161	297	37	7	14	1	1019	CHAR
CURRY,JESSE E.	14	34	458	158	323	5	6	4	8	1002	LHO
MARTIN,JAMES	10	6	562	196	168	35	0	2	10	979	CHAR
PAUL,RALPH	14	30	411	118	360	15	1	7	0	956	CHAR
RUBY,EARL	28	7	585	124	182	13	0	8	0	947	CHAR
GRANT,EVA	11	26	442	132	201	96	1	9	8	918	CHAR
MURRET,LILLIAN	7	19	272	122	364	42	10	45	0	881	CHAR
FRITZ, WILL	9	11	268	130	412	10	2	1	1	843	JFK
FRAZIER,ROBT.	11	26	392	130	213	21	7	4	8	804	JFK
RUBY,JACK	10	79	277	322	67	5	0	0	4	760	LHO
WEISMAN,BERNARD	12	18	368	107	208	7	0	18	0	738	JFK
KELLERMAN,ROY	9	67	271	168	154	32	8	15	1	724	JFK
SHANEYFELT, L.	14	30	259	160	217	17	1	1	4	699	JFK
RUBENSTEIN,HYMAN	268	22	190	99	91	12	0	2	0	684	CHAR
SIMS,RICHARD	6	48	294	51	199	16	3	16	0	633	JFK
OSWALD, MARG.	9	48	169	317	39	8	3	22	1	615	CHAR
RICH,NANCY PERRI	103	31	228	77	159	1	0	2	0	601	CHAR
SORRELS,FORREST	19	57	251	54	194	12	4	7	0	598	JFK
LATONA,SEBASTIAN	7	27	192	99	225	16	4	1	9	571	JFK
FRAZIER,BUELL W.	16	12	218	127	180	3	5	5	0	566	JFK
DELGADO,NELSON	25	14	219	72	200	24	5	4	1	563	CHAR
GIBSON,MRS.DON	8	6	215	33	261	22	2	13	0	560	CHAR
DEMOHRENSCHILDT,	23	18	176	66	241	15	1	15	1	555	CHAR
DEAN,PATRICK	22	23	308	131	66	2	0	2	6	554	LHO
ARNETT,CHARLES	25	19	301	97	88	5	0	0	3	535	LHO
BLEDSOE,MARY	6	7	212	77	190	7	10	13	1	522	CHAR
SURREY,ROBERT A.	17	15	188	126	142	8	7	10	0	513	WALKE
CUNNINGHAM,CORT.	8	15	152	142	129	24	7	11	1	488	JFK
REVILL,JACK	25	11	187	103	155	3	0	4	1	488	LHO
HOSTY,JAMES P.	9	17	235	118	94	3	5	3	4	484	JFK
TRULY,ROY	12	10	214	74	150	12	8	2	2	482	JFK
DAY, J.C.	8	10	248	87	120	2	3	0	0	478	JFK
McWATTERS, C.	13	81	198	68	50	3	35	29	1	477	JFK
TAYLOR,GARY E.	21	5	225	42	131	17	4	27	3	472	CHAR
COLE,ALWYN	13	25	263	65	86	9	1	0	8	462	JFK
BAKER,MARRION	8	21	199	64	144	6	5	7	5	454	JFK
HARRISON,WILLIAM	19	27	260	52	84	8	1	1	4	452	LHO
MAMANTOV,ILYA	29	32	156	45	146	15	6	15	4	444	JFK
MARKHAM,HELEN	4	16	165	79	176	0	2	0	0	442	JDT
LAWSON,WINSTON	9	18	173	89	124	4	5	2	7	424	JFK
GLOVER,EVERETT	32	7	180	53	131	11	1	9	1	424	CHAR
BATCHELOR,CHARLE	10	26	230	50	94	9	0	3	3	422	LHO
THORNLEY,KERRY	10	8	157	42	161	32	1	6	0	417	CHAR

WITNESS	PRE	TP	NV	CL	LH	C	FC	N	OTR	TOTAL	TYPE
CROY.KENNETH	17	13	265	42	54	5	2	2	0	400	LHO
OLIVER,REVILO	17	3	169	105	104	0	0	1	4	399	UNR
CARLIN,KAREN B.	10	14	182	13	162	7	0	6	1	394	LHO
ROWLAND,ARNOLD	20	14	210	78	48	14	0	5	0	389	JFK
WILLIAMS,BONNIE	10	22	172	44	131	1	4	4	0	388	JFK
TOBIAS,MRS.MAHLO	4	4	108	47	187	4	2	28	0	384	CHAR
MURRET,MARILYN	23	12	151	41	119	22	7	8	0	383	CHAR
FEHRENBACH,GEORG	105	14	135	32	83	9	0	5	0	383	CHAR
STOMBAUGH,PAUL	6	9	169	69	113	5	3	5	1	379	JFK
FORD,KATHERINE	5	4	178	75	100	14	1	1	0	378	CHAR
OLSEN,HARRY N.	34	27	273	16	11	12	0	4	2	377	LHO
BOYD, ELMER	5	40	187	26	94	6	0	12	0	370	JFK
POWELL,NANCY M.	22	6	226	42	60	12	0	1	0	369	CHAR
SNYDER,RICHARD	7	20	141	71	110	13	2	3	1	367	CHAR
CADIGAN,JAMES	12	22	145	69	106	5	1	1	4	361	JFK
MONTGOMERY,L.D.	22	23	165	72	63	4	0	3	2	352	LHO
FAIN,JOHN W.	7	5	178	82	65	2	6	1	2	346	CHAR
GRAVES, L.C.	29	45	152	33	76	6	0	5	3	346	LHO
ROWLEY,JAMES	7	23	145	67	75	15	5	8	8	345	SEC
TALBERT,CECIL	15	14	161	41	110	4	0	0	9	345	LHO
PERRY,MALCOLM	13	10	204	42	51	11	10	3	2	344	JFK
RAIGORODSKY,P.	8	2	182	43	85	16	1	5	8	342	CHAR
CROWE,WILLIAM	30	19	159	27	97	8	0	2	0	342	CHAR
OLSEN,KAY HELEN	31	16	236	25	19	5	0	8	0	340	LHO
VOSHININ,MRS.IGO	30	0	96	66	120	13	1	8	1	334	CHAR
NEWMAN,WILLIAM	34	23	183	33	55	6	0	0	0	334	LHO
WADE, HENRY	5	18	175	64	52	4	2	11	4	331	JFK
VOSHININ, IGOR	30	2	89	93	106	6	0	5	0	331	CHAR
SCOGGINS, WM.	11	9	150	37	114	3	0	2	2	326	JDT
BARNES, W.E.	15	36	152	26	74	10	5	7	1	325	JDT
OFSTEIN,DENNIS	12	18	162	13	106	11	0	3	0	325	CHAR
DAVIS, C.V.	13	22	145	44	95	0	2	2	0	323	JDT
POWERS.DANIEL P.	3	10	136	57	87	19	5	3	1	320	CHAR
ODIO,SYLVIA	14	27	121	15	127	8	0	4	1	316	CHAR
WALKER,GEN.EDWIN	7	19	123	37	116	5	2	6	6	315	CHAR
JARMIN,JAMES	8	11	158	23	107	4	1	0	0	312	JFK
CHEEK,BERTHA	11	5	197	40	52	5	0	0	0	310	CHAR
BRENNAN,HOWARD	15	72	47	143	27	1	1	1	1	307	JFK
NICHOLS,ALICE R.	18	18	215	24	27	5	0	0	0	307	CHAR
BOUHE,GEORGE	17	22	128	23	90	20	3	3	0	306	CHAR
HOLMES,HARRY D.	11	30	103	41	97	3	3	11	2	299	JFK
CUTCHSHAW,WILBUR	13	15	178	26	54	10	0	0	2	296	LHO
SHAW,ROBERT	12	13	142	60	58	5	3	0	6	293	JFK
HILL, JEAN L.	6	44	107	65	65	2	1	2	1	292	JFK
McMILLON,THOMAS	18	14	172	38	43	2	0	1	1	288	LHO
KANTOR,SETH	14	18	154	54	44	3	0	0	1	287	CHAR
WHALEY,WILLIAM	7	9	87	68	110	2	0	1	0	284	JFK
WALL,BRECK	40	14	178	16	27	4	0	5	0	284	CHAR
STUCKEY,WILLIAM	5	2	108	46	108	8	0	5	0	282	CHAR
CARLIN,BRUCE RAY	22	9	120	26	98	3	0	2	0	280	LHO
PENA,OREST	8	25	93	19	125	1	0	5	0	276	CHAR

WITNESS	PRE	TP	NV	CL	LH	C	FC	N	OTR	TOTAL	TYPE
ROWLAND,BARBARA	24	14	116	23	80	3	3	11	0	274	JFK
GREER,WM.	6	12	156	31	46	17	1	3	1	272	JFK
HUTCHISON. L.E.	9	5	87	22	131	5	1	1	0	261	CHAR
MILLER,LOUIS D.	16	17	192	18	14	2	0	2	1	261	LHO
EVANS,MYRTLE	2	4	96	40	85	18	6	6	0	257	CHAR
LEAVELLE,JAMES	20	24	103	19	84	2	0	2	1	254	JFK
STEVENSON,M.W.	12	15	112	24	78	8	1	3	1	253	LHO
STUDEBAKER,ROBT.	5	15	78	42	102	6	1	3	0	252	JFK
LANE, MARK	8	7	81	98	40	7	0	7	0	248	CHAR
NORMAN,HAROLD	11	8	123	18	83	2	1	1	2	247	JFK
DYMITRUK,LYDIA	34	0	60	36	92	3	2	17	0	244	CHAR
GREGORY,PAUL R.	11	16	120	8	66	14	3	6	0	244	CHAR
CUNNINGHAM,HELEN	10	1	105	44	72	1	0	10	1	243	CHAR
BOUCK,ROBERT	6	9	83	46	87	3	3	2	5	239	JFK
HALL,ELENA	14	13	114	16	61	14	1	6	0	239	CHAR
MOORE,RUSSELL L.	23	10	152	21	22	10	0	1	0	239	CHAR
CHAYES,ABRAM	5	15	46	60	98	6	1	3	6	234	CHAR
VAUGHAN,ROY	9	23	110	13	68	7	1	3	0	234	LHO
SHELLEY. WILLIAM	10	10	93	25	85	2	3	5	0	233	JFK
BELMONT,ALAN H.	7	10	74	76	51	7	2	2	1	229	SEC
TOBIAS,MAHLON	3	3	79	18	110	4	4	8	1	229	CHAR
CRAIG, ROGER	21	29	82	29	56	2	4	3	0	226	JFK
GIVENS,CHARLES	33	10	100	18	54	3	0	7	0	225	JFK
HILL,GERALD	9	21	88	35	66	2	0	2	0	223	JFK
LITCHFIELD,W.W.	33	18	58	16	89	6	1	1	0	222	CHAR
RUBY.SAM	9	3	136	17	51	5	0	0	0	221	CHAR
BEATY,BUFORD L.	14	11	112	47	30	3	0	0	0	217	LHO
VOEBEL,EDWARD	5	5	106	10	66	15	1	8	0	216	CHAR
HUMES,JAMES J.	7	30	17	79	41	21	13	7	1	215	JFK
REEVES, HUEY	14	14	99	17	63	4	0	1	0	212	LHO
GRAEF,JOHN	5	2	76	22	85	5	5	10	1	210	CHAR
OLIVIER, ALFRED	7	20	76	55	27	23	0	0	2	208	JFK
NEWMAN,JOHN	11	6	107	13	66	3	0	0	0	206	CHAR
NICOL,JOSEPH	2	10	58	50	78	3	3	1	2	205	JFK
SHASTEEN,CLIFTON	4	1	68	22	106	1	0	3	0	205	CHAR
DOUGHERTY,JACK	22	7	89	14	68	0	2	2	0	204	JFK
BATES,PAULINE V.	12	5	68	55	58	3	0	3	0	204	CHAR
ANDREWS,DEAN A.	3	8	89	8	95	1	0	0	1	204	CHAR
EBERHARDT,A.M.	12	6	126	24	27	9	0	0	2	204	CHAR
CARRICO,CHARLES	13	25	105	24	20	5	9	2	1	203	JFK
ROBERTS,EARLENE	13	13	89	21	63	0	2	2	0	203	JFK
BRANCH,JOHN	14	2	85	15	76	4	2	3	0	201	CHAR
REID,MRS.ROBT	10	2	79	19	82	3	3	2	0	200	JFK
MEYERS,LAWRENCE	22	16	117	27	12	5	0	1	1	200	CHAR
DAVIS,MRS.B.J.	1	6	95	31	64	2	0	0	1	199	JDT
RYDER,DIAL D.	26	12	59	11	82	9	0	0	0	199	CHAR
KLAUSE,ROBERT	2	7	100	18	70	1	0	0	0	198	JFK
PETERSON, JOSEPH	29	6	118	15	21	4	1	2	0	196	LHO
GREGORY,CHARLES	11	8	112	40	16	4	1	2	1	194	JFK
WATERMAN,BERNICE	4	3	49	54	78	2	2	2	2	194	CHAR
TURNER,F.M.	18	22	93	15	43	1	0	2	0	194	JFK

WITNESS	PRE	TP	NV	CL	LH	C	FC	N	OTR	TOTAL	TYPE
GARNER,MRS.JESSE	7	3	77	6	88	2	1	6	0	190	CHAR
PITTS,ELNORA	8	15	75	19	69	2	0	2	0	190	LHO
WORRELL,JAMES R.	13	12	90	45	23	3	0	2	0	188	JFK
BENAVIDES,DOMING	22	14	77	25	47	0	0	1	0	186	JDT
O'DONNELL,KENNET	3	17	129	3	23	3	3	5	0	186	JFK
JONES,O.A.	9	11	67	33	61	0	0	3	4	184	LHO
BRINGUIER,CARLOS	10	3	59	42	65	2	0	2	5	183	CHAR
SMART,VERNON	14	8	109	25	23	3	0	0	2	182	LHO
PAPPAS,ICARUS	9	17	108	26	17	4	0	1	0	182	LHO
FORD,DECLAN	11	4	68	30	52	14	0	1	0	180	CHAR
KAMINSKY,EILEEN	48	3	71	25	25	3	1	3	0	179	CHAR
SEELEY,CARROLL	15	11	69	13	69	0	0	1	0	178	CHAR
MURRET,C.DUTZ	11	6	65	10	77	4	1	2	0	176	CHAR
JOHNSON,ARNOLD S	2	5	109	21	27	9	0	3	0	176	CHAR
HILL,CLINT	6	13	102	25	18	5	3	3	0	175	JFK
JOHNSON,GLADYS	6	6	82	4	74	2	0	1	0	175	CHAR
DHORITY, C.N.	7	15	79	18	51	2	0	1	0	173	JFK
STEELE,CHAS JR.	7	3	83	9	63	1	0	5	0	171	CHAR
CLARDY,BARNARD	10	8	61	16	67	8	0	1	1	171	LHO
McKINZIE,LOUIS	15	2	53	7	92	0	0	1	0	170	LHO
PRYOR,ROY	11	6	60	9	72	10	0	2	0	170	CHAR
McDONALD,M.N.	9	12	74	8	62	2	2	0	0	169	JDT
BALLEN,SAMUEL B.	10	11	101	6	31	7	2	1	0	169	CHAR
TURNER,JIMMY	12	10	60	22	59	6	0	0	2	169	LHO
BENTON,NELSON	7	8	91	16	46	0	0	1	0	169	LHO
DONOVAN, JOHN E.	6	13	89	10	28	14	3	3	0	166	CHAR
WHITWORTH,EDITH	10	8	77	8	50	5	1	7	0	166	CHAR
JOHNSON,A.C.	13	3	101	1	46	1	0	0	0	165	CHAR
PIZZO,FRANK	8	6	27	20	95	0	0	9	1	165	CHAR
CONNALLY,JOHN	3	17	94	24	21	0	3	2	0	164	JFK
BRIAN,V.J.	6	2	69	42	41	0	0	4	0	164	CHAR
O'BRIEN,LAWRENCE	1	8	100	4	46	0	1	3	0	163	JFK
DANIELS,NAPOLEON	10	9	40	21	79	1	0	2	0	162	LHO
SAWYER, J.H.	15	13	51	24	52	1	2	3	0	161	JFK
GRAVITIS,DOROTHY	26	2	75	18	28	7	4	1	0	161	CHAR
PRICE,MALCOLM	11	9	58	8	72	2	0	1	0	161	CHAR
RIGGS,ALFREADIA	18	0	62	8	73	0	0	0	0	161	LHO
WALKER, C.T.	21	12	67	17	34	5	1	3	0	160	JFK
RICHEY,MARJORIE	31	5	88	20	12	4	0	0	0	160	LHO
WILCOX,LAURANCE	5	1	54	15	82	2	0	0	0	159	CHAR
ADAMCIK, JOHN	21	18	74	11	28	3	0	1	0	156	JFK
MELLER,ANNA	13	8	69	20	31	10	1	4	1	156	CHAR
WORLEY, G.E.	14	5	101	22	14	0	0	0	0	156	LHO
ALBA,ADRIAN	8	14	61	6	55	7	1	1	0	153	CHAR
CLARK,WILLIAM K.	8	20	71	19	22	4	6	2	0	152	JFK
TASKER, HARRY	5	6	65	22	50	3	0	1	0	152	LHO
WESTBROOK, W.R.	7	6	57	36	43	0	0	1	0	150	JFK
KRYSTINIK,RAYMON	11	3	66	8	45	13	3	0	0	149	CHAR
WOOD,STERLING	8	9	70	5	53	3	0	1	0	149	CHAR
WATHERWAX,ARTHUR	13	9	58	7	54	7	0	1	0	149	CHAR
MUMFORD,PAMELA	6	2	79	4	54	3	0	0	0	148	CHAR

WITNESS	PRE	TP	NV	CL	LH	C	FC	N	OTR	TOTAL	TYPE
HERNDON, BELL	13	25	57	36	10	7	0	0	1	148	LHO
BREWER,JOHNNY	17	10	69	9	40	1	0	1	0	147	JDT
EUINS,AMOS LEE	11	20	48	37	23	5	0	2	0	146	JFK
MICHAELIS,HEINZ	17	16	41	14	55	0	0	2	1	145	JDT
GUINYARD,SAM	12	21	46	5	58	1	1	1	0	145	JDT
COMBEST, B.H.	10	16	52	8	54	5	0	0	0	145	LHO
COUCH,MALCOLM	14	19	43	13	50	1	4	0	0	144	JFK
CARROLL,BOB K.	12	21	70	8	29	0	4	0	0	144	JFK
MOONEY,LUKE	9	10	57	17	49	0	0	1	0	143	JFK
EVANS,JULIAN	5	3	38	11	71	13	2	0	0	143	CHAR
JACKSON,ROBT.H.	14	12	55	32	21	6	1	1	0	142	JFK
HARKNESS,D.V.	18	10	62	19	31	2	0	0	0	142	JFK
BOOKHOUT,JAMES	5	20	64	10	35	4	2	2	1	142	JFK
BAKER,MRS.DON	3	18	22	29	59	4	2	5	0	142	JFK
JAMES,VIRGINIA	6	3	65	15	52	1	0	0	0	142	CHAR
LEWIS,AUBREY L.	16	4	68	5	49	0	0	0	0	142	CHAR
STOVALL,RICHARD	9	9	50	20	49	0	1	2	1	140	JFK
HELMICK,WANDA	18	2	84	17	15	4	0	0	0	140	LHO
REYNOLDS, WARREN	11	8	48	4	58	8	0	2	0	139	JDT
JOHNSON,SPEEDY	14	1	55	14	43	10	0	2	0	139	CHAR
HOLLAND.S.M.	5	9	33	35	53	2	1	0	2	138	JFK
PATTERSON, R.C.	16	3	85	13	21	0	0	0	0	138	CHAR
HALL,MARVIN E.	10	3	75	7	35	2	1	5	0	138	LHO
KNIGHT,FRANCES	7	2	33	24	61	3	1	6	0	137	CHAR
NORTON.ROBERT	26	1	47	8	55	0	0	0	0	137	CHAR
APPLIN, GEORGE	12	11	40	24	46	0	0	3	0	136	JFK
FISCHER,RONALD	21	20	46	28	19	0	1	0	0	135	JFK
HUTSON,THOMAS	20	9	54	17	27	0	4	4	0	135	JFK
WALDMAN,WILLIAM	8	23	48	16	30	1	4	4	1	134	JFK
CLARK,MAX	8	12	68	10	27	7	2	0	1	134	CHAR
LANE,DOYLE E.	9	7	66	3	47	0	0	2	0	134	LHO
GOIN, DON E.	12	4	72	10	31	0	0	3	0	132	LHO
PALMER,THOMAS	14	6	85	8	11	8	0	0	0	132	CHAR
QUIGLEY,JOHN L.	8	5	63	29	19	5	0	1	2	130	CHAR
HAYGOOD,CLYDE	16	8	55	18	29	0	1	3	0	130	JFK
McVICKAR,JOHN	7	4	33	24	54	4	2	0	1	128	CHAR
RAY,MRS.FRANK H.	16	6	55	9	28	12	2	0	0	128	CHAR
CALLAWAY.TED	8	11	49	11	48	0	0	0	1	127	JDT
RAY,MRS.THOMAS	12	9	56	14	29	3	3	1	0	127	CHAR
PULLMAN,EDWARD	14	2	81	14	15	1	0	0	0	127	CHAR
WEST, TROY	17	5	67	10	27	0	0	0	0	126	JFK
SMITH,JOE M.	9	12	48	4	50	1	1	1	0	126	JFK
HUDSON, EMMETT	6	11	47	9	48	4	0	1	0	126	JFK
SIMMONS,RONALD	7	5	47	31	26	6	2	1	0	125	JFK
PETERMAN,VIOLA	6	0	31	15	41	7	0	25	0	125	CHAR
HUNTER,GERTRUDE	8	6	53	2	51	4	0	1	0	125	CHAR
ROMACK.JAMES E.	31	7	47	14	20	2	1	2	0	124	JFK
MURRET.JOHN	12	5	52	7	38	8	1	1	0	124	CHAR
STATMAN,IRVING	4	0	37	27	50	2	0	4	0	124	CHAR
PIERCE,EDWARD E.	9	4	50	6	54	1	0	0	0	124	LHO
GREGORY,PETER P.	5	1	43	21	36	15	0	2	0	123	CHAR

WITNESS	PRE	TP	NV	CL	LH	C	FC	N	OTR	TOTAL	TYPE
BARGAS,TOMMY	6	0	52	5	50	3	1	6	0	123	CHAR
PIPER, EDDIE	12	7	50	14	37	0	1	1	0	122	JFK
PUTNAM,JAMES	17	6	30	17	47	2	0	3	0	122	JDT
ARCHER,DON RAY	10	10	45	13	41	3	0	0	0	122	LHO
KING,GLEN D.	12	10	41	12	43	4	0	0	0	122	UNR
HODGE,ALFRED	12	3	42	9	54	2	0	0	0	122	CHAR
CABELL,EARLE	6	10	48	3	50	0	1	2	0	120	JFK
HALL,C.RAY	9	4	36	13	52	3	0	2	0	119	LHO
COX,ROLAND A.	8	5	57	8	40	1	0	0	0	119	LHO
FLEMING,HAROLD	11	5	50	10	42	1	0	0	0	119	LHO
MANDELLA,ARTHUR	5	3	30	34	40	3	2	1	0	118	JFK
SHIRES,GEORGE	9	19	44	17	21	6	2	0	1	118	JFK
BREWER, E.D.	9	4	65	11	24	0	2	2	0	117	JFK
ADAMS,VICTORIA	13	8	59	13	22	0	1	1	0	117	JFK
ROBERTSON,VICTOR	11	9	79	3	8	7	0	0	0	117	LHO
BELLOCCHIO,FRANK	5	2	58	7	40	4	0	1	0	117	CHAR
SANDERS,RICHARD	4	4	56	13	38	1	0	1	0	117	CHAR
RANDLE,LINNIE M.	3	2	28	19	55	6	1	2	0	116	JFK
JOHNSON,PRISCILL	5	4	44	27	27	7	0	2	2	116	CHAR
DECKER,BILL	12	5	32	20	47	0	0	0	0	116	LHO
JOHNSTON,DAVID L	15	6	42	6	43	3	0	1	0	116	JFK
RICHEY,WARREN E.	9	10	46	11	38	1	0	0	0	115	LHO
FOSTER,J.W.	14	13	31	19	37	0	0	0	2	114	JFK
CONWAY,HIRAM	8	0	55	13	27	5	0	6	1	114	CHAR
HALL,JOHN R.	15	10	41	6	28	13	0	1	0	114	CHAR
MARTIN,FRANK M.	11	5	43	12	33	8	1	1	0	114	LHO
TICE,WILMA	20	6	40	18	25	3	1	1	0	114	CHAR
HANSEN,T.M.	14	5	59	26	7	3	0	0	0	114	CHAR
SMITH,GLENN E.	15	2	52	1	40	3	0	0	0	113	CHAR
ALTGENS,JAMES	9	9	22	21	48	0	0	3	0	112	JFK
BROCK,ALVIN R.	13	2	52	7	35	0	0	3	0	112	LHO
WALKER, IRA N.	10	10	38	7	43	2	0	1	0	111	LHO
MOORE, HENRY	21	7	44	5	29	0	2	2	0	110	JFK
ARCE, DANNY	13	7	50	13	24	0	1	1	0	109	JFK
LAWRENCE, PERDUE	16	4	74	9	3	1	2	0	0	109	JFK
HARTOGS,RENATUS	9	1	46	16	34	2	0	1	0	109	CHAR
DOBBS, FARRELL	3	2	49	30	24	1	0	0	1	109	CHAR
DAVIS,FLOYD G.	7	11	30	6	45	7	2	1	0	109	CHAR
MAYO,LOGAN W.	13	10	52	8	25	0	0	1	1	109	LHO
GREENER,CHARLES	2	8	43	7	42	5	0	1	0	108	CHAR
WIGGINS,WOODROW	16	10	36	10	32	2	0	2	0	108	LHO
McCULLOUGH,JOHN	6	7	57	20	11	5	0	1	0	107	LHO
LOVELADY, BILLY	6	4	42	18	32	1	2	1	0	106	JFK
CLARK,RICHARD	10	3	53	7	31	0	0	2	1	106	JFK
EVANS,SIDNEY	12	5	38	5	44	0	0	2	0	106	LHO
WALDO,THAYER	10	3	37	7	46	2	0	1	0	106	LHO
EDWARDS,ROBERT	13	14	33	24	18	0	0	3	0	105	JFK
TOMLINSON,D.	17	3	32	19	31	0	2	0	1	104	JFK
BROWN, EARLE	7	11	35	18	32	0	0	1	0	104	JFK
PIC,EDWARD	10	0	44	8	38	1	0	3	0	104	CHAR
BEERS,IRA J.	11	6	62	12	10	3	0	0	0	104	LHO

WITNESS	PRE	TP	NV	CL	LH	C	FC	N	OTR	TOTAL	TYPE
PHENIX,GEORGE	12	5	31	11	41	3	0	1	0	104	LHO
STOVALL,ROBERT	10	6	27	9	46	1	1	3	1	103	CHAR
HULEN,RICHARD L.	7	2	29	3	53	2	0	7	1	103	CHAR
SLACK,WILLIE	11	5	42	9	31	1	0	4	0	103	LHO
POSTAL,JULIA	14	3	36	9	39	0	0	1	0	102	JDT
FRAZIER,CAPT.W.	11	4	42	13	32	0	0	0	0	102	LHO
SMITH,JOHN ALLIS	8	13	34	8	39	0	0	0	0	102	LHO
JOHNSON, MARVIN	18	10	16	18	29	3	6	1	0	101	JFK
VINSON,PHILIP E.	16	0	39	10	28	2	1	5	0	101	CHAR
WRIGHT,NORMAN E.	11	2	72	4	7	4	0	1	0	101	CHAR
HOOVER,J.EDGAR	5	3	31	26	28	3	0	4	3	100	JFK
RAY,THOMAS M.	11	4	37	10	30	6	1	1	0	100	CHAR
POTTS,WALTER	7	5	35	14	32	0	1	5	0	99	JFK
SEMIGSEN,W.W.	7	0	35	5	52	0	0	0	1	99	CHAR
DIETRICH,EDWARD	20	1	35	11	31	0	0	1	0	99	LHO
YOUNGBLOOD,R.	7	5	54	17	9	3	1	2	0	98	JFK
LUJAN, DANIEL	18	2	33	7	38	0	0	0	1	98	JFK
SERVANCE, JOHN	7	2	33	5	50	1	0	0	0	98	LHO
ZAPRUDER,ABRAHAM	8	7	39	7	34	0	0	2	0	97	JFK
KAISER,FRANKIE	14	2	41	18	21	0	0	0	0	96	JFK
BARNHORST,COLIN	8	0	27	15	46	0	0	0	0	96	CHAR
BOGARD,ALBERT G.	15	7	34	4	31	3	0	2	0	96	CHAR
RODRIGUEZ,EVARIS	12	6	46	5	23	1	0	3	3	96	CHAR
HUFFAKER,ROBERT	12	2	45	14	21	2	0	0	0	96	LHO
STANDRIDGE,RUTH	8	4	48	10	16	0	3	6	0	95	JFK
MARTELLO,FRANCIS	5	4	42	3	35	6	0	0	2	95	CHAR
REA,BILLY	19	0	38	7	28	2	1	0	0	95	CHAR
RACKLEY,GEORGE	19	5	29	10	23	0	5	3	0	94	JFK
JENKINS,RONALD L	12	3	44	4	27	0	0	4	0	94	LHO
FOLSON,ALLISON G	6	7	37	11	32	0	0	0	0	93	CHAR
MAXEY,BILLY JOE	10	2	30	19	28	2	0	2	0	93	LHO
MILLER,DAVE L.	12	1	70	5	5	0	0	0	0	93	CHAR
McCLELLAND,ROBER	11	14	36	16	5	7	2	1	0	92	JFK
CRULL,ELGIN	11	7	33	12	27	1	0	1	0	92	UNR
ABLES,DON R.	13	5	43	4	25	0	0	1	1	91	JFK
WATSON,JAMES C.	8	4	26	13	35	3	0	2	0	91	LHO
BOWRON,DIANA	11	7	56	3	11	0	1	1	0	90	JFK
MARTIN,B.J.	8	12	36	9	23	0	0	2	0	90	JFK
SMITH,BENNIERITA	9	0	51	10	19	1	0	0	1	90	CHAR
LEBLANC,CHARLES	11	1	33	2	35	2	1	5	0	90	CHAR
HARDIN,MICHAEL	12	2	43	5	27	0	1	0	0	90	LHO
REILLY,FRANK	8	6	29	19	25	0	0	2	0	89	JFK
TAGUE, JAMES	5	11	17	18	34	1	2	1	0	89	JFK
DILLARD,TOM	9	8	19	13	37	0	1	0	2	87	JFK
GERACI,PHILIP	6	0	37	13	28	3	0	0	0	87	CHAR
BLALOCK,VANCE	9	2	50	1	22	1	1	0	0	86	CHAR
SMITH,WILLIAM	13	6	36	7	23	0	0	0	0	85	JDT
LOWERY, ROY LEE	11	6	29	12	27	0	0	0	0	85	LHO
DOWE,KENNETH	23	1	41	13	4	3	0	0	0	85	CHAR
POE,J.M.	19	9	29	9	17	0	1	0	1	84	JDT
KRISS,HARRY	8	1	24	14	37	0	0	0	0	84	LHO

WITNESS	PRE	TP	NV	CL	LH	C	FC	N	OTR	TOTAL	TYPE
SLAUGHTER,MALCOL	8	9	34	7	23	3	0	0	0	84	LHO
HALLMARK,GARNETT	8	4	25	6	38	3	0	0	0	84	CHAR
WALTHERS, EDDY	6	7	17	11	34	5	1	2	0	83	JFK
PIERCE,RIO S.	15	6	32	12	13	3	0	1	0	82	LHO
CABELL,MRS.E.	3	9	25	7	33	2	0	3	0	82	JFK
BARNETT,WELCOME	4	9	16	7	37	5	2	2	0	82	JFK
BOWERS,LEE	5	14	26	13	20	1	0	2	0	81	JFK
HINE, GENEVA	7	7	41	7	16	2	0	1	0	81	JFK
BROOKS,DONALD	9	0	36	8	28	0	0	0	0	81	CHAR
KAUFMAN,STANLEY	7	4	30	14	20	5	0	0	0	80	CHAR
MURPHY,JOE	6	8	29	13	23	0	0	0	0	79	JFK
ROSE, GUY F.	8	7	29	4	30	0	0	1	0	79	JFK
BROWN, C.W.	18	9	24	6	20	0	0	2	0	79	JFK
BOUDREAUX,ANNE	9	0	30	10	24	5	0	1	0	79	CHAR
RHEINSTEIN,FRED	7	1	29	8	33	0	0	1	0	79	LHO
GOODSON,CLYDE	7	1	40	4	27	0	0	0	0	79	LHO
DILLON,DOUGLAS	4	4	29	18	18	1	3	1	0	78	SEC
HENCHCLIFFE,M.	7	6	47	6	10	0	2	0	0	78	JFK
GIBSON,JOHN	8	7	33	12	17	1	0	0	0	78	JDT
WEITZMAN,SEYMOUR	11	8	18	20	20	0	1	0	2	78	JFK
FUQUA,HAROLD	8	2	30	5	33	0	0	0	0	78	LHO
STANDIFER,ROY	8	1	40	0	28	1	0	0	0	78	LHO
HOLLY, HAROLD	11	5	29	9	22	0	0	1	1	77	LHO
HELMS/McCONE	6	7	28	15	16	2	0	2	1	76	JFK
MOLINA, JOE	8	3	41	8	16	0	0	0	0	76	JFK
ADAMS,R.L.	5	0	36	7	28	0	0	0	1	76	CHAR
DUNCAN,WILLIAM	2	4	35	5	27	3	0	0	0	76	CHAR
FINCK,PIERRE	10	7	6	26	8	12	5	1	0	75	JFK
LEE,VINCENT T.	1	5	35	19	14	0	0	1	0	75	CHAR
DAVIS, V.L.	6	3	31	4	29	0	0	2	0	75	CHAR
KELLY,THOMAS J.	6	4	35	15	9	2	2	1	0	74	JFK
WILLIS,PHILLIP	9	11	12	5	33	2	1	1	1	74	JFK
PRICE,CHARLES	5	0	55	7	6	0	0	0	0	73	ADM
HAWKINS, RAY	6	8	25	12	13	0	1	8	0	73	JFK
HANKAL,ROBERT	7	3	25	6	29	1	0	1	0	72	LHO
PERRY, W.E.	8	2	40	2	19	0	0	0	1	71	JFK
JACKSON,THEODORE	10	3	31	5	20	1	0	1	0	71	LHO
JOHNSON,JOSEPH	29	2	27	4	5	4	0	0	0	71	CHAR
BOONE,EUGENE	7	9	17	8	29	0	0	0	0	70	JFK
SLACK,GARLAND	8	7	25	4	26	0	0	0	0	70	CHAR
WOOD,DR.HOMER	7	8	20	4	27	2	0	2	0	70	CHAR
PRIDDY, HAL	6	1	28	9	25	0	0	0	0	69	LHO
JONES,RONALD	6	8	38	7	7	2	0	0	0	68	JFK
STRONG, JESSE	8	7	29	7	15	1	0	1	0	68	LHO
KLEINMAN,ABRAHAM	15	2	41	4	4	2	0	0	0	68	CHAR
McCURDY,DANNY	4	0	29	6	26	3	0	0	0	68	CHAR
GALLAGHER,JOHN	7	9	27	5	14	4	0	1	0	67	JFK
ROBERTSON,MARY J	7	2	20	5	31	1	0	0	0	66	JFK
WULF,WILLIAM E.	14	2	19	2	25	4	0	0	0	66	CHAR
FENLEY,ROBERT	10	0	27	2	27	0	0	0	0	66	CHAR
CARRO,JOHN	13	3	12	13	21	3	0	0	0	65	CHAR

WITNESS	PRE	TP	NV	CL	LH	C	FC	N	OTR	TOTAL	TYPE
BIEBERDORF,FRED	7	5	28	5	20	0	0	0	0	65	LHO
WHITE,J.C.	17	2	16	6	22	0	0	1	0	64	JFK
ROGERS,ERIC	3	4	28	0	24	2	0	3	0	64	CHAR
BAXTER,CHARLES	10	8	24	6	5	6	4	0	0	63	JFK
BURROUGHS,W.	7	2	31	3	19	0	0	1	0	63	JDT
JIMISON,R.J.	11	1	35	2	13	0	0	0	0	62	JFK
MILLER,AUSTIN	12	7	21	8	14	0	0	0	0	62	JFK
SOLOMON,JAMES M.	8	1	21	4	27	1	0	0	0	62	LHO
HUNT,JACKIE	9	7	34	5	6	0	0	0	0	61	JFK
NELSON, DORIS	11	0	36	6	7	0	0	1	1	61	JFK
CRAWFORD,JAMES	8	5	25	3	19	0	0	0	0	60	JFK
SIEGEL,EVELYN	13	1	11	7	26	0	1	1	0	60	CHAR
ISAACS,MARTIN	10	3	18	7	21	0	1	0	0	60	CHAR
SCHMIDT,HUNTER	7	1	22	6	23	1	0	0	0	60	CHAR
PATTERSON,BOBBY	15	4	17	2	22	0	0	0	0	60	LHO
PETERS, PAUL	6	4	26	7	10	1	1	4	0	59	JFK
WESTER,AJANE	11	0	37	6	4	0	0	1	0	59	JFK
ANDERSON,MAJ.E.	11	3	35	0	5	5	0	0	2	59	EXP
ROSSI,JOSEPH	11	4	31	6	6	1	0	0	0	59	CHAR
CASON,FRANCES	8	0	28	2	18	0	0	2	0	58	LHO
JENKINS,MARION	9	6	21	7	8	4	1	1	2	57	JFK
SKELTON,ROYCE	9	6	18	7	16	0	0	1	0	57	JFK
THOMPSON, LLEWEL	3	3	28	5	11	5	1	0	1	56	DIPL
CURTIS,DONALD	10	3	30	6	6	1	0	0	0	56	JFK
CLEMENTS,MANNING	5	11	28	1	8	3	0	0	0	56	JFK
O'SULLIVAN,FREDE	12	8	13	2	20	0	0	0	1	55	CHAR
STEELE,DON F.	8	1	31	6	7	1	0	1	0	55	LHO
AKIN,GENE	11	3	16	11	6	3	3	1	0	54	JFK
LIGHT,FREDERICK	11	2	17	5	13	4	0	1	1	53	JFK
HICKS,J.B.	8	5	18	5	15	2	0	0	0	53	JFK
DANIELS,JOHN	8	4	20	2	17	1	0	1	0	53	LHO
OWENS,CALVIN	9	5	12	9	12	4	0	0	1	51	JDT
LESLIE,HELEN	10	0	19	7	13	1	0	1	0	51	CHAR
AYCOX,JAMES	6	1	30	7	5	1	0	0	0	50	CHAR
KRAVITZ,HERBERT	13	2	21	3	6	4	0	0	0	49	CHAR
RUSK,DEAN	4	4	19	12	9	0	0	0	2	48	DIPL
SMITH,EDGAR	4	3	14	5	21	0	1	0	0	48	JFK
PENA,RUPERTO	4	3	19	2	15	1	0	4	0	48	CHAR
HULSE,C.E.	11	0	19	0	17	0	0	0	0	47	LHO
GIESECKE,ADOLPH	8	4	17	6	7	0	3	0	0	45	JFK
BURNS, DORIS	13	4	8	7	12	0	0	0	0	44	JFK
LEHRER,JAMES	12	0	11	1	18	2	0	0	0	44	CHAR
BASHOUR,FOUAD	7	2	18	7	8	0	1	0	0	43	JFK
DZEMIAN, ARTHUR	11	3	5	7	7	8	0	0	0	41	JFK
HENSLEE, GERALD	9	0	16	5	9	0	0	1	0	40	JFK
RITCHIE,JAMES	8	1	14	1	15	1	0	0	0	40	CHAR
ZAHM,SGT.JAMES	12	2	13	0	6	7	0	0	1	40	EXP
BEAVERS, WILLIAM	8	5	6	8	5	8	0	0	0	40	CHAR
PINKSTON,NAT	9	0	17	1	11	0	0	0	0	38	JFK
HAMBLEN,C.A.	3	4	10	2	18	0	0	1	0	38	CHAR
SCIBOR,MITCHELL	6	8	13	1	8	0	0	1	0	37	JFK

WITNESS	PRE	TP	NV	CL	LH	C	FC	N	OTR	TOTAL	TYPE
SHIELDS.EDWARD	7	2	20	0	7	0	0	1	0	37	JFK
MITCHELL,MARYANN	5	2	13	7	9	0	0	0	0	36	JFK
GAUTHIER,LEO	3	0	17	11	2	0	0	1	0	34	JFK
HARGIS,BOBBY W.	4	5	10	6	9	0	0	0	1	34	JFK
SAWYER,MILDRED	6	2	12	0	13	0	0	1	0	34	CHAR
DONABEDIAN,GEORG	4	0	11	7	10	0	0	0	0	32	CHAR
KENNEDY,MRS.JOHN	2	2	10	8	8	1	0	0	0	31	JFK
SALYER, KENNETH	9	4	13	4	1	0	0	0	0	31	JFK
UNDERWOOD,JAMES	4	1	10	2	13	0	0	1	0	31	JFK
CASTER,WARREN	7	6	13	0	4	0	0	0	0	30	CHAR
WHITE,MARTIN	10	2	13	1	3	0	0	0	0	29	JFK
OLDS,GREGORY L.	6	2	14	4	2	0	0	0	0	28	CHAR
NICHOLS,H.LOUIS	7	1	8	4	8	0	0	0	0	28	CHAR
TORMEY,JAMES J.	1	2	16	3	5	0	0	0	0	27	CHAR
KELLY,EDWARD	9	0	9	1	8	0	0	0	0	27	LHO
CONNALLY,MRS.J.	2	3	11	3	4	1	0	0	0	24	JFK
ROSS, HENRIETTA	5	0	14	1	3	0	0	1	0	24	JFK
COULTER,HARRIS	11	0	5	2	5	0	0	0	0	23	UNR
DULANY,RICHARD	9	1	10	1	2	0	0	0	0	23	JFK
STEELE,CHAS.SR.	8	0	5	0	8	0	0	1	0	22	CHAR
BIGGIO,WILLIAM	3	1	4	2	10	0	0	0	0	20	LHO
WILLIS,LINDA	3	4	4	1	6	0	0	0	1	18	JFK
HOWLETT,JOHN JOE	2	1	3	4	6	0	0	0	1	16	JFK
WOOD,THERESA	3	0	7	0	5	0	0	1	0	16	CHAR
BOSWELL, J.T.	5	3	0	2	3	1	0	0	0	14	JFK
CARR,WAGGONER	2	2	3	2	2	0	0	0	0	11	JFK
ABT, JOHN J.	3	0	2	1	3	0	0	0	0	9	CHAR
BAKER.T.L.	3	0	1	1	3	0	0	0	0	8	JFK
CARSWELL,ROBERT	2	0	2	1	0	0	0	0	0	5	UNR

WITNESS	PRE	TP	NV	CL	LH	C	FC	N	OTR	TOTAL	TYPE
OSWALD, MARINA	22	217	1411	444	361	46	56	58	5	2615	CHAR
SENATOR,GEORGE	131	87	1282	540	656	81	2	13	2	2792	CHAR
CRAFARD,CURTIS L	223	83	2296	270	985	67	4	44	2	3972	CHAR
McWATTERS, C.	13	81	198	68	50	3	35	29	1	477	JFK
RUBY,JACK	10	79	277	322	67	5	0	0	4	760	LHO
BRENNAN,HOWARD	15	72	47	143	27	1	1	1	1	307	JFK
KELLERMAN,ROY	9	67	271	168	154	32	8	15	1	724	JFK
SORRELS,FORREST	19	57	251	54	194	12	4	7	0	598	JFK
ARMSTRONG,ANDREW	42	53	790	121	547	19	3	17	1	1592	CHAR
SIMS,RICHARD	6	48	294	51	199	16	3	16	0	633	JFK
OSWALD, MARG.	9	48	169	317	39	8	3	22	1	615	CHAR
GRAVES, L.C.	29	45	152	33	76	6	0	5	3	346	LHO
HILL, JEAN L.	6	44	107	65	65	2	1	2	1	292	JFK
DEMOHRENSCHILDT,	18	43	585	239	649	38	6	50	0	1628	CHAR
BOYD, ELMER	5	40	187	26	94	6	0	12	0	370	JFK
BARNES, W.E.	15	36	152	26	74	10	5	7	1	325	JDT
CURRY,JESSE E.	14	34	458	158	323	5	6	4	8	1002	LHO
OSWALD,ROBT	15	33	1179	560	400	124	8	32	15	2351	CHAR
MAMANTOV,ILYA	29	32	156	45	146	15	6	15	4	444	JFK
RICH,NANCY PERRI	103	31	228	77	159	1	0	2	0	601	CHAR
PAUL,RALPH	14	30	411	118	360	15	1	7	0	956	CHAR
SHANEYFELT, L.	14	30	259	160	217	17	1	1	4	699	JFK
HOLMES,HARRY D.	11	30	103	41	97	3	3	11	2	299	JFK
HUMES,JAMES J.	7	30	17	79	41	21	13	7	1	215	JFK
CRAIG, ROGER	21	29	82	29	56	2	4	3	0	226	JFK
LATONA,SEBASTIAN	7	27	192	99	225	16	4	1	9	571	JFK
HARRISON,WILLIAM	19	27	260	52	84	8	1	1	4	452	LHO
OLSEN,HARRY N.	34	27	273	16	11	12	0	4	2	377	LHO
ODIO,SYLVIA	14	27	121	15	127	8	0	4	1	316	CHAR
GRANT,EVA	11	26	442	132	201	96	1	9	8	918	CHAR
FRAZIER,ROBT.	11	26	392	130	213	21	7	4	8	804	JFK
BATCHELOR,CHARLE	10	26	230	50	94	9	0	3	3	422	LHO
PAINE,RUTH	10	25	2181	801	1995	155	31	38	15	5236	CHAR
COLE,ALWYN	13	25	263	65	86	9	1	0	8	462	JFK
PENA,OREST	8	25	93	19	125	1	0	5	0	276	CHAR
CARRICO,CHARLES	13	25	105	24	20	5	9	2	1	203	JFK
HERNDON, BELL	13	25	57	36	10	7	0	0	1	148	LHO
LEAVELLE,JAMES	20	24	103	19	84	2	0	2	1	254	JFK
DEAN,PATRICK	22	23	308	131	66	2	0	2	6	554	LHO
MONTGOMERY,L.D.	22	23	165	72	63	4	0	3	2	352	LHO
ROWLEY,JAMES	7	23	145	67	75	15	5	8	8	345	SEC
NEWMAN,WILLIAM	34	23	183	33	55	6	0	0	0	334	LHO
VAUGHAN,ROY	9	23	110	13	68	7	1	3	0	234	LHO
WALDMAN,WILLIAM	8	23	48	16	30	1	4	4	1	134	JFK
RUBENSTEIN,HYMAN	268	22	190	99	91	12	0	2	0	684	CHAR
WILLIAMS,BONNIE	10	22	172	44	131	1	4	4	0	388	JFK
CADIGAN,JAMES	12	22	145	69	106	5	1	1	4	361	JFK
DAVIS, C.V.	13	22	145	44	95	0	2	2	0	323	JDT
BOUHE,GEORGE	17	22	128	23	90	20	3	3	0	306	CHAR
TURNER,F.M.	18	22	93	15	43	1	0	2	0	194	JFK
BAKER,MARRION	8	21	199	64	144	6	5	7	5	454	JFK

WITNESS	PRE	TP	NV	CL	LH	C	FC	N	OTR	TOTAL	TYPE
HILL.GERALD	9	21	88	35	66	2	0	2	0	223	JFK
GUINYARD,SAM	12	21	46	5	58	1	1	1	0	145	JDT
CARROLL,BOB K.	12	21	70	8	29	0	4	0	0	144	JFK
SNYDER,RICHARD	7	20	141	71	110	13	2	3	1	367	CHAR
OLIVIER, ALFRED	7	20	76	55	27	23	0	0	2	208	JFK
CLARK,WILLIAM K.	8	20	71	19	22	4	6	2	0	152	JFK
EUINS.AMOS LEE	11	20	48	37	23	5	0	2	0	146	JFK
BOOKHOUT.JAMES	5	20	64	10	35	4	2	2	1	142	JFK
FISCHER,RONALD	21	20	46	28	19	0	1	0	0	135	JFK
MURRET.LILLIAN	7	19	272	122	364	42	10	45	0	881	CHAR
ARNETT.CHARLES	25	19	301	97	88	5	0	0	3	535	LHO
CROWE.WILLIAM	30	19	159	27	97	8	0	2	0	342	CHAR
WALKER,GEN.EDWIN	7	19	123	37	116	5	2	6	6	315	CHAR
COUCH,MALCOLM	14	19	43	13	50	1	4	0	0	144	JFK
SHIRES,GEORGE	9	19	44	17	21	6	2	0	1	118	JFK
WEISMAN,BERNARD	12	18	368	107	208	7	0	18	0	738	JFK
DEMOHRENSCHILDT,	23	18	176	66	241	15	1	15	1	555	CHAR
LAWSON,WINSTON	9	18	173	89	124	4	5	2	7	424	JFK
WADE, HENRY	5	18	175	64	52	4	2	11	4	331	JFK
OFSTEIN,DENNIS	12	18	162	13	106	11	0	3	0	325	CHAR
NICHOLS,ALICE R.	18	18	215	24	27	5	0	0	0	307	CHAR
KANTOR.SETH	14	18	154	54	44	3	0	0	1	287	CHAR
LITCHFIELD,W.W.	33	18	58	16	89	6	1	1	0	222	CHAR
ADAMCIK, JOHN	21	18	74	11	28	3	0	1	0	156	JFK
BAKER,MRS.DON	3	18	22	29	59	4	2	5	0	142	JFK
HOSTY,JAMES P.	9	17	235	118	94	3	5	3	4	484	JFK
MILLER,LOUIS D.	16	17	192	18	14	2	0	2	1	261	LHO
O'DONNELL,KENNET	3	17	129	3	23	3	3	5	0	186	JFK
PAPPAS,ICARUS	9	17	108	26	17	4	0	1	0	182	LHO
CONNALLY,JOHN	3	17	94	24	21	0	3	2	0	164	JFK
MARKHAM,HELEN	4	16	165	79	176	0	2	0	0	442	JDT
OLSEN.KAY HELEN	31	16	236	25	19	5	0	8	0	340	LHO
GREGORY,PAUL R.	11	16	120	8	66	14	3	6	0	244	CHAR
MEYERS,LAWRENCE	22	16	117	27	12	5	0	1	1	200	CHAR
MICHAELIS,HEINZ	17	16	41	14	55	0	0	2	1	145	JDT
COMBEST. B.H.	10	16	52	8	54	5	0	0	0	145	LHO
SURREY.ROBERT A.	17	15	188	126	142	8	7	10	0	513	WALKE
CUNNINGHAM,CORT.	8	15	152	142	129	24	7	11	1	488	JFK
CUTCHSHAW,WILBUR	13	15	178	26	54	10	0	0	2	296	LHO
STEVENSON,M.W.	12	15	112	24	78	8	1	3	1	253	LHO
STUDEBAKER,ROBT.	5	15	78	42	102	6	1	3	0	252	JFK
CHAYES.ABRAM	5	15	46	60	98	6	1	3	6	234	CHAR
PITTS,ELNORA	8	15	75	19	69	2	0	2	0	190	LHO
DHORITY, C.N.	7	15	79	18	51	2	0	1	0	173	JFK
DELGADO,NELSON	25	14	219	72	200	24	5	4	1	563	CHAR
CARLIN,KAREN B.	10	14	182	13	162	7	0	6	1	394	LHO
ROWLAND,ARNOLD	20	14	210	78	48	14	0	5	0	389	JFK
FEHRENBACH,GEORG	105	14	135	32	83	9	0	5	0	383	CHAR
TALBERT.CECIL	15	14	161	41	110	4	0	0	9	345	LHO
McMILLON,THOMAS	18	14	172	38	43	2	0	1	1	288	LHO
WALL,BRECK	40	14	178	16	27	4	0	5	0	284	CHAR

WITNESS	PRE	TP	NV	CL	LH	C	FC	N	OTR	TOTAL	TYPE
ROWLAND,BARBARA	24	14	116	23	80	3	3	11	0	274	JFK
REEVES, HUEY	14	14	99	17	63	4	0	1	0	212	LHO
BENAVIDES,DOMING	22	14	77	25	47	0	0	1	0	186	JDT
ALBA,ADRIAN	8	14	61	6	55	7	1	1	0	153	CHAR
EDWARDS,ROBERT	13	14	33	24	18	0	0	3	0	105	JFK
McCLELLAND,ROBER	11	14	36	16	5	7	2	1	0	92	JFK
BOWERS,LEE	5	14	26	13	20	1	0	2	0	81	JFK
PIC,JOHN E.	18	13	509	147	569	38	1	30	2	1325	CHAR
PAINE,MICHAEL	8	13	482	161	297	37	7	14	1	1019	CHAR
CROY,KENNETH	17	13	265	42	54	5	2	2	0	400	LHO
SHAW,ROBERT	12	13	142	60	58	5	3	0	6	293	JFK
HALL,ELENA	14	13	114	16	61	14	1	6	0	239	CHAR
ROBERTS,EARLENE	13	13	89	21	63	0	2	2	0	203	JFK
HILL,CLINT	6	13	102	25	18	5	3	3	0	175	JFK
DONOVAN, JOHN E.	6	13	89	10	28	14	3	3	0	166	CHAR
SAWYER, J.H.	15	13	51	24	52	1	2	3	0	161	JFK
FOSTER,J.W.	14	13	31	19	37	0	0	0	2	114	JFK
SMITH,JOHN ALLIS	8	13	34	8	39	0	0	0	0	102	LHO
FRAZIER,BUELL W.	16	12	218	127	180	3	5	5	0	566	JFK
MURRET,MARILYN	23	12	151	41	119	22	7	8	0	383	CHAR
GREER,WM.	6	12	156	31	46	17	1	3	1	272	JFK
RYDER,DIAL D.	26	12	59	11	82	9	0	0	0	199	CHAR
WORRELL,JAMES R.	13	12	90	45	23	3	0	2	0	188	JFK
McDONALD,M.N.	9	12	74	8	62	2	2	0	0	169	JDT
WALKER, C.T.	21	12	67	17	34	5	1	3	0	160	JFK
JACKSON,ROBT.H.	14	12	55	32	21	6	1	1	0	142	JFK
CLARK,MAX	8	12	68	10	27	7	2	0	1	134	CHAR
SMITH,JOE M.	9	12	48	4	50	1	1	1	0	126	JFK
MARTIN,B.J.	8	12	36	9	23	0	0	2	0	90	JFK
FRITZ, WILL	9	11	268	130	412	10	2	1	1	843	JFK
REVILL,JACK	25	11	187	103	155	3	0	4	1	488	LHO
JARMIN,JAMES	8	11	158	23	107	4	1	0	0	312	JFK
BEATY,BUFORD L.	14	11	112	47	30	3	0	0	0	217	LHO
JONES,O.A.	9	11	67	33	61	0	0	3	4	184	LHO
SEELEY,CARROLL	15	11	69	13	69	0	0	1	0	178	CHAR
BALLEN,SAMUEL B.	10	11	101	6	31	7	2	1	0	169	CHAR
APPLIN, GEORGE	12	11	40	24	46	0	0	3	0	136	JFK
CALLAWAY,TED	8	11	49	11	48	0	0	0	1	127	JDT
HUDSON, EMMETT	6	11	47	9	48	4	0	1	0	126	JFK
DAVIS,FLOYD G.	7	11	30	6	45	7	2	1	0	109	CHAR
BROWN, EARLE	7	11	35	18	32	0	0	1	0	104	JFK
TAGUE, JAMES	5	11	17	18	34	1	2	1	0	89	JFK
WILLIS,PHILLIP	9	11	12	5	33	2	1	1	1	74	JFK
CLEMENTS,MANNING	5	11	28	1	8	3	0	0	0	56	JFK
TRULY,ROY	12	10	214	74	150	12	8	2	2	482	JFK
DAY, J.C.	8	10	248	87	120	2	3	0	0	478	JFK
PERRY,MALCOLM	13	10	204	42	51	11	10	3	2	344	JFK
POWERS,DANIEL P.	3	10	136	57	87	19	5	3	1	320	CHAR
MOORE,RUSSELL L.	23	10	152	21	22	10	0	1	0	239	CHAR
SHELLEY, WILLIAM	10	10	93	25	85	2	3	5	0	233	JFK
BELMONT,ALAN H.	7	10	74	76	51	7	2	2	1	229	SEC

WITNESS	PRE	TP	NV	CL	LH	C	FC	N	OTR	TOTAL	TYPE
GIVENS,CHARLES	33	10	100	18	54	3	0	7	0	225	JFK
NICOL,JOSEPH	2	10	58	50	78	3	3	1	2	205	JFK
TURNER,JIMMY	12	10	60	22	59	6	0	0	2	169	LHO
BREWER,JOHNNY	17	10	69	9	40	1	0	1	0	147	JDT
MOONEY,LUKE	9	10	57	17	49	0	0	1	0	143	JFK
HARKNESS,D.V.	18	10	62	19	31	2	0	0	0	142	JFK
ARCHER,DON RAY	10	10	45	13	41	3	0	0	0	122	LHO
KING,GLEN D.	12	10	41	12	43	4	0	0	0	122	UNR
CABELL,EARLE	6	10	48	3	50	0	1	2	0	120	JFK
RICHEY,WARREN E.	9	10	46	11	38	1	0	0	0	115	LHO
HALL,JOHN R.	15	10	41	6	28	13	0	1	0	114	CHAR
WALKER, IRA N.	10	10	38	7	43	2	0	1	0	111	LHO
MAYO,LOGAN W.	13	10	52	8	25	0	0	1	1	109	LHO
WIGGINS,WOODROW	16	10	36	10	32	2	0	2	0	108	LHO
JOHNSON, MARVIN	18	10	16	18	29	3	6	1	0	101	JFK
STOMBAUGH,PAUL	6	9	169	69	113	5	3	5	1	379	JFK
SCOGGINS, WM.	11	9	150	37	114	3	0	2	2	326	JDT
WHALEY,WILLIAM	7	9	87	68	110	2	0	1	0	284	JFK
CARLIN,BRUCE RAY	22	9	120	26	98	3	0	2	0	280	LHO
BOUCK,ROBERT	6	9	83	46	87	3	3	2	5	239	JFK
DANIELS,NAPOLEON	10	9	40	21	79	1	0	2	0	162	LHO
PRICE,MALCOLM	11	9	58	8	72	2	0	1	0	161	CHAR
WOOD,STERLING	8	9	70	5	53	3	0	1	0	149	CHAR
WATHERWAX,ARTHUR	13	9	58	7	54	7	0	1	0	149	CHAR
STOVALL,RICHARD	9	9	50	20	49	0	1	2	1	140	JFK
HOLLAND,S.M.	5	9	33	35	53	2	1	0	2	138	JFK
HUTSON,THOMAS	20	9	54	17	27	0	4	4	0	135	JFK
RAY,MRS.THOMAS	12	9	56	14	29	3	3	1	0	127	CHAR
ROBERTSON,VICTOR	11	9	79	3	8	7	0	0	0	117	LHO
ALTGENS,JAMES	9	9	22	21	48	0	0	3	0	112	JFK
POE,J.M.	19	9	29	9	17	0	1	0	1	84	JDT
SLAUGHTER,MALCOL	8	9	34	7	23	3	0	0	0	84	LHO
CABELL,MRS.E.	3	9	25	7	33	2	0	3	0	82	JFK
BARNETT,WELCOME	4	9	16	7	37	5	2	2	0	82	JFK
BROWN, C.W.	18	9	24	6	20	0	0	2	0	79	JFK
BOONE,EUGENE	7	9	17	8	29	0	0	0	0	70	JFK
GALLAGHER,JOHN	7	9	27	5	14	4	0	1	0	67	JFK
THORNLEY,KERRY	10	8	157	42	161	32	1	6	0	417	CHAR
NORMAN,HAROLD	11	8	123	18	83	2	1	1	2	247	JFK
ANDREWS,DEAN A.	3	8	89	8	95	1	0	0	1	204	CHAR
GREGORY,CHARLES	11	8	112	40	16	4	1	2	1	194	JFK
SMART,VERNON	14	8	109	25	23	3	0	0	2	182	LHO
CLARDY,BARNARD	10	8	61	16	67	8	0	1	1	171	LHO
BENTON,NELSON	7	8	91	16	46	0	0	1	0	169	LHO
WHITWORTH,EDITH	10	8	77	8	50	5	1	7	0	166	CHAR
O'BRIEN,LAWRENCE	1	8	100	4	46	0	1	3	0	163	JFK
MELLER,ANNA	13	8	69	20	31	10	1	4	1	156	CHAR
REYNOLDS, WARREN	11	8	48	4	58	8	0	2	0	139	JDT
HAYGOOD,CLYDE	16	8	55	18	29	0	1	3	0	130	JFK
ADAMS,VICTORIA	13	8	59	13	22	0	1	1	0	117	JFK
GREENER,CHARLES	2	8	43	7	42	5	0	1	0	108	CHAR

WITNESS	PRE	TP	NV	CL	LH	C	FC	N	OTR	TOTAL	TYPE
DILLARD,TOM	9	8	19	13	37	0	1	0	2	87	JFK
MURPHY,JOE	6	8	29	13	23	0	0	0	0	79	JFK
WEITZMAN,SEYMOUR	11	8	18	20	20	0	1	0	2	78	JFK
HAWKINS, RAY	6	8	25	12	13	0	1	8	0	73	JFK
WOOD,DR.HOMER	7	8	20	4	27	2	0	2	0	70	CHAR
JONES,RONALD	6	8	38	7	7	2	0	0	0	68	JFK
BAXTER,CHARLES	10	8	24	6	5	6	4	0	0	63	JFK
O'SULLIVAN,FREDE	12	8	13	2	20	0	0	0	1	55	CHAR
SCIBOR,MITCHELL	6	8	13	1	8	0	0	1	0	37	JFK
RUBY,EARL	28	7	585	124	182	13	0	8	0	947	CHAR
BLEDSOE,MARY	6	7	212	77	190	7	10	13	1	522	CHAR
GLOVER,EVERETT	32	7	180	53	131	11	1	9	1	424	CHAR
LANE, MARK	8	7	81	98	40	7	0	7	0	248	CHAR
DOUGHERTY,JACK	22	7	89	14	68	0	2	2	0	204	JFK
KLAUSE,ROBERT	2	7	100	18	70	1	0	0	0	198	JFK
LANE,DOYLE E.	9	7	66	3	47	0	0	2	0	134	LHO
ROMACK,JAMES E.	31	7	47	14	20	2	1	2	0	124	JFK
PIPER, EDDIE	12	7	50	14	37	0	1	1	0	122	JFK
MOORE, HENRY	21	7	44	5	29	0	2	2	0	110	JFK
ARCE, DANNY	13	7	50	13	24	0	1	1	0	109	JFK
McCULLOUGH,JOHN	6	7	57	20	11	5	0	1	0	107	LHO
ZAPRUDER,ABRAHAM	8	7	39	7	34	0	0	2	0	97	JFK
BOGARD,ALBERT G.	15	7	34	4	31	3	0	2	0	96	CHAR
FOLSON,ALLISON G	6	7	37	11	32	0	0	0	0	93	CHAR
CRULL,ELGIN	11	7	33	12	27	1	0	1	0	92	UNR
BOWRON,DIANA	11	7	56	3	11	0	1	1	0	90	JFK
WALTHERS, EDDY	6	7	17	11	34	5	1	2	0	83	JFK
HINE, GENEVA	7	7	41	7	16	2	0	1	0	81	JFK
ROSE, GUY F.	8	7	29	4	30	0	0	1	0	79	JFK
GIBSON,JOHN	8	7	33	12	17	1	0	0	0	78	JDT
HELMS/McCONE	6	7	28	15	16	2	0	2	1	76	JFK
FINCK,PIERRE	10	7	6	26	8	12	5	1	0	75	JFK
SLACK,GARLAND	8	7	25	4	26	0	0	0	0	70	CHAR
STRONG, JESSE	8	7	29	7	15	1	0	1	0	68	LHO
MILLER,AUSTIN	12	7	21	8	14	0	0	0	0	62	JFK
HUNT,JACKIE	9	7	34	5	6	0	0	0	0	61	JFK
MARTIN,JAMES	10	6	562	196	168	35	0	2	10	979	CHAR
GIBSON,MRS.DON	8	6	215	33	261	22	2	13	0	560	CHAR
POWELL,NANCY M.	22	6	226	42	60	12	0	1	0	369	CHAR
NEWMAN,JOHN	11	6	107	13	66	3	0	0	0	206	CHAR
EBERHARDT,A.M.	12	6	126	24	27	9	0	0	2	204	CHAR
DAVIS,MRS.B.J.	1	6	95	31	64	2	0	0	1	199	JDT
PETERSON, JOSEPH	29	6	118	15	21	4	1	2	0	196	LHO
MURRET,C.DUTZ	11	6	65	10	77	4	1	2	0	176	CHAR
JOHNSON,GLADYS	6	6	82	4	74	2	0	1	0	175	CHAR
PRYOR,ROY	11	6	60	9	72	10	0	2	0	170	CHAR
PIZZO,FRANK	8	6	27	20	95	0	0	9	1	165	CHAR
TASKER, HARRY	5	6	65	22	50	3	0	1	0	152	LHO
WESTBROOK, W.R.	7	6	57	36	43	0	0	1	0	150	JFK
PALMER,THOMAS	14	6	85	8	11	8	0	0	0	132	CHAR
RAY,MRS.FRANK H.	16	6	55	9	28	12	2	0	0	128	CHAR

WITNESS	PRE	TP	NV	CL	LH	C	FC	N	OTR	TOTAL	TYPE
HUNTER,GERTRUDE	8	6	53	2	51	4	0	1	0	125	CHAR
PUTNAM,JAMES	17	6	30	17	47	2	0	3	0	122	JDT
JOHNSTON,DAVID L	15	6	42	6	43	3	0	1	0	116	JFK
TICE,WILMA	20	6	40	18	25	3	1	1	0	114	CHAR
BEERS,IRA J.	11	6	62	12	10	3	0	0	0	104	LHO
STOVALL,ROBERT	10	6	27	9	46	1	1	3	1	103	CHAR
RODRIGUEZ,EVARIS	12	6	46	5	23	1	0	3	3	96	CHAR
REILLY,FRANK	8	6	29	19	25	0	0	2	0	89	JFK
SMITH,WILLIAM	13	6	36	7	23	0	0	0	0	85	JDT
LOWERY, ROY LEE	11	6	29	12	27	0	0	0	0	85	LHO
PIERCE,RIO S.	15	6	32	12	13	3	0	1	0	82	LHO
HENCHCLIFFE,M.	7	6	47	6	10	0	2	0	0	78	JFK
JENKINS,MARION	9	6	21	7	8	4	1	1	2	57	JFK
SKELTON,ROYCE	9	6	18	7	16	0	0	1	0	57	JFK
CASTER,WARREN	7	6	13	0	4	0	0	0	0	30	CHAR
TAYLOR,GARY E.	21	5	225	42	131	17	4	27	3	472	CHAR
FAIN,JOHN W.	7	5	178	82	65	2	6	1	2	346	CHAR
CHEEK,BERTHA	11	5	197	40	52	5	0	0	0	310	CHAR
HUTCHISON, L.E.	9	5	87	22	131	5	1	1	0	261	CHAR
VOEBEL,EDWARD	5	5	106	10	66	15	1	8	0	216	CHAR
BATES,PAULINE V.	12	5	68	55	58	3	0	3	0	204	CHAR
JOHNSON,ARNOLD S	2	5	109	21	27	9	0	3	0	176	CHAR
RICHEY,MARJORIE	31	5	88	20	12	4	0	0	0	160	LHO
WORLEY, G.E.	14	5	101	22	14	0	0	0	0	156	LHO
QUIGLEY,JOHN L.	8	5	63	29	19	5	0	1	2	130	CHAR
WEST, TROY	17	5	67	10	27	0	0	0	0	126	JFK
SIMMONS,RONALD	7	5	47	31	26	6	2	1	0	125	JFK
MURRET,JOHN	12	5	52	7	38	8	1	1	0	124	CHAR
COX,ROLAND A.	8	5	57	8	40	1	0	0	0	119	LHO
FLEMING,HAROLD	11	5	50	10	42	1	0	0	0	119	LHO
DECKER,BILL	12	5	32	20	47	0	0	0	0	116	LHO
MARTIN,FRANK M.	11	5	43	12	33	8	1	1	0	114	LHO
HANSEN,T.M.	14	5	59	26	7	3	0	0	0	114	CHAR
EVANS,SIDNEY	12	5	38	5	44	0	0	2	0	106	LHO
PHENIX,GEORGE	12	5	31	11	41	3	0	1	0	104	LHO
SLACK,WILLIE	11	5	42	9	31	1	0	4	0	103	LHO
POTTS,WALTER	7	5	35	14	32	0	1	5	0	99	JFK
YOUNGBLOOD,R.	7	5	54	17	9	3	1	2	0	98	JFK
RACKLEY,GEORGE	19	5	29	10	23	0	5	3	0	94	JFK
ABLES,DON R.	13	5	43	4	25	0	0	1	1	91	JFK
HOLLY, HAROLD	11	5	29	9	22	0	0	1	1	77	LHO
LEE,VINCENT T.	1	5	35	19	14	0	0	1	0	75	CHAR
BIEBERDORF,FRED	7	5	28	5	20	0	0	0	0	65	LHO
CRAWFORD,JAMES	8	5	25	3	19	0	0	0	0	60	JFK
HICKS,J.B.	8	5	18	5	15	2	0	0	0	53	JFK
OWENS,CALVIN	9	5	12	9	12	4	0	0	1	51	JDT
BEAVERS, WILLIAM	8	5	6	8	5	8	0	0	0	40	CHAR
HARGIS,BOBBY W.	4	5	10	6	9	0	0	0	1	34	JFK
TOBIAS,MRS.MAHLO	4	4	108	47	187	4	2	28	0	384	CHAR
FORD,KATHERINE	5	4	178	75	100	14	1	1	0	378	CHAR
EVANS,MYRTLE	2	4	96	40	85	18	6	6	0	257	CHAR

WITNESS	PRE	TP	NV	CL	LH	C	FC	N	OTR	TOTAL	TYPE
FORD.DECLAN	11	4	68	30	52	14	0	1	0	180	CHAR
LEWIS,AUBREY L.	16	4	68	5	49	0	0	0	0	142	CHAR
GOIN. DON E.	12	4	72	10	31	0	0	3	0	132	LHO
McVICKAR,JOHN	7	4	33	24	54	4	2	0	1	128	CHAR
PIERCE,EDWARD E.	9	4	50	6	54	1	0	0	0	124	LHO
HALL,C.RAY	9	4	36	13	52	3	0	2	0	119	LHO
BREWER, E.D.	9	4	65	11	24	0	2	2	0	117	JFK
SANDERS.RICHARD	4	4	56	13	38	1	0	1	0	117	CHAR
JOHNSON.PRISCILL	5	4	44	27	27	7	0	2	2	116	CHAR
LAWRENCE. PERDUE	16	4	74	9	3	1	2	0	0	109	JFK
LOVELADY. BILLY	6	4	42	18	32	1	2	1	0	106	JFK
FRAZIER.CAPT.W.	11	4	42	13	32	0	0	0	0	102	LHO
RAY.THOMAS M.	11	4	37	10	30	6	1	1	0	100	CHAR
STANDRIDGE.RUTH	8	4	48	10	16	0	3	6	0	95	JFK
MARTELLO,FRANCIS	5	4	42	3	35	6	0	0	2	95	CHAR
WATSON.JAMES C.	8	4	26	13	35	3	0	2	0	91	LHO
HALLMARK,GARNETT	8	4	25	6	38	3	0	0	0	84	CHAR
KAUFMAN,STANLEY	7	4	30	14	20	5	0	0	0	80	CHAR
DILLON.DOUGLAS	4	4	29	18	18	1	3	1	0	78	SEC
DUNCAN.WILLIAM	2	4	35	5	27	3	0	0	0	76	CHAR
KELLY.THOMAS J.	6	4	35	15	9	2	2	1	0	74	JFK
ROGERS.ERIC	3	4	28	0	24	2	0	3	0	64	CHAR
PATTERSON.BOBBY	15	4	17	2	22	0	0	0	0	60	LHO
PETERS. PAUL	6	4	26	7	10	1	1	4	0	59	JFK
ROSSI.JOSEPH	11	4	31	6	6	1	0	0	0	59	CHAR
DANIELS.JOHN	8	4	20	2	17	1	0	1	0	53	LHO
RUSK,DEAN	4	4	19	12	9	0	0	0	2	48	DIPL
GIESECKE.ADOLPH	8	4	17	6	7	0	3	0	0	45	JFK
BURNS, DORIS	13	4	8	7	12	0	0	0	0	44	JFK
HAMBLEN,C.A.	3	4	10	2	18	0	0	1	0	38	CHAR
SALYER. KENNETH	9	4	13	4	1	0	0	0	0	31	JFK
WILLIS.LINDA	3	4	4	1	6	0	0	0	1	18	JFK
OLIVER.REVILO	17	3	169	105	104	0	0	1	4	399	UNR
TOBIAS,MAHLON	3	3	79	18	110	4	4	8	1	229	CHAR
RUBY.SAM	9	3	136	17	51	5	0	0	0	221	CHAR
WATERMAN.BERNICE	4	3	49	54	78	2	2	2	2	194	CHAR
GARNER.MRS.JESSE	7	3	77	6	88	2	1	6	0	190	CHAR
BRINGUIER,CARLOS	10	3	59	42	65	2	0	2	5	183	CHAR
KAMINSKY.EILEEN	48	3	71	25	25	3	1	3	0	179	CHAR
STEELE.CHAS JR.	7	3	83	9	63	1	0	5	0	171	CHAR
JOHNSON.A.C.	13	3	101	1	46	1	0	0	0	165	CHAR
KRYSTINIK,RAYMON	11	3	66	8	45	13	3	0	0	149	CHAR
EVANS.JULIAN	5	3	38	11	71	13	2	0	0	143	CHAR
JAMES.VIRGINIA	6	3	65	15	52	1	0	0	0	142	CHAR
PATTERSON. R.C.	16	3	85	13	21	0	0	0	0	138	CHAR
HALL.MARVIN E.	10	3	75	7	35	2	1	5	0	138	LHO
HODGE,ALFRED	12	3	42	9	54	2	0	0	0	122	CHAR
MANDELLA,ARTHUR	5	3	30	34	40	3	2	1	0	118	JFK
CLARK,RICHARD	10	3	53	7	31	0	0	2	1	106	JFK
WALDO.THAYER	10	3	37	7	46	2	0	1	0	106	LHO
TOMLINSON,D.	17	3	32	19	31	0	2	0	1	104	JFK

WITNESS	PRE	TP	NV	CL	LH	C	FC	N	OTR	TOTAL	TYPE
POSTAL,JULIA	14	3	36	9	39	0	0	1	0	102	JDT
HOOVER,J.EDGAR	5	3	31	26	28	3	0	4	3	100	JFK
JENKINS,RONALD L	12	3	44	4	27	0	0	4	0	94	LHO
MOLINA, JOE	8	3	41	8	16	0	0	0	0	76	JFK
DAVIS, V.L.	6	3	31	4	29	0	0	2	0	75	CHAR
HANKAL,ROBERT	7	3	25	6	29	1	0	1	0	72	LHO
JACKSON,THEODORE	10	3	31	5	20	1	0	1	0	71	LHO
CARRO,JOHN	13	3	12	19	21	9	0	0	0	66	CHAR
ISAACS,MARTIN	10	3	18	7	21	0	1	0	0	60	CHAR
ANDERSON,MAJ.E.	11	3	35	0	5	5	0	0	2	59	EXP
THOMPSON, LLEWEL	3	3	28	5	11	5	1	0	1	56	DIPL
CURTIS,DONALD	10	3	30	6	6	1	0	0	0	56	JFK
AKIN,GENE	11	3	16	11	6	3	3	1	0	54	JFK
SMITH,EDGAR	4	3	14	5	21	0	1	0	0	48	JFK
PENA,RUPERTO	4	3	19	2	15	1	0	4	0	48	CHAR
DZEMIAN. ARTHUR	11	3	5	7	7	8	0	0	0	41	JFK
CONNALLY,MRS.J.	2	3	11	3	4	1	0	0	0	24	JFK
BOSWELL, J.T.	5	3	0	2	3	1	0	0	0	14	JFK
RAIGORODSKY,P.	8	2	182	43	85	16	1	5	8	342	CHAR
VOSHININ, IGOR	30	2	89	93	106	6	0	5	0	331	CHAR
STUCKEY,WILLIAM	5	2	108	46	108	8	0	5	0	282	CHAR
GRAEF,JOHN	5	2	76	22	85	5	5	10	1	210	CHAR
BRANCH,JOHN	14	2	85	15	76	4	2	3	0	201	CHAR
REID,MRS.ROBT	10	2	79	19	82	3	3	2	0	200	JFK
McKINZIE,LOUIS	15	2	53	7	92	0	0	1	0	170	LHO
BRIAN,V.J.	6	2	69	42	41	0	0	4	0	164	CHAR
GRAVITIS,DOROTHY	26	2	75	18	28	7	4	1	0	161	CHAR
MUMFORD,PAMELA	6	2	79	4	54	3	0	0	0	148	CHAR
HELMICK,WANDA	18	2	84	17	15	4	0	0	0	140	LHO
KNIGHT,FRANCES	7	2	33	24	61	3	1	6	0	137	CHAR
PULLMAN,EDWARD	14	2	81	14	15	1	0	0	0	127	CHAR
BELLOCCHIO,FRANK	5	2	58	7	40	4	0	1	0	117	CHAR
RANDLE,LINNIE M.	3	2	28	19	55	6	1	2	0	116	JFK
SMITH,GLENN E.	15	2	52	1	40	3	0	0	0	113	CHAR
BROCK,ALVIN R.	13	2	52	7	35	0	0	3	0	112	LHO
DOBBS, FARRELL	3	2	49	30	24	1	0	0	1	109	CHAR
HULEN,RICHARD L.	7	2	29	3	53	2	0	7	1	103	CHAR
WRIGHT,NORMAN E.	11	2	72	4	7	4	0	1	0	101	CHAR
LUJAN, DANIEL	18	2	33	7	38	0	0	0	1	98	JFK
SERVANCE, JOHN	7	2	33	5	50	1	0	0	0	98	LHO
KAISER,FRANKIE	14	2	41	18	21	0	0	0	0	96	JFK
HUFFAKER,ROBERT	12	2	45	14	21	2	0	0	0	96	LHO
MAXEY,BILLY JOE	10	2	30	19	28	2	0	2	0	93	LHO
HARDIN,MICHAEL	12	2	43	5	27	0	1	0	0	90	LHO
BLALOCK,VANCE	9	2	50	1	22	1	1	0	0	86	CHAR
FUQUA,HAROLD	8	2	30	5	33	0	0	0	0	78	LHO
PERRY. W.E.	8	2	40	2	19	0	0	0	1	71	JFK
JOHNSON,JOSEPH	29	2	27	4	5	4	0	0	0	71	CHAR
KLEINMAN,ABRAHAM	15	2	41	4	4	2	0	0	0	68	CHAR
ROBERTSON,MARY J	7	2	20	5	31	1	0	0	0	66	JFK
WULF,WILLIAM E.	14	2	19	2	25	4	0	0	0	66	CHAR

WITNESS	PRE	TP	NV	CL	LH	C	FC	N	OTR	TOTAL	TYPE
WHITE.J.C.	17	2	16	6	22	0	0	1	0	64	JFK
BURROUGHS.W.	7	2	31	3	19	0	0	1	0	63	JDT
LIGHT.FREDERICK	11	2	17	5	13	4	0	1	1	53	JFK
KRAVITZ.HERBERT	13	2	21	3	6	4	0	0	0	49	CHAR
BASHOUR,FOUAD	7	2	18	7	8	0	1	0	0	43	JFK
ZAHM.SGT.JAMES	12	2	13	0	6	7	0	0	1	40	EXP
SHIELDS,EDWARD	7	2	20	0	7	0	0	1	0	37	JFK
MITCHELL.MARYANN	5	2	13	7	9	0	0	0	0	36	JFK
SAWYER,MILDRED	6	2	12	0	13	0	0	1	0	34	CHAR
KENNEDY.MRS.JOHN	2	2	10	8	8	1	0	0	0	31	JFK
WHITE,MARTIN	10	2	13	1	3	0	0	0	0	29	JFK
OLDS,GREGORY L.	6	2	14	4	2	0	0	0	0	28	CHAR
TORMEY.JAMES J.	1	2	16	3	5	0	0	0	0	27	CHAR
CARR,WAGGONER	2	2	3	2	2	0	0	0	0	11	JFK
CUNNINGHAM,HELEN	10	1	105	44	72	1	0	10	1	243	CHAR
SHASTEEN.CLIFTON	4	1	68	22	106	1	0	3	0	205	CHAR
WILCOX,LAURANCE	5	1	54	15	82	2	0	0	0	159	CHAR
JOHNSON,SPEEDY	14	1	55	14	43	10	0	2	0	139	CHAR
NORTON,ROBERT	26	1	47	8	55	0	0	0	0	137	CHAR
GREGORY,PETER P.	5	1	43	21	36	15	0	2	0	123	CHAR
HARTOGS,RENATUS	9	1	46	16	34	2	0	1	0	109	CHAR
DIETRICH,EDWARD	20	1	35	11	31	0	0	1	0	99	LHO
MILLER,DAVE L.	12	1	70	5	5	0	0	0	0	93	CHAR
LEBLANC,CHARLES	11	1	33	2	35	2	1	5	0	90	CHAR
DOWE,KENNETH	23	1	41	13	4	3	0	0	0	85	CHAR
KRISS.HARRY	8	1	24	14	37	0	0	0	0	84	LHO
RHEINSTEIN.FRED	7	1	29	8	33	0	0	1	0	79	LHO
GOODSON.CLYDE	7	1	40	4	27	0	0	0	0	79	LHO
STANDIFER,ROY	8	1	40	0	28	1	0	0	0	78	LHO
PRIDDY. HAL	6	1	28	9	25	0	0	0	0	69	LHO
JIMISON,R.J.	11	1	35	2	13	0	0	0	0	62	JFK
SOLOMON,JAMES M.	8	1	21	4	27	1	0	0	0	62	LHO
SIEGEL,EVELYN	13	1	11	7	26	0	1	1	0	60	CHAR
SCHMIDT.HUNTER	7	1	22	6	23	1	0	0	0	60	CHAR
STEELE,DON F.	8	1	31	6	7	1	0	1	0	55	LHO
AYCOX.JAMES	6	1	30	7	5	1	0	0	0	50	CHAR
RITCHIE,JAMES	8	1	14	1	15	1	0	0	0	40	CHAR
UNDERWOOD.JAMES	4	1	10	2	13	0	0	1	0	31	JFK
NICHOLS,H.LOUIS	7	1	8	4	8	0	0	0	0	28	CHAR
DULANY.RICHARD	9	1	10	1	2	0	0	0	0	23	JFK
BIGGIO,WILLIAM	3	1	4	2	10	0	0	0	0	20	LHO
HOWLETT,JOHN JOE	2	1	3	4	6	0	0	0	1	16	JFK
VOSHININ,MRS.IGO	30	0	96	66	120	13	1	8	1	334	CHAR
DYMITRUK,LYDIA	34	0	60	36	92	3	2	17	0	244	CHAR
RIGGS,ALFREADIA	18	0	62	8	73	0	0	0	0	161	LHO
PETERMAN,VIOLA	6	0	31	15	41	7	0	25	0	125	CHAR
STATMAN.IRVING	4	0	37	27	50	2	0	4	0	124	CHAR
BARGAS.TOMMY	6	0	52	5	50	3	1	6	0	123	CHAR
CONWAY.HIRAM	8	0	55	13	27	5	0	6	1	114	CHAR
PIC.EDWARD	10	0	44	8	38	1	0	3	0	104	CHAR
VINSON,PHILIP E.	16	0	39	10	28	2	1	5	0	101	CHAR

WITNESS	PRE	TP	NV	CL	LH	C	FC	N	OTR	TOTAL	TYPE
SEMIGSEN,W.W.	7	0	35	5	52	0	0	0	1	99	CHAR
BARNHORST,COLIN	8	0	27	15	46	0	0	0	0	96	CHAR
REA,BILLY	19	0	38	7	28	2	1	0	0	95	CHAR
SMITH,BENNIERITA	9	0	51	10	19	1	0	0	1	90	CHAR
GERACI,PHILIP	6	0	37	13	28	3	0	0	0	87	CHAR
BROOKS.DONALD	9	0	36	8	28	0	0	0	0	81	CHAR
BOUDREAUX.ANNE	9	0	30	10	24	5	0	1	0	79	CHAR
ADAMS,R.L.	5	0	36	7	28	0	0	0	1	76	CHAR
PRICE,CHARLES	5	0	55	7	6	0	0	0	0	73	ADM
McCURDY,DANNY	4	0	29	6	26	3	0	0	0	68	CHAR
FENLEY,ROBERT	10	0	27	2	27	0	0	0	0	66	CHAR
NELSON, DORIS	11	0	36	6	7	0	0	1	1	61	JFK
WESTER,AJANE	11	0	37	6	4	0	0	1	0	59	JFK
CASON,FRANCES	8	0	28	2	18	0	0	2	0	58	LHO
LESLIE,HELEN	10	0	19	7	13	1	0	1	0	51	CHAR
HULSE,C.E.	11	0	19	0	17	0	0	0	0	47	LHO
LEHRER,JAMES	12	0	11	1	18	2	0	0	0	44	CHAR
HENSLEE. GERALD	9	0	16	5	9	0	0	1	0	40	JFK
PINKSTON,NAT	9	0	17	1	11	0	0	0	0	38	JFK
GAUTHIER,LEO	3	0	17	11	2	0	0	1	0	34	JFK
DONABEDIAN,GEORG	4	0	11	7	10	0	0	0	0	32	CHAR
KELLY,EDWARD	9	0	9	1	8	0	0	0	0	27	LHO
ROSS, HENRIETTA	5	0	14	1	3	0	0	1	0	24	JFK
COULTER,HARRIS	11	0	5	2	5	0	0	0	0	23	UNR
STEELE.CHAS.SR.	8	0	5	0	8	0	0	1	0	22	CHAR
WOOD,THERESA	3	0	7	0	5	0	0	1	0	16	CHAR
ABT. JOHN J.	3	0	2	1	3	0	0	0	0	9	CHAR
BAKER,T.L.	3	0	1	1	3	0	0	0	0	8	JFK
CARSWELL,ROBERT	2	0	2	1	0	0	0	0	0	5	UNR

WITNESSES NOT CALLED BY THE WARREN COMMISSION

Due to many factors, some of which included police ineptitude in not sealing crime scenes or taking names when they should have, bureaucratic snafus, interagency rivalries, compartmentalization of the investigation by the Warren Commission, or simply a desire to see justice obstructed, a veritable cadre of valuable witnesses was never heard by the Warren Commission.

Some were admittedly unknown to them, for reasons cited above, and the commission cannot be held fully responsible for those omissions. Others, however, were known to them and ignored, as their story seemed at odds with the preconceived official verdict.

In casting through this veritable Who's Who of the Kennedy assassination, it should strike the reader that there is *quality* in this list, as opposed to *quantity,* which is presented in Table 5, "Witness Totals by Category." The people cited below could fill another fifteen volumes of testimony, and it would probably be more meaningful than page after page of testimony from the porters at police headquarters, a barber who supposedly cut Oswald's hair, or Jack Ruby's cleaning lady.

Of course, those cited below, like those called by the commission, would have been of value only if they had been asked meaningful questions.

You decide.

Julia Ann Mercer—eyewitness to events in Dealey Plaza hours before the assassination, she claimed to see a gun unloaded from a panel truck at the base of the knoll.

William Newman and Gayle Newman—Dealey Plaza eyewitnesses who believed the shots originated somewhere in the neighborhood of cameraman Zapruder.

Gordon Novel—covert operative believed to have been in Dealey Plaza.

Silvia Duran and Eusebio Azcue—consulate employees who could best testify as to the identity of the individual who appeared at the Cuban embassy in Mexico City.

Eugene Wilson—Albert Bogard coworker who, at five feet, eight inches tall, identified "Oswald" as being five feet, when the real Oswald was taller than Wilson.

Carolyn Walther—saw gun extruding from the TSBD sixth floor.

Frank Wright—resident in neighborhood where Tippit was slain.

Tom Tilson—Dallas police officer who chased a suspect in his auto, and reported the event and the plate number to higher authorities—all for naught.

William Walter—FBI night clerk who alleged he received a bureau telex regarding possible assassination attempt on JFK for November 22.

Alan Sweatt—high-ranking member of Dallas sheriff's department; had some knowledge of Oswald's "operative" status.

O. V. Campbell—TSBD employee who told of knoll shots, in affidavit.

Marilyn Sitzman—Zapruder's secretary who shared his perch during the filming of the motorcade.

David Cherry—alleged organizer of meetings that involved gun-running to Cuba, a mysterious colonel, and Jack Ruby.

H. B. Reynolds—Dallas police officer who spoke of rumor that Ruby exited a police vehicle in the basement.

Acquila Clemons—resident of neighborhood in which Tippit was slain.

Hal Hendrix—a.k.a. "The Spook"—provided Seth Kantor with a biography of Oswald very shortly after 12:30 P.M. on November 22.

Capt. Alexis Davidson—gave physicals to Oswalds before their departure from USSR; knew Oleg Penkovsky, Soviet officer executed for passing secrets to the United States; Oswald was believed to have the Davidson family address in Atlanta, and his flight to Texas made a stopover there.

Spas Raikin—met the Oswalds upon their arrival back in the United States; linked to a group that gathered intelligence for the CIA.

Maurice Orr—Elm Street eyewitness.

S/A Glen Bennett, S/A Paul Landis, S/A Sam Kinney, S/A Emory Roberts, S/A John Ready, S/A George Hickey, and S/A McIntyre—Secret Service in follow-up.

Gordon Arnold—soldier on leave who photographed event and hit the dirt. Arnold's film was seized and he has not seen it since.

Mary Woodward, Maggie Brown, Aurelia Lorenzo, and Ann Don-aldson—employees of *Dallas Morning News* who were eyewitnesses in Dealey Plaza; Mary Woodward would later file a story that the shots came from the knoll area and that the second and third shots were fired in very close time sequence.

John Chism and Mary Chism—eyewitnesses in Dealey Plaza.

John Powell—county jail inmate with excellent view of the TSBD sixth floor who made claims to having seen things there that are contrary to the official version.

Charles Bronson—eyewitness who filmed the event. The film strongly suggests movement by more than one person on the TSBD sixth floor, but was ignored.

Robert Hughes—eyewitness who filmed the event. The content of his film is similar in nature to Bronson's, and also was ignored.

Georgia Mayor—*Dallas Morning News* employee who was Ruby's alibi.

Hugh Aynesworth—*Dallas Morning News* employee who noted Ruby's absence from the newspaper office for twenty key minutes on November 22.

E. Howard Hunt—Mexican-based CIA officer; implicated in JFK plot by testimony of Marita Lorenz.

Ed Butler—other member of Oswald/Bringuier debate.

Guy Banister—former ONI and FBI agent; anti-Castro zealot associated with Ferrie, Oswald, and possibly Clay Shaw.

Sergio Arcacha Smith—anti-Castro Cuban with knowledge of the entire movement.

Mary Brengel—secretary to Guy Banister.

Delphine Roberts—another Banister employee; reportedly saw Oswald and his Cuban leaflets, but was told by Banister that all was well.

Loran Hall—admitted he was "Oswald" at Odio residence, in deposition; denied it shortly thereafter.

Joseph Milteer—right-wing zealot who was tape-recorded predicting and verifying events of November 22; was given clean bill of health by FBI.

Alonzo Hudkins—reporter who "broke" Oswald-as-informant story.

Norman Lee Elkins—the "radical" who was the only premotorcade focus of concern.

Willie Mitchell—another inmate of the county jail who had a commanding view of the TSBD sixth floor.

David B. Grant—Secret Service agent present at Oswald questioning.

Robert Nash—U.S. marshal present at Oswald questioning.

Mrs. Tippit—Mrs. Oswald and Mrs. Kennedy both testified; Mrs. Tippit could also have fleshed out some details about J. D.

Father Oscar Huber—gave last rites to JFK. I have always maintained that his silence was due to understandable sacramental reasons; however, I have learned of correspondence of his in which he spoken openly of what he saw of JFK, and it was not reportage identical to that in the Warren Report.

Tom Robinson—Gawler's funeral home, which prepared JFK for burial; his comments to researchers suggest JFK was more seriously damaged than we have been led to believe.

Jerrol Custer—X-ray technician at Bethesda Naval Hospital.

Thomas A. Vallee—suspect placed under arrest in Chicago on November 1; was perceived as a threat to JFK, although he was a John Birch Society member and ex-marine, with marksmanship skills (a parallel Oswald?).

John Martino—allegedly had evidence of a pro-Castro plot; his appearance was urged on the commission by counsel Slawson.

Edward Partin—Teamsters official under watchful eye of FBI who had knowledge of threats against RFK and JFK.

J. C. Price—eyewitness to events from his post atop the Terminal Annex Building; noted individuals behind the picket fence leaving in haste.

James Chaney—motorcade motorcycle escort.

Milton Jones—passenger confused with Oswald by bus driver McWatters.

Adm. George Burkley—JFK's physician and the only doctor present at both Parkland and Bethesda; "verified" autopsy face sheet later denied by autopsy doctors.

John T. Stringer—photographer at Bethesda whose work is as yet unseen.

James Siebert and Francis X. O'Neill—two FBI agents detailed to Bethesda to receive bullets or evidentiary material received at autopsy.

Gary Underhill—CIA contract agent who spoke of CIA involvement.

S/A Robert Barrett—FBI man present at Dealey Plaza and Texas Theater.

Pat Kirkwood—proprietor of "The Cellar" where Secret Service agents visited the night before the motorcade; alleged to have underworld ties and believed to have departed for Mexico in haste following assassination.

David Sanders—orderly at Parkland who helped prepare JFK for placement in the original coffin.

Jerry Boyd Belknap—the epileptic in Dealey Plaza.

Sgt. Miguel Rodriguez—the noncom Oswald poured a drink over, which led to his second court-martial.

J. Walton Moore—George DeMohrenschildt's CIA contact.

Aubrey Rike, Dennis McGuire, and Vernon O'Neal—all employed by O'Neal Ambulance/Funeral; had knowledge of JFK as well as epileptic event.

William Bruce Pitzer—took photos in autopsy room that were immediately destroyed; later, "a suicide."

James L. Simmons, Walter L. Winborn, Nolan H. Potter, Curtis F. Bishop, Richard C. Dodd, Thomas J. Murphy, Clemon E. Johnson, Ewell W. Cowsert, and George A. Davis—railroad-related people who viewed the motorcade from atop the triple underpass.

Mary Moorman—accompanied Jean Hill to Dealey Plaza; eyewitness; took Polaroid photographs considered crucial.

Jack Franzen—eyewitness.

Charles Brehm—eyewitness.

Patricia Lawrence—eyewitness.

Dolores Kounas—eyewitness.

Bill Wentfre—Jack Beers's photo partner.

Clayton Butler and Eddie Kinsley—Tippit ambulance staff.

Chief Lumpkin—Dallas police; too high-ranking not to have been called.

H. L. Hunt—wealthy oilman who had the clout to know everything happening in Dallas in 1963.

Orville Nix—took movie as revealing as Zapruder's; his estate is still in litigation to have it returned.

Mary Muchmore—also filmed Dealey Plaza.

William Gaudet—a CIA type who just happened to get the Mexican tourist card issued immediately before Oswald's; knew of Banister-Ferrie doings.

John Wilson—detained in Cuba along with a "Santos," and recalled Ruby making a visit.

Mrs. Lovell Penn—chased riflemen (who left behind 6.5mm shells) off her property.

Eugene Hale Brading, Donald Wayne House, Jack Lawrence, Larry Florer, Donald Sharp, and any other Dealey Plaza "detainees," regardless of the duration of their stay.

Gus Abrams, John F. Gedney, and Harold Doyle—the three "tramps."

Dr. Earl Rose—the man who should have performed the autopsy that was never done on JFK in Dallas.

Carroll Jarnigan—an attorney who made accusations linking Ruby and Oswald.

O. P. Wright—the head of security at Parkland who handled the "magic bullet."

S/A Richard Johnsen—the Secret Service man who received the "magic bullet" from Wright, pocketed it with no thought of giving it to local authorities, and turned it over to James Rowley in the White House.

S/A Richard Harrison—FBI agent who visited Miller's Funeral Home with a rifle and fingerprint ink.

Paul Groody—director of Miller Funeral Home who had to clean fingerprint ink off the corpse of Oswald.

Chester Breneman and Bob West—the surveyors who performed the intricate measurements involved in the reenactment of the assassination, only to find their figures later changed.

Jim Hicks—photographed in Dealey Plaza, he claimed he was the radioman coordinating the teams of shooters.

Mrs. Louise Latham—Texas Employment Commission employee involved in Oswald's checkered employment history; subsequent to the assassination, she and her husband relocated in haste.

Lt. Col. Robert E. Jones—112th Military Intelligence Group commander, which did not protect the president in Dallas but did have a file on "Hidell/Oswald."

H. R. "Bum" Bright—put up some of the money, along with Nelson Baker Hunt, for the unfriendly newspaper ad "welcoming" JFK to Dallas.

Bill Wiseman—saw Mary Moorman's Polaroid photos of the TSBD sixth floor at the time of the shooting.

Thomas Atkins—official photographer for JFK White House; had a journalist's sense for the event, yet thought shots were coming from street level.

Roy Stamps—corroborated Seth Kantor's story of seeing Ruby at Parkland; saw JFK's foot hanging over limousine as car arrived.

Jim Willmon—*Dallas Morning News;* recognized that attention was focused on knoll, not TSBD.

Beverly Oliver—"babushka lady" who lost a roll of film to police officials in Dealey Plaza.

Lilian Mooneyham—clerk of 95th District Court; saw someone in TSBD sixth floor a few minutes after the shooting.

Dave Wegman—NBC photographer who jumped out of the press car and filmed the knoll.

James Wilcott—CIA finance officer; would later tell HSCA that Oswald was an agency operative, from his own knowledge of payments.

Ed Hoffman—deaf-mute who witnessed events in the railroad yards, reported to the local authorities, and was ignored.

T. F. Bowley—used Tippit's radio to call in the emergency there.

William H. Griffin—spoke of Oswald as FBI informant; later retracted.

Walter Kirk Coleman—witness to "Walker events" of April 10, 1963.

James Powell—army intelligence operative in Dealey Plaza.

Malcolm Summers—eyewitness; threatened by person unknown, but armed, on the knoll.

Jack Davis—Texas Theater patron whom Oswald sat next to briefly, possibly in search of a "contact."

Paul O'Connor—Humes's lab technician at Bethesda who apparently saw a different JFK than the photos show.

Julius Hardie—saw men with rifles on the triple underpass before assassination; reported to FBI after the event; ignored.

Gerry Patrick Hemming—may well have key information; implicated by Marita Lorenz.

José Aleman—knew of mob threats against JFK.

William Harper and Allen Harper—found bone fragment in Dealey Plaza on November 23.

S/A Abraham Bolden—Secret Service agent who got in deep trouble for being concerned that the Chicago attempt on JFK might have been part of something even larger.

James Curtis Jenkins—also assisted Humes et al. at Bethesda.

Dr. John Ebersole—radiologist at Bethesda; autopsy indicated no spinal damage to JFK; X rays show otherwise; he could clear that up.

Adm. Calvin Galloway—Humes's commanding officer at Bethesda who was present at JFK's autopsy.

Capt. John Stover—commanding officer at the U.S. Navy Medical School; also present at JFK's autopsy.

Capt. Robert Canada—commander of Bethesda Naval Hospital; present at JFK's autopsy.

Marita Lorenz—key witness who implicated Hunt, Sturgis, and Gary Hemming among Dallas plotters.

Dr. Charles A. Crenshaw—Parkland Hospital surgical resident on November 22 and November 24; allegedly took phone call from LBJ demanding deathbed confession from Oswald on November 24.

S/A Roger Warner—Secret Service agent who interviewed suspect Donald Wayne House.

Richard Case Nagell—career government servant who was so concerned with having an alibi for November 22 that he fired a pistol into a bank wall, so as to be in jail.

Thomas Buchanan—author of *Who Killed Kennedy?* who was trashed by the commission.

Nerin E. Gun—another author who disagreed with official verdict and was vilified by the commission.

David Atlee Phillips—high-level CIA operative who might well possess a great deal of data.

Clay Shaw—director of New Orleans Trade Mart and CIA contract agent; would later run afoul of the law.

Yuri Nosenko—Soviet KGB officer who defected to the United States, claiming full knowledge of Oswald's activities in the Soviet Union.

U. E. Baughman—head of Secret Service at outset of JFK term; certainly had knowledge of protective responsibilities, without having to cover his own butt.

Gerald Behn—head of White House detail of the Secret Service; did not make Dallas trip despite obvious concerns.

Hugh Betzner—took valuable photographs in Dealey Plaza.

Richard R. Carr—valuable eyewitness.

Starvis Ellis—motorcycle in motorcade; saw hole through limo windshield.

Godfrey McHugh—high-ranking JFK aide on Dallas trip; "with body" entire time.

Rosemary Willis—daughter of Phil Willis who stops running at a key point in the Zapruder film; her sister was mistakenly called to testify.

Rose Cheramie—told of plot against JFK before it happened; Louisiana authorities showed concern but got no response.

Francis Fruge—knew of Rose Cheramie's story before Dallas.

Tom Howard—attorney with strong ties to Ruby.

Regis Kennedy—FBI agent who shows up too many times for coincidence.

"Muggsy" O'Leary—Secret Service agent present at autopsy.

Albert Osborne, a.k.a. John Howard Bowen—bus passenger with "Oswald" on Mexican adventure.

Gary Powers—Lee Harvey Oswald claimed to see him in Moscow.

William Reily—Lee Harvey Oswald employer in New Orleans; strongly anti-Castro; other employers called, why not he?

Eva Springer—Dean Andrews's secretary; knew Andrews had been contacted to defend Oswald.

General Philip Wehle—head of ceremonial casket team; present at autopsy.

Audrey Bell—Parkland Hospital operating room nurse; had knowledge of Connally wounds, metal.

Wilma Bond—took photographs in Dealey Plaza.

Dennis David—Bethesda enlisted man with knowledge of JFK autopsy.

Hurchel Jacks—Texas state trooper who drove LBJ in motorcade.

Edward Kenney—high-ranking officer at Bethesda Naval Hospital.

Charles Killion—Secret Service agent on Dallas detail.

Jerry Kivett—Secret Service agent on Dallas detail.

Lem Johns—Secret Service agent on Dallas detail.

Steve Landregan—Parkland Hospital administrator who had hospital prepared in case of Lee Harvey Oswald injury but not JFK.

J. S. Ledbetter—autopsy-related.

James Metzler—autopsy-related.

David Osborne—autopsy-related.

Edward Reed—technician at autopsy.

Floyd Reibe—assisted at autopsy.

Elmer Todd—FBI agent who received "magic bullet" on evening of November 22.

Tom Alyea—news cameraman inside TSBD on November 22.

Gloria Calvery—witness.

Aline Mosby—journalist who interviewed Lee Harvey Oswald in Moscow.

Jim Towner—took photographs in Dealey Plaza.

Robert Webster—another "returned defector."

Charles Flynn—FBI agent who used Ruby as an informant.

Milton Kaack—FBI agent aware of Oswald case before November 22.

H. B. McLain—motorcycle in motorcade.

Dan Rather—local news source in 1963.

Gordon Shanklin—FBI special agent in charge who gave order to destroy evidence.

Jean West, a.k.a. Jean Aase—connected to Ruby and syndicate.

Two hundred individuals are listed, each with knowledge at least as valuable as that given by the 488 commission witnesses. Perhaps there was a perception that America was not prepared for the truth in 1963 and 1964, and the sin of it all is that we haven't gotten it yet. And most of the people listed above can no longer help.

Many are gone forever. The rest cling to thirty-year-old perceptions and the hope that their testimony will someday be heard or accepted.

NONSENSE

The Warren Commission published twenty-six volumes of hearings and exhibits. The first fifteen volumes contain only testimony, and make up 7,909 pages of small print. The remaining eleven volumes contain exhibits and comprise 9,831 pages. Much of what is in there is not to the point, to say the least. But the following exhibits fit into the category suggested by the above heading.

Subsequent to the publication of the twenty-six volumes, it was learned that the Warren Commission sequestered 357 *cubic feet* of additional materials. Part of the justification for that was that supposedly much of the 357 cubic feet was just nonrelated nonsense and not worth the lives of trees. That theory is called into question by demonstrating below that they *did* publish the nonsense. Since then, much of the 357 cubic feet of material has been released, and in most cases where they have not been censored into oblivion, they are more valuable than the junk cited below. The FBI telex of November 17, warning of an assassination attempt on November 22–23 in Dallas, is but one of many examples of useful but unpublished material.

The source follows the item; the number in parentheses is the number of pages it takes up.

CE 43—Unreadable; 16H 175 (1)
CE 107—LHO's factory pass in Minsk; 16H 475 (1)
CE 108–9—Lyrics of a Russian song; 16H 476–78 (3)
CE 110—A blank page; 16H 480 (1)
CE 113—Texas driver's handbook; 16H 485 (0.5)
CE 116—Spanish-English dictionary; 16H 487–89 (3)

CE 119–121—"Various medical items"; 16H 492 (1)

CE 128—Map of Fort Worth; 16H 495–98 (4)

CE 129–131—Marina's birth certificate, a duplicate, and a copy of the duplicate; 16H 499–502 (4)

CE 146–49—"Man's shoes"; 16H 514 (1)

CE 165–68, 170–79—Photos—LHO's funeral; 16H 522–23, 525–29 (7)

CE 239—USMC scorebook—mostly empty; 16H 639–79 (41)

CE 258—Transcript of Marguerite Oswald press conference of 1/29/64; 16H 720 (1)

CE 276–80—Marina's contracts with business agents; 16H 770–800 (31)

CE 326–30—News clippings: "Marina Oswald attended Mass, had Quiet Yule"; and others; 16H 918–21 (4)

CE 332—Copy of invoice showing rental by James Martin of tape recorder; 16H 924 (1)

CE 375—A side view of McWatters' bus; 16H 970 (0.5)

CE 379–80—Two photos of interior of bus; 16H 972–73 (2)

CE 436—"Photograph of door leading to backyard of Paine home"; 17H 161 (0.5)

CE 535–36—Newspaper photos of Mark Lane; 17H 235 (1)

CE 700—Connally's tie; 17H 356 (1)

CE 748—Photo of headless man with Mannlicher; 17H 522 (0.5)

CE 752—Negative of CE 748; 17H 525 (0.5)

CE 762—Secret Service PRS threats, including one to Truman; 17H 536–85 (50)

CE 837—Article from *National Enquirer;* 17H 837 (1)

CE 851—An X ray of a fractured goat rib from a "Connally" reenactment; 17H 847 (1)

CE 949—State Department to WC, listing revoked passports, with every name deleted; 18H 249–54 (6)

CE 993—Marina Oswald narrative, in Russian; 18H 548–95 (48)

CE 994—Translation of CE 993; translator not noted; 18H 596–642 (47)

CE 1012—A photo of General Walker's clothesline; 18H 658 (0.5)

CE 1030—Secret Service to WC, 6/11/64—legislative suggestions; 18H 629–34 (6)

CE 1041—Statement of purposes, goals, of Conservatism U.S.A.; 18H 868–72 (5)

CE 1053A—Treasury Department report on Secret Service facilities; 18H 898–926 (29)

CE 1053B—D. Dillon, Treasury Department budget, 8/31/64; 18H 927–28 (2)

CE 1053F—D. Dillon to WC; Secret Service budgets, 1960–65; 18H 935–36 (2)

Allen ex. 1–15 Letters of Marguerite Oswald to private schools, 1940s 19H 1–15 (15)

Armstrong, Andrew 5300 A–F, 5301 A–E; eleven photos of Rudy and strippers 19H 24–34 (11)

Armstrong, Andrew 5305 A–S Ruby's spiral notebook; unreadable 19H 43–61 (19)

Barnes, W. E. A–F Six photos of Tippit's patrol car 19H 113–15 (3)

Bowron, Diana ex. 4 "30 Min. Diana will never forget" British newspaper clipping marked "Top Secret" 19H 170 (1)

Carro, John ex. 1 Report of J. Carro on Oswald's truancy, 3/12/53 19H 308–23 (16)

Cheek, Bertha 5353 FBI report of 11/29/63; ends in midsentence 19H 326–28 (L3)

Clardy, B. 5061 Clardy to J. Curry; three pages and three typefaces 19H 331–33 (3)

Crafard, Curtis 5227 Letter, "Deal Gail . . ." 19H 361–62 (2)

Fehrenbach, George 1 Sketch of office in Muncie, Ind. 19H 649 (0.5)

Fehrenbach, George 2–3 Photos of his friends 19H 649 (0.5)

Graves, Jean 1 Oswald time cards—Leslie Welding 20H 19–21 (3)

Helmick, Wanda ex. 1 Sketch of Bull Pen drive-in 20H 91 (1)

Herndon, Bell P. 1–12 Charts of Ruby's polygraph 20H 92–155 (64)

Holmes, Harry D. 1-A Sample post office box application 20H 173 (1)

Hulen, Richard 1–15 YMCA paperwork 20H 189–99 (11)

James, V. 3, 4, 5, 7, 11 Documents with a lot of whiteout 20H 238, 241–42, 245, 251 (5)

Kaiser, Frankie E. C. Photo of windowsill in Domino Room, TSBD 20H 335 (1)

King, Glen 5 A copy of Glen King 4 20H 462–69 (8)

McMillon, Thomas 5020 A handwritten copy of McMillon 5018 20H 565–70 (6)

Miller, Austin A. A sketch of the triple underpass 20H 620 (1)

Murphy, Joe E. A sketch of the triple underpass 20H 638 (1)

Murret, Lillian 1 Photo of Marguerite Oswald and E. Ekdahl, May 1945 20H 639 (1)

Odum, Bardwell Photo of unknown individual furnished to FBI by CIA (repeat of CE 237) (the exhibit has value, but it is a repeat) 20H 691 (0.5)

Oliver, Revilo P. 1, 2 Fictional articles using uncited sources to prove that the communist conspiracy killed JFK 20H 692–717 and 718–35 (44)

Oliver, Revilo P. 5 *National Enquirer* (repeat of CE 837) 20H 749 (1)

Oliver, Revilo P. 10 Transcript of speech given by Oliver on his U.S. tour, August to September 1964, which repeated the thesis suggested in Oliver 1, 2. 20H 753–93 (41)

Paine, Ruth 277A $10 check to Marina, 12/28/63 21H 13 (0.5)

Paine, Ruth 278, 278A Christmas card, Marina to Ruth Paine, with envelope 21H 14–16 (2.5)

Pic, John E. 1–60 Irrelevant materials from 1940s, '50s; photo of LHO with dog, 1949; 21H 50–127 (78)

Rachal, John R. Louisiana Department of Labor documents—inaccurate data 21H 282–86 (5)

Rich, Nancy P. A "To whom it may concern" letter of reference for Ms. Rich 21H 295 (1)

Rubenstein, Hyman 1–2 Appeals for money for Ruby defense 21H 315–16 (1.5)

Ruby, Earl ex. 1 "Why Ruby Shot Oswald" by S. Dann (an act of patriotism by a man temporarily insane and other specious arguments) 21H 321–50 (30)

Sawyer, Herbert A, B Radio logs—repeats 21H 388–400 (12.5)

Siegel, Evelyn S. Youth House social worker reports on Oswald, 5/7/53 21H 484–509 (26)

Skelton, Royce Sketch of triple underpass 21H 519 (1)

Staples, Albert E. 1 Marina's dental records, Baylor University 21H 550–56 (7)

Wilcox, Laurence R. 3010–14 Unrelated telegrams 21H 748–51 (3.5)

CE 1107—Three prescriptions in Russian; LHO's high-school ID; 22H 64 (1)

CE 1110—LHO's Soviet book for payment of factory union dues; 22H 69–71 (3)

CE 1117—WC internal memo—books read by Oswald (James Bond, *Profiles in Courage, Ben Hur, Blue Nile, Bridge over the River Kwai*); 22H 82–84 (3)

CE 1153—Secret Service report, LHO in New Orleans; unreadable; 22H 187–88 (2)

CE 1165—A duplication of CE 1161, LHO expenditures; 22H 222–32 (10.5)

CE 1167—A duplication of CE 1161, 1165; 22H 239–67 (28.5)

CE 1170—Oswald's subscription to *Time*; 22H 270 (0.5)

CE 1173—Thirteen canceled Leslie Welding paychecks of LHO; 22H 273–77 (5)

CE 1179—Social Security data on *Earl* Ruby; 22H 292–94 (2.5)

CE 1189—Ruby's military record—qualified as sharpshooter on 2/10/44; 22H 309 (1)

CE 1190–1226—FBI interviews with Ruby cronies from 1940s; 22H 310–35 (25.5)

CE 1252—Naturalization records of Ruby family; 22H 361 (1)

CE 1274—Selective Service reports on Ruby's military "career"; 22H 378–79 (2)

CE 1281—Ruby's *mother's* medical records; 22H 386–410 (25)

CE 1291—Clinical evaluation of Ruby in 1922; 22H 429–32 (4)

CE 1297—Ruby's records from Illinois Institute for Juvenile Research, 1922; 22H 445–75 (31)

CE 1316–17—Photos of Leningrad; 22H 492 (1)

CE 1339—Youth House report on LHO, 1953; 22H 558–59 (1.5)

CE 1340–47—Excerpts from *The Militant*; 22H 560–77 (18)

CE 1384—LHO school records, 1953; several blank pages; 22H 688–700 (12.5)

CE 1391—Soviet blood analysis for LHO, with translation; 22H 718 (1)

CE 1392–95—Worthless photos; 22H 719–20 (2)

CE 1413—Louisiana Department of Public Safety—LHO background, school records; 22H 808–28 (20)

CE 1457–69—FBI reports: Ruby as phone pervert, sodomist, queen, boy-lover; 22H 879–89 (11)

CE 1494—Treatment for Ruby's baldness; 22H 913 (0.5)

CE 1552—FBI interview with J. Leipsic, who bought pizza crusts from Ruby; 23H 43 (0.5)

CE 1649—FBI interview with E. Castro, who worked with Ruby in 1960, never saw LHO; 23H 121 (0.5)

CE 1698—Social Security data—Ruby's sister Eileen; 23H 173–75 (3)

CE 1699—Ruby's behavior, 1922; 23H 176 (1)

CE 1706–7—Ruby's military records; 23H 182–202 (21)

CE 1708—FBI interview with Ruby, 1947; 23H 203–4 (2)

CE 1709–10—Investigation of Ruby, 1947; 23H 205–6 (2)

CE 1713–19—Ruby's tax returns, 1956–62; 23H 208–69 (62)

CE 1760—FBI report on burlesque houses, 1962; 23H 368 (0.5)

CE 1803—Hoover letter re Revilo Oliver; 23H 423–41 (19)

CE 1807—FBI report, LHO's custody, 1940s; 23H 445–52 (7.5)

CE 1850–56—LHO time sheets, Jaggers-Chiles-Stovall; 23H 529–625 (97)

CE 1873, 1873—A–L LHO school records, year by year; 23H 651–75 (24.5)

CE 1873–0—Marguerite Oswald's divorce report; 23H 677 (0.5)

CE 1874—LHO's possible attendance at day nursery; 23H 677–80 (3.5)

CE 1916–27—Interviews with LHO cousins, nonrelatives; 23H 716–22 (6.5)

CE 1958–60E—Marguerite Oswald's divorce papers, 1933 ff; 23H 780–94 (15)

CE 1964—Russian book *Certificate of a Hunter and Fisherman*; 23H 804–15 (12)

CE 1969—LHO passport, no entries; 23H 818–23 (6)

CE 1971—"Book of useful advice" in Russian; 23H 827–30 (3)

CE 2000—Marguerite Oswald's marriage certificate, 1933; 24H 35 (0.5)

CE 2067—*The New York Times*, "Kennedy's Car Refitted"; 24H 494 (0.5) (it wasn't JFK's anymore)

CE 2113–18—Photos of overpass; 24H 543–48 (6)

CE 2123—State Department re Mexico, in Spanish; 24H 663–91 (29)

CE 2158, 2161—Transcripts of media interviews with strippers; 24H 795–98, 806–7 (4.5)

CE 2183–85—Media editorials; 24H 856–58 (2.5)

CE 2188—A–E History of Elm Street and triple underpass; 24H 861–65 (5)

CE 2190—Six Mexican postcards; 25H 1–3 (3)

CE 2197—Property owned by LHO relatives; 25H 76 (1)

CE 2199—Interview with David Lutenbacher, LHO's brother's principal, 1932; 25H 79 (1)

CE 2201—Check with New Orleans Credit Bureau for LHO's mother; 25H 80–81 (1)

CE 2202–3—Interview with LHO's 1940 neighbors; 25H 81–83 (2.5)

CE 2205—Marguerite Oswald's insurance policies; 25H 84–86 (2.5)

CE 2220—Interview with LHO's fourth-grade teacher; 25H 119 (1)

CE 2223—LHO, New York, 1953; interview with V. Connell—caught LHO in Bronx Zoo; 25H 121–22 (6.5)

CE 2235—Interview with LHO classmates; 25H 133–34 (2)

CE 2242—Interview with Dr. Jacobsen—treated Ruby for fungus; 25H 142 (1)

CE 2310—Records of pay telephone at Phil's Deli; 25H 255 (0.5)

CE 2360—Interview with Ruby's sister's doctor; 25H 342 (1)

CE 2405–13, 2816—Ruby trial transcripts—*selected witnesses*; 25H 386–505; 26H 237–43 (126)

CE 2426—Photo of Ruby's bedroom; 25H 525 (0.5)

CE 2475—A–B Photos of box holding *tape* of newscast; 25H 663 (1)

CE 2487—Photo of book *Learning Russian*; 25H 686–88 (3)

CE 2488—Tourist map of Mexico City; 25H 689–704 (16)

CE 2490—LHO's 1962 Russian library card; 25H 706 (1)

CE 2491—Photo, "Impeach Earl Warren" sign; 25H 717 (0.5)

CE 2526—Manifest of *Air Force One*, Fort Worth-Dallas; 25H 735 (1)

CE 2551—Six pages on creation of the FBI, by C. Bonaparte; 25H 778–83 (6)

CE 2585—FBI memo re Buchanan, *Who Killed Kennedy?*; 25H 857–62 (5)

CE 2595–2630—Photos of Russian strangers; 25H 876–93 (18)

CE 2705—Marina's clinical tests before leaving Russia; 26H 76 (1)

CE 2759—LHO's love life in Russia, pre-Marina; 26H 144 (0.5)

CE 2791—Photo of Ruby's "twistboard" brochure; 26H 180 (1)

CE 2801–32—passim Ruby, LHO—"nut allegations"; 26H 190–236, 244–74 (77)

CE 2884–85—Interview with D. Stuart, who once fixed a microphone for Ruby; 26H 339–40 (1.5)

CE 2946—Plot of Chinese communists and Castro to kill JFK; 26H 407–9 (3)

CE 3018—FBI report, twistboards; 26H 556–57 (1.5)

CE 3043—Transcripts of Ruby trial; 26H 590–94 (4.5)

CE 3050—FBI report of photo of Ruby watching motorcade, but no photo; 26H 602–4 (2)

CE 3141—Photos of LHO's clipboard; 26H 824–25 (2)

CE 3154—Numbers assigned to previous CEs; 26H 862–935 (74)

There are many more than these samples; however, the list cited above adds up to 1,661 pages, or just over one sixth of the total exhibits. If, as some contend, there were 8,000 sets of the 26 volumes published, this tripe wasted 13,288,000 pages of paper.

NOTES

PROLOGUE

1. The media's hasty willingness to accept the rapidly emerging "official version" is well demonstrated by their total apathy with respect to the televised interview with Jean Hill on November 22. Before the president was even known to the media to be dead, Hill indicated that shots came from "the hill over there." Yet the depository soon became the focal point, and witnesses with other data, like Hill, were ignored. See Brown, "November 22: Origin of Media apathy," *Dateline Dallas*, Vol. I, No. 1, April 1994.
2. The methodology and thinking behind this evolution is given excellent treatment in Peter Dale Scott's *Deep Politics and the Death of JFK* (Berkeley, Calif., 1993), passim.
3. Sylvia Meagher placed the number as high as seventy-seven; the precise quantification is moot, as no inferences can be proved except that *not enough* officers were actually performing protective duties. In one case, L. D. Montgomery testified that it was his duty to walk *behind* Oswald to prevent the prisoner from *escaping*. (See 13H 27.)
4. RFK would also die under mysterious and as yet unsolved circumstances.
5. The confusion here stems from a misunderstanding of issues; news files would have known who Oswald was, and could have had material available reasonably quickly; Oswald, however, was not *officially* seen as the presidential assassin until well after some journals announced the fact. The cover story hit the fan too soon.

CHAPTER 2

1. Jim Moore, *Conspiracy of One* (Fort Worth, 1990); Dr. John K. Lattimer, *Kennedy and Lincoln* (New York, 1980); to Dr. Lattimer's credit, his one-

man study of the case is far more persuasive for the lone assassin than was the report of the president's commission.

2. Jim Garrison, *Heritage of Stone* (New York, 1970), p. 142.
3. CE 1784, 23H 411.
4. 19H 470, 19H 473, 24H 203.
5. 19H 475, CE 2003, 24H 207.
6. CE 2086, 24H 522; CE 2089, 24H 524.
7. CE 2098 24H 531.
8. HSCA *Report,* cited in Anthony Summers, *Conspiracy* (New York, 1980), p. 76.
9. Dillard exhibit C 19H 565.
10. CE 3076, 26H 679; see also Leo Sauvage, *The Oswald Affair* (Cleveland, 1966), pp. 31–33.
11. Interview with Larry Pressman, August 15, 1992.
12. Interviews with Marina Porter, January 22, 1993, and February 24, 1995.
13. CE 2562, 25H 808.
14. CE 2559, 25H 797.
15. Sauvage, *Oswald Affair,* p. 58.
16. CE 2560, 25H 799; CE 2147, 24H 779.
17. CE 1335–37, 22H 546–49.
18. 4H 261; this convinced Day it was an old print.
19. 4H 23.
20. Jim Garrison, *On the Trail of the Assassins* (New York, 1988), p. 97n.
21. 1H 21.
22. CE 1156, 22H 197; CE 1401, 22H 750, 763; CE 1404, 22H 785.
23. CE 1934, 23H 729.
24. CE 3049, 26H 600.
25. CE 2003, 24H 228; Decker 5323, 19H 456–57; Weitzman's (or someone's) comments on November 22 were broadcast on KBOX, CE 3043, 26H 599.
26. CE 2011, 24H 412; see also Price exhibits 2–35, which tell of Connally fragments being submitted to the Parkland Pathology Department, 21H 268.
27. Robert Groden and Harrison E. Livingstone, *High Treason* (New York, 1989), p. 55.
28. See testimony of Royce Skelton, 6H 236 ff; also Jim Marrs, *Crossfire* (New York, 1989), p. 316.
29. CE 1407, 22H 791.
30. CE 1974, 23H 914.
31. Dick Russell, *The Man Who Knew Too Much* (New York, 1992), p. 332.
32. CE 2084, 24H 520.
33. Interview, Mary Woodward, November 22, 1992.
34. CE 1024, 18H 755.

35. CE 1024, 18H 762.

36. Deposition is in CE 2003, 24H 213; testimony, 7H 560.

37. Jean Hill with Bill Sloan, *JFK: The Last Dissenting Witness* (New Gretna, La., 1992), p. 23.

38. Decker 5323, 19H 511.

39. See 7H 487 for Mrs. Cabell's comments; for a more thorough discussion of the gunpowder/cordite smell, see Summers, *Conspiracy*, p. 62.

40. CE 1974, 23H 913; both comments cited are a few seconds apart.

41. CE 1974, 23H 884, 885, 888, 881.

42. CE 1974, 23H 843–44, 845.

43. On Roger Craig, see CE 1967, 23H 817; CE 1992, 24H 23.

44. See Marrs, *Crossfire*, p. 531 ff; Summers, *Conspiracy*, p. 53; and G. Robert Blakey and Richard N. Billings, *The Plot to Kill the President* (New York, 1981), pp. 106–7.

45. I HSCA 344.

46. For Clint Hill, see CE 1024, 18H 744–45; for the Warren Commission's artistic rendering, see CE 385, 16H 977; the heart theory is the author's; try it with a sportcoat and the measured specs!

47. *Dallas Morning News*, November 23, 1963, p. 1.

48. CE 2147, 24H 771.

49. 5H 235.

50. 9H 275.

51. 11H 426.

52. 3H 154; in Brennan's posthumous memoir, *Eyewitness to History*, there is so much nonsensical embellishment that the work would be better titled *I, Witless to History*.

53. Russell, *Man*, p. 438.

54. 11H 419.

55. Renatus Hartogs and Lucy Freeman, *Two Assassins* (New York, 1965), pp. 106–7.

56. Gerald Posner, *Case Closed* (New York, 1993), p. 178.

57. Ibid., p. 3.

58. Ibid.

59. Ibid., pp. 20, 67n.

60. Ibid., p. 309.

61. Ibid., pp. 35, 49, passim.

62. Ibid., p. 112.

63. Ibid., p. 278.

64. Ibid., pp. 310–11.

65. Ibid., p. 411.

66. See Walt Brown, "You Can't Close a Case if You Can't Count," in *Probable*

Cause 6, June 1994; *Dateline Dallas,* Vol. I, No. 2, July 1994; and *The Fourth Decade,* Vol. 1, No. 5, July 1994.

67. Posner, *Case Closed,* p. 242; Harold Norman strongly denied much of what was attributed to him by Posner. Interview with author, June 15, 1994.

CHAPTER 3

1. Blakey, *Plot,* p. 6.
2. Blakey puts the exact number at 83; see Blakey, *Plot,* p. 7.
3. House Assassination *Report,* pp. 230–31, suggests that a motorcade was canceled; recently uncovered material suggests that the motorcade was proposed/considered, but never carved in stone, hence not necessarily "canceled," a subtle but worthwhile distinction.
4. Interviews with Roy Kellerman, c. 1974, William Greer, c. 1970.
5. Interview with Greer; some of this material appears in slightly different language in CE 1024, 18H 723, or in his all-too-brief testimony in 2H 112–32.
6. CE 1021, 18H 710, quoting Secret Service manual.
7. Secret Service manual, Section 10, Chapter I, p. 7, cited in CE 1018, 18H 665.
8. See Harrison E. Livingstone, *High Treason* (New York, 1992), p. 245, for a full discussion.
9. Vincent Palamara, "The JFK Murder-Criminal Conspiracy or Willful Misconduct?" Peter Kross, ed., in *Backchannels,* Vol. II, No. 4.
10. Harrison E. Livingstone, *Killing the Truth* (New York, 1993), p. 544.
11. Ibid., p. 532.
12. 2H 61 gives the date *and location* of Greer's testimony; the weather is available in the Washington, D.C., press of the following day.
13. L. Fletcher Prouty, *JFK* (New York, 1992), p. 138.
14. CE 2112, 24H 542.
15. CE 1024, 18H 760.

CHAPTER 4

1. Prouty, *JFK,* p. 50.
2. "James Hepburn," *Farewell America* (Liechtenstein, 1968), p. 338. This thesis is echoed by R. C. Nagell in Russell, *The Man Who Knew Too Much,* p. 50.
3. William R. Corson, *Armies of Ignorance,* cited in Garrison, *Trail of the Assassins,* p. 60.
4. See L. Fletcher Prouty, *The Secret Team* (Costa Mesa, Calif., 1973).
5. Prouty, *JFK,* p. 153.

6. Mark Lane, *Plausible Denial* (New York, 1991), pp. 55–56.

7. Russell, *The Man Who Knew Too Much*, p. 205, discusses Powers' concerns; for Oswald's CIA file, see Sylvia Meagher, *Accessories After the Fact* (New York, 1967), p. 220 ff.

8. CE 870, 17H 866.

9. 8H 336.

10. See Hugh C. McDonald, *Appointment in Dallas: The Final Solution to the Assassination of JFK* (New York, 1975) for the full treatment of "Saul."

11. See Robert Morrow, *Firsthand Knowledge: How I Participated in the CIA-Mafia Murder of President Kennedy* (New York, 1992), for the Morrow-Ferrie relationship.

12. House Assassinations Hearings, 10H 132; 4H 432; House Assassinations *Report*, pp. 142–43; Garrison, *Trail of the Assassins*, pp. 106–7.

13. Henry Hurt, *Reasonable Doubt* (New York, 1985), and Garrison, *Trail of the Assassins*, pp. 106–7.

14. Garrison, *Trail of the Assassins*, p. 37; CE 2901, 26H 357. For Andrews' blunt comments to the commission, see 11H 330.

15. Lane, *Plausible Denial*, pp. 209–303; the disinclination of the HSCA to believe Ms. Lorenz is detailed in Blakey and Billings, *Plot to Kill the President*, p. 175.

16. Lane, *Plausible Denial*, p. 3.

17. Russell, *The Man Who Knew Too Much*, p. 416.

18. Summers, *Conspiracy*, p. 64; CE 2121, 24H 576; CE 2195, 25H 25, 25H 45.

19. Cited in Groden and Livingstone, *High Treason*, p. 298.

CHAPTER 5

1. Marrs, *Crossfire*, p. 221.

2. John Davis, *Mafia Kingfish* (New York, 1989), pp. 238–39.

3. For the best overall Hoover-Kennedy-LBJ interaction, see Mark North, *Act of Treason* (New York, 1991); for a recent revisionist biography of Hoover, see Anthony Summers, *Official and Confidential: The Secret Life of J. Edgar Hoover*.

4. For a printout of the teletype, see Groden and Livingstone, *High Treason*, in the photo section following p. 180.

5. Russell, *Man Who Knew Too Much*, pp. 56–57 and 114.

6. CE 762, 17H 566.

7. See Gary Shaw, *Cover-Up* (Austin, Tex., 1992), pp. 182–83.

8. See 5H 97 ff.

9. A sampling of witnesses who strongly disagreed with FBI reports of their testimony would include B. R. Williams, 3H 172; H. Norman, 3H 196;

Robert E. Edwards, 6H 205; Nelson Delgado, 8H 238; Martin Isaacs, 8H 327; Max Clark, 8H 349; Capt. W. B. Frazier, 12H 57; G. E. Worley, 12H 379; and Ira J. Beers, 13H 104.

10. U.S. Senate Intelligence Report, JFK Assassination, pp. 33, 23.
11. 5H 98.
12. See North, *Act of Treason*, pp. 71, 77, and passim.

CHAPTER 6

1. 4H 322–23.
2. 2H 110.
3. Cited in 26H 72.
4. Schmidt to Weissman, October 29, 1963; 18H 836.
5. See CE 1814, 23H 471; also 5H 504, 509.
6. CE 1882, 23H 687; see also Sauvage, *Oswald Affair*, p. 76.
7. See "Hepburn," *Farewell America*, pp. 185, 234–35, 217, 237–38.
8. 9H 106.
9. Cited in Russell, *Man Who Knew Too Much*, p. 606.
10. 5H 198.
11. Summers, *Conspiracy*, p. 35; Marrs, *Crossfire*, p. 1.
12. 25H 194.
13. Walker bullet cited in *Dallas Morning News*, April 11, 1963; *New York Times*, April 12, 1963.
14. See "Hepburn," *Farewell America*, pp. 121, 151, 155.
15. Summers, *Conspiracy*, p. 246; CE 2003, 24H 324; 24H 329.
16. Hill, *JFK: Last Dissenting Witness*, p. 92.
17. Morrow, *Firsthand Knowledge*, p. xvi, *passim*.
18. Garrison, *Heritage of Stone*, p. 151.
19. CE 2981, 26H 473.
20. W. R. Morris and R. B. Cutler, *Alias Oswald* (Manchester, Mass., 1985), p. xiv.
21. "Hepburn," *Farewell America*, p. 84 ff.

CHAPTER 7

1. Davis, *Mafia Kingfish*, p. 65.
2. See North, *Act of Treason*, p. 56; Davis, *Mafia Kingfish*, p. 139.
3. JFK allegedly told Ben Bradlee, in February 1963, of the Hoffa threat vs. RFK; Marrs, *Crossfire*, p. 173.
4. North, *Act of Treason*, p. 369.
5. Davis, *Mafia Kingfish*, p. 121.

6. CE 2998, 26H 509.

7. Davis, *Mafia Kingfish,* p. 129; Scheim, *Contract on America,* p. 93.

8. Blakey and Billings, *Plot,* p. 312.

9. CE 2253, 25H 177.

10. CE 1693, 23H 166–67; CE 1442, 1443, 22H 859.

11. CE 1559, 23H 48; CE 1300, 22H 478.

12. CE 1228, 22H 336; CE 1184, 22H 300–3; CE 1763, 23H 372; CE 1202, 22H 318.

13. See Scheim, *Contract on America,* p. 99.

14. CE 1729, 1730, 23H 334; CE 1734, 23H 340.

15. CE 1318, 22H 493; Blakey and Billings, *Plot,* p. 289.

16. See Blakey and Billings, *Plot,* p. 257.

CHAPTER 8

1. See Marrs, *Crossfire,* p. 295; Zirbel, *Texas Connection,* p. 158; North, *Act of Treason,* p. 219.

2. Zirbel, *Texas Connection,* p. 122.

3. Marrs, *Crossfire,* p. 6; Zirbel, *Texas Connection,* p. 194.

4. Charles Crenshaw, *Conspiracy of Silence* (New York, 1992), discusses some of LBJ's phone calls. Also 5H 259.

5. Fletcher Prouty, in *JFK,* dissents, insisting that Nixon was still in Dallas when the shots were fired.

6. In an interview on December 10, 1993, Madeline Brown told me that she, along with Clint Peoples and Billy Sol Estes, had decided to film their stories and go public. Days before the scheduled filming, Peoples was run off the highway and killed. Thereafter, Ms. Brown said, Billy Sol was a man not wanting to go public. "Or drive on highways?" I asked. After that conversation, which included a promise of documents from Ms. Brown, someone got to her, as she has not returned repeated phone calls and letters. The best bet for "who got to her" is, sadly, someone within the research community who seeks to "own" her story.

CHAPTER 9

1. 5H 365.

CHAPTER 10

1. Cited in Scheim, *Contract on America,* p. 187.

2. Decker 5323, 19H 534.

3. Groden and Livingstone, *High Treason,* p. 365.
4. CE 2213, 25H 97, 102; CE 2946, 26H 407

BOOK ONE
CHAPTER 2

1. Thomas Buchanan, *Who Killed Kennedy?* pp. 10, 151 ff.
2. 5H 101.
3. 9H 106.
4. 11H 417, 419.
5. Sloan and Hill, *JFK: Last Dissenting Witness,* p. 53.
6. Marrs, *Crossfire,* p. 1; 5H 198.
7. 2H 250.
8. CE 1265, 22H 370.
9. Sloan and Hill, *JFK: Last Dissenting Witness,* p. 75.
10. Garrison, *Heritage of Stone,* p. 161.
11. Ibid., p. 63.
12. Penn Jones, *Forgive My Grief* (Waxahachie, Tex., by author), III, 15.
13. Davis, *Mafia Kingfish,* p. 140; Blakey and Billings, *Plot to Kill the President,* p. 322.

CHAPTER 3

1. CE 1365, 22H 617.
2. 2H 111.
3. 7H 338.
4. Cited in Davis, *Mafia Kingfish,* pp. 175–76.
5. 19H 483.
6. 17H 457.
7. 12H 132.
8. King ex. 4, 20H 454.
9. 24H 259.
10. 3H 244.
11. See Groden and Livingstone, *High Treason,* p. 135.
12. Kantor ex. 3, 20H 391.
13. CE 771, 17H 628.
14. Decker 5323, 19H 458.
15. HAH, 9H 530.
16. Hepburn, *Farewell America,* p. 349; 21H 548.
17. CE 705, 17H 368.

CHAPTER 4

1. CE 1974, 23H 839.
2. CE 1407, 22H 791.
3. CE 1381, 22H 632.
4. 3H 283.
5. 3H 283.
6. CE 1358, 22H 604.
7. Decker 5323, 19H 467–68.
8. Prouty, *JFK*, photo caption before p. 221.
9. 2H 177.
10. 3H 211.
11. CE 1381, 22H 681.
12. 3H 227.
13. 3H 283.
14. 7H 348.
15. 17H 398.
16. 17H 465.
17. 23H 914, 24H 406, 23H 915, 17H 464.
18. 23H 847, 916.
19. 17H 467.
20. 23H 924.
21. 20H 499.
22. See Groden and Livingstone, *High Treason*, p. 162; for a more detailed discussion, see Shaw and Harris, *Cover-Up*, p. 144, 144n; Shaw and Harris agree that Connally was not shot from the TSBD.
23. Shaw and Harris, Ibid. Decker 5323, 19H 502.
24. HAH, 5H 690, 723; 8H 49–50; Warren Report, p. 68.
25. 17H xvi describes the wounds; 17H 346 depicts them.
26. 19H 511.
27. 7H 564.
28. 7H 510.
29. 6H 247.
30. Sloan and Hill, *JFK: Last Dissenting Witness*, pp. 24, 26–27.
31. "The Ricky White Materials," an unpublished synopsis of a news conference.
32. Jones, *Forgive My Grief*, III, 53

CHAPTER 5

1. See Marrs, *Crossfire*, p. 361, or the film itself. This issue has never been

thoroughly resolved, however. Some suggest that after passing Curry, the limo stopped for directions at the on-ramp to Stemmons Freeway.

2. CE 705, 17H 465.
3. CE 705, 17H 465.
4. CE 705, 17H 462; CE 1974, 23H 914; 23H 855.
5. Decker 5323, 19H 511, 516, 530–31.
6. Sloan and Hill, *JFK: Last Dissenting Witness*, p. 32.
7. Talbert ex. 5069, 21H 666; see also Brewer, 7H 6–7.
8. See Davis, *Mafia Kingfish*, p. 176.
9. Hurt, *Reasonable Doubt*, p. 157; author interview with Madeline Brown, December 10, 1993.
10. 4H 232–39.
11. CE 2003, 24H 264.
12. Crull ex. 1, 19H 394.
13. CE 705, 17H 397.
14. CE 1974, 23H 850.
15. Meagher, *Accessories After the Fact*, pp. 262–63. This is disputable, because the tape exists.
16. CE 2781, 26H 165.
17. The testimony of William Whaley refers to a "timing" of Oswald's movements that proved he could not have arrived at the Tippit scene until 1:21 P.M.
18. See Buchanan, *Who Killed Kennedy?*, pp. 130–31.
19. CE 1974, 23H 922–23, 880.
20. CE 1976, 24H 1.
21. CE 1148, 22H 178.
22. Davis, *Mafia Kingfish*, p. 195 ff.
23. 7H 126.
24. CE 705, 17H 470.
25. 17H 218.
26. See Sauvage, *Oswald Affair*, p. 42.
27. 21H 643–49.
28. 17H 495.
29. 11H 397–98.
30. CE 2145, 24H 759.
31. Kelley ex. A, 20H 443.
32. 7H 315.
33. 20H 499; CE 3078, 26H 686.
34. Richard Stovall ex. C, 21H 599–602.
35. 2H 425–26.
36. CE 2554, 25H 787; CE 705, 17H 380.

37. CE 705, 17H 374–430, passim.
38. CE 705, 17H 379, 432.
39. 20H 255.
40. 21H 708–9; 20H 413.

CHAPTER 6

1. 22H 1–2.
2. See Meagher, *Accessories After the Fact*, p. 183 ff.
3. 5H 229.
4. CE 1351, 22H 582–83.
5. 11H 294.
6. CE 1351, 22H 586.
7. Decker 5323, 19H 533; Marrs, *Crossfire*, p. 78.
8. 22H 632–86, passim.
9. 4H 30.

CHAPTER 7

1. CE 2003, 24H 356; C. E. Talbert (5067) 21H 660.
2. 24H 356; 12H 45.
3. 12H 5–7; 12H 389–90.
4. CE 3006, 26H 529.
5. Price ex. 21H 170, 182.
6. 21H 215.
7. 21H 171.
8. 19H 411–12.
9. CE 2003, 24H 352.
10. CE 1757, 23H 365.
11. 24H 451–52.
12. 1H 81; CE 1155, 22H 194.
13. CE 1794, 23H 413.
14. CE 2053, 24H 470.
15. Croy 5051, 19H 387; Vaughan 5335–36, 21H 684–91; Pierce 5077, 21H 132; Putnam 5073, 21H 280; Maxey 5094, 20H 606–11; Talbert's statement is in 15H 189–90.
16. Solomon 5106, 21H 532–33.
17. Stevenson 5053, 21H 581.
18. See Marrs, *Crossfire*, p. 269.
19. CE 1272, 22H 377; CE 1273, 22H 377.
20. CE 1741, 23H 349.

21. CE 1693, 23H 166–67; CE 1442–43, 22H 859; Davis, *Mafia Kingfish*, pp. 141–44.

22. CE 1518, 23H 8–9.

23. CE 1528, 23H 17–19.

24. CE 1746, 23H 354.

25. CE 1466, 22H 886; CE 1224, 22H 334.

26. Sam Ruby ex. 1, 21H 378; Alice R. Nichols 5355, 20H 680; CE 1696, 23H 169; CE 1227, 22H 335.

27. CE 1187, 22H 307.

28. CE 1228, 22H 336; Alfred Hodge ex. 1, 20H 159.

29. Sorrels ex. 1, 21H 537; CE 1615, 23H 95.

30. CE 2002, 24H 48–194, passim.

31. CE 1515, 23H 4; CE 1646, 23H 119.

32. CE 1659, 23H 132; CE 1467, 22H 886–87.

33. 14H 359.

34. CE 1753, 23H 363.

35. CE 1300, 22H 478.

36. Cited in Blakey and Billings, *Plot to Kill the President*, p. 312.

37. CE 2264, 25H 189; CE 2003, 24H 313.

38. Buchanan, *Who Killed Kennedy?*, p. 141.

39. Rea ex. 1, 21H 293; Saunders ex. 1, 21H 385.

40. CE 2281, 25H 205; Senator 5400, 21H 431.

41. CE 2254, 25H 178–79; 20H 159.

42. Earl Ruby ex. 1, 21H 328, 332.

43. CE 2253, 25H 177.

44. Branch ex. 1, 19H 171.

45. CE 1810, 23H 461.

46. CE 2029, 24H 442.

47. CE 1748, 23H 356–57.

48. 5H 206, 12H 308.

49. S. Kantor ex. 3, 20H 382.

50. C. Ray Hall ex. 3, 20H 55.

51. CE 2038, 24H 453.

52. CE 2389, 25H 363.

53. CE 2821, 26H 254–61.

54. CE 2275, 25H 198–99; CE 1744, 23H 352; CE 1222, 22H 332; CE 2250, 25H 174.

55. CE 1184, 22H 303.

56. CE 1245, 22H 355; CE 1561, 23H 49–52; CE 2495, 25H 709–10.

57. 23H 334; 21H 33–41; 21H 381; CE 1028, 18H 823.

58. CE 2003, 24H 271; CE 2078, 24H 513.

59. Buchanan, *Who Killed Kennedy?*, pp. 28, 140.
60. "Hepburn," *Farewell America*, p. 242.
61. CE 2292, 25H 221.
62 Marrs, *Crossfire*, p. 433.
63. Livingstone, *Killing the Truth*, p. 551.
64. Blakey and Billings, *Plot to Kill the President*, p. 338.
65. 5H 237.
66. 15H 39.

Book Two
CHAPTER 1

1. Philip Melanson, *Spy Saga: Lee Harvey Oswald and U.S. Intelligence* (New York, 1990), p. xiii.
2. For an excellent treatment of the medical procedures, and a fascinating tour of the world of medicine as it relates to the assassination, see Crenshaw, *Conspiracy of Silence*.
3. *Life*, "John F. Kennedy Memorial Edition," November 1963.
4. Ibid.
5. Ibid.
6. *Life*, February 21, 1964.
7. *Life*, November 24, 1966.
8. *Life*, November 27, 1967.

CHAPTER 2

1. Gray ex. 2, 20H 25–26.
2. CE 1962, 23H 797–98.
3. Edward J. Epstein, *The Assassination Chronicles* (New York, 1992), p. 357. This work is a compilation of his three works on the JFK assassination: *Inquest*, *Legend*, and *Counterplot*.
4. Hurt, *Reasonable Doubt*, p. 197; Melanson, *Spy Saga*, p. 11.
5. Melanson, *Spy Saga*, p. 11.
6. Lane, *Plausible Denial*, p. 12.
7. See Sauvage, *Oswald Affair*, p. 5; Epstein, *Assassination Chronicles*, pp. 360–61; Marrs, *Crossfire*, p. 106.
8. Melanson, *Spy Saga*, p. 8.
9. CE 833, 17H 789.
10. CE 1961, 23H 796.
11. Russell, *Man Who Knew Too Much*, p. 145.

12. Cited in Summers, *Conspiracy*, p. 174; Marrs, *Crossfire*, p. 116, citing Summers.
13. Allison G. Folsom ex. 1, 19H 656, 662, 720.
14. CE 822, 17H 709.
15. WC, *Report of Proceedings*, January 27, 1964, p. 192.
16. Epstein, *Assassination Chronicles*, p. 388.
17. See Blakey and Billings, *Plot to Kill the President*, p. 31.
18. CE 1150, 22H 180–81.
19. See 19H 248–49, and 250–74, passim.
20. CE 1403, 22H 780.

CHAPTER 3

1. 16H 94.
2. Priscilla Johnson ex. 2, 20H 287.
3. CE 1385, 22H 702–8.
4. Morris and Cutler, *Alias Oswald*, p. 24.
5. CE 2750, 26H 126.
6. CE 2758, 26H 143–44.
7. Morrow, *Firsthand Knowledge*, p. 171.
8. 5H 414.
9. CE 870, 17H 866.
10. CE 917, 18H 115.
11. CE 97, 16H 422–30.
12. 5H 407, 410, 617.
13. CE 315, 16H 870–73.
14. Epstein, *Assassination Chronicles*, p. 565.
15. See Summers, *Conspiracy*, pp. 220–21.
16. CE 1403, 22H 775.
17. CE 1403, 22H 773.
18. Marrs, *Crossfire*, p. 126.
19. CE 2703, 26H 75.
20. Virginia James ex. 2, 20H 236.
21. Virginia James ex. 6, 20H 242, 244.
22. 1H 429.
23. 2H 8–9.
24. 2H 339; 8H 368; 8H 476; 9H 30, 130, 147.
25. CE 950, 18H 277.
26. 18H 131–32.
27. CE 975, 18H 374.

28. CE 970, 18H 367.
29. Virginia James ex. 3, 20H 239.
30. 5H 332.
31. 1H 133.

CHAPTER 4

1. 17H 289.
2. CE 796–97, 17H 682; CE 823, 17H 718–32; Cadigan ex. 10, 19H 283–84; CE 1114, 22H 77–79; CE 1944, 23H 740–44.
3. CE 801–2, 17H 686; CE 821, 17H 700–706; CE 980, 18H 383–95; CE 2751, 26H 126–31.
4. CE 826, 17H 753–69.
5. G. Donabedian ex. 1, 19H 581–617.
6. CE 228, 16H 621–25; CE 823, 17H 718–32; Cadigan ex. 10, 19H 283–84; G. Donabedian ex. 1, 19H 581–617; CE 1944, 23H 743–44.
7. 19H 397–98.
8. For the best treatment of Hoover and Oswald, see North, *Act of Treason.*
9. Marina mentioned the stopover in Atlanta in CE 994, 18H 626, 629; also believable, as direct flights were not then available from New York to Love Field.
10. Russell, *Man Who Knew Too Much,* p. 276.
11. *Ibid.,* p. 361; 9H 275; see also Epstein, *Assassination Chronicles,* p. 557 ff, and Garrison, *Trail of the Assassins,* p. 56.
12. Summers, *Conspiracy,* p.164.
13. CE 1894, 23H 896; CE 1144, 22H 162.
14. CE 1901, 23H 705; CE 1894, 23H 696; see also CE 1144, 22H 162.
15. CE 1940, 23H 735; CE 1154, 22H 188.
16. CE 1905, 23H 707; could this have been Oswald's understanding of the name "Charles Harrelson"?
17. V. T. Lee ex. 3, 20H 515, 519.
18. CE 1414, 22H 828.
19. CE 1412, 22H 807; James DiEugenio, *Destiny Betrayed* (New York, 1992), p. 219.
20. CE 1410, 22H 796–99; CE 2195, 25H 58–59.
21. CE 2542, 25H 769; CE 1411, 22H 800–802.
22. 5H 9; 1H 24.
23. CE 1412, 22H 804.
24. 10H 36.
25. CE 2210, 25H 90.

26. CE 1140, 22H 125.
27. CE 1942, 23H 737–39.
28. CE 1154, 22H 190.
29. CE 2951, 26H 424–25.
30. 11H 420.
31. CE 1784, 23H 392.
32. CE 994, 18H 626–29; CE 1403, 22H 777.
33. CE 1401, 22H 751–58; CE 1156, 22H 195.
34. CE 2001, 24H 38, 39, 41, 47.
35. Russell, *Man Who Knew Too Much*, p. 318.
36. A. Johnson ex. 7, 20H 272.
37. Meagher, *Accessories After the Fact*, pp. 286–87.
38. 1H 71.
39. *House Assassination Report*, 142–43.
40. CE 1404, 22H 786–88; CE 1972, 23H 830–31; CE 849, 23H 414–16; CE 2522, 25H 731.
41. CE 1401, 22H 750, 763; CE 1404, 22H 785; CE 1156, 22H 197; CE 1788, 23H 400.
42. CE 1114, 22H 77–79; CE 781, 17H 666–67; they are not presented in the correct chronology, allowing the casual reader to think that Oswald wanted to visit Cuba on his second passport . . . not so!
43. A. Johnson ex. 4-A, 20H 265; A. Johnson ex. 5, 20H 266–68; A. Johnson ex. 6, 20H 270.
44. CE 1070, 22H 20.
45. 5H 381; Senate Select Committee, *Investigation into the Assassination of JFK* (Washington, D.C., 1979), p. 54.
46. CE 822, 17H 707 ff; CE 824, 17H 733.
47. CE 822, 17H 715.
48. 3H 128 and passim; 2H 393; Epstein, *Assassination Chronicles*, p. 485.
49. CE 826, 17H 767.

CHAPTER 5

1. 1H 4.
2. CE 1859, 23H 629.
3. Ibid.
4. Summers, *Conspiracy*, p. 99; for Michael Paine's statements regarding his viewings of the "backyard photos" on Friday, see 9H 444.
5. CE 2977, 26H 458–9.
6. Russell, *Man Who Knew Too Much*, p. 361.

7. CE 2446, 25H 587.

8. CE 3146, 26H 834–35; Blakey and Billings, *Plot to Kill the President,* p. 165.

9. CE 1143, 22H 154–55.

10. CE 2763, 26H 148.

11. CE 2862, 26H 302; CE 2789, 26H 178–79.

12. North, *Act of Treason,* p. 328; for the A&P check-cashing episode, see CE 1165, 22H 225.

13. CE 1327, 22H 524; CE 1335–37, 22H 546–49; CE 1403, 22H 782.

14. CE 1330, 22H 526.

15. CE 3031, 26H 577–78.

16. CE 2003, 24H 304.

17. Ibid; CE 2370, 25H 349.

18. CE 1530, 23H 21; CE 1529, 23H 20.

19. CE 2003, 24H 304; CE 2547, 25H 772.

20. The "Abilene Incident" is best chronicled in North, *Act of Treason,* p. 366.

21. CE 1967 (dated November 23, 1963), 23H 817; also in CE 1992, 24H 23.

22. See Russell, *Man Who Knew Too Much,* p. 542 ff; Garrison, *On the Trail of the Assassins,* p. 70 ff.; see also George Michael Evica, *And We Are All Mortal* (West Hartford, Conn., 1978), passim, as excellent source material on Masen.

CHAPTER 6

1. CE 1984, 24H 16.

2. CE 1988, 24H 18.

3. 3H 257.

4. CE 705, 17H 416.

5. CE 1974, 23H 870.

6. See Marrs, *Crossfire,* p. 353.

7. CE 2003, 24H 246.

8. CE 1931, 23H 726.

9. CE 835, 17H 816.

10. 4H 239.

11. Seth Kantor ex. 3, 20H 369.

12. Harry Holmes ex. 4, 20H 179.

13. Cited in Groden and Livingstone, *High Treason,* p. 204.

14. 5H 231.

15. See Summers, *Conspiracy,* p. 434.

16. CE 630, 17H 285.

17. Commission document 205, p. 148.

18. CE 1780, 23H 385–86.
19. CE 1783, 23H 390.
20. CE 1780, 23H 385.
21. CE 2002, 24H 151.

Book Three

CHAPTER 1

1. *Dallas Morning News,* November 23, 1963, p. 1.
2. For a more complete discussion, see Marrs, *Crossfire,* p. 355.
3. CE 835, 17H 816.
4. CE 1021, 18H 710.
5. Racine, *La Thebaide* (1664), Act IV, Scene iii.
6. 1H 426.
7. CE 1953, 23H 757 ff.
8. U.S. Senate Intelligence Report, John F. Kennedy Assassination, p. 33.
9. Ibid., p. 23.
10. See Davis, *Mafia Kingfish,* p. 213; also, Blakey and Billings, *Plot to Kill the President,* p. 257.
11. Davis, *Mafia Kingfish,* p. 119.
12. See North, *Act of Treason,* p. 411.
13. Ibid., p. 349.
14. 11H 226.
15. Davis, *Mafia Kingfish,* p. 236; U.S. Senate Intelligence Report, John F. Kennedy Assassination, pp. 5, 47.
16. Hill and Sloan, *JFK: Last Dissenting Witness,* p. 66.
17. Discussed in Epstein, *Assassination Chronicles,* p. 106.
18. Interview with Joseph Ball in Ibid., p. 107; Warren Commission executive session transcript, January 27, 1964, p. 171.
19. Hoover's testimony appears in 5H 97 ff.
20. CE 2778, 26H 161.
21. CE 2448, 25H 588.
22. CE 1416, 22H 833.
23. Summers, *Conspiracy,* pp. 231, 321. The original discovery was made by Jim Garrison and/or his staff in the course of the Shaw investigation.
24. CE 1980, 24H 7.
25. CE 1381, 22H 632–86.
26. HSC Report, p. 128; available more readily in Hurt, *Reasonable Doubt,* p. 27.
27. ABC Television, *Nightline,* December 1, 1993.

CHAPTER 2

1. Meagher, *Accessories after the Fact*, p. xxvi.
2. *The New York Times*, November 25, 1963.
3. Kai Bird, *The Chairman* (New York, 1992), p. 548.
4. Lane, *Plausible Denial*, p. 43n; see also North, *Act of Treason*, pp. 548–49.
5. Bird, *The Chairman*, pp. 549–50.
6. In only one interview, with Marina Oswald on September 6, did the commissioners ask a sizable portion of the questions.
7. Epstein, *Assassination Chronicles*, p. 35.
8. Ibid., pp. 35, 45.
9. Shaw, *Cover-Up*, p. 2.
10. Murray Kempton, *The New Republic*, June 13, 1964.
11. DiEugenio, *Destiny Betrayed*, p. 91, citing research done by John Judge, confirmed by this author in a discussion with Mr. Judge on October 17, 1992.

CHAPTER 3

1. 3H 55–56.
2. 2H 339; 8H 368, 476; 9H 30, 130, 147.
3. 4H 74.
4. 2H 364.
5. 3H 159–60 and passim. Had Brennan made his collection of specious claims at Oswald's trial in a court of law and under oath, it is arguable that he would have served more time than Oswald. (He would have testified at Oswald's trial, had Oswald lived.)
6. 3H 144; 24H 522; 2H 161–62; 2H 207.
7. 12H 57.
8. 12H 379.
9. 13H 104.
10. 3H 267; 4H 329; 7H 342; 2H 138.
11. CE 2578, 25H 845.
12. CE 768, 17H 609.
13. Decker ex. 5323, 19H 573.
14. CE 2554, 25H 787.
15. CE 1974, 23H 881.
16. CE 762, 17H 566.
17. 9H 275.
18. 5H 332.
19. Seth Kantor ex. 3, 20H 366.

20. CE 1325, 22H 523.
21. CE 1156, 22H 196.
22. Epstein, *Assassination Chronicles*, p. 21.
23. CE 2195, 25H 25.
24. Ibid., 25H 45.
25. CE 767, 17H 593–600.
26. CE 2395, 25H 375.
27. CE 1365, 22H 617.
28. CE 1974, 23H 917.
29. CE 697–98, 17H 354.
30. CE 2003, 24H 212.
31. Bowron ex. 4, 19H 170.
32. 6H 136–37, 141.
33. CE 760, 17H 530.
34. Crafard 5226, 19H 356.
35. 19H 360.
36. CE 602–5, 17H 230–31.
37. Shaw, *Cover-Up*, p. 72; see also Walt Brown, *People v. Lee Harvey Oswald* (New York, 1992), p. 201.
38. Decker 5323, 19H 536.
39. 7H, 254.
40. Cited in Hurt, *Reasonable Doubt*, p. 47.
41. See Scheim, *Contract on America*, pp. 99, 174–75; sanitized version appears in CE 1536, 23H 27.
42. Newman 5038 C, D, 20H 648–49.
43. 1H 162.
44. Decker ex. 5321, 19H 452; see also Marrs, *Crossfire*, p. 14.
45. King ex. 4, 20H 453.
46. Cited in North, *Act of Treason*, p. 496.
47. President's Commission, *Report of Proceedings*, pp. 152–53.
48. 2H 47.
49. Sloan and Hill, *JFK: Last Dissenting Witness*, pp. 102–3.
50. CE 2644, 25H 903–8.
51. Report, p. 790.
52. CE 1435, 22H 845.
53. Brennan, *Eyewitness to History* (Waco, Tex., 1987), p. 63.
54. See Summers, *Conspiracy*, p. 109.
55. Shaw, *Cover-Up*, p. 32.
56. See North, *Act of Treason*, p. 528.
57. Report, p. 194.
58. 20H 571.

59. Cited in Summers, *Conspiracy,* p. 117.
60. 18H 118.
61. CE 2562, 25H 808.
62. 21H 230.
63. 24H 367 ff., 394 ff.
64. 18H 249–54.
65. 23H 710–11.
66. 22H 11.
67. 20H 2.
68. Cited in Blakey and Billings, *Plot to Kill the President,* p. 40.
69. Livingstone, *High Treason 2,* p. 261.
70. 2H 363.
71. 21H 151.
72. 6H 70.
73. 6H 67, 47, 34.
74. 20H 333; 6H 54, 40–41.
75. 6H 20.
76. For Olivier, see 5H 89.

SELECT BIBLIOGRAPHY

Anson, Robert S. *They've Killed the President! The Search for the Murderers of John F. Kennedy*. New York: Bantam Books, 1975.

Bird, Kai. *The Chairman: John J. McCloy and the Making of the American Establishment*. New York: Simon & Schuster, 1992.

Blakey, G. Robert, and Billings, Richard N. *The Plot to Kill the President; Organized Crime Assassinated JFK*. New York: Times Books, 1981.

Brennan, Howard L., with Cherryholmes, J. Edward. *Eyewitness to History*. Waco, Tex.: Texian Press, 1987.

Brown, Walt. *The People v. Lee Harvey Oswald*. New York: Carroll & Graf, 1992.

Buchanan, Thomas G. *Who Killed Kennedy?* New York: G. P. Putnam's Sons, 1964.

Canfield, Michael, and Weberman, Alan J. *Coup d'État in America: The CIA and the Assassination of John F. Kennedy*. New York: The Third Press, 1975.

Craig, John R., and Rogers, Philip A. *The Man on the Grassy Knoll*. New York: Avon Books, 1992.

Crenshaw, Dr. Charles A., with Hansen, Jens, and Shaw, J. Gary. *JFK: Conspiracy of Silence*. New York: Signet, 1992.

Curry, Jesse E. *JFK Assassination File*. Dallas, by author, 1969.

Davis, John H. *Mafia Kingfish: Carlos Marcello and the Assassination of John F. Kennedy*. New York: McGraw-Hill, 1989.

Eddowes, Michael. *The Oswald File*. New York: Clarkson Potter, 1977.

Epstein, Edward Jay. *The Assassination Chronicles* [a compendium of Epstein's separate works]. New York: Carroll & Graf, 1992.

Evica, George Michael. *And We Are All Mortal: New Evidence and Analysis in the Assassination of John F. Kennedy*. West Hartford, Conn.: University of Hartford Press, 1978.

Fensterwald, Bernard, and Ewing, Michael, eds. *Coincidence or Conspiracy?* New York: Zebra Books, 1977.

Flammonde, Paris. *The Kennedy Conspiracy: An Uncommissioned Report on the Jim Garrison Investigation.* New York: Meredith Press, 1969.

Fonzi, Gaeton. *The Last Investigation.* New York: Thunder's Mouth Press, 1993.

Fox, Sylvan. *The Unanswered Questions About President Kennedy's Assassination.* New York: Award Books, 1965.

Garrison, Jim. *A Heritage of Stone.* New York: G. P. Putnam's Sons, 1970.

———. *On the Trail of the Assassins: My Investigation and Prosecution of the Murder of President Kennedy.* New York: Sheridan Square Press, 1988.

Groden, Robert J., and Livingstone, Harrison E. *High Treason.* New York: The Conservatory Press, 1989.

Hepburn, James [pseud.]. *Farewell America.* Vaduz, Liechtenstein: Frontiers Publishing Company, 1968.

Hurt, Henry. *Reasonable Doubt: An Investigation Into the Assassination of John F. Kennedy.* New York: Holt, Rinehart, & Winston, 1986.

Joesten, Joachim. *Oswald: Assassin or Fall Guy?* New York: Marzani & Munsell, 1964.

Jones, Penn, Jr. *Forgive My Grief* (five volumes). Midlothian, Tex.: Midlothian Mirror, 1966 ff.

Kantor, Seth. *Who Was Jack Ruby?* New York: Everest House, 1978.

Lane, Mark. *A Citizen's Dissent: Mark Lane Replies.* New York: Holt, Rinehart, & Winston, 1968.

———. *Plausible Denial: Was the CIA Involved in the Assassination of JFK?* New York: Thunder's Mouth Press, 1991.

———. *Rush to Judgment.* New York: Holt, Rinehart, & Winston, 1966.

Lattimer, Dr. John K. *Kennedy and Lincoln: Medical and Ballistic Comparisons of Their Assassinations.* New York: Harcourt Brace Jovanovich, 1980.

Lifton, David S. *Best Evidence: Disguise and Deception in the Assassination of John F. Kennedy.* New York: Macmillan, 1980.

Livingstone, Harrison Edward. *High Treason 2.* New York: Carroll & Graf, 1992.

———. *Killing the Truth.* New York: Carroll & Graf, 1993.

McDonald, Hugh C. *Appointment in Dallas: The Final Solution to the Assassination of JFK.* New York: H. McDonald Publishing Co., 1975.

Marchetti, Victor, and Marks, John. *The CIA and the Cult of Intelligence.* New York: Alfred A. Knopf, 1974.

Marrs, Jim. *Crossfire: The Plot That Killed Kennedy.* New York: Carrol & Graf, 1989.

Meagher, Sylvia. *Accessories after the Fact: The Warren Commission, the Authorities, and the Report.* New York: Vintage books, 1976.

Melanson, Philip H. *Spy Saga: Lee Harvey Oswald and U.S. Intelligence*. New York: Praeger, 1990.

Menninger, Bonar. *Mortal Error: The Shot That Killed JFK*. New York: St. Martin's Press, 1992.

Model, F. Peter, and Groden, Robert J. *JFK: The Case for Conspiracy*. New York: Manor Books, 1976.

Moore, Jim. *Conspiracy of One*. Forth Worth: The Summit Group, 1990.

Morris, W. R., and Cutler, R. B. *Alias Oswald*. Manchester, Mass.: GKG, 1985.

Morrow, Robert D. *Firsthand Knowledge: How I Participated in the CIA-Mafia Murder of President Kennedy*. New York: Shapolsky, 1992.

North, Mark. *Act of Treason: The Role of J. Edgar Hoover in the Assassination of President Kennedy*. New York: Carroll & Graf, 1991.

Oliver, Beverly, with Buchanan, Coke. *Nightmare in Dallas*. Lancaster, Pa.: Starburst Publishers, 1994.

Oswald, Robert, with Land, Myrick and Barbara. *Lee: A Portrait of Lee Harvey Oswald*. New York: Coward-McCann, 1967.

O'Toole, George. *The Assassination Tapes: An Electronic Probe into the Murder of John F. Kennedy and the Dallas Cover-Up*. New York: Penthouse Press, 1975.

Popkin, Richard H. *The Second Oswald*. New York: Avon Books, 1966.

Posner, Gerald. *Case Closed*. New York: Random House, 1993.

Prouty, L. Fletcher. *JFK: The CIA, Vietnam, and the Plot to Assassinate John F. Kennedy*. New York: Carol Publishing Group, 1992.

————. *The Secret Team: The CIA and Its Allies in Control of the United States and the World*. Englewood Cliffs, N.J.: Prentice-Hall, 1973.

Russell, Dick. *The Man Who Knew Too Much*. New York: Carroll & Graf, 1992.

Sauvage, Leo. *The Oswald Affair: An Examination of the Contradictions and Omissions of the Warren Report*. Cleveland: World Publishing, 1966.

Scheim, David E. *Contract on America: The Mafia Murder of President John F. Kennedy*. New York: Shapolsky Books, 1988.

Scott, Peter Dale. *Deep Politics and the Death of JFK*. Berkeley: University of California Press, 1993.

Scott, Peter Dale; Hoch, Paul L.; and Stetler, Russell. *The Assassinations, Dallas and Beyond: A Guide to Cover-ups and Investigations*. New York: Random House, 1976.

Shaw, J. Gary, and Harris, Larry R. *Cover-Up: The Governmental Conspiracy to Conceal the Facts About the Public Execution of John Kennedy*. Cleburne, Tex.: by authors, 1976.

Sloan, Bill, and Hill, Jean. *JFK: The Last Dissenting Witness*. New Gretna, La.: Pelican Press, 1992.

State of Texas, Attorney General's Office. *Texas Supplemental Report on the Assassination of President John F. Kennedy and the Serious Wounding of Governor John B. Connally, November 22, 1963.* Austin: Attorney General's Office, 1964.

Summers, Anthony. *Conspiracy.* New York: McGraw-Hill, 1980.

Thompson, Josiah. *Six Seconds in Dallas: A Micro-Study of the Kennedy Assassination.* New York: Bernard Geis, 1967.

U.S. House of Representatives. *The Final Assassinations Report: Report on the Select Committee on Assassinations.* New York: Bantam Books, 1979.

————. Select Committee on Assassinations. *Hearings before the Select Committee: Investigation of the Assassination of President John F. Kennedy* (five volumes). 95th Cong., 2nd sess., 1978.

————. Select Committee on Assassinations. *Investigation of the Assassination of President John F. Kennedy: Appendix to Hearings Before the Select Committee on Assassinations* (seven volumes), 95th Cong., 2nd sess., 1979.

U.S. Rockefeller Commission. *Report to the President by the Commission on CIA Activities Within the Untied States.* New York: Manor Books, 1975.

U.S. Warren Commission. *Hearings Before the President's Commission on the Assassination of President Kennedy* (twenty-six volumes). Washington, D.C.: U.S. Government Printing Office, 1965.

Wecht, Cyril. *Cause of Death.* New York: Dutton, 1993.

Weisberg, Harold. *Oswald in New Orleans: Case for Conspiracy with the CIA.* New York: Canyon Books, 1967.

————. *Post Mortem: JFK Assassination Cover-up Smashed!* Frederick, Md.: by author, 1965.

————. *Whitewash: The Report on the Warren Report.* New York: Dell, 1966.

————. *Whitewash II: The FBI-Secret Service Cover-up.* New York: Dell, 1967.

Wilber, Charles. *Medicolegal Investigation of the President John F. Kennedy Murder.* Springfield, Ill.: Charles Thomas & Sons, 1978.

Zirbel, Craig I. *The Texas Connection: The Assassination of John F. Kennedy.* Scottsdale, Ariz.: The Texas Connection Company, 1991.

Additional materials: Journal articles are cited as used, and appear in *Back Channels,* ed. Peter Kross, Franklin Park, N.J.; *Probable Cause,* ed. Steve Gerlach, 105 Yarra Road, North Croydon, Victoria, Australia; and *The Third (Now the Fourth) Decade,* ed. Jerry Rose, S.U.N.Y., Fredonia, N.Y.

INDEX